COMPUTING
AN ACTIVE-LEARNING APPROACH

P.M. Heathcote B.Sc.(Hons), M.Sc

Pat Heathcote is a Senior Lecturer in Computing at Suffolk College, Ipswich, where she has taught since 1982 on A Level Computing, BTEC and Accountancy courses, as well as a range of other computing courses. Prior to coming to Suffolk College she was for many years a programmer at McGill University in Montreal, Canada, and also held posts as a Systems Analyst with a large hospital, and subsequently with a firm of computer consultants. She is an Assistant Examiner for Advanced Level Computing with the Associated Examining Board.

2nd Edition

DP Publications Ltd
Aldine Place
142/144 Uxbridge Road
Shepherds Bush Green
London W12 8AW

1994

Acknowledgements

I would like to thank Tim Glover for his substantial and valued contributions to this book. Thanks are also due to all my colleagues in the Computing Section who have helped in many different ways, specifically Matthew Todd for material on databases, Prolog and control systems. Special thanks go to my husband without whom this book would never have been completed. I would also like to thank all the many lecturers who made useful suggestions for improvements in the second edition, and I hope that most will find that their suggestions have been incorporated. If any suggestions seem to have been ignored, this is probably because of the contradictory requirements of different courses and a desire to keep the book at a reasonable length.

I also wish to thank the following:

Owen Southwood for illustrations in the text (Figures 8.1, 8.2, 9.1, 69.1, 71.2, 72.1, 73.4, 73.5, 75.2, 75.4, 75.6);

The New Scientist for permission to reproduce two drawings by Peter Gardiner from 'Inside Science', 29 September 1990 (Figures 82.2, 82.3)

Anritsu Corporation, Graphtec (UK) Ltd, Liberator Ltd, Sensory Visionaid, Sharp Ltd, Time Computer Systems Ltd, Ellinor Touch Technology, Apple Computer Inc for permission to reproduce photographs of their equipment;

the following Examination Boards for permission to use questions from past examination papers:

The Associated Examining Board (AEB), University of Cambridge Local Examinations Syndicate (UCLES), Joint Matriculation Board (JMB), Northern Examinations and Assessment Board (NEAB), University of London Schools Examinations Board (London), Northern Ireland Schools Examinations and Assessment Council (NISEAC), Scottish Examination Board (SEB), University of Oxford Delegacy of Local Examinations (Oxford), Welsh Joint Education Committee (WJEC).

The answers in the book and in the teacher's supplement are the sole responsibility of the author and have neither been provided nor approved by the examination boards.

First Edition 1991. Reprinted 1991,1992, 1993
Second Edition 1994

A catalogue entry for this book is available from the British Library.

ISBN 1 85805 080 4
Copyright © P. M. Heathcote 1994
Cover illustrations © Robert Heathcote 1994
Line drawing illustrations copyright © Owen Southwood 1991
Diagrams at Figs 82.2 and 82.3 copyright © Peter Gardiner, New Scientist,
IPC Magazines Ltd, World Press Network 1990

Cover design by Robert Heathcote

Printed by
The Guernsey Press Co Ltd
Vale, Guernsey

PREFACE

Aim

The aim of this book is to provide the **classroom support material** needed on those computer courses adopting an **active-learning approach**. It covers comprehensively the core topics of the various **Advanced Level Computing** syllabuses and is relevant for **BTEC** and **BCS** courses. In the second edition, material has been brought up to date wherever necessary and reflects trends in current syllabi.

Need

There are many excellent course text books on computing at this level (including *Computer Science* by C. S. French) which give valuable support and wider reading/reference for the student **outside** classroom time.

This book, however, addresses the need for material that is an **integral** part of the classroom teaching, providing a **lesson plan** for the lecturer and incorporating the following features:-

1) Concise explanation of principles;

2) Questions at **appropriate points** within the text (with space allowed for the students to fill in answers) to enable the students to test and broaden their knowledge and understanding, develop ideas, supply discussion points and test how well the student can apply the principles.

Apart from its value **during** the course, this is also an ideal book around which each student can build his/her revision programme.

Approach

The text has been designed as an **interactive** teaching and learning aid, and eliminates the need for handouts or copious note-taking by students. There are ten self-contained sections designed to allow for two sections being covered each term over a two year period. Within each section, units equate to lesson periods. The sections can be tackled non-sequentially, although it is advisable to begin with Section 1 as an introduction to the course.

Teacher's supplement

The teacher's supplement allows the book to be incorporated easily into lesson plans. It provides tips on implementation of the course and outline answers to all in-text questions and chapter-end exercises/exam questions. It is available free of charge to teachers using the book as a course text.

Alternative ways of using the book

1. **Classroom workbook:** teachers can explain each part of a topic in whatever way they like and use the concise explanations as the 'skeleton' of the classroom work. Students take an active part in the learning process via the questions interspersed throughout the text, but are freed from the need to copy out pages of notes.

2. **Open learning or directed unsupervised study:** students can read through units themselves, and supplement their studies with wider reading from the suggested reading list given in the Bibliography. They then come together in the classroom to **discuss** answers.

3. **Combination of the above:** mix as the teacher sees fit, using the teacher's supplement as a guide to lesson planning.

Note:- there are no answers in the book to the in-text questions (but see teacher's supplement). However, the gaps left in the text can be, for example, completed in pencil with the student's attempt, and inked in after classroom discussion to provide a permanent reference. In this second edition, extra questions have been added at the end of most units, with answers provided at the back of the book to selected exercises.

It is expected that the theoretical part of the course will be accompanied by approximately an equal amount of practical work. The choice of specific packages used is left up to the individual lecturer.

TABLE OF CONTENTS

Section 1 — Introduction to Computers and Business Data Processing

Unit 1 — Introduction to Computer Hardware

The components of a computer

All computers, whatever their size, have the same basic components: input devices, a processor, (the Central Processing Unit or CPU), main memory (internal memory), output devices and auxiliary storage devices, also known as **backing store**. All devices external to the CPU and main memory are known as **peripherals**.

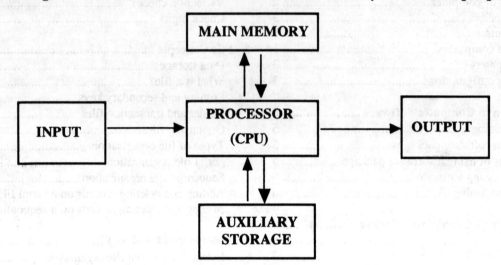

Figure 1.1 — Block diagram of a computer system

Q1: Name some input devices, output devices, and auxiliary storage devices.

Storage capacities

Both the internal memory size of the computer and the storage capacity of peripherals such as disk and magnetic tape are commonly measured in **bytes** (or larger units such as kilobytes and megabytes), with one byte typically able to store one character in coded binary form.

1 kilobyte	= 1K byte (KB)	=	1,024 bytes (This is 2^{10} bytes)
1 megabyte	= 1M byte (MB)	=	1,000K bytes = 1,024,000 bytes

Q2: How many characters can be stored on a floppy disk with a capacity of (a) 720K bytes

(b) 1.4M bytes

Categories of computers

There are four main categories of computer: microcomputers, minicomputers, mainframe computers and supercomputers. These classifications are based on physical size, speed, processing capabilities, memory size, disk storage capacities and cost. However, rapid advances in technology mean that the boundaries are constantly shifting and many computers might be put into more than one category. Essentially there is no difference, for example, between a large or powerful micro and a small mini.

Microcomputers

This category includes personal computers, portable micros and laptop computers. They are usually equipped with a hard disk, floppy disc drive, between 1 and 32 megabytes of memory, a keyboard and a VDU (Visual Display Unit). Floppy disks come in 2 standard sizes: 5¼" disks typically holding between 360K (kilobytes) and 1M bytes of data, and 3½" with a somewhat greater capacity. A high density 3½" disk holds 1.44M bytes of data.

Q3: If a page of text in a book such as this has an average 50 lines, with 60 characters (including spaces) on each line, estimate how many pages could be stored on a floppy disk with 250K of free storage capacity. What other characters apart from the actual text and graphics would have to be stored?

Minicomputers

These are more powerful than micros and can support typically up to 100 or so terminals with users performing different tasks. They may cost tens or even hundreds of thousands of pounds.

Mainframe computers

These are large systems that can hold huge amounts of data and support perhaps hundreds of user terminals. A mainframe computer with all its associated peripherals such as disk drives, tape drives and printers may occupy a whole floor of a fair sized building.

Supercomputers

This is the most powerful category of computer, costing several million pounds. They are used in applications that require huge amounts of processing or thousands of long, complex calculations. They are used, for example, to perform the detailed calculations required to model the air flow over a car or the wings of a plane in order to improve the design. The Airbus 310's fuel efficiency has been improved by 20% compared with previous models, thanks to simulations of air flow performed by supercomputers.

Numerical weather forecasting is another area requiring massive numbers of calculations to be performed, both for short-term weather forecasts, and for long-term climatic predictions, assessing conditions decades or even centuries hence.

Computer configurations

The term **computer configuration** is used to describe the collection of hardware used in an organisation or by an individual. Thus a typical computer configuration in a school office might consist of an Apple Macintosh with a 120MB hard disk, a 3½" floppy disk drive and a dot matrix printer. A larger computer configuration might comprise several microcomputers within a building linked together by cabling to form a **local area network**, so that users can share software, data and peripherals.

Q4: What would be a suitable computer configuration for use by a class of students in a school or college?

Exercises:

1. Which category of computer would be most suitable in the following situations?

   (a) A computer controlling space exploration rocket launches.

   (b) A large branch of a national grocery chain using the computer to run the EPOS (Electronic Point of Sale) terminals.

   (c) A firm of accountants employing 12 people handling customers' accounts.

   (d) A College administration system for handling student enrolments, class lists etc.

   (e) A large insurance brokers handling hundreds of millions of pounds worth of business every year.   (6 marks)

   (f) A public library in a medium sized town with a computerised system for the lending and return of books.

2. A floppy disk has a capacity of 1.44M bytes. Will this be sufficient to store 3 files of 700K, 710K and 20K respectively? How many megabytes in total will the three files occupy?   (2 marks)

3. A file of 68,600 bytes needs to be stored. Will it fit on a floppy disk with 67K of free disk space?   (1 mark)

4. Name 10 different ways in which you or any member of your family comes in contact with or is affected by computer technology in your daily lives. In general, do you think that the use of computers has improved the quality of life? Justify your answer.   (12 marks)

5. Describe briefly THREE situations in which the actions of a customer in a supermarket might generate data which is entered into a computer system.   (3 marks)

   AEB Paper 2 1989

6.* What are the differences between a floppy disk and a hard disk?   (3 marks)

7.* Some PCs are now equipped with a CD ROM drive. What are the differences between CD ROM and a hard disk? Name TWO applications for which CD ROM would be useful.   (4 marks)

* *Answers to questions marked with an asterisk are at the back of the book.*

Unit 2 — Introduction to Computer Software

Data processing

All computers are capable of performing four general operations: **input, process, output** and **storage**. Data (raw facts and numbers) are input to the computer from a keyboard or other input device, manipulated by the computer in a predetermined manner, and some form of output is produced. Some of the raw or processed data may be stored on disk, magnetic tape, or other device, or used to update information already held on one of these devices.

For a computer to perform its processing, it has to be given a detailed set of instructions called a **computer program, program instructions,** or **software**.

Application software packages

Most people who use a computer ('**end users**') do not write their own programs. Large companies employ systems analysts and programmers who design and write specialized systems for them. Small businesses often buy off-the-shelf **application packages** to perform common business tasks.

Q1: Name some common categories of business application package.

Advantages of using a software package

If a small company decides to computerise, for example, its customer invoicing system, there are many advantages in buying a software package rather than hiring a consultant to write the software, or getting an employee to write it, always assuming that a suitably skilled person is available.

Conversely, there are also some disadvantages in buying an off-the-shelf package as opposed to acquiring a tailor-made set of programs.

Q2: Make a list of these advantages and disadvantages.

5

Word processing software

Word processing software is used to write letters, reports, books and articles, and any other document that in the past would have been typed on a typewriter. As the user keys in the text, it appears on the screen and is held in the computer's memory. The user can easily edit the text, correct spelling mistakes, change margins and so on before printing out the final version. The document can also be saved on disk for future amendment or use. Until the instruction is given to save, however, the document held in memory will be lost if for example there is a power cut. Memory is a **volatile** storage medium, and users are well advised to save their work frequently.

Desktop publishing

Desktop publishing is an extension of word processing, allowing the user to lay out the page exactly as he or she wants it. This book was prepared using PageMaker desktop publishing software.

It is easy to change fonts and write in columns, and to draw simple diagrams. Often, a document is prepared using a word processor and then imported into PageMaker where it can be put into columns, different typefaces used, or diagrams added. Complex pictures and graphics can be prepared in other specialised drawing packages, or 'scanned' using a scanner and then imported onto the page before printing. Tasks that would previously have taken a graphic artist or printer hours of laborious work can now be achieved easily in a few minutes.

A College logo is imported...   *sized...*

'squashed'...   *and cropped.*

In order to make the best use of desktop publishing, of course, the proper hardware is essential. This includes a reasonably powerful microcomputer with a hard disk drive, a high capacity floppy disk drive, and a laser printer. A suitable printer would cost around £1200. In general, as software becomes more powerful and sophisticated, correspondingly more powerful, faster micros with more memory are required to run it.

There is no substitute for practical experience, so if at all possible you should use a desktop publishing package yourself and make notes on its capabilities.

Exercises:

1.　(a)　Use a word processing package to prepare a curriculum vitae.

　　(b)　Use a word processing package to write a report on the different features offered in the package you use. Structure the report by describing the main menu options and the most useful features available within each of these options. For example, your wordprocessor may have a **Format** menu which gives you facilities to change the font, make text **bold** or *italic*, align paragraphs left, right or centre and so on.

　　　　Include in your report examples of the features you describe. Be sure to try out the spellchecker!

2.　Word processing and spreadsheet packages are widely used in the office environment.

　　Outline the features which you consider to be essential in a word-processing package, and illustrate your answer with reference to a package with which you are familiar.　　　　　　　(10 marks)

NISEAC Paper 2 June 1989

3. Give an example of one organisation in which the introduction of a word-processing system might be beneficial. Explain what the benefits might be. (8 marks)

    UCLES Specimen AS Level 1989

4. Outline the technological developments that have enabled desktop publishing to be performed within an office environment. Indicate the effects of these developments on the office staff involved. *(6 marks)*

    UCLES AS Level May 1990

5. Word processors and desk top publishing systems are becoming widely used. List *three* drawbacks which have emerged with the use of these systems. (6 marks)

    NISEAC Paper 2 June 1989

6. A business word processing package contains a text-editor to enable documents to be prepared on a computer. The package also contains several data files and additional programs.

    Give **two** possible data files which might be included and state the possible use of **two** of the additional programs.

    (4 marks)

    London Paper 1 June 1989

7. Text prepared using a word processor can have its spelling checked using a spellchecking facility. When this is activated each word in the prepared text is checked against a dictionary of over 50,000 words held in ROM.

    (a) In principle, how can a spellchecker confirm the correct spelling of a word? (1 mark)

    (b) Certain rejected words may be correctly spelt. Describe, with examples, **two** distinct cases when this could occur and describe how a spellchecker could accommodate such words for future reference. (3 marks)

    (c) When may a spellchecker not be able to recognise a misspelling? Give an example. (2 marks)

    (d) Once any misspelt words have been found and isolated, describe what might be done in order to correct them. Describe any other facilities that a spellchecker might provide to assist the word processor operator.

    (6 marks)

    (Note: The next part of the question is included for completeness, but cannot be answered until data structures have been covered)

    (e) Describe, using diagrams, an appropriate data structure to hold the dictionary in order to provide a fast access route to any given word. Explain how the dictionary is accessed. (8 marks)

    JMB Paper 2 May 1989

8.* A secretary creates a file of text using a word processor and subsequently attempts to display the file by using the standard operating system command for outputting text files to the screen.

    Describe and explain the resulting screen display. (4 marks)

    NISEAC Paper 1 May 1990

9.* Some word-processing packages contain routines which periodically save the currently active file.

    (a) Explain the purpose of this feature.

    (b) Describe how the same purpose can be achieved when using a word-processing package which does not have this automatic feature.

    (c) Identify *one* factor which affects the frequency of the saves. (3 marks)

    London Paper 2 June 1992

Unit 3 — Spreadsheets and Integrated Packages

Spreadsheets

Spreadsheet software is used by people who work with numbers: accountants, banks and building society employees, engineers, financial planners. The user enters the data and the formulae to be used in manipulating the data, and the program calculates the results. One of the most useful features of a spreadsheet is its ability to perform **'What If'** calculations: "What if we produce 30% more widgets and wages increase by 10% — how much will we have to charge in order to show a profit?" Spreadsheets are therefore often used in **planning and budgeting**, but are also widely used by anyone working with figures — for example, keeping a set of students' marks.

Below is a diagram of the opening screen in the Lotus 1-2-3 Release 3 spreadsheet package.

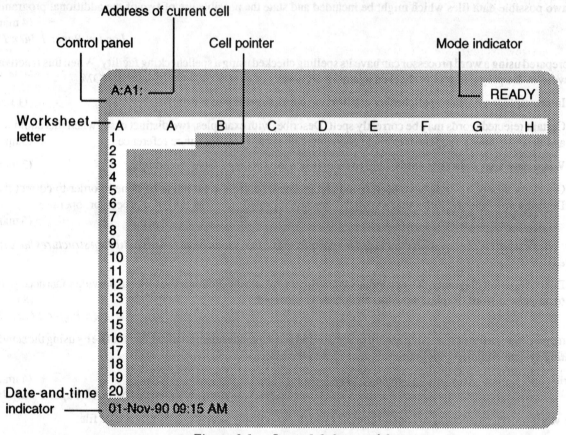

Figure 3.1 — Lotus 1-2-3 spreadsheet

Using the Spreadsheet

The user can move around the spreadsheet using the cursor keys (arrow keys), and enter text, numbers or formulae which will be automatically calculated. A menu of options can be displayed on the screen by pressing the / (slash) key. When an option is chosen, such as File, a further menu is displayed to allow the user to Save or Retrieve a file. This is known as a **hierarchical menu system**.

Other options allow the user to increase or decrease column width, insert or delete rows and columns, display numbers to a given number of decimal places, copy or move blocks of cells, etc. An advanced feature of spreadsheets is the ability to automate a series of steps using a **macro**, which is a sequence of instructions typed into the spreadsheet. The macro (which is in fact a computer program) can then be activated and those steps will be performed. A simple macro could for example display part of a spreadsheet, allow the user to enter some figures, then save and print the spreadsheet.

Computer graphics software

Using graphics software such as Harvard Graphics or Lotus Freelance, numeric values can quickly be transformed into different types of graph for a more easily grasped presentation. Most spreadsheet packages provide the ability to draw graphs such as bar graphs, pie charts and line graphs from a series of numbers.

Integrated packages

An increasingly important feature of modern software is its ability to **integrate** with other packages. For example a user may have some figures stored in a database which he wants to import into a graphics package, or he may have prepared some figures in a spreadsheet which he wants to insert into a word processed document. Many **integrated packages** such as Smart and Lotus Symphony have a spreadsheet module, a database module and a word-processing module and data can readily be transferred between modules. Other packages such as the spreadsheet Lotus 3 or SuperCalc 5 will accept data from, for example, dBase III+.

Exercises:

1. (a) Give **two** situations in which spreadsheet packages could be appropriately used. (2 marks)

   (b) Describe the form of entry of data, the manipulation of data and the output facilities provided by typical spreadsheet packages. (6 marks)
   UCLES Paper 2 Nov 1989

2. What are the key features of a *spreadsheet* package? In what way can a spreadsheet support decision-making processes? (3 marks)
   London Specimen Paper 2 1989

3. A small office coffee fund consists of six people contributing variable amounts of money weekly for supplies of the commodities coffee, sugar, milk and biscuits.

   One person (the organiser) is put in charge of this fund and decides to use a spreadsheet to keep the following accounts.

   (1) Incomings — record how much is received from each person each week and calculate a running total of how much each person has paid.

   (2) Outgoings — record weekly how much is spent on each commodity and calculate a running total of the cost of each commodity.

   (3) Balance — calculate a running balance showing the difference between incomings and outgoings.

   Whenever the outgoings exceed the incomings, indicated by a negative balance, the organiser goes around asking people for more contributions to the fund.

   The fund is cleared annually and any outstanding balance carried forward to the following year.

   (i) Draw a diagram to show the layout of the spreadsheet. (8 marks)

   (ii) Describe how the spreadsheet is initially set up with names, amounts, date, headings and formulae. Show clearly how the formulae cater for the proposed calculations. (8 marks)

   (iii) Describe how the spreadsheet is updated. (2 marks)

   (iv) Describe any necessary security procedures. (2 marks)
   JMB Paper 2 May 1990

4.   The following small spreadsheet indicates the examination results of 6 students in a series of seven examinations:

	A	B	C	D	E	F	G	H	I	J
1		EXAMINATION NUMBER								STUDENT
2	NAME	1	2	3	4	5	6	7	TOTAL	AVERAGE
3										
4	Bloggs,F	45	65	45	53	36	47	53	a	b
5	Brown,G	36	56	54	55	34	48	51		
6	Green,G	55	39	55	53	42	55	62		
7	Magenta,V	43	44	34	46	30	46	48		
8	Pink,A	56	62	53	58	51	52	66		
9	White,D	50	48	50	51	46	53	60		
10										
11	SUBJ.AVERAGE	c								d

Produce formulae (using functions where appropriate) to give *a*, *b*, *c*, and *d* on the sheet.   (6 marks)

NISEAC Paper 2 June 1990

5.   In a certain college, each student is examined in six subjects. To gain an overall certificate a student must attain a weighted average calculated by multiplying each of his subject scores by a given factor and summing the products.

It is required to:

(i)   Produce a results sheet containing the examination results and weighted average for each student, and the average mark for each subject.

(ii)   Provide a look-up facility to find students who match certain specified criteria:

e.g.   Physics > 70 AND Weighted average > 55

(iii)   Produce a written report on the examination including summary tables.

(a)   For each of the tasks outlined above, identify an appropriate software package and justify your choice by outlining the essential features of the package.   (24 marks)

(b)   Discuss the advantages and disadvantages of using a single integrated package rather than three distinct dedicated packages.   (6 marks)

NISEAC Paper 1 May 1990

6.*   Spreadsheet packages are now widely used in business.

(a)   Explain why spreadsheets are so useful.

(b)   Spreadsheet files are sometimes saved for use by other software packages. Give an example of such use.

(c)   Explain why spreadsheet packages offer a choice of data formats.   (5 marks)

London Paper 2 June 1992

Unit 4 — Human Computer Interface

Introduction

The 'human computer interface' (or 'man machine interface') is a term used to describe the interaction between a user and a computer; in other words, the method by which the user tells the computer what to do, and the responses which the computer makes.

The aim of any human computer interface is to make communication with the computer as easy as possible. This is one aspect of **user-friendly** software.

User-friendly software

The task of creating easy-to-use software is not an easy one, and an enormous amount of study, experimentation and effort has gone into ways of making software user-friendly. Such software usually has most of the following qualities:

- It is so simple that you can start using it before reading the documentation.

- It allows you to do your job, and nothing more.

- It does not get you lost, unable to continue no matter what key you press.

- It is consistent throughout, so that you can start to predict how the software will react to certain commands. An action or command must mean the same thing in different contexts.

- It should have helpful error messages so that you know what to do when you make a mistake or something unexpected happens.

- It should never 'crash', no matter what the user enters — with the exception of the 'Break' key or equivalent being pressed!

- It may have different ways of giving a command for different users — for example shortcuts for more experienced users.

- It should have a (pocket-sized) user manual which tells you what you want to know in easily understandable terms.

Q1: Suggest another attribute of user-friendly software.

Menu interface

In this type of interface the user is presented at each stage with a numbered 'menu' of choices and makes his choice by highlighting it or by keying in the number identifying his chosen option. In a **hierarchical menu system** he will then be presented with a further menu, and so on until the desired function is identified. Generally speaking menus should not be nested too deeply or it becomes difficult for a user to find his way around the system.

The Sage Accounting software provides an example of a hierarchical menu-driven interface.

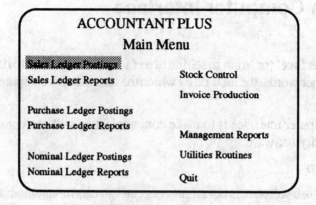

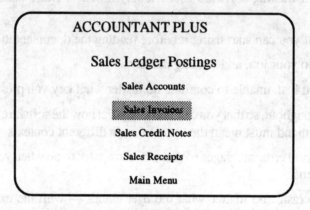

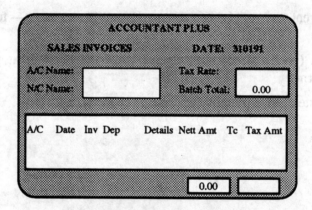

Figure 4.1 — Hierarchical menu interface

Pull-down menus

These are a variation of the menu interface. The top level of menu is displayed along the top of the screen and the user can make a choice either by using a given keystroke combination or by using a mouse to point at the chosen option. A second level of menu then appears and the user again makes a choice.

Pop-up menus

These are similar in operation to pull down menus, and as the name implies, appear on the screen in response to a user command.

12

Q2: Name a piece of software using   (a)   pull-down menus

                                               (b)   pop-up menus

The WIMP interface

WIMP stands for Windows, Icons, Mouse and Pull-down menus.

A **window** is an area on the screen through which a particular piece of software or data file may be viewed. The window may occupy the whole screen, or the user can choose to have several windows on the screen with a different application running in each one. Windows can be moved, sized, stacked one on top of the other, opened and closed. A Windows environment mimics a desktop on which a worker may have several books or pieces of paper spread out for reference.

An **icon** is a small picture representing an item such as a piece of software, a file, storage medium (such as disk or tape) or command. By pointing with a mouse at a particular icon and clicking the mouse button the user can select it.

Microsoft Windows enables the user to run several different software packages such as MS Word (a word processor), MS Excel (a spreadsheet), MS Paint (a graphics package) simultaneously and to move data and graphics from one package to another. Software packages written by other manufacturers, such as Aldus PageMaker, have been written to run under Windows because of the convenience to the user of this easy-to-use environment.

All these packages use a consistent interface and have a similar 'look and feel' so that a user familiar with one package can quickly learn a second. For example, in each package a single click of the mouse button **selects** an item, and a double click **activates** the item. In each package, the methods for opening, closing, sizing and moving windows is identical.

Q3: Design icons to represent   (a) a game of chess   (b) a word-processor   (c) an accounts package.

Forms and dialogue boxes

When a user is required to enter data such as, for example, sales invoices or customer names and addresses, it is common to have a 'form' displayed on the screen for the user to fill in. The following points should be noted when designing forms of this type:

- The display should be given a title to identify it.
- The form should not be too cluttered. Spaces and blanks in a display are important.
- It should give some indication of how many characters can be entered in each field of data.
- The user should be given a chance to go back and correct any field before the data is accepted.
- Items should appear in a logical sequence to assist the user.
- Default values should wherever possible be pre-written onto the form so that a minimum of data entry is required.
- Full exit and 'help' facilities should be provided. For example, the user could enter '?' in a field if he

requires more information.

- Lower case in a display is neater and easier to read than upper-case.

- 'Attention-getting' devices such as blinking cursors, high-intensity, reverse video, underlining etc should not be over-used.

Dialogue boxes are a special type of form often associated with the Windows environment; an example shown below is the dialogue box which appears when the instruction to Print a File is given in PageMaker.

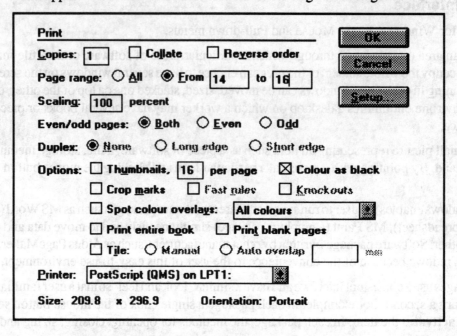

Figure 4.2 — Dialogue box

Command-driven interfaces

With this type of interface very little help is given to the user, who has to type a command such as, for example, DELETE FILE1 to delete a file. Commands enable a user to quickly and concisely instruct the computer what to do, but they do require the user to have a knowledge of the commands available and the syntax for using them. How for example do you delete two files?

Q4: Identify TWO situations in which a command-driven interface would be appropriate.

Speech input (voice recognition)

The ultimate in user-friendly interfaces would probably be one in which you could simply tell your computer what to do in ordinary speech. Two distinct types of voice recognition system are emerging; small vocabulary command and control systems and large vocabulary dictation systems.

- **command and control systems** can be relatively small and cheap because they need only a small, tightly defined vocabulary of technical terms. Such systems are coming rapidly into use as automatic call-handling systems for applications such as bank account enquiries. In PC systems, voice command can be used to bring up files, control printing and so on, effectively replacing the mouse. In some systems the computer is 'trained' by an individual user speaking in a vocabulary of words and keying them in at the same time; it then stores a recording of the user's speech pattern for each word or syllable.

14

- **Large vocabulary dictation systems** can handle whole sentences and extensive vocabularies but need much greater processing power and memory space. These systems use elaborate probability distributions to estimate which word the accoustic pattern it has picked up is most likely to be, partly by looking at other words in the developing sentence and predicting what sort of word (noun or verb, for example) is likely to be used. IBM in September 1993 demonstrated a PC that after suitable 'training' will take dictation at 70 words per minute and gets 97% of them correct. Voice recognition is however still an expensive technology and widespread use is some way off.

Q5: Name some other situations in which voice input would be appropriate.

Advantages and disadvantages of natural language dialogue

Advantages:

- Most natural form of dialogue for humans — no need for training in a specialised command language.

- Extremely flexible and powerful.

- The user is free to construct his own commands, frame his own questions, etc.

Disadvantages:

- People find it difficult to stick to strictly grammatical English.

- A well designed 'artificial language' can often say the same thing more concisely than 'natural language'.

- A smooth, natural language can easily mislead the naive user into believing the computer is much more intelligent than it actually is.

Speech/sound output

A speech synthesis system works as follows:

Individual words and sounds are spoken into a microphone by a human being and recorded by the system, thereby training it to speak. Output that would normally be printed can then be spoken, so long as the word is contained in its vocabulary. Sometimes words which are not recognised are spelt out.

Such a system has limited use but could for example be used by a bank computer connected by telephone line to customers' homes and offices. The customer could key in his account number using the telephone keypad, and the computer could then access his account and speak out the customer's account balance.

Special purpose human-computer interfaces

Sometimes the HCI is provided by special hardware and software, for example in a cash dispensing machine, or in an automatic pilot system in an aircraft where special dials convey information to the human pilot. **Embedded computers** are computers built into special purpose equipment and controlled by an interface specific to that purpose, like a washing machine.

Q6: Give other examples of special-purpose interfaces.

Exercises:

1.   Much early software was thought to be unfriendly to the user as little consideration was given to the user interface. Describe three examples of techniques that have been introduced in an attempt to reduce some of the problems of the user interface.   (5 marks)

AEB Specimen AS paper 1990

2.   In June 1990 Lotus Development, which markets the LOTUS 1-2-3 package (one of the most profitable computer programs in history) successfully sued Paperback Software, a small company in Boston, for selling a computer program that looked and worked just like LOTUS 1-2-3. Ashton-Tate, creator of dBase, sued two other companies for writing software that used the same programming language as dBase. In each case, the code used was quite different but the 'look and feel', the **user interface**, is identical to the original program.   (4 marks)

Produce arguments for and against the view that software manufacturers should be allowed to copy good ideas from other programmers.

3.   A travel agent's enquiry and booking system is used by staff with various levels of technological expertise.

Explain how careful selection and design of

      (i)   the hardware

      (ii)   the software

      (iii) the user documentation

      (iv)   the user interface

can aid in the development of a user-friendly system for such an application.   (8 marks)

UCLES Paper 2 Nov 1989

4.   By means of a suitable application in each case, explain what is meant by

      (a)   a menu selection dialogue

      (b)   a command dialogue with a help list

      (c)   a forms dialogue   (6 marks)

London Specimen Paper 1 1989

5.*   Considerable efforts have been made to provide powerful yet intuitive user interfaces to a wide range of application packages, operating systems and programming languages.

      (a)   Identify a range of facilities that could be provided and discuss the perceived need for such facilities. (4 marks)

      (b)   Describe how you might assess the effectiveness of such interfaces.   (1 mark)

London Paper 2 June 1991

Unit 5 — Business Information Systems

"In the end, all business operations can be reduced to three words: people, product and profit. People come first. Unless you've got a good team, you can't do much with the other two".

Lee Iacocca, Chairman of Chrysler Motors (An Autobiography)

All businesses exist to make money. In order to increase profits, a business has basically two options:

1. Increase revenue from sales or services
2. Decrease costs

Each of these objectives can be broken down into several more levels of detail.

Q1: What steps could a manufacturing business take to increase sales?

Q2: Name two general types of costs which a manufacturing business will incur.

Q3: Continue the 'structure diagram' to show how the main objective of making a profit can be broken down:

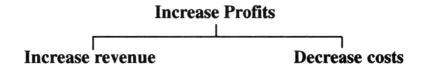

Types of information system

In general, there are three **levels** in the hierarchy of a business organization.

1. The **strategic** level, consisting of senior management responsible for long term planning and policy-making decisions.

2. The **tactical** level, consisting of middle management in charge of one particular department or area of the business such as Sales and Marketing, Accounts, or Production.

3. The **operational** level consisting of the workforce who are taking sales orders, keeping the accounts, making the product, and so on.

Each of these three levels needs information suited to their particular needs. Information systems can be classified into the following types:

- operational systems

- management information systems

- decision support systems

- expert systems

Operational systems

An operational system is designed to process data generated by the day-to-day business transactions of a company. Examples of operational systems are accounting systems, invoicing systems, stock control systems and order entry systems. For example, a clerk processing customer orders needs to know:

- whether the item is in stock

- what the price of the item is

- what discount if any the customer should be given

- customer details such as address, credit status, etc.

Q4: What information would a wages clerk need to enter into a payroll system which calculates weekly wages for factory workers? What information about each worker would be held in the computer system?

Management information systems

In the early days of business computing, computers were usually used to replace an existing manual system. This often resulted in faster processing, reduced clerical costs, and improved customer service.

Managers then began to see that the computer's ability to process large quantities of data very fast could be used to produce useful information for management purposes. Often the same data that is used as part of an operational system can be used to produce management information. For example, in a system for processing sales orders, the item sold, quantity and customer's details would be entered, and the **operational system** would update the customer's balance, print an invoice and make a deduction from the stock file. The related **management information system** could produce reports showing, for example:

- what the total sales of each item were last period

- how that compares with the same period last year

- which sales areas had the highest sales

- which customers have had amounts outstanding for more than three months, and so on.

Q5: What management information could be extracted from a payroll system?

Decision support systems

Managers will often need information that is not routinely provided by operational or management information systems. For example, a company chairman may want to know the effect on profits if sales increase by 10% and costs increase by 5%.

A decision support system is a system designed to help someone reach a decision by summarising all the available relevant information. Some of this information may be held in the company's database, and some may be external to the company, such as current interest rates, the price of oil, population trends, or new competitors starting up in the area. Decision support systems often include **query languages** to enable managers to make spontaneous requests from databases, **spreadsheet models** which enable 'What if' calculations to be made, and **graphics** to provide a clear representation of the available data.

A common characteristic of decision support systems is interactivity. The systems need to be easy to use, and to be really useful they need to be able to accept input from the user and then provide the required answer. Expert systems are a special type of decision support system.

Expert systems

An expert system is a computer program which is capable of emulating human reasoning. It does this by combining the knowledge of human experts on a given subject, and then following rules that it has been given to draw inferences. To use the system, the user sits at a terminal and answers questions posed by the computer, which eventually reaches a diagnosis or decision and will also tell the user how it has reached a particular conclusion.

Expert systems have been used in such fields as medical diagnosis, fault diagnosis in a steel rolling mill, geological prospecting, processing Social Security claims, and management of stock portfolios. (Expert systems are discussed in more detail in Unit 80.)

Exercises:

1. Give THREE general reasons why businesses use computers to assist in their administration.   (3 marks)
    AEB Paper 2 1986

2. "The increased use of computers and information technology in commerce and industry has made life more convenient and less complicated for the ordinary person".

    Give **two** points in support of this proposition and **two** points against it.   (4 marks)
    AEB Paper 2 1987

3. "The introduction of new technology into the workplace may produce a decline in job satisfaction."

    Give **one** argument in support of this claim and **one** argument against it.   (2 marks)
    AEB Paper 2 1988

4. Distinguish between information systems for

    — Data Processing

    — Office Support

    — Decision Support   (6 marks)
    NISEAC Paper 2 June 1990

5.* The manager of a cinema is facing a dilemma, whether to raise admission prices by a small amount to ensure total income continues just to cover running expenses or to risk a much larger increase. Suggest a suitable *type of general purpose package* for the manager to use to study the implications of the options. Explain how the manager could use this package to assist the decision making process and the setting of admission prices.   (4 marks)
    AEB Paper 1 1992

19

Unit 6 — Methods of Processing

An overview of processing techniques

'Input — Process — Output'; all computers perform these three general tasks. Within this broad framework, the ways in which we use computers to perform various tasks can be broken down into different categories. Consider the following examples:

- a computer being used to control the landing of an aircraft has to respond instantly to information received from sensors measuring height, speed, position etc, and to commands the human pilot might give.

- an Electronic Point-of-Sale (EPOS) terminal at the checkout in a supermarket may be connected to a minicomputer holding the description and price of each barcoded item. As the item is passed over the scanner the details are displayed on a screen and printed on the customer's receipt.

- a mainframe computer which is used to calculate the payroll for a large company can be given the data and within certain limits the payroll program can be run at any time without any further interaction with the user.

These three situations are examples of **real-time**, **on-line** and **batch processing** respectively.

Real-time processing

Real-time processing means that the computer has to keep pace with some external operation, processing the data that it receives more or less instantaneously and producing immediate results.

Real-time systems are used in a variety of situations and generally speaking fall into one of two categories:

1. process control
2. information storage and retrieval

Process control

This is the control of machinery or industrial processes by means of a computer. Sensors continuously monitor data such as temperature, pressure, composition of substances and so on and the computer reacts accordingly. Thousands of tasks including the operation of a nuclear power station, controlling processes in chemical engineering, monitoring and controlling medical equipment in hospitals and the manufacture of a wide range of goods provide examples of process control.

Q1: Name some items of data that would be input to a computer which was controlling the landing of an aircraft. In your opinion, can this task be safely performed without human intervention?

Information storage and retrieval ('interactive processing')

A different type of real-time system is one in which a single user or a number of users needs to be able to make queries and update information held in a file. Often such systems will involve large databases held on mainframe computers, as for example in an airline reservation system. A user sitting at a terminal will type in the details of the customer's request, and details of suitable flights will be displayed. A booking can then be made and will be recorded immediately. Such systems need sophisticated procedures for ensuring that the same seat is not sold simultaneously to two different customers in different places.

This type of interactive processing, where the user enters all the data pertaining to one transaction and the computer then processes it, is called **'transaction processing'**.

Real-time systems are also used in small businesses, for example in stock control systems where as soon as a sale is made the invoice is printed out and the appropriate amount deducted from the quantity in stock. A library system where books borrowed are immediately recorded as being out to a particular person is another example of a real-time system.

The expression **'pseudo real-time'** is sometimes used to describe a real-time system where a delay of a few seconds may occur before the system responds. Such a delay is usually quite acceptable in an enquiry system.

'Interactive processing' is another term used to mean that data is processed upon entry and output produced immediately.

Q2: Briefly describe TWO examples of real-time systems which you have seen being used.

On-line processing

For real-time processing, the input device (which may be a terminal, a barcode reader, a device to read the magnetic strip on a credit card, etc) must be **on-line** to the computer. This expression simply means that it is connected to the computer and it is therefore possible to access information held on the computer. Some systems may permit a user to access information, but not to change it. An example of this would be a cash register in a supermarket or department store which can look up the description and price of an article, but does not update the stock information when a sale is made. This is a simpler and cheaper system to run and does not require such a powerful computer or such sophisticated software and backup procedures to handle computer breakdowns.

Q3: Many banks operate an on-line system for customers to draw out cash via a cashpoint machine. Others have a real-time system. What is the difference from the customer's point of view?

Note that the term 'on-line' is also applied to files of data held on backing storage such as disk. If a file is 'on-line' it is accessible at that particular time to the program currently running. Data stored on a floppy disk which is lying on your desk is 'off-line'!

Batch processing

In a typical batch processing environment, large volumes of data are received at a centralised data processing department, usually in the form of typed or handwritten forms. These **source documents** are then counted into batches of say 50 or 100 and entered into the computer to be held on a **transaction file** until they can be processed. Batch processing is often (although not always) carried out on mainframe computers, which are also being used for real-time processing. Since there is generally no immediate urgency for a batch of data to be processed, this is often done at night when the computer would otherwise be idle.

Batch processing is considered in more detail in the next Unit.

Combined interactive and batch processing

Some applications use both interactive and batch processing. This is illustrated in the following example, describing a banking application.

1. Bank customers use cashpoint machines to withdraw cash by inserting their cards, typing in their PIN (Personal Identification Number) and the amount of cash to be withdrawn.

2. As soon as the data is entered, the program directs the computer to retrieve the customer's record from the customer file.

3. The program reduces the customer's balance by the amount withdrawn, or refuses the transaction if the balance is insufficient. The new balance is sent back to the customer's display, the card is positioned for the customer to retrieve it and the cash is issued when he has done so.

4. The new balance is written back to the customer file.

5. The program adds a record to the transaction file. This file contains a record for each transaction made during the day.

6. At 2am, the cashpoint machine is closed and the transaction file is input to a program that produces a daily summary of cashpoint transactions.

Q4: Which of the steps above involve interactive processing and which involve batch processing?

Q5: Some important details have been left out of the above description! What are they?

Centralised versus distributed processing

In the 1960s when computers began to be widely used in business and commerce, the trend was to have a centralised data processing department with a mainframe computer and a staff of systems analysts, programmers, computer operators and other data processing staff. All data would be sent to this department for input and processing and the reports would be sent back to the department originating the request.

With the advent of minis and microcomputers, this trend has been reversed over the past decade or more, with each branch or department in an organization having its own processing power in the form of workstations attached to a local minicomputer, or microcomputers forming a local area network, possibly also connected to a mainframe at head office. This is known as **distributed processing**.

Q6: A large company has a central mainframe computer, and employees throughout the company have 'dumb' terminals on their desks — that is, terminals consisting of a VDU and keyboard only, from which they can enter data and run programs. The terminals are all connected to the mainframe computer. Is this 'distributed' or 'centralised' computing?

Q7: What are the advantages of distributed processing as opposed to centralised processing? What are the disadvantages?

Exercises:

1. What is meant by a real time transaction system? Describe the operation of such a system by considering a relevant application with which you are familiar. (6 marks)
   WJEC AS May 1990

2. In some applications, data entry takes place at the site where the data is generated ('distributed data entry') but processing takes place centrally. Give an example of distributed data entry used in conjunction with centralised data processing.

3. Name a processing method suitable for use in each of the following situations. Justify your answers.

   (a) A submarine uses a computer to monitor sonar readings which determine its height above the sea bed. The computer maintains the submarine at a constant height above the sea bed.

   (b) Monthly sales information from each shop in an international chain is electronically transferred to a central computer. The data is processed to try to identify fashion trends. (4 marks)
   AEB Paper 2 1989

4. (a) Distinguish between a *batch processing system* and a *multi-user on-line system*. Identify those additional features required in a *multi-user on-line system* that are not needed in a *batch processing system*. Give one example of the realistic use of each type of system. (7 marks)

   (b) What is meant by a *distributed computer system*? Why might an educational establishment consider purchasing a distributed system in preference to other types of computer system? (8 marks)
   UCLES AS Level May 1989

5.* A bank's computer system supports on-line enquiries during the day and batch processing at night.

   Describe *three* tasks which the bank's computer might perform in batch processing mode. (3 marks)
   London Paper 1 1992

6.* Clearly distinguish between batch and real-time processing. (2 marks)

   Describe an application that is suitable for batch processing. What are the advantages and disadvantages of batch processing for this application over real-time processing? (4 marks)
   JMB Paper 1 1991

Unit 7 — Batch Processing

Data entry for batch processing

As explained in the previous Unit, computer applications use either interactive or batch processing methods to process data. The methods used to input data for batch processing will be different from those used for interactive processing.

While data entry for interactive processing is necessarily **on-line** (meaning that the device used for data entry is connected to the computer used for processing it), data entry for batch processing is frequently **off-line**. In this case, the data is input to a computer other than the one on which it will eventually be processed. Frequently the computer used for data entry is used for nothing else and is said to be **dedicated** to data input (see for example the **key-to-disk** unit discussed in Unit 71).

In **on-line** batch data entry, data is input directly to the computer on which it will be processed, but it is stored on disk or tape for processing later, in a batch.

The steps in batch processing

In a large scale batch environment, thousands of input documents may be received every day for input and processing. Stringent procedures have to be followed in order to make sure that no documents are lost or entered twice by mistake, and that all data is correctly **transcribed** (ie copied from the source document). The following procedures are commonly followed:

1. The documents are **scrutinised** by a **data control clerk**, who is in charge of the data entry department. She will make sure that the documents are legible and contain all the necessary information.

2. The source documents are then counted into batches of 50 or 100, and a **batch header slip** or **batch cover note** is filled in for each batch, and attached to the front of the batch. Each batch is given a number, which is entered on the batch header slip and recorded in a **batch register**. It will be the responsibility of the data control clerk to monitor the progress of each batch through the data preparation and processing system, recording its progress in the register.

Q1: Design a batch header for a batch of customer orders received by a mail order firm, 'WorldWide Fashions Limited'. A sample form is shown with Q3.

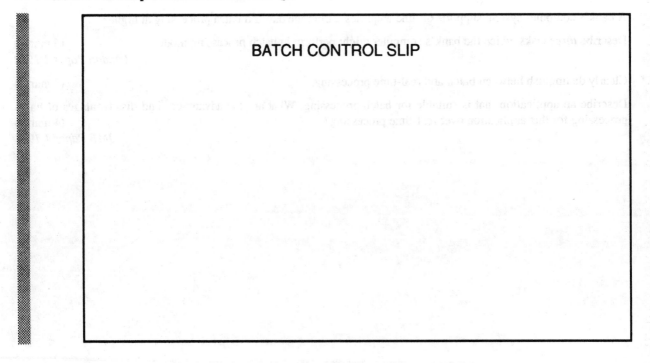

BATCH CONTROL SLIP

3. **Control totals** are calculated manually for the batch. In a batch of data recording customer payments, for example, the total of all payments would be calculated and entered on the batch header.

    Control totals are of two types — totals that are meaningful in some way, such as total payments, total hours worked by employees in a week, etc and totals that are meaningless but are useful for checking that the data has been entered correctly. This type of control total is known as a **hash total**.

4. The batch of data, including the batch header, is keyed in by a **data preparation clerk** and stored on disk or tape.

5. The batch is now passed to a second data preparation clerk who switches the terminal to **verify** mode, and keys the data in a second time. If any discrepancies are detected, the clerk will be able to check the source document and make a correction if necessary.

6. The batch of data on disk or tape is now ready to be **validated** by means of a computer program. This will be done on the computer used for processing the data. A variety of checks will be carried out, as described later in this Unit.

7. If any errors are discovered by the validation program, these will be printed on a validation report and the incorrect records in the batch will be retrieved and rekeyed. Steps 6 and 7 will be repeated until no errors are found.

8. The valid data is now held on a **transaction file** on disk or tape and is ready to be processed.

Q2: Draw a block diagram showing the stages in batch processing up to the point where the data is ready to be processed.

Validation checks

The validation program mentioned in steps 6 and 7 above will carry out a series of checks appropriate to the source data, in an attempt to ensure that the data has been correctly entered.

The following checks may be carried out:

1. **Presence check.** The program checks that all items of data are present. For example, the customer account number could not be omitted on a sales order.

2. **Character count.** Some items such as a customer code or product code are of fixed length, say 8 characters.

3. **Picture check.** This ensures that certain fields are in the correct format, for example 3 letters followed by 6 digits.

4. **Range check.** This checks that a field lies within a particular range — for example week number must be between 1 and 53.

5. **Check digit checks.** see below

6. **File lookup.** If the validation program has access to master files, then input data can be validated by reference to those files. For example a stock file could be looked up to verify that a given product code exists.

7. **Batch header checks.** Any control totals on the batch header which have been manually calculated will be calculated by the computer and the totals compared. This will include the total number of records in the batch, and any hash totals that have been calculated.

Q3: What checks could be carried out on a batch of mail order forms, a sample of which is given below?

Worldwide Fashions Limited Bradford West Yorkshire BD17 6DA					**CUSTOMER ORDER FORM**		
Customer name:							
Full postal address:							
				Postal code			
date							
description	colour number	catalogue number	size	price each £ p		how many	office use

Check digits

Code numbers such as customer number, employee number or product number are often lengthy and prone to errors when being keyed in. One way of preventing these errors occurring is to add an extra digit to the end of a code number, which has been calculated from the digits of the code number. In this way the code number with its extra check digit is self-checking.

The best-known method of calculating check digits is the modulus-11 system, which traps over 99% of all errors. The calculation of a check digit is shown below.

1. Each digit of the code number is assigned a weight. The right hand (least significant) digit is given a weight of 2, the next digit to the left 3, and so on.

2. Each digit is multiplied by its weight and the products added together.

3. The sum of the products is divided by 11 and the remainder obtained.

4. The remainder is subtracted from 11 to give the check digit. The two exceptions are:
   - If the remainder is 0, the check digit is 0.
   - If the remainder is 1, the check digit is X.

Example:

To calculate the check digit for the number 1587:

original code number	1	5	8	7
weights	5	4	3	2
multiply digits by its weight	5	20	24	14
Add products together	5 + 20 + 24 + 14 = 63			
Divide by 11	5 remainder 8			
Subtract remainder from 11	11 - 8 = 3			

Check digit = 3. The complete code number is therefore 15873.

Q4: Calculate the check digit for the number 1578. Is the number 15783 a valid code?

Q5: Most books have an **ISBN** (International Standard Book Number) printed on the back cover. This number incorporates a modulus-11 check digit. Find a book with an ISBN and use the above method to check that it is a valid code number.

Note that in order to check that a code number is valid, it is not necessary to recalculate the check digit completely. If the check digit itself is assigned a weight of 1, and the products of the digits (including the check digit) and their respective weights are calculated, their sum will be divisible by 11 if the check digit is correct.

Exercises:

1. State **three** circumstances when batch processing is more appropriate than real-time processing. (3 marks)
   AEB Paper 2 1990

2. The transaction file in a company's payroll process includes employee number, hours worked, department, and week number. How might each of the following validation checks be applied to this data:

   (a) control total?

   (b) range check?

   (c) check digit? (3 marks)
   AEB Paper 2 1990

3. (a) Explain the main characteristics of the following processing methods:

   batch

   pseudo real time (or interactive) processing (6 marks)

   (b) State **one** advantage of each of these methods in comparison with the other. (2 marks)

   (c) Name a processing method which would be suitable for the following jobs, justifying your answers:

   (i) Processing issues and renewals of books in a library

   (ii) Processing the monthly payroll for a large company

   (iii) Processing mail order requests for car insurance quotations (6 marks)
   AEB Paper 2 1987

4. The data capture process for a particular computerised stock control system begins when a standard form is filled in at the stock issue counter. These forms are received and batched by data control. The data is then keyed to floppy disk for processing.

   Give examples of the types of error likely to occur. (4 marks)
   London Specimen AS Paper 1989

5.* Distinguish between *verification* and *validation* in the context of data entry. Give examples to illustrate your answer. (3 marks)
   London Paper 1 1991

6.* A large hardware shop supplies a wide variety of kitchen and dining room utensils, bathroom equipment, and many items for the "do-it-yourself" handyman. There are usually eight assistants serving customers and an office staff of two who handle the paperwork and administration, all under the supervision of a manager.

   The shop is about to install a single microcomputer system for the use of the office staff. One use of the system will be to process the payroll.

   (a) Suggest **two** other purposes for which the system is likely to be used in the office. For each of these uses explain in general terms what data will be supplied to the system, how it might be captured, what processing the system might apply to the data, what output would be expected and how it might be displayed. (10 marks)

   (b) What will be the chief advantages of the new system from the point of view of the office staff? Are there any disadvantages? How will the new system affect the privacy of the personal information held in the office about the shop employees? What effect will it have on the risk of fraud or dishonesty on the part of the staff or manager? (6 marks)

   (c) It has been suggested that the shop would have done better to invest in a more complex system, with a number of terminals in the shop as well as in the office. Give reasons for and against this suggestion. (2 marks)
   UCLES Paper 2 November 1992

Unit 8 — File Concepts

Data storage

In a manual system, data may be stored in folders in a filing cabinet, loose leaf pages in a ledger, cards in a cardbox, or numerous other ways.

In a computer system, data is commonly stored on magnetic media such as disk or tape. These provide a more permanent form of storage than main memory because they are **non-volatile**, ie the data is retained when the power is switched off.

However the data is stored, it must be capable of being quickly retrieved for inspection or processing, and the purpose of this Unit is to explain the various ways in which files can be organised.

What is a file?

A file is an organised collection of data. In computer terminology an employee file, for example, consists of a collection of data about **all** employees, a stock file consists of a collection of data about **all** stock items, and so on. A file therefore consists of a number of **records**.

A **record** is the collection of data pertaining to **one** item or individual. It consists of a number of **fields**, which each hold one piece of data such as name, date of birth etc. Some fields will hold **characters**, and some fields will be **numeric** and used in calculations, such as price or quantity in stock. If a field consists of digits only, such as a telephone number, but is never going to be used in a calculation, it is often convenient to define it as a character field in any case. Once a field has been defined as a numeric field it is impossible to store any other characters in it.

Q1: Why should you not store a telephone number as a numeric field?

Primary and secondary keys

Each record usually has some way of identifying it uniquely, with one of the fields within the record acting as a **primary key field**. Thus each record in a file must have a different **primary key** in order to distinguish it from all the other records. Sometimes there is no one field which is unique to each record and a second field is used as part of the primary key, which is then called a **composite primary key**.

In addition to having one primary key, records may have one or more **secondary keys**. These are fields which are not unique to each record, but which may be put in an index and used to retrieve records. For example, in a stock file, the primary key might be a unique stock number, and secondary keys could be supplier and type of item.

Q2: Which field or fields on a telephone directory file will act as the primary key?

Q3: In a file of library books, what field could be used as a primary key? What fields could be used as secondary keys?

The word 'file' is frequently misused by people new to computer terminology to mean a *record,* that is, the data relating to a single individual or item, because this is how the term is used in everyday English. However, this is *wrong, wrong, wrong*! So do not talk about retrieving or updating a file when you mean retrieving or updating a record.

Master and transaction files

Most large companies have hundreds or even thousands of files that store data pertaining to the business. Some of the files will be **transaction files** and some will be **master files**.

Transaction files contain details of all transactions that have occurred in the last period. A period may be the time that has elapsed since business started that day, or it may be a day, a week, a month or more. For example a sales transaction file may contain details of all sales made that day. Once the data has been processed it can be discarded (although backup copies may be kept for a while).

Master files are permanent files kept up to date by applying the transactions that occur during the operation of the business. They contain generally two basic types of data:

- Data of a more or less permanent nature such as on a payroll file, name, address, rate of pay etc.

- Data which will change every time transactions are applied to the file — for example, gross pay to date, tax paid to date, etc.

Q4: A file of student records is to be kept holding student number, personal details such as name and address, course number and course grade (A-F). Design a record structure for the file, under the following headings:

Field description **Field length** **Field type (character or numeric)**

Organising files

Files stored on magnetic media can be organised in a number of ways, just as in a manual system. There are advantages and disadvantages to each type of file organisation, and the method chosen will depend on several factors such as:

- how the file is to be used

- how many records are processed each time the file is updated

- whether individual records need to be quickly accessible.

Types of file organisation

The available methods include:

- serial
- sequential
- indexed sequential
- random

Serial file organisation

The records on a serial file are not in any particular sequence, and so this type of organisation would not be used for a master file as there would be no way to find a particular record except by reading through the whole file, starting at the beginning, until the right record was located. Serial files are used as temporary files to store transaction data.

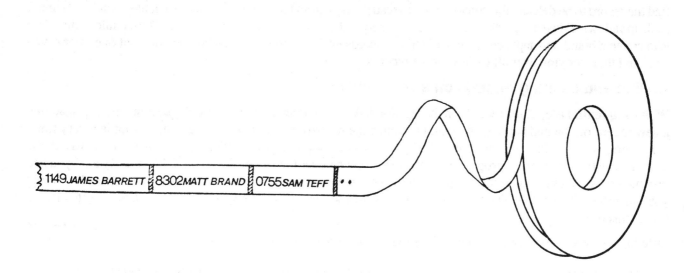

Figure 8.1 — A serial file

Sequential file organisation

As with serial organisation, records are stored one after the other, but in a sequential file the records are sorted into **key sequence**. Files that are stored on tape are **always** either serial or sequential, as it is impossible to write records to a tape in any way except one after the other. From the computer's point of view there is essentially no difference between a serial and a sequential file. In both cases, in order to find a particular record, each record must be read, starting from the beginning of the file, until the required record is located. However, when the whole file has to be processed (for example a payroll file prior to payday) sequential processing is fast and efficient.

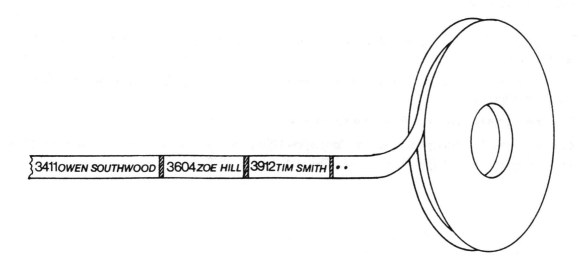

Figure 8.2 — A sequential file

Adding and deleting records on a serial file

Most computer languages that are used for data processing include statements which allow the file to be opened at the end of existing records. Then, if one or more new records has to be added to a serial file, there is no problem; the new records can simply be appended to the end of the file.

Deleting a record is more complex. It is easy to understand the problem if you imagine the file is held on magnetic tape, and understand that in any particular program run you can **either** read from the tape **or** write to the tape. To find the record to be deleted, the computer has to read the tape from the beginning; but once it has found it, it cannot back up and 'wipe' just that portion of the tape occupied by the record, leaving a blank space. The technique therefore is to create a brand new tape, copying over all the records up to the one to be deleted, leaving that one off the new tape, and then copying over all the rest of the records.

Adding and deleting records on a sequential file

With a **sequential** file, all the records on the tape (or disk) are in order, perhaps of employee number, so just adding a new record on the end is no good at all. Of course the records could then be sorted but sorting is a very time-consuming process. The best and 'correct' way is to make a new copy of the file, copying over all records till the new one can be written in its proper place, and then copying over the rest of the records. It's exactly as if you had just made a list on a nice clean sheet of paper of all the students in the class in order of surname, and then discovered you had left out Carter, A.N. The only way to end up with a perfect list is to copy it out again, remembering to include Carter this time.

Deleting a record is exactly the same as for serial organisation.

Q5: How would you **change** a record on a sequential file held on magnetic tape? (e.g. if you had got Carter's initials wrong?)

Exercises:

1. Distinguish between the terms **primary key** and **secondary key** as applied to files and give an example of each from within a payroll master file.
    (6 marks)
    NISEAC Paper 1 1991

2. What is meant by the term file organisation? Name four different types of file organisation and describe briefly how records are held in TWO of these organisations.
    (10 marks)

    Name an application suitable for each of the choices you have described, giving reasons why the file organisation is particularly appropriate.
    (8 marks)

3. Distinguish between a **master file** and a **transaction file**.
    (2 marks)

    In a computerised electricity billing system, three types of file are used; master files, transaction files and reference files. Describe the possible contents of ONE file of each type in this system.
    (8 marks)

Unit 9 — Indexed and Random Files

Indexed sequential file organisation

Just as in a sequential file, records are stored in sequence based on the value in the key field of each record. In addition, however, an indexed file contains an index consisting of a list of key field values and the corresponding disk address for each record in the file. The index is usually stored with the file when the file is first created, and retrieved from disk and placed in memory when the file is to be processed.

For a large file held on a disk pack, more than one **level** of index is required. The simplest indexing technique is called **cylinder-surface-sector** indexing. For each disk pack in the file, there is a **cylinder index**, or **primary index**, which will normally all be read into memory and held there while the file is in use. It contains a list of the highest keys held in each cylinder of the file, as shown in the example on the next page. When looking for a record with a particular key, this index is searched from the beginning until an entry is found which is greater than or equal to the key required. The cylinder holding the record is thus ascertained and the read-write heads can be moved there (a process known as **seeking**).

A **cylinder** on a disk pack is made up of all the tracks that can be accessed from one position of the read-write heads; thus if each disk has 200 tracks, there will be 200 cylinders on the disk pack. The cylinders do not of course really exist in any touchable form, it is merely a convenient concept. When a large number of records is written to a file, all the tracks in one cylinder are filled first and then the read-write heads move across to the next cylinder. This minimises the movement of the read-write heads and results in faster data transfer than filling up one surface after another.

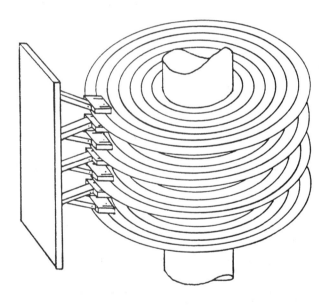

Figure 9.1 — A disk pack

Having reached the correct cylinder, a further index is read and searched. This is the **surface index**, or **secondary index**, which holds a list of the surface numbers and the highest key to be found there. There is one of these indexes for each cylinder of the file. By comparing these hi-keys with the one required, the correct surface can be selected (a process known as **switching**).

Once on the right track, a third level of index, the **sector index** can be read and searched as before, to give the sector number at which the record is to be found.

For example, suppose we wish to access the record with key 5584. The cylinder index might look like this:

cylinder	hi-key
0	193
1	346
.	...
.	...
19	4382
20	5495
** 21	6608
.	...
.	...
199	49999

Searching this index, the first number which is greater than or equal to 5584 is 6608. This shows that our record, if it exists, is on cylinder 21.

Thus, the read/write heads are moved to cylinder 21. On arrival, the surface index is located on surface 0 and is read:

surface	hi-key
0	5510
** 1	5622
2	5843
.	...
.	...
7	6608

This means that record 5584 should be on surface 1, so the read head for that surface is activated.

The sector index located on sector 0 of cylinder 21, surface 1 is then read:

sector	hi-key
0	5521
1	5538
2	5560
3	5568
4	5583
** 5	5597
6	5606
7	5622

This tells the system that the record with key 5584 should be in sector 5, so that sector 5 is read into main store. It will then be serially searched until the correct record is located. If it is not found, then

- *either* the record does not exist

- *or* when the record was added to the file, there was no room for it in cylinder 21, surface 1, sector 5, and so the record was **overflowed** elsewhere (see below).

All this disk accessing and searching is time consuming, but still much faster than a serial search of a sequential file for finding an individual record. However, the indexes take up quite a lot of space, and this is a disadvantage of indexed sequential organisation. The major advantage of this file organisation is that it can be processed either **randomly** using the indexes, or **sequentially** without using the indexes.

Overflow

When a record, either a variable length record which has become longer during updating, or a record which is being newly inserted into the file, will not fit into the sector which should accommodate it (ie its **home sector**), then an overflow has occurred. To allow for such a happening, an **overflow area** is created on the disk pack. When a record will not fit onto its home sector, it is placed into an overflow sector and a message or **tag** is left in its home sector giving the key field of the record and the address of the overflow sector in which it can be found. A second access then takes place and the record can be retrieved. Where possible, overflow sectors should be in the same cylinder as the corresponding home sectors so as to minimize head movement.

Q1: On which cylinder will record 4508 be located?

Where will record 5512 be located?

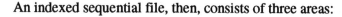

An indexed sequential file, then, consists of three areas:

1. a **home** area where the records are initially stored

2. one or more **index** areas set aside to hold the indexes

3. one or more **overflow areas** to hold records that are added at a later date and will not fit in their correct home sectors or **blocks.**

Blocks

When a file is recorded on disk or tape, the physical space in which data is recorded is unlikely to be exactly the same size as the record, which is the logical unit of the file.

Both disks and tapes transfer data between CPU and backing store in chunks called **blocks.** The number of logical records stored in a block is called the **blocking factor** of the file.

We have seen that data is recorded on a disk around concentric circles called **tracks**, and that each track is divided up into **sectors.** A block on disk takes up one sector, and so the word 'sector' is often used interchangeably with 'block' when referring to disk.

When an indexed sequential file is first set up, the user can specify how many records are to be placed in each block. The aims which he will take into consideration include:

*   making file access as quick as possible

*   dealing with additions and deletions to the file as efficiently as possible

*   making the most efficient use of storage space.

A common **blocking strategy** is to put several records in one block, but to leave enough free space for extra records to fit in each block before overflow occurs. This is particularly important if the file is expected to grow and shrink frequently. The term **block packing density** refers to the ratio of space allocated to records in each block to the total space available. Similarly, **cylinder packing density** is the ratio of tracks initially set aside for records to total number of available tracks on the cylinder. It is common practice to allow some free space on each cylinder to act as the **overflow area.**

Example: A disk pack has 20 usable surfaces, and each block consists of 512 bytes. Three records each of 100 bytes are placed in each block, giving a **block packing density** of approximately 300/500 = 60%.

Four tracks are left free on each cylinder, giving a **cylinder packing density** of 16/20 = 80%

Q2: An indexed sequential file of 10000 records is to be created, and it has been calculated that a maximum of 6 records could fit into each block. However, the programmer has decided to use a block packing density of 66.67%. How many blocks will be required for the **home area**?

File reorganisation

After a period of time, if records are continually being added to and deleted from an indexed sequential file, a large proportion of records will end up in the overflow area. Indeed even the cylinder overflow areas may become full and a secondary overflow area may come into use. This means that several blocks may have to be read to locate a record, and access time increases dramatically. Sooner or later it becomes necessary to **reorganise** the file. This entails reading the records in their **logical sequence** and copying them to another file, once again allowing free space in each home block for additional records, and recreating the indexes at the same time.

Indexed files on floppy disks

For a small file, such as one that might be held on a floppy disk, a less sophisticated procedure is used. The records are not held in sequence, and the index contains an entry for **every** record in the file. The index has to be held in such a way that it can be quickly searched, and it is usually held as a **binary tree**, which will be explained in the Section on data structures.

Random files

A random file (also called a **hash file, direct** or **relative** file) has records that are stored and retrieved according to either their disk address or their relative position within the file. This means that the program which stores and retrieves the records has first to specify the address of the record in the file.

This is done by means of an **algorithm** or formula which transforms the record key into an address at which the record is stored. In the simplest case, record number 1 will be stored in block 1, record number 2 in block 2 and so on. This is called **relative** file addressing, because each record is stored at a location given by its key, relative to the start of the file.

More often, however, record keys do not lend themselves to such simple treatment. If for example we have about 1000 records to store, and each record key is 5 digits long, it would be a waste of space to allow 99999 blocks in which to store records. Therefore, a **hashing algorithm** is used to translate the key into an address.

One hashing method is the division/remainder method. Using this method, a prime number close to the number of records to be stored on the file is chosen and the key of the record is divided by this number. The remainder is taken as the address of the record.

For example, using the prime number 997, the address of record number 75481 would be calculated as follows:

75481/997 = 75 remainder 706.

Address = 706.

Q3: Calculate the address of record number 48562

Synonyms

This method of file organization presents a problem: however cunning the hashing algorithm, synonyms are bound to occur, when two record keys generate the same address. One method of resolving synonyms is to place the record that caused the collision in the next available free space. Another technique is to have a separate overflow area and leave a tag in the original location to indicate where to look next.

As with indexed sequential files, when the file becomes very full and many records are not in their correct 'home', it will be necessary to reorganise the file in order to improve access time. This may mean allocating more space to the file, and/or changing the hashing algorithm. The records can then be read serially from the old file and mapped to their recalculated addresses on the new file.

(Note: Hash files are discussed further in Unit 28.)

Fixed and variable length records

In some circumstances records in a file may not all be the same length. **Variable length records** may be used when either

- the number of characters in any field varies between records

- records have a varying number of fields.

A variable length record has to have some way of showing where each field ends, and where the record ends, in order that it can be processed. There are two ways of doing this;

- use a special end-of-field character at the end of each field, and an end-of-record marker at the end of the record, as shown below. (* is used as the end-of-field marker, and # is used as the end-of-record marker.)

      SH12345*laser printer*QMS PS410*750.00*999.99*7#

      MH452*colour flatbed scanner*Microtek Scanmaker II*150.00*289.00*3#

- use a character count at the beginning of each field, and an end-of-record marker. In the implementation shown below, the byte holding the count is included in the number of characters for the field, and a real number is assumed to occupy 4 bytes, an integer 2 bytes. (You could also have a character count for the entire record instead of the end-of-record marker.)

      8SH1234514laser printer10QMS PS4105750.005999.9937#

      6MH45223colour flatbed scanner22Microtek Scanmaker II5150.005289.0033#

The **advantage** of allowing variable length records is that it is more economical in terms of disk storage space. The advantage of fixed length records is that they are simpler to process, and allow an accurate estimate of storage requirements. When held in a direct access file, fixed length records can be updated 'in situ' (see page 41) because the new record will occupy exactly the same amount of space as the old record.

Exercises:

1. (a) Within the context of random access files:

    (i) explain, with the aid of a simple example, what is meant by a hashing algorithm; (4 marks)

    (ii) outline the steps needed to insert a record into a random access file. These should include a method to overcome any difficulties which may occur as the space allocated for the file fills up. (4 marks)

   (b) An indexed sequential file consists of a two level index, home area and overflow areas.

    (i) What would be contained in the indexes? (2 marks)

    (ii) What is the purpose of two indexes? (1 mark)

    (iii) Outline the steps needed to insert a record into this file. These should include a method of overcoming any difficulties which may occur as the space allocated for the file fills up. (7 marks)

   (c) State **one** advantage and **one** disadvantage of random access files over indexed sequential files. (2 marks)

AEB Paper 1 1990

2. An indexed sequential file has half-a-million records and occupies more than 100 megabytes of backing store.

    With the aid of diagrams,

    (a) show how the file might be organised;   (4 marks)

    (b) give an algorithm to retrieve a record with a particular key value.   (5 marks)
    UCLES Paper 1 Nov 1989

3. When records are stored using a direct access file organisation, collisions can occur.

    (i)   Explain briefly what is meant by a collision.

    (ii) Describe one method of dealing with collisions.   (4 marks)
    NISEAC Paper 2 1992

4. A file is to be created on a magnetic disk so that 500 fixed length records can be stored. The records each have a four-digit key field and each record is to occupy one block. The location of each record on the disk is obtained by a hashing algorithm which takes the right-hand three digits as the block address. If the hashing algorithm yields a block that is already occupied, the next block is tested for the presence of a record and so on until the next free block is found. The record is then written into this free block.

    (a) The first five records, in input sequence, have key fields

         1269   4267   0267   7270   5268

         Show, using a table, the locations of the blocks into which the records are placed.   (4 marks)

    (b) Explain how the record with key field 1269 may be deleted without having to reorganise the whole file.   (2 marks)

    (c) Why may it be necessary to reorganise the file when many records have been added and deleted? Describe how this could be done.   (4 marks)
    London Paper 1 June 1990

5. (a) A University stores details of 12000 students in a random access file.

         (i)   Explain how a hashing algorithm may be used to locate a particular student's record.   (2 marks)

         (ii)   Outline the steps needed to insert a new student's record into the file.   (2 marks)

         (iii) Describe a method to overcome any problems which might occur as the space allocated for the file fills up.   (2 marks)

    (b) A supermarket stores details of its stock in an indexed sequential file. Each entry has a two level index, a home area and an overflow area.

         (i)   Describe the format of one of these indexes.   (2 marks)

         (ii)   Explain why two levels of index are used in this application.   (2 marks)

         (iii) Outline the steps needed to insert a record for a new stock item into this file.   (3 marks)

         (iv)   Briefly describe the problems that may occur as the space allocated for the file fills up.   (2 marks)
    London Paper 2 1992

6.* A random (relative) file organisation is to be used to store details of 800 customers of a particular electrical wholesaler. Customers are identified by a 5 digit customer number. The file is to be loaded at 80% capacity, and the method of hashing used is the division-remainder method.

    Show how the address of customer 23456 might be computed.   (5 marks)
    NISEAC Paper 2 1991

Unit 10 — File Processing

The role of various files in a computer system

All data processing systems except the most trivial will need to store data in files. These files can be categorised as

- master files
- transaction files (sometimes called **movement** files)   **or**
- reference files

Master and transaction files were defined in the previous Unit. A **reference file** is a file that contains data used by a program during processing. For example, in a payroll system:

- the **master file** contains details on each employee
- the **transaction file** contains details of the hours worked, holiday and sick days etc last period
- the **reference file** contains data on tax bands, union rates, etc.

Q1: In an electricity billing system, briefly outline the contents of the customer master file, the transaction file and a reference file.

Q2: Why not hold the data in the reference file either on the customer master file or within the program which calculates the customers' bills?

Operations on files

The following operations are commonly carried out on files:

- Interrogating/referencing
- Updating
- Maintaining
- Sorting.

Interrogating or referencing files

When a file is interrogated or referenced it is first searched to find a record with a particular **key**, and that record is then displayed on a screen, printed out or used in further processing, without itself being altered in any way.

How the record is located will depend entirely on how the file is organised. If the file is **sequential**, each record will have to be read until the required one is found. If the file is **indexed**, the indexes will first be read and the address of the record obtained so that the record can be read directly. If the file is **random** the hashing algorithm will be applied to get the address of the record.

Note that **database** systems are organised differently from the individual files discussed in this Unit and the previous one, and are considered separately in another Section.

Q3: A bicycle shop selling bicycles and spare parts has a computerised stock control system so that the salespersons can see whether any item is in stock via a terminal in the shop. What file organisation would you recommend for the master file of all stock items? Justify your answer.

Updating files

A master file is **updated** when one or more records is altered by applying a transaction or a file of transactions to it. First of all the correct record has to be located and read into memory, then updated in memory, and written back to the master file.

Once again, the method of doing this will depend on the file organisation.

If the master file is sequentially organised, it is impossible to read a record into memory, update it and then write it back to the same location.

The method used to update a sequential file was developed when virtually all master files were stored on magnetic tape (or even on punched cards or paper tape!). Although disks are often used nowadays to store sequential files, the same method is still used because it is very efficient under certain circumstances.

The method is called '**updating by copying**' and it requires the transaction file to be sorted in the same order as the master file.

The steps are as follows:

1. A record is read from the master file into memory

2. A record is read from the transaction file into memory

3. The record keys from each file are compared. If no updating is required to the master file record currently in memory (there being no corresponding transaction record) the master record is copied from memory to a **new master file** on a different tape or area of disk, and another master file record is read into memory, overwriting the previous one. This step is then repeated.

4. If there **is** a transaction for the master record currently in memory, the record is updated. It will be retained in memory in case there are any more transactions which apply to it. Steps 2-4 are then repeated.

After a sequential file has been updated, two versions or **generations** of the master file exist; the **old master file**, still in the same state it was in prior to the update, and the **new master file** just created. The next time the file is updated, a third version of the master file will be created, and so on.

It is obviously not necessary to keep dozens of out-of-date master files, and the general practice is to keep three generations, called **grandfather, father** and **son** for obvious reasons, and then re-use the tapes or disk space for the next update that takes place.

The following diagram illustrates the process.

Day 1

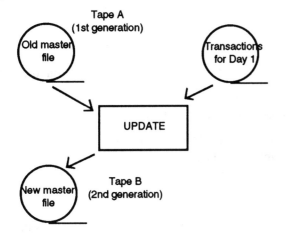

After the update on Day 1, Tape A is the 'Father' tape and Tape B is the 'Son' tape.

Day 2

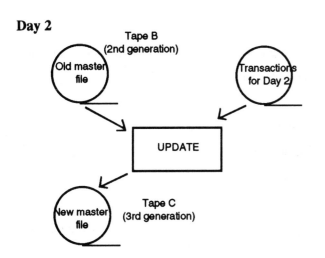

After the update on Day 2, Tape A is the 'Grandather' tape, Tape B is the 'Father' tape and Tape C is the 'Son' tape.

Figure 10.1 - Granfather-Father-Son method of updating

Updating by overlay

If the file to be updated is indexed sequential or random, it is possible to access a record directly, read it into memory, update it, and write it back to its original location. This is called **updating by overlay, updating in place** or **updating in situ** if you are a Latin speaker. It is possible to do this because unlike in sequential file processing, the record is accessed by means of its address on the file and so can be written back to the same address.

File maintenance

File maintenance is similar to file updating, but refers to the updating of the more permanent fields on each record such as in a stock file, for example, the description of the item, price, location in warehouse, etc. It also involves adding new records to the file and deleting records for items that are no longer held.

Once again, depending on the file organisation, either the grandfather-father-son technique will be used, or, if the file is indexed or random, **updating by overlay** may be used.

Sorting a file

Both transaction files and master files may need to be sorted. Transaction files need to be sorted into the same sequence as the master file if sequential updating is to be used, and master files are sometimes sorted if a report is needed in a different sequence from the one in which the records are held.

Sorting methods are considered in Unit 29.

File access methods

How a file is **organised** determines how it can be **accessed**.

- a sequential file can only be accessed sequentially

- a random file would normally only be accessed randomly (it *could* be accessed serially but the records would not be in any particular sequence so this would be unusual)

- an indexed sequential file can *either* be accessed sequentially *or* randomly.

An indexed sequential file is thus the most versatile file organisation, and is used in many different situations. One example would be customer billing systems (electricity, gas, etc) where the master file can be processed sequentially when sending out bills to all customers, and randomly when payments come in in dribs and drabs.

Criteria for use of sequential and direct access files

The choice of file organisation will be one of the most important decisions made by the file designer. A number of questions need to be answered, including:

- Must the user have immediate access to the data, with a response time of no more than a few seconds?

- Must the information be completely up to date, or will last night's or last week's information be sufficient?

- Can requests for information be batched, sequenced and processed all together?

- Are reports needed in a particular sequence?

- What is the most suitable storage medium for the volume of data involved?

- What will happen if the information on the files is lost or destroyed?

In addition two further factors need to be considered; hit rate and volatility.

Hit rate

Hit rate measures the proportion of records being accessed on any one run. It is calculated by dividing the number of records accessed by the total number of records on the file, and expressed as a percentage.

For example, on a payroll run if 190 out of 200 employees were to be paid the hit rate would be 95%. In a system for processing car insurance renewals in weekly batches, the hit run would be about 2% if renewals were spread more or less evenly through the year.

Sequential updating is inefficient with a low hit rate; random access would be better.

Volatility

This refers to the number of additions and deletions from a file over a period of time. A highly volatile file has a lot of additions and deletions. Sequential organisation is suitable here because the whole file is copied during processing, and new records are automatically incorporated and deleted records left out during copying.

Q4: What is the effect of high volatility on an indexed sequential file?

Use of serial files

Serial files are normally only used as transaction files, recording data in the order in which events take place; for example, sales in a shop, customers taking cash from a cash machine, orders arriving at a mail order company. The transactions may be batched and the master files updated at a later time, or alternatively in a real-time system, the files may be updated straight away but the transaction file is kept for record-keeping purposes. It will also be used in the event of a disaster like a disk head crash, to restore the master file from the previous night's backup.

Use of sequential files

Sequential files are used as master files for high hit rate applications such as payroll. The main bulk of processing time is taken up with the weekly or monthly payroll, when every employee's record needs to be accessed and the year-to-date fields brought up to date, and sequential organisation is fast and efficient. It is **not** efficient when only a few records need to be accessed; for example if an employee changes address and the record needs to be updated, since the entire file has to be read and copied over to a new master file. However as this happens relatively infrequently it still makes sense to use a sequential file organisation.

Use of indexed sequential files

Indexed files are extremely useful as they can be sequentially processed when all or most of the records need updating or printing, and randomly when only a few need to be directly accessed. They are suitable for real-time stock control systems, because each time a customer makes a purchase, the master file can be looked up, using the index, to find the appropriate record and ascertain the description and price to print on the receipt. The quantity in stock can be immediately updated, and the record written back to the file ('updating in situ'). When reports of sales or stock are needed in stock number sequence, the file can be processed sequentially, not using the index at all. Sequential processing of an indexed file is fast, but not as fast as the processing of a sequential file because each block probably contains some empty space, and some records will be in a separate overflow area; the records are not all in **physical** sequence even though they are in **logical** sequence (ie they appear to the user/programmer to be in sequence).

Use of random files

Random files are used in situations where extremely fast access to individual records is required. To find a record, the hashing algorithm is applied to the record key and the record address immediately found, so no time is wasted looking up various levels of index. In a network system, user ids and passwords could be stored on a random file; the user id would be the key field from which the address is calculated, and the record would hold the password (encrypted for security reasons) and other information on access rights. Random file organisation might also be used in an airline booking system, where thousands of bookings are made every day for each airline from terminals all over the country. A fast response time to the desired record is crucial here. Note that random file organisation is **not** suitable if reports are going to be needed in key sequence, as the records are scattered 'at random' around the file.

Exercises:

1. Describe **each** of the following types of file organisation:

    (i)   serial file

    (ii) sequential file

    (iii) random file.

    Suggest a situation in which each type of file would be the appropriate choice. In **each** case indicate briefly how records can be saved and retrieved.   (8 marks)
    UCLES AS May 1989

2. Suggest **three** distinct reasons why a large food warehouse should use an indexed sequential file organisation for their stock file in an on-line computerised stock control system.   (3 marks)
    AEB Paper 2 1989

3. (a) Give an example of an application where it is sensible to use an indexed sequential file, explaining why this file structure is appropriate.   (3 marks)

(b)　Sometimes a multi-level index is used in an indexed sequential file.

(i)　Explain briefly why this is necessary.　(1 mark)

(ii)　Show, by means of a diagram and notes, how a record is accessed in such a situation.　(3 marks)

UCLES Paper 2 May 1990

4.　(a)　(i)　Describe briefly *three* methods by which a file on a direct access device may be organised. In each case suggest how a record in the file may be accessed. It is not necessary to describe how overflow is handled.

(6 marks)

(ii)　What are the advantages and disadvantages of storing the records as fixed length records rather than variable length records?　(4 marks)

(b)　A hospital maintains patients' medical records on a computer. The system is to be used for the prompt on-line retrieval of a patient's medical history.

Choose a suitable record structure and a suitable file structure for this application.

Give detailed reasons for your choice.

(5 marks)

London June 1989

5.*　A particular computer application uses the Grandfather-Father-Son system for maintaining backup copies of its master file. The working copy of the master file is found to be corrupt. On examination, the Father file is also found to be corrupt but all other components of the backup system are intact. Describe clearly how it is still possible to recreate the working copy of the master file.　(6 marks)

NISEAC Paper 1 1992

6.*　State what is meant by the term **hit-rate** (file activity ratio). What is the hit rate for a small master file of 10 records which is to be updated by the following batch of transactions: (the transaction type is indicated but not relevant).

record id.	trans. type
123	2
123	1
45	3
400	1
45	1
123	2
400	3
246	3
45	2

(4 marks)

NISEAC Paper 1 1991

Section 2 — Programming in Pascal

Unit 11 — Introduction to Programming

Programming involves writing the instructions to enable a computer to do a specific task. These instructions have to be written according to the rules of the particular programming language chosen for the task.

Low-level languages and machine code

The only instructions that a computer can actually execute are **machine code** instructions, coded in binary 0's and 1's. In the very early days of computers, programs were written in machine code — a very laborious process!

Programming languages such as **assembly language** were developed to eliminate the need to use binary codes for each instruction. These languages use mnemonic codes such as ADD for 'add', SUB for 'Subtract', BEQ for 'Branch if Equal' and so on. Assembly language is used when the programmer needs to write a program that will execute very quickly, or use as little memory as possible, or perform a task that involves manipulating the bits and bytes of the computer in minute detail.

Such a language is called a **low-level** language and is usually rather difficult to learn and understand.

High-level languages

Some programming languages are fairly similar to English, and these are known as **high-level** languages. **Pascal** is a typical high-level language, but there are many others and programmers generally choose the one best suited to their needs. FORTRAN, for example, stands for FORmula TRANslation and is particularly suited to scientific applications. COBOL (COmmon Business Oriented Language) is widely used for business applications. Pascal, invented in 1971 by Niklaus Wirth, has been chosen for this course because it is a general purpose language that can be used to demonstrate in a practical way many aspects of the theory covered in other Sections, namely:

- it encourages the use of well structured programs

- it corresponds closely to **pseudocode**, a design language similar to English used for formulating solutions to problems

- it has facilities for procedure calling, parameter passing, testing and branching, iteration and recursion

- all of the data structures such as linked lists, stacks, queues and trees can be conveniently implemented in Pascal

- it has the facility for **dynamic memory allocation** using pointer variables.

Q1: Name some other high level languages.

Q2: Where does the name 'Pascal' originate from?

A Pascal program

As a first example, consider a program that calculates an electricity bill. The standing charge is £7.41 per quarter, and the unit rate is 6.5 pence per unit. The number of units used this quarter is 1200.

```pascal
program elec(input,output);
{a program to calculate electricity bills}

var
     standing_charge     :real; {the fixed quarterly charge}
     unit_rate           :real;
     units_used          :integer;
     total_bill          :real;

begin
     standing_charge:=7.41;
     unit_rate:=0.065;  {converted to £}
     units_used:=1200;
     total_bill:=standing_charge+(unit_rate*units_used);
     writeln('Total amount payable',total_bill)
end.
```

The parts of a program

The Pascal program shown above consists of three parts:

1. the **program heading**, consisting of the word **program** and a program name of our choice, followed by the words **input, output** in brackets.

2. A **declaration** of each item of data to be used by the program.

3. A sequence of actions (statements) enclosed between the words **begin** and **end**.

Certain words in the program have been written in boldface type to show that these are **reserved words**, or **keywords**. They are part of the Pascal language and can only be used for the purpose defined by the rules of the language. A complete list of reserved words can be found in the Pascal manual for your version of Pascal.

The program heading

All Pascal programs start with a program heading. The words **input, output** in brackets indicate that the program may perform both input (reading in of data from some medium external to the program) and output (writing out of data to an external medium).

Q3: Does the above program perform both **input** and **output**? Find out whether your particular version of Pascal requires you to include (**input, output**) in the program heading.

Comments

The second line of the program is a **comment**; a comment may occur anywhere in the program and is enclosed in curly brackets { }, or alternatively (* *) may be used. Comments are ignored by the compiler but provide essential documentation for anyone who wants to know such things as:

*   who wrote the program

*   when it was written

*   what the program does

*   how parts of it work

*   what certain variables are used for, and so on.

Variable declaration

This section of the program is headed **var** which stands for **variable**. All the data items used, read in or calculated by the program must be declared in this section. Each data item has a name called an **identifier**; for example, **standing_charge**, **unit_rate**, etc., and this should be chosen by the programmer to be self-explanatory wherever possible. **Standing_charge** is a better name than **sc** even if it takes longer to type in!

Some of the items are defined as **real**, meaning that they will hold numbers with a decimal point such as 123.45, -23.0, or 0.15. **Integer** values are whole numbers such as -7 or 1990.

A real number has to have a number preceding the decimal point in Pascal; you will get an error message if you write a statement such as

```
rate := .5
```

Q4: What should you write instead, if you want to assign the value .5 to a real variable called rate?

The statement part of the program

The part of the program where the actual work is done is enclosed between the key words **begin** and **end**. The punctuation is important and will be explained in due course.

Q5: Type in and run the program **elec**.

Would it be permitted to write the following?
```
var
      standing_charge,unit_rate,total_bill:real;
      units_used:integer;
```

There is one way to find out; try it! You will find that it is quite permissible to declare more than one variable on a line. However, some people prefer to write only one variable per line, and line up all the semi-colons by using the tab key, which makes the program look neat, and it also makes it easier to spot where variables have been declared, and to check that a variable declaration has not been omitted by mistake.

Q6: What happens if you simply put as the program header:
```
program elec;
```

Again, you should try this out. The answer will depend on the particular version of Pascal you are using. If you are using Turbo Pascal, this form of program heading is quite acceptable.

Q7: Change the writeln statement to

```
writeln('Total amount payable',total_bill:8:2);
```

What can you deduce about the 8:2?

Try changing it to 8:3, 12:2, 4:2 and running the program each time.

Formatting the output

If you have tried out the suggestions in the question above, you will have deduced that writing

```
total_bill:8:2
```

causes the number to be displayed to 2 decimal places. The number 8 is the **total field width**; for example the number 123.45 has a total field width of 6 (including the decimal point). Writing it with the format 8:2 will mean that it will be padded out with 2 blank spaces on the left hand side.

Exercises:

1. Using **elec** as a model, write a program which defines the bills received in each quarter of the year as £35.00, £37.78, £22.53 and £43.85 respectively and calculates and outputs the total bill for the year.

2. Complete the following program, which calculates the number of rolls of wallpaper required to cover a wall of any dimensions.

```
program wallpaper(input,output);
{written by:                    }

var
     length:real;
     (missing statements here)


     paper_width, paper_length    :real;
     wall_area, no_of_rolls       :real;

begin
     {enter dimensions of wall and wallpaper roll}
     write('Enter the length of the wall: ');
     readln(length);
     write('Enter the height of the wall: ');
     (missing statement here)

     write('Enter the width of the roll: ');
     (missing statements here)




     {calculate number of rolls required}
     wall_area:=length*height;
     roll_area:=(complete this statement)
     no_of_rolls:=wall_area/roll_area;
     no_of_rolls:=1.10*no_of_rolls;         {add 10% for matching pattern}

     writeln('You will need ',no_of_rolls:6:1,' rolls of wallpaper')
end.
```

3. Amend the program to accept the price per roll and display the total cost of wallpaper. Write down some test data and check that your program is giving the expected answers.

4. Write a program to enable a student to calculate how much money will be needed per week to buy a meal and two drinks each weekday. The program should ask how much a meal costs, and how much a drink costs, and then calculate and display the total weekly cost.

5. Amend the above program to calculate and display the total cost for a 13-week term, assuming that the student also has to buy books and stationery costing an average of £x per month. (User to enter a value for x).

Unit 12 — Variables, Assignments, Reading and Writing

Types of data

There are four primitive built-in data types defined in the Pascal language. These are

- integer (whole numbers)
- real (numbers with a decimal point)
- character (any ASCII character such as a letter, number or 'special character' like @, or #)
- boolean (a variable which can only hold the value **true** or **false**)

Note: Turbo Pascal defines 5 different integer types, which are listed below:

type	Range	Format
shortint	-128 .. 127	signed 8-bit
integer	-32768 .. 32767	signed 16-bit
longint	-2147483648 .. 2147483647	signed 32-bit
byte	0 .. 255	unsigned 8-bit
word	0 .. 65535	unsigned 16-bit

Each of these is stored in a different way in the computer's memory. Therefore before we attempt to store any data in memory, either by reading it in or by the use of an **assignment** statement, we must tell the compiler what sort of data we intend to store in any particular variable. This is done using the **var** declaration. For example:

```
var
    grade:char;
    mark1:integer;
    mark2:integer;
    average:real;
```

If a variable has been declared as an integer, for example, we cannot store a character or a real number in it.

In addition, we need some way of storing a **string** of characters such as a student's name, and most versions of Pascal allow a string to be defined as, for example,

```
student_name:string;
```

which in Turbo Pascal allows up to 255 characters to be stored in student_name, using a statement such as

```
student_name:='Mary Jones';
```

Note that the string has to be enclosed in single quote marks.

Rules for identifiers

The program name and the variable names are all called **identifiers**, and the following rules apply:

- they must always start with a letter
- they can consist of letters, digits and the underscore character
- uppercase and lowercase letters are treated as identical

Q1: Which of the following are valid identifiers?

(i)	Prog-1	(iii)	student mark	(v)	K.O'R.
(ii)	TaxProgram	(iv)	1st_grade	(vi)	program1.pas

Assignment statements

In Pascal a value or expression is **assigned** to a variable using the symbol ':='. Here is an example of an assignment statement:-

```
daily_cost := cost_of_lunch + 2 * cost_of_drink;
```

The following mathematical symbols are used in constructing expressions:

Operator	Operation	Operand types	Result type
+	addition	integer type	integer type
		real type	real type
−	subtraction	integer type	integer type
		real type	real type
*	multiplication	integer type	integer type
		real type	real type
/	division	integer type	real type
		real type	real type
div	integer division	integer type	integer type
mod	remainder	integer type	integer type

In addition, brackets ( ) are used wherever necessary, or to clarify the meaning of the expression. The same rules of precedence apply as in ordinary arithmetic; multiplication and division are performed before addition and subtraction, and expressions in brackets are evaluated first.

Q2: Evaluate x in the following expressions: (assume x is an **integer** variable)

(i)   x:=5*7+3*4

(ii)   x:=5*(7+3)*4

(iii)   x:=5*(7+3*4)

(iv)   x:=27 div 4

(v)   x:=27 mod 4

(vi)   x:=24/4

Q3: Find the errors in the following program (you should find about ten!):

```
program   error;
var
     student-name:string;
     mark1,mark2,mark3;integer;
     total,average:integer;

begin
     student_name='Jo';
     mark_1:=50;
     mark_2:=52;
     mark_3:=68;
     total_mark:=mark_1+mark_2+mark_3
     average:=total_mark*3;
     writeln('Average mark='AVERAGE:8:2)
end
```

Notice that there are two types of error in the above program; **syntax** errors — errors in the way the Pascal language has been used — and a **logic** error. The compiler will detect all the syntax errors but it cannot detect the logic error.

Reading in data from a keyboard

Data is read into a Pascal program using either a **read** or a **readln** statement. We could read in three student marks from the keyboard with the statement

```
read(mark_1,mark_2,mark_3);
```
or
```
read(mark_1);
read(mark_2);
read(mark_3);
```

where mark_1, mark_2 and mark_3 are integer values all typed on one line, separated by at least one space.

readln has the effect of skipping to a new line after reading the variable.

```
read(mark_1);
readln;
```

has the same effect as

```
readln(mark_1);
```

Displaying data on the screen

The **write** and **writeln** statements are used to display data. As with **readln**, writeln causes a skip to a new line after writing the data. Thus

```
write('Average=');
writeln(average);
```

has the same effect as

```
writeln('Average=',average);
```

Formatting output

It is convenient to be able to control the number of spaces used by the computer to print integers, and to be able to specify the number of decimal places to be displayed in the case of a real number. This is done by specifying the total field width and number of places after the decimal point, separated by colons. Thus if the value of **average** is say 74.0,

```
writeln('Average=',average:5:1);
```

will print

```
Average= 74.0
```
(leaving one space after the = sign, for a total field width of 5).

Compound statements and punctuation

All the statements between **begin** and **end** can be regarded as a single compound statement, with the semi-colon acting as a **separator** between statements. (The significance of a **compound statement** will become clearer later on when looping and branching are covered). All statements between **begin** and **end** need to be separated from each other, but there is no need to put a semi-colon after the final statement before **end**. However it will not cause an error if you do so.

Notice also that the last statement of the program, **end**, has to be followed by a full-stop.

Q4: How do you clear the screen?

Q5: How do you position the cursor on the screen?

Improving the readability of a program

You will find your programs are easier to understand and debug if they are clearly laid out. You should

- be generous with your comments
- use tabs to indent sections of code. For example, indent all the code between **begin** and **end.**
- use meaningful variable names
- leave blank lines between chunks of code to make it more readable

Q6: Can you put more than one statement on one line?

Exercises:

1. Write a program which allows a user to input a student's name and 3 marks, then calculates the average and displays the result in the following format:

    Student name: xxxxxxxxxxxxxxxxxxx

    Marks: 99   99   99

    Average: 99.9

2. On a screen layout chart, a coding sheet or a piece of squared paper, draw up the layout for the till receipt in exercise 3. (Do not draw the box around the receipt; this represents the screen.)

3. Write a program to display a receipt for a customer who has purchased a single item. The program should display the blank receipt, accept the item description, quantity and price, calculate the value and display it. Then input the amount tendered and display the change due.

```
                    TAYLOR GROUP PLC

                            UNIT
        ITEM            QTY PRICE      VALUE
        xxxxxxxxxxxxxx   99 999.99     99999.99

        amount tendered              99999.99
                                     ------------
        change due                   99999.99

              PLEASE RETAIN YOUR RECEIPT
              THANK YOU FOR YOUR CUSTOM
```

4. Imagine that you and a friend are planning to set up a hamburger stand. The initial setting up cost will be £200.00 for the stand. Write a program which will input the cost price and proposed selling price of a hamburger, and the estimated number of hamburgers that you will sell in a day, and calculate how long it will take to recoup the cost of the stand.

    What other software could you use for this type of problem instead of writing a Pascal program? What are the relative advantages of each method of solution?

Unit 13 — An Introduction to Looping and Branching

Looping (also called iteration or repetition)

In the last Unit we looked at a program for calculating the average of 3 marks. The method used could be summarised as

```
Read in the marks
Add them up
calculate the average
output the result
```

This worked well enough for three numbers but would be quite impractical for 30 or 300!

We will consider a slightly different problem: the program is to input the marks for any number of students, calculate the average mark and display the number of students and the average mark.

What we need to do is to keep a running total; keep reading in the next mark and adding it to the total until there are no more marks to enter. The number of marks entered must be counted too, so that the average can be calculated.

The outline solution is, then, as follows:

```
Set total_mark, no_of_marks to 0

while there is another mark to enter
    read a mark
    add it to total_mark
    add 1 to no_of_marks
endwhile

calculate the average mark
display no_of_marks and average
```

How will the program know when there are no more marks to enter? There are three ways of handling this.

1. The program asks before reading each mark: "Are there any more marks to enter?" and waits for the user to answer Yes or No.

2. As soon as a mark is entered, the program tests to see if a special value such as -1 or 999 which would not normally occur as a data item, has been entered. This value is called a **sentinel** or **dummy** value, or sometimes a **rogue** value, and can be recognised by the program as a signal that all of the actual data items have been processed.

Q1: Can you think of the third way?

Q2: Which of the three methods do you prefer? Why?

The WHILE..DO statement in Pascal

The syntax of the **while..do** statement is shown by the following **syntax diagram:**

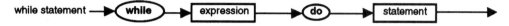

The expression controlling the repetition must be of type *boolean;* that is, one which evaluates to *true* or *false*.

The following operators may be used in making comparisons:

```
>           greater than
<           less than
>=          greater than or equal
<=          less than or equal
<>          not equal
in          member of (eg  while num in [70..100] )
```

Note that when using the 'in' operator, the values in the square brackets must be integers or characters, not real numbers or strings.

For example:

```
write('Please enter the first mark; enter -1 to end');
readln(student_mark);
while student_mark<>-1 do
    begin
         total_mark:=total_mark+student_mark;
         no_of_marks:=no_of_marks+1;
         write('Please enter the next mark; enter -1 to end');
         readln(student_mark)
    end; {endwhile}
```

Notice the **compound** statement which includes the **begin** and **end** and all the statements in between. If there was only one action to be performed, the **begin** and **end** would not be necessary.

The program will continue to execute the compound statement until a mark of -1 is entered.

Note that the condition 'student_mark<>-1' is tested **before** entering the loop.

Q3: Why not put the **write** and **readln** statements at the beginning of the loop?

Q4: What happens if the first mark entered is -1?

Q5: Write statements to perform the following:

(i)   Add up the numbers from 1 to 100 and display the result

(ii)   Read in a number between 1 and 75 and then print that number of asterisks in a line.

An introduction to procedures

Three main tasks can be identified in the program to calculate the average of a set of marks:

```
Initialise
Input and process marks
Output results
```

This could be called the **top-level** solution to the problem; recognising the major steps that are to be performed without specifying in any detail how they are to be achieved.

The program can thus be broken down into **modules**; and the preferred way of writing a program is to code each of these tasks as a separate **procedure**. The main program will then reflect the top-level solution, and call each of these procedures in turn. Note that

- each procedure is given a name, and has the same structure as a program. (More on that later).

- the procedure is **called** from the main procedure simply by writing its name.

- any procedure that is called must be written **before** it is called; that is, it must be placed physically above the statements in the main program.

Program to calculate the average of a set of marks

A complete program to input a set of student marks and calculate the average is shown below.

Notice that '**input_and_process**' is **one** procedure; you should **not** try to write separate procedures for '**input**' and '**process**', which complicates things unnecessarily.

```
Program mark_avg(input,output);
{program to calculate average of a set of students' marks}

var
    student_mark, total_mark, no_of_marks:integer;
    average:real;


Procedure initialise;
begin
    no_of_marks:=0;
    total_mark:=0;
end; {end of procedure}


Procedure input_and_process;
begin
    write('Please enter the first mark, -1 to end: ');
    readln(student_mark);
    while student_mark<>-1 do
        begin
        total_mark:=total_mark+student_mark;
        no_of_marks:=no_of_marks+1;
        write('Please enter the next mark, -1 to end: ');
        readln(student_mark)
    end; {endwhile}
end;     {end of procedure}


Procedure output_result;
begin
    average:=total_mark/no_of_marks;
    writeln('Average mark is ',average:5:2);
    writeln('Total number of students: ',no_of_marks:3)
end; {end of procedure}



{******   MAIN PROGRAM  - EXECUTION STARTS HERE   *******}

begin
    initialise;
    input_and_process;
    output_result
end.
```

(Exercises 1, 2 and 3 may be done before covering Selection)

Selection (IF..THEN..ELSE)

It is often necessary to take different routes through a program depending on some condition. This can be achieved in Pascal by the **if..then..else** statement, the syntax of which is shown below:

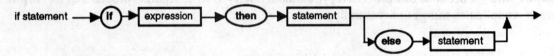

The expression must produce a result of type *boolean* (*true* or *false*).

Example:

```
if mark>=70 then

    writeln('Merit')


else
    if mark>=50 then
        writeln('Pass')
    else


        writeln('Fail');



    {endif}
```

The above is an example of a 'nested if' statement.

Q6: Amend the above statement so that if the mark is 70 or above the program prints 'Well Done' on the line beneath the grade; and if the mark is less than 50 the program prints 'You are required to resit this assignment' on the line beneath the grade.

Compound conditions can be constructed using **and, or,** and **not**. For example:

```
if (status='m') and (salary<2400) then tax:=0;
```

or

```
if (hours>40) and (hours<48) then
    begin
        overtime_rate:=1.5*normal_rate;
        calculate_pay
    end
else
    double_time;
```

Note the brackets round the conditions, and note that you **cannot** write

```
If hours>40 and <48 then       etc etc
```

Example: Write a Pascal statement to mean "if reply not equal to 'Y' call a procedure no_more"

Answer: `if not (reply ='Y') then no_more;`

Trace tables

When a program is not working correctly (perhaps producing a wrong answer, or getting into an infinite loop), it is useful to trace through the program manually, writing down the values of the variables as they change. The variable names can be written as column headings and their values underneath the headings to form a trace table. Being able to trace manually through the steps of a program is an essential skill in program debugging.

Example: Use a trace table to show the values of the variables student_mark, total_mark, no_of_marks and average when the program mark_avg is run (see Page 57). You may assume that the user enters the marks 7, 5, 9, -1.

Answer: Take a look at the program and write down the variable names across the page. The order is not particularly important; in the example below, they have been written in the order in which they will first be encountered. Then start at the first instruction in the main program and trace the instructions in the order that the computer will execute them.

no_of_marks	total_mark	student_mark	average
0	0	7	?
1	7	5	
2	12	9	
3	21	-1	7

Q7: The following extract from a program is intended to calculate the sum of the squares of a series of numbers entered by the user. The end of data entry is signalled by the dummy value -1. Use a trace table to find out why the program is not giving the right answer when the user enters the values 2, 5, 3, 1, -1. The first couple of lines of the trace table have been filled in for you; notice that a column has been allocated for the condition n <> -1, and this can only take the values True or False.

What output would you expect the program to produce if it was working correctly?

```
total:=0;
while n<>-1 do
begin
    write ('Please enter a number');
    readln(n);
    total:=total+n*n;
end; {while}
writeln('Total=',n:8:2);
```

n	n*n	total	n<>-1
		0	True
2	4	4	True

Note that a programming environment such as Turbo Pascal has facilities for stepping through a program one instruction at a time, setting breakpoints in a program, showing the values of selected variables as you step through, and many more useful programming aids. You should make sure you find out all you can about how to use such features, which can save hours of debugging time.

Exercises:

1. Use a **trace table** to show the values of var1, n and the condition **n < 5** when the following statements are executed:

```
var1 := 3;
n := 0;
while n < 5 do
    begin
        var1 := var1 + n;
        n := n + 1
    end;
```

var1	n	n < 5

*For each of the programs below write a **top-level** solution in ordinary English, breaking down the problem into its major components, then code the program using procedures.*

2. Write a program which calculates a simplified payroll. For each employee the user enters name, hourly rate and number of hours worked. The program calculates gross pay, deducts tax at 25% of gross, and prints out the employee name, hours, rate, gross pay, tax and net pay. At the end of the program the total gross, total tax and total net pay for all employees is to be printed out together with the number of employees.

3. Write a program to print out a triangle of stars, with 41 stars in the last row:

```
         *
        ***
       *****
      *******
        etc
```

(n.b. Do not use 41 writeln statements! The statement part of the main program should consist of two procedure calls: **Initialise** and **Print_stars**.)

4. Write a program which allows the user to input a date, eg March 1, followed by the noon temperature on that day for the last several years, from meteorological records. The program has to calculate the maximum, minimum and average temperature and display the results.

5. A computer language has variable names which must conform to the syntax shown below.

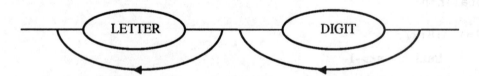

State which of the following are legal variable names. For each incorrect variable name, explain why it is incorrect.

(a) 5thyear

(b) class6a

(c) st561   (5 marks)

6.* Which of the following are valid Boolean conditions in Pascal?

(a) value => 100.0   {value is a real variable}

(b) (max>37.5) and (max<42.0)   {max is a real variable}

(c) day in ['Mon','Tue','Wed','Thu','Fri'] {day is a string variable}

(d) (mark not > 80)   {mark is an integer variable}

Unit 14 — Top-down Structured Programming

Top-down design

Top-down design is the technique of breaking down a problem into the major tasks to be performed; each of these tasks is then further broken down into separate subtasks, and so on until each subtask is sufficiently simple to be written as a self-contained **module** or procedure. The program then consists of a series of calls to these modules, which may themselves call other modules.

Jackson structure diagrams

It is useful to have some way of representing the **structure** of a program — how the modules all relate to form the whole solution — and a Jackson structure diagram is one way of doing this. When a program is large and complex, it becomes especially important to plan out the solution before doing any coding, and a structure diagram also serves a useful purpose as documentation when the program is complete.

The diagram resembles a family tree, with the main program statements written **across** the top line.

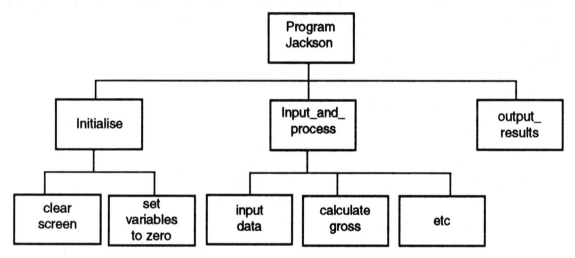

Figure 14.1 — A Jackson structure diagram

Q1: Draw a structure diagram showing a 'program' for preparing a meal consisting of soup, main course and dessert.

The building blocks of a structured program

Only three different 'building blocks' or **program constructs** are needed to write a structured program. These are

- **sequence** — in which one statement follows another and the program executes them in the sequence given

- **selection** — 'if..then..else' is an example of selection, where the next statement to be executed depends on the value of an expression

- **iteration** — a section of the program is repeated many times, as for example in the 'while..do' statement.

Notice the absence of the GO TO statement! Experience has shown that programs which are written without using GO TO statements are easier to follow, easier to debug and easier to maintain.

Programs that are written using **top-down** techniques, and using only the three constructs described, are called **structured programs**. May you live to be a hundred, and may all your programs be structured!

Representation of a loop

An asterisk in a box, with the condition written outside the box and the statements or modules within the loop written on the next level down, is used to indicate a section of code repeated many times.

```
eg   while a<b do
         begin
             statement1
             statement2
             statement3
         end   {endwhile}
```

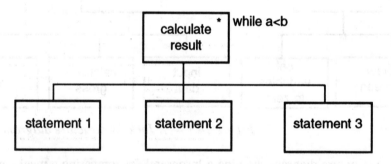

Figure 14.2 — Iteration

Representation of selection

Selection is represented by a small circle in each of the boxes representing the alternative paths:

```
if (answer='Y') or (answer='y') then
    statement 1
else
    statement 2
```

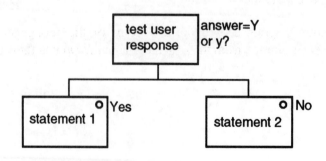

Figure 14.3 — Selection

Example: Draw a structure diagram and code a progam to input a number of sales transaction records each of which contains a salesperson's number (between 1 and 3) and a sales amount in £. Accumulate the total sales for each salesperson and the total overall sales, and output these figures at the end of the program.

The structure diagram can be drawn as follows:

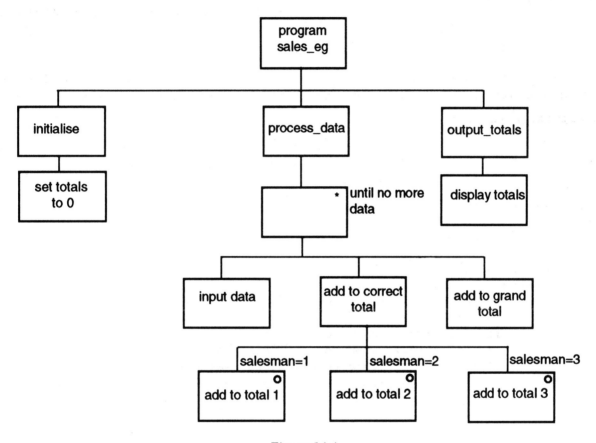

Figure 14.4

A guideline for drawing Jackson structure diagrams is that you should not put boxes representing loops (ie boxes containing asterisks) on the same level as other types of boxes. This is why in the diagram above, the box containing the asterisk appears **below** the 'process_data' box.

The same guideline applies to boxes containing circles representing selection; **all** the boxes on the same level must be 'selection' boxes if any of them are.

Q2: Compare the structure diagram above with the coding on the next page. What details of the procedure **process_data** have been omitted from the structure diagram? Do you think the omissions matter?

```pascal
program sales_eg;
{program to accumulate sales totals for three salesmen}

uses crt;    {calls in Turbo Pascal's library routines}

var
    grand_total, total1, total2, total3, amount:real;
    salesman:integer;



procedure initialise;
begin
    clrscr; {clear screen}
    grand_total:=0;
    total1:=0;
    total2:=0;
    total3:=0;
end; {procedure}



procedure process_data;
begin
    write('Please enter salesperson''s number (0 to finish): ');
    readln(salesman);
    while salesman<>0 do
        begin
            write('Enter sales amount: ');
            readln(amount);
            if (salesman=1) then total1:=total1+amount;
            if (salesman=2) then total2:=total2+amount;
            if (salesman=3) then total3:=total3+amount;
            grand_total:=grand_total + amount;
            write('Please enter next salesperson''s number (0 to finish): ');
            readln(salesman)
        end;
    {endwhile}
end; {procedure}


procedure output_totals;
begin
    writeln;
    writeln('Total for salesperson 1: ',total1:8:2);
    writeln('Total for salesperson 2: ',total2:8:2);
    writeln('Total for salesperson 3: ',total3:8:2);
    writeln('Grand total of all sales: ',grand_total:8:2)
end; {procedure}


{***** MAIN PROGRAM ******}

begin
    initialise;
    process_data;
    output_totals
end.
```

Modular programming

Any programs that you write for this course are likely to be relatively short; however, in industry and commerce some problems will require thousands or even tens of thousands of lines of code to solve. The importance of splitting up the problem into a series of self-contained **modules** then becomes obvious. A module should not exceed 100 or so lines, and preferably be short enough to fit on a single page; some modules may be only a few lines.

Advantages of modular programming

1. Some modules will be standard procedures used again and again in different programs or parts of the same program; for example, a routine to display a standard opening screen.

2. A module is small enough to be understandable as a unit of code. It is therefore easier to understand and debug, especially if its purpose is clearly defined and documented.

3. Program **maintenance** becomes easier because the affected modules can be quickly identified and changed.

4. In a very large project, several programmers may be working on a single program. Using a modular approach, each programmer can be given a specific set of modules to work on. This enables the whole program to be finished sooner.

5. More experienced programmers can be given the more complex modules to write, and the junior programmers can work on the simpler modules.

6. Modules can be tested independently, thereby shortening the time taken to get the whole program working.

7. If a programmer leaves part way through a project, it is easier for someone else to take over a set of self contained modules.

8. A large project becomes easier to monitor and control.

Program maintenance

Q3: It has been estimated that up to 80% of programming involves 'maintenance' rather than writing new programs. What is 'program maintenance' and why should it be necessary?

Bottom-up design

When faced with a large and complex problem it may be difficult to see how the whole thing can be done. It may be easier to attack parts of the problem individually, taking the easier aspects first and thereby gaining the insight and experience to tackle the more difficult tasks, and finally to try and bolt them all together to form the complete solution. This is called a **bottom-up** approach. It suffers from the disadvantage that the parts of the program may not fit together very easily, there may be a lack of consistency between modules, and considerable re-programming may have to be done.

Program constants

Every program that we have encountered has had a **variable declaration**, starting with the reserved word **var**. In addition to variable identifiers, some programs use **constant** values which never change throughout the program. For example, in the program which printed a triangle of asterisks, we could define a constant identifier called, say, *asterisk*, to hold the character '*'. To do this, we insert above the **var** declaration, a **const** declaration as follows:

```
program triangle;
const
     asterisk='*';   {note the syntax carefully; = and not := is used here}
var etc
```

Although it is perfectly possible to write any program without a **const** declaration, it sometimes is convenient to use constants, and as an added bonus the program will run a microsecond or two faster because the compiler will replace all references to a constant by its actual value at compile time. The two programs below will give you an opportunity to try them out.

Exercises:

1. Draw a structure diagram for Exercise 4 in the previous Unit (inputting temperatures and calculating maximum, minimum and average.)

2. Draw a structure diagram for a program which calculates and prints staff mileage allowances. Allowances are paid at the rate of 28p per mile if the purpose of the trip is to visit one or more students, and 22p per mile for any other type of journey. The program should clear the screen and display a heading with today's date, then continue to input data and calculate and print mileage allowances until the user indicates that there is no more data. Include statements to check that a valid journey type is entered.

3. Code and test the above program.

4. Draw a structure diagram and write a program which allows a user to input a sentence terminated by a full-stop. The program is to count and display the number of words in the sentence, and also count and display the number of words over 3 letters.

5. Explain why computer programs have to be maintained. Give *three* factors which ease the task of program maintenance.

   (4 marks)
   London Paper 1 June 1990

6.* What is meant by the term **maintenance** when applied to an applications package such as a payroll package?

   (2 marks)

   Describe briefly two events that could necessitate the maintenance of such a package. (4 marks)
   London Specimen Paper 1 1989

7. A program accepts as input two positive integers. It initialises a running total and enters a loop containing the following logic:

   - at any stage when the first number is odd, the second is added to the running total;

   - the first number is halved (disregarding any fraction produced) and the second doubled;

   The loop is repeated until the first number is equal to zero, and on exiting the loop the running total is output.

   Using 50 and 12 as the input, and showing the steps in the process, deduce the program's purpose. (6 marks)
   NISEAC Paper 1 1991

Unit 15 — Selection and Iteration

The CASE statement

We have already seen one type of conditional statement; the **if..then..else** construct. The **case** statement is useful when a choice has to be made between several alternatives. The syntax diagram is as follows:

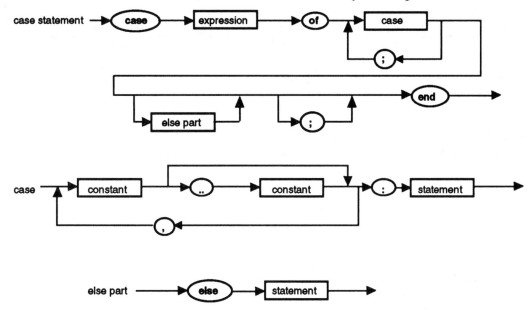

Q1: Are the two examples below valid **case** statements?

```
(i)  case choice of
        0,2,4,6,8 :    writeln('This is an even digit');
        1,3,5,7,9 :    writeln('This is an odd digit');
        10..100   :    writeln('This is a  number between 10 and 100');
     else
        writeln('Negative or >100');
     end; {case}

(ii) case month of
        'Jan','Mar','May','Jul','Aug','Oct','Dec'  :no_of_days:=31;
        'Apr','Jun','Sep','Nov'                    :no_of_days:=30;
        'Feb':    if year mod 4=0 then
                        no_of_days:=29
                  else
                        no_of_days:=28;
                  {endif}
     end; {case}
```

Q2: Write a **case** statement instead of a nested **if** statement for the problem posed in **Q6** in Unit 13. (Set grade to 'Merit' for a mark of 70 or over, etc)

The REPEAT..UNTIL statement

The **repeat..until** statement is rather similar to the **while..do** statement, except that the expression controlling the loop is tested **after** the execution of each sequence, so that the loop is always performed at least once.

The syntax is as follows:

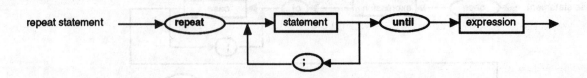

Example:

```
repeat
      write('Do you wish to continue? Answer Y or N');
      readln (answer);
until answer in ['Y','y','N','n'];
```

The FOR statement

The third type of loop is a **for** loop, which causes a statement (which may be a compound statement) to be repeatedly executed a predetermined number of times.

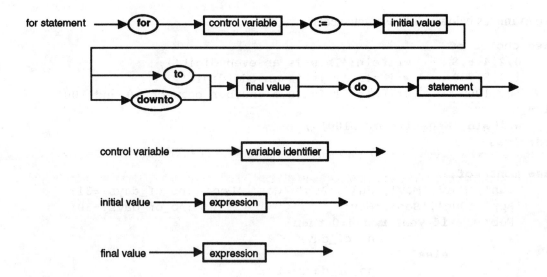

Example:

```
total:=0;
for day:=1 to 7 do
    begin
          readln(sales);
          total:=total+sales;
    end;
```

Pseudocode

In the last Unit we looked at structure diagrams as a way of developing a solution to a problem, and saw how useful they are in implementing a top-down approach. If, however, we try to write down all the details of every module in a structure diagram, it becomes unwieldy. It is most useful in specifying the structure of a program down to the module level.

Pseudocode provides a means of expressing algorithms without worrying about the syntax of a particular language.

Example: Write pseudocode for an algorithm to find the maximum, minimum and average of a set of marks.

```
Procedure FindMaxMark
begin
    set max no. of marks and total to zero
    set min to 100
    read the first mark
    while not end of data
        if mark > max set max = mark
        endif
        if mark < min set min = mark
        endif
        add mark to total
        add 1 to no. of marks
        read the next mark
    endwhile
    calculate average
    print results
end procedure
```

Note that

- keywords such as **begin, end, while, endwhile, if**, and **endif** mark the limits of procedures, loops and conditional statements

- the actual statements of the algorithm can be written in ordinary English

- the indentation is important — it gives a visual picture of the extent of loops and conditional statements

There are no absolute rules for writing pseudocode; for example both versions of the **repeat** construct shown below would be quite acceptable:

```
repeat until end of data
    statements
    .....
    .....
    .....
end repeat


repeat
    statements
    .....
    .....
    .....
until end of data
```

Generating random numbers

In many types of problem it is useful to be able to generate a series of random numbers in a given range. Different versions of Pascal have different functions for doing this, but all work on the same principle. A 'seed' is supplied either by the user or automatically by the system, using the system clock, to generate the first random number, which will be in the range 0 <= random number < 1. Subsequent numbers are all generated from the previous one in the series. If you wish to repeat the same sequence of numbers then you provide the 'seed', otherwise you leave it to the computer.

Example: In Turbo Pascal, a random number between 2 and 12 can be generated by first initializing the random number generator with a call to **randomize,** or by assigning a specific integer value to the predefined identifier **randseed,** and then calling the function **random**. **Random(n)** returns a random number of type **word** within the range 0 <= x < n. If no argument is supplied, it returns a random argument of type **real** in the range 0 <= x < 1.

ie
```
    begin
        ......
        randomize;
        {or randseed := 5; (or any other integer) to generate the same
        sequence of random numbers each time}
    repeat
        ......
        test_num := random(11) + 2;{to get an integer between 2 and 12}
        etc

    until ....
```

The random number generator's seed (which is obtained from the system clock) is stored in a predeclared integer variable called **randseed**. By assigning a specific value to **randseed**, a specific sequence of random numbers can be generated over and over. This is particularly useful in data encryption and simulation.

Exercises:

1. Draw a structure diagram for a program used to help young students learn multiplication tables. The program should:

    (a) accept entry of student's name and use the name in any interaction between computer and student.

    (b) ask the student what table they wish to be tested on.

    (c) ask 5 random questions from the table, by calling a standard random number generator such as **random** in Turbo Pascal, giving the correct answer if the student gets it wrong.

    (d) on completion, give the score out of 5, make a suitable remark, and offer the student another go.

    (e) when the student decides to end, make a suitable closing remark and end the program.

2. Devise suitable test data for this program. Can you be absolutely sure that the program is working correctly?

3. What improvements can you suggest could be incorporated in your program?

4. Many high-level languages provide several ways of controlling loops in a program. Describe **three** ways of implementing a sequence of steps within a loop, giving an example of each and stating how they differ from each other.

5. Write a program for a game in which the user guesses what random number between 1 and 1000 the computer has "thought of", until he or she has found the correct number. The computer should tell the user for each guess whether it was too high, too low or spot on! How many carefully chosen guesses should the user need before getting the right answer?

6. Write a program to let the computer guess what number YOU have thought of, within a specified range.

Unit 16 — Arrays and Data Types

Introduction

In Unit 14 there is a sample structure diagram (figure 14.4) and program for accumulating total sales for each of three salespersons. Now clearly if there were, say, 150 salespeople, the method used would be quite impractical. We need some way of defining all 150 totals in one statement, and this is where **arrays** come in. The statement

```
var
      total:array[1..150] of real;
```

defines 150 real variables, which will be referred to as total[1], total[2], ...total[150]. The number in brackets is called the **index** or **subscript** of the array. In this example it can be an integer, or an integer variable, or an integer expression; for example total[i+1] , where i is an integer variable. Of course we must be careful that the value of i+1 lies between 1 and 150 or a run-time error will occur, and a message 'subscript out of range' or something similar will be displayed.

An array is a way of **organising** data in memory, and is an example of a **data structure.** Data structures are covered in Section 3.

Q1: Add a line of code to initialise all 150 elements of the array **total** to zero.

```
for i:=1 to 150 do
```

Q2: Define an array of integers called **temp** whose index varies between -10 and +50.

An array may also be used to hold strings of characters. For example we could define an array to hold the names of the months:

```
var
      month_name:array[1..12] of string[9];
```

The array could be initialised with a procedure containing 12 statements of the form

```
month_name[1]:='January  ';
month_name[2]:='February ';
etc
```

Q3: Write statements to input a month number between 1 and 12 , together with a sales amount, and display 'The sales figure for xxxxxxxxx is 9999.99' (where xxxxxxxxx represents the month number, and 9999.99 the sales amount. You may assume the existence of a procedure to initialise the month names, as given above).

Declaring data types

Pascal allows the programmer to define data types other than the simple types **real, integer**, etc. If for example we wish to access individual characters in a string, the string has to be defined as an **array of char**. We can define a **type** consisting of an array of characters as follows:

```
type
        input_string=array[1..6] of char;
var
        number:input_string;
```

The Boolean function eoln

The built-in Pascal function **eoln** is used to detect the **end of line** when data is being read in from a keyboard character by character. It is set to **true** when the *next* character to be entered is a <Return> character. You may wonder how the computer can perform this mind-reading feat — the answer is that as the characters are typed, they are placed in a **line buffer** and none of them is processed until <Return> is pressed. The computer therefore has all the characters in the line of input available to it and can scan ahead to check the next character.

Example: Write a procedure which allows the user to enter up to **max** digits, terminated by <Return>, and checks that each character entered is a valid digit between 0 and 9. If any invalid character is encountered a 'flag' **error_detected** is set to **true**. (This type of routine is useful for validating input, so as to ensure that a program will not crash when a user enters a non-numeric character when a numeric character is expected. Instead, the program could print out an error message and ask the user to re-enter a numeric value. A variation is shown on page 75).

```
procedure validate_integer;
    {assume all variables have been declared in the main program}

begin
    count:=0;
    error_detected:=false;

    while not eoln do
      begin
          count:=count+1;
          if count > max then error_detected:=true {too many digits}
          else
            begin
                read(number[count]);
                if not(number[count]in['0'..'9'])then
                    error_detected:=true;
                {endif}
            end; {endif}
      end;
    {endwhile}
    readln; {this is needed to go to the next line}
end; {procedure}
```

Looking up tables of values

Arrays are frequently used to store tables of values. For example, suppose we have 3 arrays, one containing the names of the 12 countries in the Common Market, and the other two containing the name of each country's currency and the current exchange rate. Given a particular country's name, we can look it up in the appropriate array and then, having determined the array subscript, print the corresponding currency name and exchange rate.

Q4: Assuming the existence of three arrays **country_name**, **currency**, and **exchange_rate**, and assuming each element of all the arrays has been initialised with an appropriate value, write statements to input the name of a country, look it up in the array **country_name**, and display the name of the country together with the corresponding currency name and exchange rate. You should allow for the possibility that the country name is not in the array, in which case the message 'Country not known' should be displayed.

```
        {arrays defined as follows}
var
        country_name    :array[1..12] of string[15];
        currency        :array[1..12] of string[15];
        exchange_rate   :array[1..12] of real;
        country         :string[15];
        ....
        ....
begin

        {first two lines are as follows:}
        write('Please input the name of the country: ');
        readln(country);
```

Multi-dimensional arrays

An array can have more than one dimension; for example, a two-dimensional array could be declared as follows:

```
total:array[1..150,1..5] of real;
```

The first index could represent a particular salesperson, and the second index a particular department in a store.

Q5: Suppose that input consists of a salesperson number between 1 and 150, a department number between 1 and 5 and a sales amount. Write statements to input **salesman_no, dept,** and **amount** and add the sales amount to the correct element of **total**.

Exercises:

1. Draw a structure diagram or write pseudocode for the following program, and then code and test it:

   (a) input a number of sales transactions, each consisting of a salesperson's number (between 1 and 150), a Department number (between 1 and 5) and a sales amount.

   (b) accumulate and print out the total sales for each employee with non-zero sales, and the total sales for each Department together with the name of the Department. (Departments are as follows: 1=Electrical, 2=Household goods, 3=Toys and Games, 4=Menswear, 5=Ladies' Fashion).

2. Write a program to simulate throwing a die a number of times, and display the number of times each face appears. Your program should allow the user to specify how many 'throws' he wants to make.

3. (a) Explain what is meant by 'top down design' of programs. Give **two** advantages of designing programs this way.
   (5 marks)

   (b) A program is required to enter a set of student's examination marks, to count the number of students who obtained each mark and to output the count for each mark. Examination marks are integers in the range 0 to 500.

   Use the method of top down design to produce a pseudocode description of an efficient algorithm. Give just two design levels, the first using a suitable graphical method or ordinary English, the second in pseudo-code. Give also the design of a suitable data structure to process the examination marks. Discuss briefly the efficiency of your design.
   (9 marks)

   (c) Suggest **two** different application packages in which the program described in (b) may be contained as one of a number of modules.
   (2 marks)

   (d) It is proposed to add a validation module to the program described in (b) in order to avoid errors due to erroneous input. Give a high level design for a suitable module and explain at what point it is called by the program in (b).
   (4 marks)
   AEB Paper 2 1989

4. Write the program for Exercise 3 incorporating the validation module.

Unit 17 — Procedures and Functions

Program structure

In standard Pascal, all programs have to conform to a particular format given below:

```
program heading;
label
     labels;
const
     constant declarations;
type
     data type definitions;
var
     variable declarations;

procedures and functions;

begin
     main program
end.
```

Procedure and function structure

Procedures have an almost identical structure:

```
procedure procname(formal parameters);
label
     labels;
const
     constant declarations;
type
     data type definitions;
var
     variable declarations;

procedures and functions;

begin
     main body of procedure;
end;
```

Functions have exactly the same structure as procedures except that a function starts with a function header:

```
function funcname(formal parameters):data type;
```

Global and local identifiers

Any procedure or function can include the declaration of constants and variables using **const** and **var** statements. Identifiers declared within a subprogram (that is, a procedure or function) are **local** identifiers and exist only during a call to the subprogram. Identifiers which are declared in the **main** program are called **global** variables and can be used throughout the program and all subprograms.

Note: The control variable of a FOR loop must be a local variable.

Block structure

Pascal is said to be a **block structured** language. A **block** consists of a **declaration** part, which includes constant, variable, label and type definitions and procedure and function declarations, and a **statement** part.

A sample program outline

```
program mainprog;
var  var1:real;
     var2,xxx:integer;

     procedure first_proc;
     var a,b,c:real;

         function func1;
             begin {func1}
                 .
                 .
             end;   {func1}

         begin {first_proc}
             .
             .
         end; {first_proc}

     procedure second_proc;
     var d,e,xxx,n,m:real;
```

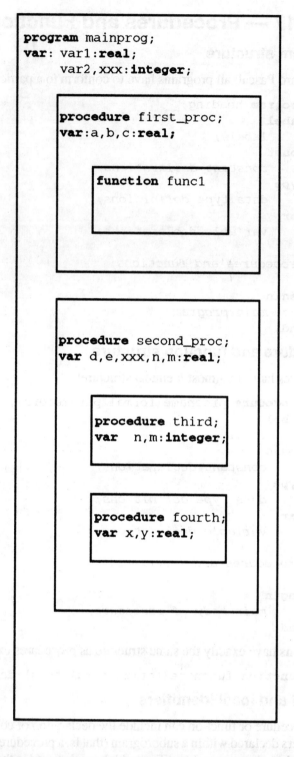

```
    begin {mainprog}
        .
        .
    end. {mainprog}
```

Q1: Complete the outline program, according to the diagram on the right hand side showing the 'blocks' that make up the program.

Scope of identifiers

All identifiers have to be declared before they can be used, and the **scope** of an identifier includes the block (program or subprogram) in which it is declared, and all blocks included within it.

An exception to this rule occurs when an identifier has the same name as one in a block which calls it, as for example the variable **xxx** in the outline program above.

Q2: Complete the following table:

Identifier	Scope
var1,var2	main_prog, first_proc, second_proc, third, fourth, func1
xxx	main_prog, first_proc, func1. Once second_proc is called, the **local** variable takes precedence. Its scope is second_proc, third and fourth.
a,b,c	
d,e	
n,m	

Parameters

The ability to declare local variables within subprograms is very useful in modular programming because it ensures that each subprogram is completely self-contained and independent of any global variables that have been declared in the main program. However, there has to be some way of passing information between outer and inner blocks (eg between the main program and its subprograms) and this is done by means of **parameters** (also sometimes referred to as the **arguments** of the subprogram).

For example, when you write the statement

```
gotoxy(35,10);
```

you are calling a procedure gotoxy with **parameters** 35 and 10. The procedure itself will have a procedure heading which looks something like the following:

```
procedure gotoxy(x,y:integer);
```

To distinguish between the parameters used when calling the routine and those which are declared in the procedure heading, the values that are passed (35 and 10 in the example) are called **actual parameters**, while the parameters in the procedure heading (x and y in the example) are called **formal parameters**.

Example: Write a procedure to move the cursor down the screen n lines, and show how you would use it to move
the cursor down the screen   (a)   5 lines

                (b)   m lines.

Answer:

```
procedure MoveDown(n:integer);
var  line_number : integer;
begin
     for line_number = 1 to n do
          writeln;
     {endfor}
end; {MoveDown}
```

To move down 5 lines, the procedure will be called with the statement

```
MoveDown(5);
```

To move down m lines the procedure will be called with the statement

```
MoveDown(m);
```

The formal parameter n in the above example does not change value in the procedure. It is called a **value parameter**, and the actual value 5, or the value of m in the second call, is passed to the memory location n from the calling procedure (or main program). This is called **passing parameters by value**.

In the next example, the procedure performs a calculation and passes the answer back to the calling procedure or main program.

Example: Write a procedure which accepts a number of seconds and converts this number to hours, minutes and seconds, passing the answer back to the calling routine.

Answer:
```
procedure TimeConversion(TotalSeconds:          ; var hours, minutes,
                                                    seconds :integer);
begin
    hours := TotalSeconds div 3600;
    minutes := (TotalSeconds mod 3600) div 60;
    seconds := (TotalSeconds mod 3600) mod 60
end; {TimeConversion}
```

Q3: How will you use this procedure to convert 4000 seconds to hours, minutes and seconds, storing the result in h, m, and s?

Hours, minutes and seconds in the above example are **variable parameters**, and must be preceded by the word **var** in the procedure heading. They are passed **by reference**; the **addresses,** not the **values,** of h, m and s are passed to the procedure.

A further example of parameter passing

On the following page is a program which allows the user to enter an integer of up to 9 digits, and then calculates a modulus-11 check digit and prints out the whole code number, incorporating the calculated check digit. The top-level solution to this problem could be expressed as

```
repeat until no more integers
    input the digits
    calculate the check digit
    output the code number
end repeat
```

The procedure **calc_checkdigit** is called with the following statement:

```
calc_checkdigit(raw_number, no_of_digits, check_digit);
```

The identifiers in brackets are the so-called **actual parameters;** they represent the actual values that will be passed to the subroutine or passed back from the subroutine. In this example, **raw_number** and **no_of_digits** are passed to the subprogram, which calculates and returns the value **checkdigit.**

The **declaration** of the procedure **calc_checkdigit** is as follows:

```
procedure calc_checkdigit(y:array_n; n:integer; var checkdigit:char);
```

The identifiers in brackets are the so-called **formal** parameters. Important points to note are summarised below:

- the **order** in which the parameters are declared is crucial; it must correspond to the **actual parameter list** in the calling statement.

- any identifier whose value will be **changed** in the subprogram (eg **checkdigit**) must be declared as a **variable** using the **var** statement. These are called **variable** parameters (or sometimes **output** parameters), and they provide two-way communication. Parameters whose values do **not** change in the subprogram are called **value** parameters (or sometimes **input** parameters).

- each identifier must have its type declared.

- the types that are allowed in a parameter list are the **simple data types** such as **real, integer, char, boolean,** or any declared type. This means that whenever a parameter is a **structured** type such as an array, the type must be defined by the programmer and the type identifier used in the procedure heading. The type **array_n** has for this reason been declared in the main program.

```
program check_dig; {program to calculate check digits}
type array_n = array[1..9] of char;
var  answer,check_digit : char;
          raw_number       : array_n;
          no_of_digits     : integer;


procedure input_integer(var x:array_n; var count:integer);
{Accepts entry of the integer digit by digit and validates each digit}
var  entry_valid    : boolean;
     next_digit      : char;

begin
    repeat
        count := 0;
        writeln('Enter an integer of up to 9 digits, followed by <Enter>');
        while not eoln do
            begin
                count := count + 1;
                read(next_digit);
                x[count] := next_digit;
                if not (next_digit  in ['0'..'9']) then
                    begin
                        writeln('Error - please redo from start');
                        entry_valid := false;
                        readln;
                    end
                else
                    entry_valid := true;
                {endif}
            end;
        {endwhile}
    until entry_valid; {end repeat}
    readln;
end; {input_integer}


procedure calc_checkdigit(y:array_n; n:integer; var checkdigit:char);
const         x = 'x';
              zero = '0';
var         count,weight,weighted_value,remainder,sum   :integer;
begin
    weight :=2;
    sum := 0;
    for count := n downto 1 do
        begin
            weighted_value := (ord(y[count])-48) * weight;
            sum := sum + weighted_value;
            weight := weight + 1;
        end;
    {endfor}
    remainder := sum mod 11;
    case remainder of
    0          : checkdigit := zero;
    1          : checkdigit := x;
    2..10      : checkdigit := chr(48 + 11 - remainder);
    end; {case}
end; {calculate checkdigit}
```

```
procedure output_code(x:array_n; n:integer; checkdigit:char);
var counter : integer;
begin
    write('The code number is ');
    for counter := 1 to n do
        write (x[counter]);
    {endfor}
    write (checkdigit);
    writeln;
end;

{***** MAIN PROGRAM ******}
begin
    repeat
        input_integer(raw_number,no_of_digits);
        calc_checkdigit(raw_number,no_of_digits,check_digit);
        output_code(raw_number,no_of_digits,check_digit);
        writeln;
        writeln('Another? (Y or N): ');
        readln(answer);
    until answer in ['n','N'];
end.
```

Q4: In the program above which calculates and outputs check digits:

(i)   Identify 4 global variables

(ii) Identify two variables which are local to the procedure input_integer.

(iii) Identify two parameters which are passed **by value** to the procedure calc_checkdigit

(iv) Identify one parameter which is passed **by reference** to the procedure calc_checkdigit. Explain the difference between passing parameters by value and passing them by reference.

Q5: Which of the following procedure headings is valid?

```
(i)        procedure proc1( a,b,c;   var d,e:integer);

(ii)       procedure proc2(var m,n:char; var s,t:real; v:real);

(iii)      procedure proc3(x:array[1..10] of integer; var z:char);

(iv)       procedure proc4;

(v)        procedure proc5(   d,e :real;f,g :integer;
                              var  p:char;q,r,s:real);
```

Q6: The last procedure above is called with the statement

```
            proc5(j,k,l,m,n,x,y,z);
```

Which are **value** parameters and which are **variable** parameters? Explain the difference.

Standard functions

Pascal has many built-in functions, some of which such as **trunc** and **random** we have already come across. A summary of some of the most frequently used functions is given below. There are many others, which will be listed in your Pascal manual.

Chr	returns a character of a specified ordinal number eg chr(69)='E'
Ord	returns the ordinal number of an ordinal-type value eg ord('A')=65
Round	rounds a type real value to an integer value eg round(3.6)=4
Trunc	truncates a type real value to an integer value eg trunc(5.8)=5
Sqr	returns the square of the argument
Sqrt	returns the square root of the argument
Length	returns the dynamic length of a string
Random	returns a random number.

For convenience, the ASCII codes for the common characters and numbers are given below:

ASCII	Char	ASCII	Char	ASCII	Char	ASCII	Char
32	space	56	8	80	P	104	h
33	!	57	9	81	Q	105	i
34	"	58	:	82	R	106	j
35	£	59	;	83	S	107	k
36	$	60	<	84	T	108	l
37	%	61	=	85	U	109	m
38	&	62	>	86	V	110	n
39	'	63	?	87	W	111	o
40	(	64	@	88	X	112	p
41	)	65	A	89	Y	113	q
42	*	66	B	90	Z	114	r
43	+	67	C	91	[	115	s
44	,	68	D	92	\	116	t
45	-	69	E	93	]	117	u
46	.	70	F	94	^	118	v
47	/	71	G	95	_	119	w
48	0	72	H	96	'	120	x
49	1	73	I	97	a	121	y
50	2	74	J	98	b	122	z
51	3	75	K	99	c	123	{
52	4	76	L	100	d	124		
53	5	77	M	101	e	125	}
54	6	78	N	102	f	126	~
55	7	79	O	103	g	127	del

User-written functions

We can also write our own functions, and everything that has been said about procedures also applies to functions; the only difference between them lies in the way they are declared and called. The example below, which returns the largest of two integers, illustrates this.

```
function max(a,b:integer):integer;
    begin
        max:=a;
        if b>a then max:=b;
    end;
```

This function would be called with the statement (for example)

```
MaxValue := max(x,y);
```

Note that

- the function has to contain an assignment statement to give it its value

- the function **type** (**real, integer** etc) has to be specified.

- a function is not normally used when more than one value is to be passed back, this value being passed back in the actual function name, e.g. **max** in the above example.

Exercises:

1. Write a procedure which positions the cursor at a given point on the screen and then writes a character string. (Use the Turbo Pascal GOTOXY procedure or equivalent).

2. Write a program to simulate storing 80 records with 4-digit keys in a random file of between 80 and 160 spaces, as specified by the user. For each 'record', the program should generate a random 4-digit integer to represent a record key, and then calculate the record address using the algorithm

   address:=record_key **mod** filesize

   The key should then be stored in the corresponding element of an array (which represents the file). If there is already a key at the address, the new key is to be stored in the next available free element, and a variable counting the number of 'collisions' should be incremented by 1.

   Print out after each 10 keys have been stored, the number of collisions which have occurred.

   From this simulation, how much space would you recommend allowing for a random file if 80 records have to be stored? Is there any other information which could usefully be obtained if appropriate enhancements were made to the program?

3. Write a function called Power which has integer arguments x, n and returns x^n .

4. Write a program which allows the user to input a sentence of up to 60 characters at the keyboard (terminated by a full-stop), and then calls a procedure which encrypts the sentence as follows:

   Generate a random number between 1 and 6. Then, for each character in turn, find its ASCII code, add to it the random number, and convert it back to a character.

   Print out the encrypted sentence, and then call another procedure which 'decrypts' it and print out the decrypted version.

5. In assembly language programming the use of jump or branch instructions is the sole means of transferring control. Early high-level programming languages effected transfer of control through the use of GOTO-type (jump) instructions too.

   (a) Explain why the use of GOTO-type instructions is no longer considered good high-level language programming practice. (4 marks)

   (b) Describe **four** features of structured programming languages which have made the use of GOTO-type instructions redundant. (8 marks)

   (c) A particular problem requires a procedure which requests, inputs and validates two numbers. For each, the user is prompted with the message "Please enter a reading". The number is input and a range check performed to ensure it is in the range 1 to 100 inclusive. If it is out of range, the message "Range error—please re-enter" is displayed and a substitute number input. This is repeated until the number is found to be in range. The two numbers input are stored in the variables 'first' and 'second', respectively.

   Write an efficient algorithm to perform this task without using GOTO-type instructions. (6 marks)

   (d) Explain how assembly language program design can minimise the problems which arise through excessive use of these instructions. (2 marks)

   JMB Paper 2 May 1990

6.* Explain what is meant by **parameter passing** in the use of subprograms in a programming language. What is the main advantage of using parameters? (4 marks)

   NISEAC Paper 1 1991

Unit 18 — Recursion

Recursive procedures

A procedure is **recursive** if it calls itself, and the process is called **recursion**. The short program below calls the recursive procedure **PrintList**.

```
program Recurs;
var abc:integer;
procedure PrintList(num:integer);
begin
     num := num-1;
     if num > 1 then PrintList(num);
     writeln(num);                        {LINE A}
end; {procedure PrintList}

{***** main program*****}
begin
     abc := 4;
     PrintList(abc);
     writeln(abc);                        {LINE B}
end.
```

When this program is run, the procedure PrintList is called with the parameter abc set to 4. (Note in passing that this parameter is passed **by value;** the formal parameter num is not declared as a variable, so the actual value 4 is passed to the procedure rather than the address of abc.)

The address of the instruction marked {LINE B} is stored on the return address stack, and execution will proceed from that line when the procedure has been executed.

Now execution of PrintList begins; num is decremented by 1 and becomes 3. The procedure calls itself, and the address of the instruction marked {LINE A} is stored on the procedure stack, together with the information that num=3. When this line is eventually executed, the number 3 will be displayed.

PrintList now begins again, with the value of the actual parameter num set to 3. It is decremented to 2, the procedure is called again, the return address stored, and the process continues until num=1 and the procedure call is not executed. At this point LINE A is executed for the first time and the number 1 is displayed. The end of the procedure has been reached, so the first return address is taken off the stack; this is also LINE A, with a parameter of 2, so the number 2 is displayed. The end of the procedure is reached again, so the next return address is taken off the stack; LINE A again, this time with a parameter of 3. Finally the end of the procedure is reached again and the address of the next instruction is LINE B, so the number 4 is written.

Value of num	return addresses
1	LINE A
2	LINE A
3	LINE A
4	LINE B

A stack is a first in, last out data structure, so the last address put on the stack will be the first one taken off. The instruction writeln(num) *with num=3 was the first to be put on the stack, so it will be executed last of the LINE A's, followed last of all by LINE B.*

The above example illustrates three essential ingredients that must be present in any recursive process.

1. A stopping condition must be included which when met means that the routine will not call itself and will start to 'unwind'.

2. For input values other than the stopping condition, the routine must call itself.

3. The stopping condition must be reached after a finite number of calls.

Another example of recursion

Recursion is a useful technique for the programmer when the algorithm itself is essentially recursive. An example of this is the calculation of a factorial, where **n!** (read as **factorial n**) is defined as follows:

If n = 0 then n! = 1

otherwise, n! = n*(n-1)*(n-2)*........*3*2*1

Thus for example 4! = 4 x 3 x 2 x 1, and 0! = 1 (by definition).

This can be defined recursively as

If n = 0 then n! = 1

otherwise n! = n*(n-1)!   (For example 4! = 4 x 3!)

The pseudocode for a recursive function to calculate n! is as follows:

```
function factorial(n)
begin
    if   n = 0 or 1 then factorial = 1
    else factorial = n*factorial(n-1)
end
```

Q1: Dry run the above function when it is called with the statement **answer = factorial(4)**.

Q2: What happens if the function is called with answer = factorial(-3)?

Which of the 3 'essential ingredients' of a recursive function is not present?

Advantages and disadvantages of recursion

In general, a non-recursive solution is more efficient in terms of both computer time and space. This is because when using a recursive solution, the computer has to make multiple procedure or function calls, each time storing return addresses and copies of local or temporary variables, all of which takes time and space. Another point to consider is that if the recursion continues too long, the stack containing return addresses may overflow and the program will crash. If for example you try to calculate factorial 2000 using a recursive routine, 2000 return addresses have to be stored before the routine begins to unwind, and the computer may run out of memory to do this.

For some problems, however, a recursive solution is more natural and easier for the programmer to write. You will encounter a good example of this later when studying tree traversals (Unit 27).

Generally speaking, if the recursive solution is not much shorter than the non-recursive one, use the non-recursive one. Going by this rule, it would be better to use iteration rather than recursion to work out a factorial; it serves as a neat example of recursion but would be more efficiently and just as simply written iteratively, using a For..Next loop, for example. This is left as an exercise for the reader!

Exercises:

1. Name one advantage and one disadvantage of recursive routines. (2 marks)

2. Distinguish between **iteration** and **recursion**. Why are both useful to a programmer? Give **one** example of the use of iteration and **one** example of the use of recursion in programming. (6 marks)
WJEC AS Level 1989

3. When developing large computer programs, it is very difficult to ensure that the procedure and variable names used are unique and are not being used elsewhere in the program.

   (a) Explain the features and mechanisms required in a high-level programming language to help programmers avoid the problem of conflicting variable or procedure names. Include in your answer an explanation of how conflict is avoided when passing parameters to and from procedures. (6 marks)

   (b) When a team is working together on a project with different programmers working on different program units, what additional features and precautions are required to avoid problems of conflicting variable and procedure names when the units are linked together? (2 marks)

   (c) In the program segment given below assume the procedure 'print' generates a new line.

```
global integer n
n := 10
reduce(n - 5)
print(n)
STOP
```

   The procedure 'reduce' is given below.

```
procedure reduce (n: local integer)
begin
    if n <> 1 then
        reduce(n - 1)
    endif
    print(n)
end
```

   (i) Using a trace table demonstrate the effect of executing the program segment clearly showing the printout. (8 marks)

   (ii) How many versions of the procedure 'reduce' are stored by the computer when executing this program segment? (2 marks)

   (iii) What changes would make the program segment more readable? (2 marks)
JMB Paper 2 May 1989

4. The following procedure prints out characters in a rather strange sequence:

```
procedure charprint(x, y, z : char; n : integer);
begin
    if n > 0 then
    begin
        write (x);
        charprint(y, z, x, n - 1);
        write (z);
    end; {if}
end; {charprint}
```

Show the output produced by each of the following three procedure calls:

   (a) `charprint('A', 'B', 'C', 1);`

   (b) `charprint('A', 'B', 'C', 2);`

   (c) `charprint('A', 'B', 'C', 3);` (6 marks)

Unit 19 — Sequential File Processing

Introduction

This Unit is concerned with writing data to disk files and reading data from disk files for further processing or producing reports. Standard Pascal supports only serial/sequential file organisation; access to an individual record is only possible by reading each record from the beginning of the file until the correct one is located.

In Turbo Pascal, records may be accessed randomly using the standard procedure **seek**, which enables the programmer to specify exactly which record is to be read. Details of this technique are not covered here.

Record declaration

A data file will consist of a number of **records**, each of which is divided into a number of **fields**. For example, a stock file could consist of records having the following fields:

field name	type
item_no	string[6]
description	string[6]
selling_price	real
qty_in_stock	integer

Pascal uses a built in composite data type **record** to define the fields in the record as follows:

```
type stock_rec_type = record
        item_no       :string[6];
        description   :string[20];
        selling_price :real;
        qty_in_stock  :integer;
    end;
```

The data type for the **file** of records now has to be declared as follows:

```
stock_file_type = file of stock_rec;
```

and finally the variables of type **file_of_stock** and **stock_rec** are declared:

```
var
    stock_file    :stock_file_type;
    stock_item    :stock_rec_type;
```

Note that item_no and description have been given a fixed length of 6 and 20 respectively. In the sample program later in this unit, character strings will be defined as arrays of characters, which makes input easier for the user because the input routine can be written to 'pad out' each field with spaces if necessary.

Q1: Imagine you are to create a file of stock transaction records, each consisting of a 6-character item number and a quantity sold. Write the **type** and **var** declarations to declare the file and associated record structure.

Assigning an external name to a file

Before a file variable can be used, it must be associated with an external file. In Turbo Pascal, this is achieved by means of the **assign** statement; for example

```
assign(stock_file,'a:\data\stock.dat');
```

In other versions of Pascal, the filename must appear in the parameter list of the program heading, and this name will then be used as the external file name:

```
program stock(input,output,stock_file);
```

Input and output

A file must be 'opened' before it can be read from or written to. An existing file can be opened for reading with the **reset** procedure, and a new file can be created and opened with the **rewrite** procedure. **Append** is used to open an existing file before appending extra records to the end of the file.

When a file is processed sequentially, it may be read from or written to with the standard procedures **read** and **write**; for example

```
read(stock_file,stock_item);
```

In Turbo Pascal (but not in standard Pascal) a file should be closed when processing is completed, using the standard procedure **close**.

```
close(stock_file);
```

The standard boolean function **eof** detects the end of a file when reading records sequentially. It will return **true** when the last record in a file has been read, and **false** otherwise.

Accessing fields in a record

In order to refer to a field of a record, the **dot notation** is used. For example, to refer to item_no in the field stock_item, we write

```
stock_item.item_no
```

Q2: If we have also defined a record called **trans_rec** which has a field **item_no**, how will this be referred to?

The dot notation can become rather cumbersome, and Pascal provides a more convenient way of referring to fields within a record, namely, the **with** statement.

```
with statement ──▶( with )──▶[ record identifier ]──▶( do )──▶[ statement ]──▶
```

```
eg   with stock_rec do
     begin
         write('Enter item number');
         readln(item_no);
         .
         .
     end; {with}
```

Writing to the printer

To write to the printer in Turbo Pascal, include **printer** in the program's **uses** clause just beneather the program header at the start of the program (e.g. **uses crt, printer**) and use

```
writeln(Lst,data)
```

A sample program

The following program demonstrates both writing to disk, and reading from disk. Stock records are accepted at the terminal and written to disk, and then when all records are written, the file is closed and re-opened for input and the records are read and displayed on the screen.

```
program s_create;

{Program to accept data from the keyboard and write to stock master file.}

uses crt;
const max = 20;
type
     string_max = array[1..max] of char;
     stock_rec_type = record
         item_no        : integer;
         description    : string_max;
         selling_price  : real;
         qty_in_stock   : integer;
     end;

     stock_file_type = file of stock_rec;

var
     stock_file   : stock_file_type;
     stock_item   : stock_rec_type;
     filename     : string[20];

procedure read_text_string(no_of_chars:integer; var text_string:string_max);
const space = ' ';
var counter:integer;

begin
     for counter := 1 to no_of_chars do
          if eoln then text_string[counter]:=space
          else read(text_string[counter]);
          {endif}
     {endfor}
     readln;
end; {procedure}


Procedure initialise;
begin
     clrscr;
     writeln('Please enter the name of the file, including pathname
       (eg a:\stockmas.dat);' );
     readln(filename);
     assign(stock_file,filename);
     rewrite(stock_file);
     write('Enter item number; 999 to finish: ');
     readln(stock_item.item_no);
 end; {procedure}
```

```
Procedure write_recs;
begin
      with stock_item do
      begin
          while item_no <>999 do
              begin
                  write('Enter description: ');
                  read_text_string(20,description);
                  write('Selling price     : ');
                  readln(selling_price);
                  write('Quantity in stock: ');
                  readln(qty_in_stock);
                  write(stock_file,stock_item);
                  write('Enter item number; 999 to finish: ');
                  readln(item_no);
              end; {while}
          close(stock_file);
      end; {with}
end; {procedure}


Procedure read_recs;
begin
    reset(stock_file);
    with stock_item do
      begin
          while not eof(stock_file) do
              begin
                  read(stock_file,stock_item);
                  writeln(item_no:7, description:22, selling_price:8:2,
                          qty_in_stock:5);
              end; {while}
      end; {with}
    close(stock_file);
end; {procedure}


{***** MAIN PROGRAM *****}

begin
      initialise;
      write_recs;
      read_recs;
end.
```

Exercises:

1. Write a program which accepts stock transactions from the keyboard giving item number and quantity sold, and writes them to a transaction file on disk. (n.b. Input the transactions in item number sequence, to avoid having to sort them before testing the update program in Exercise 2).

2. Write a program which performs a sequential file update of the stock master file, using as input the old stock master file and the transaction file, and creating a new stock master file.

Unit 20 — Program Production and Testing

Software development tools

Hopefully, by the time you get to this point you will have quite a lot of programming experience behind you. The purpose of this Unit is to summarise the role of some of the software development tools that you will have used (perhaps without being fully aware of what was going on behind the scenes), and to discuss methods of thoroughly testing a program.

Translating and running programs

The diagram below summarises the steps followed, and the software used in the creation of a source program and its conversion to executable form.

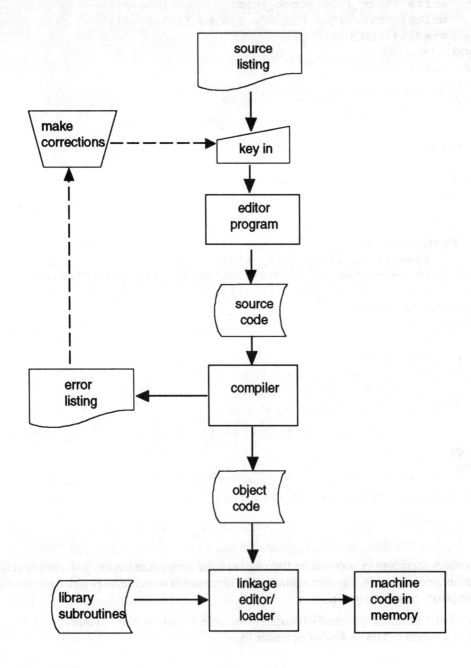

Figure 20.1

The text typed in by the programmer is known as the **source code**. This then has to be translated into machine code, which the computer can execute. The translation process is performed by a program called a **compiler**, and the output from this process is called the **object code**. This is stored on disk and can be run (executed) as many times as required without going back to the source code.

If the compiler finds any statements that it cannot translate, because the programmer has made an error in the **syntax** of the statement, it will report each wrong statement either on the screen or on an error listing, with a (sometimes rather abstruse) error message, and the program will not be translated into machine code. The programmer then has to find the errors, make the necessary corrections to the source code and recompile the program.

Editors

An editor is a piece of software which enables the programmer to enter and edit a program. Most programming environments such as Turbo Pascal or Microfocus COBOL have their own editor program, but programs can also be typed in using a wordprocessor in 'non-document mode'.

A **screen** editor allows the programmer to position the cursor anywhere on the screen and insert or delete text.

Q1: Describe briefly other facilities provided by a screen editor for entering and editing programs.

Compilers and interpreters

Compilers and interpreters are covered in detail in Unit 49. The text typed in by the programmer with the aid of the editor is known as the **source code**, and this has to be translated by either a compiler or an interpreter into machine code or **object code**.

Linkage editor

Once the code written by the programmer has been compiled, the object code is stored on disk. Before it can be executed, however, any separately compiled subroutines such as input and output routines, or routines written by the programmer, have to be **linked** into the object code. This is the function of the **linkage editor**. It puts the appropriate machine addresses in all the external call and return instructions, so that the modules are linked together properly.

Loader

When the program is ready to be run, a program called a **loader** will take the machine code program and load the instructions (perhaps from disk) into their specified storage locations.

Debuggers

A debugger is a program which helps you to find logic errors in your program. For example, Turbo Pascal contains a **Debug** menu option which allows you to display the values of chosen variables on screen. You can step through the program one line at a time by pressing the function key F7, or specify a point in the source code and have the program execute up to that point (a **break point**) before you start to step through. You can display the procedure stack, so that you can see exactly when procedures are called and in what sequence (a **trace** facility). On some systems you can have a printout of the complete contents of memory (a **store dump**) so that you can examine all variables.

No amount of description can replace practical experience, so try to find out whether your own system has debugging facilities and get in some practice!

Prettyprinter

A prettyprinter is another useful software tool which will take your source code and indent each line correctly so that, in Pascal, all the **begin** statements line up with the correct **end** statement and so on. Having a program correctly indented can be a great help in spotting missing **end** statements or finding logic errors buried in nested **if** statements.

Separate compilation of modules

It is often useful to be able to compile modules separately and subsequently recombine them without having to re-compile working modules unnecessarily. Typically, a subroutine **library** of useful routines is built up and can be shared by several programs. Since these routines are already in object code, they could have been produced in any language, regardless of the language used for the program which calls them.

A summary of program development aids

Aids to the programmer may include

- an on-line help facility giving information about any command, standard function or procedure.

- utility programs enabling the user to design input screens and have the code automatically generated.

- separate compilation of modules, allowing the programmer to build up a library of precompiled, tested code

- an **integrated development environment** combining a text editor and a compiler, with pull-down menus, windows, help facility and debugger

- a prettyprint facility to tidy up the appearance of the source code.

Types of program error

Once the program has been typed in, different types of errors may show up. These include

- **syntax errors**: e.g. a misspelling such as **redln(x)** instead of **readln(x)**

- **semantic errors**: e.g. trying to assign a **real** number to an **integer** variable.
  (The actual statement, e.g. **a := 1.5;** may look all right but if **a** is an integer the compiler will give an error message.)

- **logic errors**: e.g. writing **net := salary + tax** when you meant to write **net := salary - tax**

- **runtime errors**: e.g. attempting to read past the end of a file.

Q2: Show how the statement **a := b / c** may result in an error of **each** of the above types under different circumstances.

Q3: Give another example of each of the above types of error. How will each of these errors be detected?

Program testing

Often it is not immediately obvious that there are logic errors in a program. Indeed some programs may function correctly for months or even years before a particular circumstance, or piece of input data, causes a problem or error to surface.

It is the job of the programmer to test, as far as possible, that all parts of the program work correctly. It should be realised that **complete** testing is not possible except in the case of the most trivial program; one can never be completely certain that all errors have been removed, but sufficient tests can be performed to give a reasonable measure of confidence in the program.

The situation is analagous to testing children on multiplication tables; once a child has answered a certain number of tests correctly, at some point or other the teacher assumes that all other tests will be answered correctly and testing ceases.

Consider the simple pseudocode segment given below, which looks up a table and prints out the entry for 'OLIVER'.

```
Set search flag on
while not end of table and search flag on
    if name='OLIVER'
    then print name
        set search flag off
    endif
endwhile
if search flag on
then print 'OLIVER not in table'
endif
```

Q4: Devise test data for this segment. Does the test data test the program **completely?**

Designing a test plan

Good testing requires:

- a thorough knowledge and understanding of what the program is supposed to do
- thinking out what ought to be tested
- working out expected results for each of the test cases
- writing down the test plan.

Since we cannot test everything, each test must be carefully planned to provide more information about the program. A major benefit of preparing a comprehensive test plan with expected results is that it forces the programmer to think carefully about the program and often errors are spotted even before running the test!

Test data should test the program to its limits, and should include

- **data at the extremes of ranges,** as this is where a large number of errors occur (e.g. if you have a statement "If age >= 21 then *do something* ", test it three times with age = 20, 21 and 22)
- **invalid data** just outside valid ranges, or of the wrong type (character rather than numeric, etc) as well as **valid data.**

Q5: An important point about testing is that tests should be designed with the aim of proving the program **incorrect**, rather than designing tests to show which parts of the program work correctly. Do you think the person who wrote the program is the best person to design the test data? If not, who should design it? Give reasons for your answers.

Methods of testing

The objectives of testing can be stated in two basic questions:

1. Does the logic work properly?
   - does the program work as intended?
   - can it be made to 'crash'?
2. Is all the necessary logic present?
   - are there any functions missing?
   - does the program or module do everything specified?

There are two different ways of testing, known as **functional** and **logical** (also called **structural**) testing.

Functional testing

Functional testing is carried out independently of the code used in the program. It involves looking at the program specification and creating a set of test data that covers all the inputs and outputs and program functions. This type of testing is also known as **'black box testing'**. For example, to test the program which calculates check digits (see Unit 17) we could draw up the following test plan:

	Test	Purpose	Expected result
1.	Enter 1587	Test valid data	3
2.	Enter 9 digits 033514325	Test extreme case	3
3.	Enter 10 digits 0335143256	Too many digits	?
4.	Enter 154W	Invalid digit	'Error - please redo from start'
5.	Enter no digits	Extreme case	?

These tests seem to cover the problem quite well, but nevertheless they do not completely test the program.

Q6: What other tests can you devise which will provide more information about the program?

Logical (structural) testing

Logical testing ('**white box testing**') is dependent on the code logic, and derives from the program structure rather than its function. In other words, we study the program code and try to test each possible path in the program at least once. The problem with logical testing is that it will not detect missing functions: you cannot test what isn't there!

One method of devising a test plan is to start with a set of functional test cases, and then add additional tests to exercise each statement in the program at least once, making sure that each decision is tested for all outcomes.

Exercises:

1. (a) Write brief notes to describe the following program design strategies:

    (i)   top-down design and stepwise refinement;

    (ii)   bottom-up design

    Describe **one** advantage of each of these methodologies.   (8 marks)

   (b) Describe **one** feature of a programming language which assists the implementation of a top-down design.
                                                                         (2 marks)

   (c) Describe briefly **five** examples of software which assist in the development of computer programs. In each case explain why the example you have described is helpful.   (10 marks)
                                                                 AEB Paper 2 1988

2. Describe how you would test a program which is designed to read from a keyboard, in a random order, a number of transaction records each with several fields, to update a master file with these records causing several master file records to be modified.   (5 marks)
                                                    AEB Specimen AS Level Paper 1989

3. When a piece of software is being developed, certain errors may occur before and during program execution. State **three** types of possible errors together with suitable examples.   (6 marks)
                                                 London Specimen AS Level Paper 1989

4. (a) State and explain the fundamental steps between the definition of a problem and the successful implementation of a computer based solution to the problem.   (8 marks)

   (b) Describe briefly how a program can be checked for correct operation and explain the role of test data in this process.
                                                                         (6 marks)
                                                 UCLES Specimen AS Level Paper 1989

5.* Describe the function of program test data and explain how test data should be chosen.   (3 marks)
                                                                 AEB Paper 2 1991

Section 3 — Data Structures

Unit 21 — Strings, Arrays and Records

Introduction to data structures

All data processing on a computer involves the manipulation of data. This data can be organised in the computer's memory in different ways according to how it is to be processed, and the different methods of organising data are known as **data structures**.

Computer languages such as Pascal have built-in **elementary data types** (such as *integer*, *real*, *Boolean* and *char*) and some built-in **structured** or **composite** data types (data structures) such as *record*, *array* and *string*. These composite data types are made up of a number of elements of a specified type such as *integer* or *real*.

In subsequent Units you will see that some data structures such as stacks, queues and trees are not built in to the language and have to be constructed by the programmer.

Strings

A string is made up of a sequence of characters. In standard versions of Pascal, a string has to be defined as being of a certain length. A **type** statement is used to define the composite data type and a variable can then be declared as being of that type.

```
eg    type string = array[1..80] of char;

      var       s:string;
```

This string then has a fixed length of 80 and we cannot, for example, write

```
      s:='JOHN';
```

Seventy-six blanks would need to follow the letters JOHN to make the statement valid.

To provide for strings of varying length, most versions of Pascal (including Turbo Pascal) have a pre-defined type *string* which allows character strings of any length to be assigned to the variable. This enables a string of any length to be defined with a statement such as

```
      var s:string;
```

without a corresponding **type** statement.

Operations on strings

These include finding the length of a string, **concatenating** or joining two strings, comparing two strings and extracting substrings.

Note that strings are essentially **dynamic data structures**, that is, the number of characters in a string may vary at run time. In Turbo Pascal, the string occupies as many bytes as its maximum length (up to 255) plus 1. The first byte contains the dynamic length of the string.

Q1: Show THREE methods by which you could store the names IAN, RUSSELL, ANITA, EVA and CHRISTOPHER in a storage space of length 55 in such a way that they could subsequently be separated into individual names again.

Arrays

An array is defined as a finite ordered set of homogeneous elements.

Finite means that there is a specific number of elements in the array. The number may be large or small but it is fixed and it must be at least one. Thus an array is a **static data structure**.

Ordered implies that there is a first, second, third etc element of the array.

Q2: What do you think **homogeneous** means?

Implementation of arrays in Pascal

An array x consisting of fifty integers may be declared in Pascal as follows:

```
var
    x : array[1..50] of integer;
```

Q3: How do you reference the 21st element of the array?

Q4: Define an array TEMP with 31 elements of type *real*. The array subscripts are to range from 0 to 30.

Multi-dimensional arrays

The concept of a one-dimensional array can be extended to two or more dimensions.

A two dimensional array may be declared in Pascal as, for example,

```
x:array[0..10] of array [1..6] of integer
```

This declaration can be abbreviated to

```
x:array[0..10,1..6] of integer
```

Q5: Define a two-dimensional array which will hold the 12 monthly sales totals for 6 salesmen. Write a statement in Pascal which will assign the value 2516.25 to salesman number 3 as his June sales figure.

Q6: Write pseudocode statements to calculate the total annual sales for each salesman. (Assume the sales figures have been read into the array).

98

Records

A record is the most common data structure in computerised data processing. Many languages such as COBOL and Pascal (but not BASIC) have a built-in composite data type **record**.

Records are somewhat similar to arrays in that they consist of a number of related data items, but they differ in that the data items or fields may have different types.

A student record might have the following fields:

name	address	course	date_of_birth
Ben Ramsey	17 Elmer Street, Ipswich	PD7015	170873

The **field identifiers** here are **name, address,** and so on. We also need to be able to identify the entire record, say by the name **student**. We can then refer to a particular field of this record using the 'dot' notation, ie:

```
student.name,  student.address, etc
```

Q7: Write a statement to change the student's course code to PD7075.

In Pascal, the structure of a record is defined by means of a **type** definition. This defines the name of the structure (ie record, in this case), the name of each field and the type of the element in each field. For example:

```
type stud_rec_type = record
              name:     array [1..25] of char;
              address:  array [1..30] of char;
              course:   array [1..6] of char;
              date:     integer
          end;
```

In the variable section we can define variables to be of the type defined in the type definition. For example:

```
var
    student_1: stud_rec_type;
    student_2: stud_rec_type;
```

This declaration defines two variables student_1 and student_2 each of type stud_rec_type. Note that we can if we wish assign the complete contents of one record to another record, if they are of the same type; eg

```
student_1:=student_2;
```

Q8: Write a type definition **stock_rec_type** for a record structure which is to consist of three parts; stock code (6 characters), description (25 characters) and price (a real number). Then write the variable declaration for **s_item**, which is to be of type **stock_rec_type**.

The WITH statement

If we have a large record with many fields it becomes tedious to use the dot notation to enumerate each field. To assign values to each field of the student record would require a series of statements such as

```
student.name:='Michael Head';
student.address:='2 Burnett Road, Colchester';
student.course:='PD7015';
student.date_of_birth:=100371;
```

Instead, we can use a shorthand notation:

```
with student do
    begin
            name:='Michael Head';
            address:='2 Burnett Road, Colchester';
            course:='PD7015';
            date_of_birth:=100371
    end;
```

Note that it is impossible in Pascal to read in a complete record from the keyboard without mentioning each field explicitly. You cannot write

```
readln(student);
```

Instead, it could be written

```
with student do
    begin
            read(name,address,course,date_of_birth);
            readln
    end;
```

Fixed and variable length records

The records discussed so far have all been **fixed length records**. If all the records belong to a file, every record in the file will have the same fixed number of fields and characters.

With variable length records, all the records in the file will not be the same size. This could be for one or both of the following reasons:

- The **size** of some of the fields could vary — eg a field containing a name or an address

- The **number of fields** could vary. For example, a customer's invoice record could have a field (or several fields) for each item that he has purchased.

There is no easy way in Pascal of implementing variable length records, since records are **static** data structures and the space is allocated in the computer's memory at compilation time, not at run time.

The **advantage** of using fixed length records, therefore, is that they are the simplest for the programmer, as the fixed-length record data structure is a built-in feature of the language. The **disadvantage** of fixed length records is that they can be very wasteful of space if individual records have fields which vary in length, or which have varying numbers of fields. In addition, there is often no way of knowing how many fields might be needed for a particular record, as in the example of the customer's invoice record given above.

Exercises:

1. (a) Write down an algorithm, using pseudocode or otherwise, which will store in LARGE and SMALL the largest and smallest values among a set of positive integer values stored in elements zero to MAX of an array named PLACE.

(4 marks)

UCLES Paper 2 May 1990

2. The array TEST(1:10,1:5) contains 10 rows and 5 columns and is made up of single byte elements.

   If the base location of the array (i.e. the address of the first element) is 0, then what is the address of element TEST(7,2) if the array is stored in memory   (i) by columns,

                              (ii) by rows.   (4 marks)

   NISEAC Paper 2 June 1990

3. The following is a top level design of an algorithm for determining whether a given wordstring is palindromic, ie. it reads the same both forwards and backwards. For example the word TIPPIT is palindromic.

```
1     State the objectives of the problem
2     Input the string, character by character, into the string array WORD$,
      determining the number of characters n, which are read in.
3     Initialise the array index variables left and right.
4     While (left <= right) and (WORD$(left) = WORD$(right))
5        begin
6           left=left+1
7           right=right-1
8        end
9     endwhile
10    If C1 then     palindrome=true
11    else      palindrome=false
12    If C2 then     output "Word is palindromic."
13    else output "Word is not palindromic."
```

N.B. WORD$(i) represents the ith character in the string held in the array.

(i) Write out the conditions **C1** and **C2** in steps 10 and 12 above.   (5 marks)

(ii) Trace the word '**REPAPER**' using a trace table with the following column headings;

left	right	left<=right	WORD$(left)=WORD$(right)

    (10 marks)

(iii) Refine step 2 of the design as a separate module.   (5 marks)

London Specimen AS Paper 1989

4. Write a Pascal program for the above algorithm.

5. State one advantage of using fixed length records and one advantage of using variable length records in a computerised data processing system.   (2 marks)

AEB Sample Paper 1990

Unit 22 —Tables and Searching Methods

Records are rarely used singly; usually they are part of a **file**, or part of a composite data structure known as a **table**.

A **table** is an **array of records**; each element of the array, instead of being an elementary type such as *integer* or *real*, is itself a record.

If a file of data records is small enough to fit into memory, a table could be used to store a whole file so that it could be manipulated in some way; for example, it could be sorted and output in the new sequence.

Tables are also used for looking up information. The following table holds information about College courses.

Course_code	Title	Weeks_duration	Cost
EC5764	Spreadsheets	10	25.00
EC5765	Databases	10	25.00
EC5821	C Programming	24	70.00
EC5824	Expert Systems	36	98.50
PD3011	A-Level Computing Yr 1	36	76.00
PD3012	A-Level Computing Yr 2	33	76.00

etc

The concept of a table is similar to that of a file but there are two important differences:

• A table contains a fixed predetermined number of entries, whereas a file can contain any number of records.

• A table is held in the computer's memory whereas a file is held on some backing storage device such as disk or tape. Of course, as mentioned above, a file may be read into a table in memory, but more often only one record is held in memory at one time. When that record has been processed and output, the next record is read in and overwrites the previous one in memory.

Q1: How would you use the table of courses given above to find the cost of course PD3011? What is the advantage of holding the entries in the table in ascending sequence of course code?

Q2: How many records, on average, would have to be examined in a table of 500 courses in order to find a particular course?

Tables in Pascal

The above table could be defined in Pascal as follows:

```
type
  course_rec_type = record
          course_code    :array[1..6] of char;
          course_title   :array[1..30] of char;
          weeks_duration :integer;
          cost           :real
    end;

var        courses        :array[1..100] of course_rec_type;
```

To access one field in a particular record of **courses**, the dot notation can be used. The cost of the Expert Systems course EC5824 is referred to as

```
courses[4].cost
```

Q3: Write statements to define a table which is to hold a name and three examination marks for each of 100 students, using an array to hold the marks. How will you reference the name and the second exam mark of the thirty-fifth student?

Searching a table

A common operation on a table is to search it for a given value; for example, we could search for a given course code in order to ascertain its cost. The simplest type of search is a **linear search**, where every item in the table is searched in sequence. If the table is sorted on the field being searched (the key field) then the search can be abandoned as soon as the search value exceeds the key field.

The pseudocode for a procedure to search the table for a given course code is as follows:

```
Procedure SEARCH_TABLE
begin
     subscript = 0
     code_found = false
     repeat
        subscript = subscript+1
        if courses[subscript].course_code = item_sought
              then code_found = true
        endif
     until code_found = true or subscript = no_of_elements
          or courses[subscript].course_code > item_sought
end procedure
```

The procedure sets a boolean variable **code_found** to **true** if the course code is found.

Binary search

In a binary search, the middle item of the sorted array being searched is examined to see if it is equal to the search item. If not, then if it is greater than the search item, the upper half of the array is of no further interest. The number of items being searched is therefore halved and the process repeated until the last item is examined, with either the upper half or the lower half of the values searched being eliminated at each pass.

The search has a maximum number of searches of $\log_2$ N, where N is the size of the array; it is much faster than a linear search when the array or table is large. Note that the items must be in sequence, and the algorithm for searching the array must allow for the item not being there.

The pseudocode for a binary search on the table of course codes is given below:

```
Procedure Binary_Search
begin
(Initialize variables)
        found = false
        search_failed = false
        high_pointer = no_of_elements
        low_pointer = 1
        repeat
            (find midpoint of search area)
            midpoint = trunc((high_pointer+low_pointer)/2)
            if   courses[midpoint].course_code = item_sought
                then found = true
            else  (has the whole array been searched?)
                if low_pointer >= high-pointer
                    then search_failed = true
                else   (no, still searching)
                  if courses[midpoint].course_code < item_sought
                    then low_pointer = midpoint+1
                  else high_pointer = midpoint-1
                  endif
                endif
            endif
        until found or search_failed
end procedure
```

Q4: Perform a dry-run through the above pseudocode, showing the values of **low_pointer, high_pointer, midpoint, courses[mid_point].course_code, found** and **search_failed** at each stage when an array **courses** containing the course codes 4, 8, 15, 16, 18, 24, 28, 32, 38, 41, 43 is searched for the value 19.

Exercises:

1. Describe the principle of operation underlying each of:

    (a) sequential search;

    (b) binary search.

    (3 marks)
AEB Paper 2 1990

2. Show the steps needed to look up Birmingham using a binary search on the following list:

    Aberdeen, Birmingham, Cambridge, Exeter,

    Manchester, Newcastle, Norwich, Oxford, Reading,

    Sheffield, Southampton, York.

    (2 marks)
AEB Paper 2 1987

3. Two conditions must be satisfied for the binary search algorithm to find the key of a data item in a list of items. What are these conditions? (2 marks)
AEB Paper 2 1986

4. Write a program to test out the binary search algorithm.

    (a) First of all create a test file on disk, each record containing the name of a town and its distance in miles from London. Add records to this file in alphabetical order.

    (b) Write a program which reads the records into a table in memory, prompts the user for the name of a town, and then performs a binary search on the table to find the number of miles from London. Display this information, or, if the town is not found in the table, display a suitable error message.

5. Details of a football league table containing twenty teams are read into two arrays, NAME containing the team names and POINTS containing the total league points accumulated to date i.e. POINTS[I] contains the points accumulated by TEAM[I].

    These may be visualised as follows:

ARRAY INDEX	TEAM	POINTS
1	LIVERPOOL	14
2	ARSENAL	12
3	SPURS	10
--	------------	--
20	WEST HAM	1

    Each week the table is updated with data giving points scored by some of the teams. (Some teams may not play on a particular week).

    The form in which the data is given is shown below, not necessarily in any particular order.

    n (the number of results to follow)

Team name	Points gained.
Team name	Points gained.
--------------	----------------

    (n results)

    Write pseudocode to represent the process of updating the table. (10 marks)
NISEAC Paper 2 June 1989

Unit 23 — Linear Lists

Introduction

A linear list is an example of a **sequence**, that is, a dynamic data structure in which items of data are held one after the other in some predefined order. Lists of employees or stock items are examples of sequences which would probably be held on disk or tape files rather than in memory. In other cases a linear list may be held in memory and possibly displayed on a screen. An example is a display showing the arrival times of trains at a railway station:

Time	Starting Point
1450	Norwich
1458	Colchester
1520	Stowmarket
1545	Cambridge
1555	Liverpool Street

Implementation of sequences

The items in a sequence may be held in different ways:

1. The items are placed in memory in the same order in which they occur. This is known as **contiguous representation**, or a **linear list**.

2. The items are **not** stored in the order in which they occur in the sequence. Each item then needs an additional field called a **link** which points to the next item in the sequence, and this structure is known as a **linked list**. Linked lists will be considered in the next Unit.

In order to represent a linear list, we need to define a table large enough to hold the maximum sequence that is likely to occur, and two additional variables to hold the current size of the sequence and the limit to which the sequence can grow (ie the size of the table).

			time	starting_point
size 5	**item** 1		1450	Norwich
	2		1458	Colchester
	3		1520	Stowmarket
max 20	4		1545	Cambridge
	5		1555	Liverpool Street

The sequence may be **initialized** simply by setting **size** to 0.

Two other procedures can be performed on a linear list; **insertion** and **deletion**.

Inserting an item

Suppose we wish to insert an arrival, the 1455 from Liverpool Street. A first attempt at an insertion routine might be along the lines of the following:

```
If the list is empty, insert the item in the list.
If the list is full, display a message 'list is full'.
Otherwise, start at the beginning of the list and examine each item
until the time of the current item being examined > time of the new item.
Move all the rest of the sequence, including the current item, down 1.
Insert the new item in its correct place.
```

This is in practice rather clumsy and quite difficult to code. The algorithm can be much simplified by

(a) the addition of an extra item at the beginning of the list, with an index of 0 which is used to hold the item to be inserted, and

(b) searching backwards instead of forwards through the list.

We now have:

```
Put the new item in item[0]
If the list is full, display a message 'list is full'.
Otherwise, start at the end of the list and examine each item.
While the time of the current item is greater than the time of the new item,
       move current item down one place.
Insert the new item.
```

Example: Show how the list of arrival times and starting points of trains can be held in a **table** (an array of records) in memory.

Write pseudocode for an algorithm to insert a new element in the list.

Answer: The table to hold the list can be declared as follows:

```
type
    item_type = record
        time            : integer;
        starting_point: string;
    end;
var
    item : array[0..20]of item_type;
```

Pseudocode for inserting a new element in the list is as follows:

```
Procedure Insert_Item

begin
    get new item
    item[0] = new item
    p = size
    if size = max then write 'list full'
    else
        while item[p].time > item[0].time
            item[p+1] = item[p]
            p = p-1
        endwhile
        size = size + 1
        item[p+1] = item[0]
    endif
end procedure
```

Retrieving and deleting an item from a list

To retrieve an item from a list, we again put the given item in item[0] and search backwards from the end of the list, for a time less than or equal to the time of the given item.

The pseudocode for a procedure to find an item is shown below. If the item is in the list, a flag called **found** will be set to **true**, and **p** will indicate its position, otherwise **found** will be set to **false**.

```
procedure Find_Item
begin
    item[0].time = given_time
    p = size                        ( set pointer to end of list )
    found = false
    while item[p].time > given_time
        p = p - 1                   ( continue searching )
    endwhile
    ( if p = 0 on exit from the loop, then given_time is not in the list.
    If p is not = 0 then given_time may be present in the list  )
    if p <> 0 then
        if item[p].time = given_time
            then found = true
        endif
    endif
end procedure
```

Example: Write an algorithm to delete an item from the list. (Use the above procedure FIND_ITEM).

```
procedure Delete_Item
begin
    get item to delete
    call Find_Item to see if item is in the list
    if found = false then write error message    (ie item is not in list)
    else                         (p gives the position of the item)
        while p < size    (if it's the last item, no need to move anything)
            item[p] = item[p+1]
            p = p + 1
        endwhile
        size = size - 1
    endif
end procedure
```

Exercises:

1. In what way does a search for a **key** item differ from a search for a **non-key** item in a linear list?   (1 mark)

2. Under what circumstances would it be beneficial to use a binary search rather than a linear search on the key field of a linear list? Could you use a binary search on a non-key field?   (2 marks)

3. Write a program which displays a list of arrivals at a station, sequenced by arrival time. The program should allow additions, changes and deletions from the list, while maintaining its correct sequence, and should display a menu asking the user which function he requires.

Unit 24 — Linked Lists

Definition

A linked list is a dynamic data structure used to hold a sequence, as described below:

- The items which form the sequence are not necessarily held in contiguous data locations, or in the order in which they occur in the sequence.

- Each item in the list is called a **node** and contains an **information** field and a **next address** field called a **link** or **pointer** field. (The information field may consist of several sub-fields.)

- The information field holds the actual data associated with the list item, and the link field contains the address of the next item in the sequence.

- The link field in the last item indicates in some way that there are no further items (e.g. has a value of 0).

- Associated with the list is a **pointer variable** which points to (i.e. contains the address of) the first node in the list.

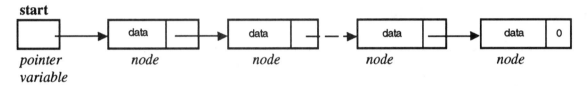

start

pointer variable   *node*   *node*   *node*   *node*

Operations on linked lists

In the examples which follow we will assume that the linked list is held in a table in memory, and that each node consists of a person's name (the information field) and a pointer to the next item in the list. We will explore how to set up or initialise an empty list, insert new data in the correct place in the list, delete an unwanted item and print out all items in the list. We will also look at the problem of managing the free space in the list.

Imagine that the table holding the list has room for 6 entries, and has already had 4 names inserted into it in such a way that they can be retrieved in alphabetical order, so that it is currently in the following state.

Address	Name	Pointer
1	Browning	4
2	Turner	0
3	Johnson	2
4	Cray	3
5		
6		

start = 1

nextfree = 5

Figure 24.1

Notice that
- a pointer **start** points to the first item in the list

- **nextfree** is a pointer to the next free location in the table

- by following the links, names can be retrieved in alphabetical order.

To insert a new name, for example Mortimer, into the list, pointers will have to be changed so that it is linked into the correct place. At this stage we have not really decided how to manage the free space in the list, so we will simply add 1 to **nextfree.**

The table will now appear as in Figure 24.2.

Address	Name	Pointer
1	Browning	4
2	Turner	0
3	Johnson	5
4	Cray	3
5	Mortimer	2
6		

start = 1

nextfree = 6

Figure 24.2

Q1: Show the state of the table and pointers after insertion of the name Allen. Can you write down the steps involved in inserting a new name to the list, so that alphabetical sequence is maintained?

Now we will delete a name. Return to the table as shown above in Figure 24.2 (before inserting Allen), and delete the name Johnson. After adjusting the pointers, the table looks like this:

Address	Name	Pointer
1	Browning	4
2	Turner	0
3	Johnson	2
4	Cray	5
5	Mortimer	2
6		

start = 1

nextfree = 6

Figure 24.3

Note that • Johnson is still physically in the table, but not part of the list any more.

• **nextfree** hasn't altered, and we have come up against a problem; there is no way to reclaim the vacancy left by Johnson. If the table is not to become full of unwanted records with no room left in it to add new records, we will have to address this problem. (Note, however, that the so-called 'management of free space' adds a degree of complexity to algorithms which is not always required in answers to exam questions unless specifically asked for.)

Management of free space

The solution is to keep **two** linked lists; one for the actual data, and one for the free space. When a new item is added, a node is grabbed from the free space list, and when a node is deleted, it is linked into the free space list.

When the table is first initialised prior to entering any names, it will consist of just one linked list of free space:

Address	Name	Pointer
1		2
2		3
3		4
4		5
5		6
6		0

start = 0

nextfree = 1

Figure 24.4

110

After the names Browning, Turner, Johnson and Cray have been added (don't worry about how they were inserted, we're coming to that) the table will look like this:

Address	Name	Pointer
1	Browning	4
2	Turner	0
3	Johnson	2
4	Cray	3
5		6
6		0

start = 1

nextfree = 5

Figure 24.5

Notice that we now have two linked lists going. We'll now work out an algorithm for inserting a name into the list. As an example, we'll insert Mortimer between Johnson and Turner.

Inserting an item

Here are the steps:

```
store the new name Mortimer in the node pointed to by nextfree
determine by following the links, where the new item should be linked in
change nextfree to point to next free location
change Mortimer's pointer to point to Turner
change Johnson's pointer to point to Mortimer
```

Some extra steps would need to be inserted to cope with various special cases such as inserting a name at the very front of the list (e.g. Allen), or inserting the first name into an empty list, but we'll ignore these cases for now.

Diagrammatically, this is what we have done:

Before insertion:

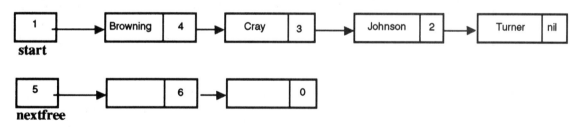

After insertion:

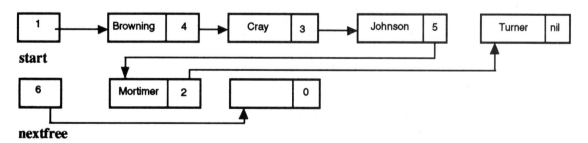

Figure 24.6

Before we go further and express this algorithm in more formal pseudocode, you need to make sure you clearly understand the notation used.

node[p].name holds the name in the node pointed to by p

node[p].pointer holds the value of the pointer in the node pointed to by p

Q2: Looking at Figure 24.5, node[3].name = Johnson, and node[3].pointer = 2.

What is the value of (i)   node[start].pointer?

                        (ii)   node[4].name?

                        (iii)   node[node[3].pointer].pointer?

                        (iv)   node[node[start].pointer].name?

Notice how we can 'peek ahead' using the pointers to see what name is in the next node, or even the node after that one, and so on. Here's a first attempt at the pseudocode for the algorithm to add a new name to the list.

```
begin procedure
      node[nextfree].name = new name        (store the new name in next free node)
      p = start
      follow pointers until node[p].pointer points to a name > new name
      temp = nextfree                        (put 5 in temp)
      nextfree=node[nextfree].pointer        (put 6 in nextfree)
      node [temp].pointer = node[p].pointer  (put 2 in Mortimer's pointer field)
      node[p].pointer = temp                 (put 5 in Johnson's pointer)
end procedure
```

This algorithm is in enough detail to get you through most questions on how to insert a node into a linked list. However, to deal with the special cases (checking for a full list and inserting at the head of the list) and to specify how to follow the pointers until you reach the correct insertion point, you need the following:

```
begin procedure
      if nextfree = 0 then write ('List if full') and exit procedure.
      node[nextfree].name = new name        (store the new name in next free node)
      if start = 0 then                      (insert into empty list)
          temp = node[nextfree].pointer
          node[nextfree].pointer = 0
          start = nextfree
          nextfree = temp
      else
          p = start
          (check for special case inserting in front of list)
          if new name < node[p].name
                then node[nextfree].pointer = start
              start = nextfree
          else                               (start general case)
              placefound = false
              while node[p].pointer<>0 and not placefound
                  if newname >= node[node[p].pointer].name    (peek ahead)
                        then p =node[p].pointer
                      else placefound = true
              endwhile
              temp = nextfree
              nextfree = node[nextfree].pointer
              node[temp].pointer=node[p].pointer
              node[p].pointer = temp
          endif (general case)
end procedure
```

Deleting an item

Returning to the table as in Figure 24.5, we will delete Johnson. The steps are as follows:

```
follow the pointers until Johnson is found
change Cray's pointer to point to Turner
change Johnson's pointer to nextfree
change nextfree to point to Johnson
```

Diagrammatically:

Before deletion:

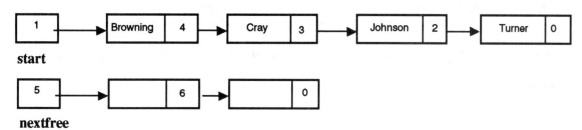

After deletion:

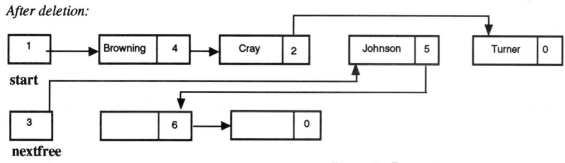

Figure 24.7

In pseudocode:

```
begin procedure
    p = start
    follow pointers until node[p].pointer points to the name to delete
    temp = node[p].pointer                  (put 3 in temp)
    node[p].pointer =  node[temp].pointer   (put 2 in Cray's pointer field)
    node[temp].pointer = nextfree           (put 5 in Johnson's pointer field)
    nextfree = temp                         (put 3 in nextfree)
end procedure
```

This is enough level of detail to show the concept of deleting from a linked list and you may wish to skip the next couple of paragraphs. However, for those who wish to go deeper, a fuller discussion follows.

Once again, deleting the first node in the list is a special case because **start** has to be altered. In the general case, following the pointers until node[p].pointer points to the name to delete again involves 'peeking ahead' to see what is in the next node, because once we are at a node we can't get back to change the previous pointer. So we want to stop following pointers not when node[p].name = name to delete, but at the node before that; i.e. when node[node[p].pointer].name = name to delete.

Note that deleting the last node (or inserting onto the end of the list, in the case of insertion) causes no special problems; try it and you will see this is true.

The full pseudocode is given on the next page.

Pseudocode for deleting an item from a linked list

```
begin procedure
     if start = 0 then write 'List is empty' and exit procedure.
     p = start
     if deletename = node[start].name then     (special case for first node)
          temp = node[start].pointer
          node[start].pointer = nextfree
          nextfree = start
          start = temp
     else                                       (general case)
          while deletename<> node[node[p].pointer].pointer
               p = node[p].pointer              (advance the pointer)
          endwhile
          (node[p] now points to the node to be deleted; adjust the pointers)
          temp = node[p].pointer
          node[p].pointer = node[temp].pointer
          node[temp].pointer = nextfree
          nextfree = temp
     endif   (general case)
end procedure
```

Printing out all the names in a linked list

To print all the names in the list, follow the pointers, printing each name in turn.

```
begin procedure
     p = start
     while p <> 0
          current = node[p]
          print current.name
          p = current.pointer
     endwhile
end procedure
```

Pointer variables

A pointer variable is one which is used for the sole purpose of pointing to another address in memory. Thus **start** and **nextfree** are pointer variables in the above examples. You may come across "pointer notation" in exam questions. In this notation, if **start** is a pointer variable, **start^** is the variable to which **start** points.

Thus, looking at Figure 24.1, start^.name = Browning, and start^.pointer = 4

Using this notation, the algorithm for printing out the names in the list becomes

```
begin procedure
     p=start
     while p <> 0
          current= p^
          print current.data
          p=current.pointer
     endwhile
end procedure
```

Doubly linked lists

In some circumstances it may be convenient to point to the previous item as well as the next item. In that case, two pointers would be required in each node.

In other cases, it may be more convenient to have backward pointers instead of forward pointers.

Exercises:

1. (a) Describe with the aid of a suitable diagram the data structure known as a linked list (or chain).   (4 marks)

   (b) An accounting system accepts data from a keyboard in the following form:

      Account number

      Description

      Value

   This data is called a posting.

   Postings are held in a randomly accessed disk file such that each new posting to an account is added to the end of the file and linked by a pointer to the previous posting for the same account. Each disk record therefore consists of the posting data (as above) plus the record number of the previous record on the same list.

   Access to the file is made through a continuously maintained table, held in main store, which is such that entry number I in this table gives the record number of the latest posting added to the file with account number I.

   (i) Construct a pseudocode algorithm or a flowchart showing how a record may be input and added to this file.

   (ii) Construct a pseudocode algorithm or a flowchart showing how a listing, in any convenient order, of all postings with account number I may be produced.

   (iii) Describe how a particular posting may be deleted from the file whilst retaining the correct list structure.

   (You may assume that the file management software for this system accesses records randomly by their record number.)   (16 marks)

   AEB Specimen Paper 1986

2. (a) What is meant by a linked list?

   (b) Explain, using diagrams showing the appropriate pointers in **each** case, how

   (i) an item can be found within an ordered linked list,

   (ii) an item can be inserted immediately before a specified item in a linked list,

   (iii) a known item can be deleted from a linked list.   (7 marks)

   WJEC AS Level May 1990

3. You are asked to write, for college use, a package to process the subject options of the students. There are about 400 students in a year group, with up to a dozen joining and leaving during the year. The records of the students in the group are initially saved in a direct access file alphabetically in name order. Leavers will have their records tagged and new-comers's records will be appended to the end of the file in the order in which they arrive. At the start of the file there will be details including the number of students at the beginning of the year and the total number of records.

   Each student record contains: the name, number of subjects studied, each subject chosen together with pointers, for each subject, which will locate the record of the next student alphabetically who is also studying that subject. At the start of the file will be pointers which locate the record of the first student studying each subject.

   (a) Describe in detail an algorithm, which minimizes the number of tests, to locate the details of a particular student, originally in the list when only the student's name is known.   (7 marks)

   (b) If the student's details had been added later, how would the relevant record be found?   (3 marks)

   (c) After the start of the year a student decides to take up an extra subject. Describe in detail how the file would be updated.   (10 marks)

   AEB Paper 2 1991

   Hints for the above question: Make up some test data; insert about 8 students in alphabetical order in addresses labelled 1,2,3 etc, with the number of subjects studied (1, 2 or 3 is plenty), show the pointers and you will find you have a number of linked lists. Part (a) requires a binary search, part (b) a linear search starting at the end of the original records. The question is much easier when you have some sample data to look at.

4. Write a program to implement a linked list of names as a table, allowing the user to initialise the list, add, delete and print names. Include a debugging option to print out the whole contents of the table so that you can examine the pointers.

Unit 25 — Queues

Definition

A queue is a **First In First Out** (FIFO) data structure. New elements may only be added at the end of the queue, and elements may only be retrieved or deleted from the front of the queue.

The sequence of the data items is determined not by their value but simply by the order in which they were inserted.

Implementation of a queue

There are several ways of implementing the storage of a queue in memory. A simple way involves using an array of fixed size, and providing pointers to the front and rear of the queue, together with two extra variables showing the maximum capacity of the queue and its current size.

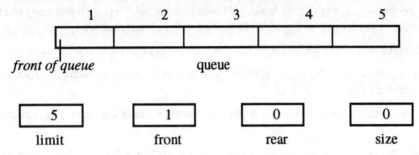

It may seem a little strange at first sight to define an empty queue in this way with rear = 0 and front = 1. However, as soon as the first item or person joins the queue, the rear pointer is incremented to 1. This single item is then at both the front and the rear of the queue, and the pointers reflect this situation.

After the addition of ROY and JAMES, the queue becomes

| ROY | JAMES | | | |

5	1	2	2
limit	front	rear	size

Q1: Three people DAVID, DEBBIE and SAMANTHA join the queue and two people leave. What is the state of the queue and pointers now?

| | | | | |

limit	front	rear	size

A problem arises when the next person joins the queue, because although there will only be 3 people in the queue the upper bound of the array has been reached.

Q2: Suggest a way of handling the problem of the queue moving down the storage space as elements are added and removed.

A circular queue

One solution to the problem of 'overflow' as the queue moves down the array is to let the rear of the queue 'wrap around' to the start of the array. An area of store used in this way is sometimes called a **circular buffer**.

The queue will be full when size = limit.

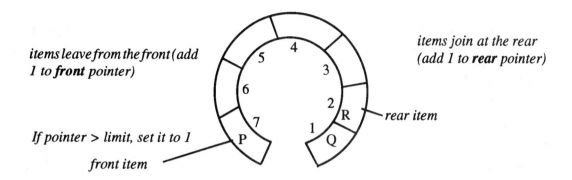

items leave from the front (add 1 to front pointer)

items join at the rear (add 1 to rear pointer)

rear item

If pointer > limit, set it to 1

front item

Figure 25.1 — A circular queue after several items have entered and left

Declaration of a queue in Pascal

A queue to hold up to 10 strings, say, may be declared in Pascal as follows:

```
const      limit=10
type queue=record
   item          :array[1..limit] of string;
   front,rear    :integer;
   size          :integer
end;
var  q:queue;
```

Q3: Given the above declaration, how do you refer to

(a) the front of the queue

(b) the rear of the queue

(c) the size of the queue?

The following is pseudocode to initialise the queue:

```
procedure initialise
begin
     q.front = 1
     q.rear = limit
     q.size = 0
end procedure
```

Note that the rear of the queue is set to LIMIT, because in the circular representation of the queue, this element immediately precedes the first element. The rear pointer is moved forward just before a new element joins the queue, as shown in the following pseudocode for inserting an element:

Pseudocode for a procedure to add an element x to the queue:

```
procedure insert
begin
    with q do
        if size = limit
            then write ('queue overflow')
        else
        ( advance the rear pointer )
            if rear = limit
                then rear = 1
            else rear = rear + 1
            endif
            item(rear) = x
            size = size + 1
        endif
    end procedure
```

Q4: Write pseudocode for a procedure to remove an item from a queue and place it in a variable called **next**. Remember to allow for an empty queue.

Q5: A circular queue q of length 4 has been initialised by setting variables as follows:

q.size = 0

q.limit = 4

q.front = 1

q.rear = 4

Show by means of diagrams the state of the queue and associated variables after each of the starred operations in the following sequence:

*1   Initialise q

2   Insert **job_1**

3   Insert **job_2**

*4   Insert **job_3**

*5   Remove one item

6   Insert **job_4**

7   Remove one item

*8   Insert **job_5**

front =   rear =

size =

front =   rear =

size =

front =   rear =

size =

front =   rear =

size =

118

Implementing a queue as a linked list

A queue can be implemented in a linked list by keeping an external pointer to the front of the queue.

We can access the front of the queue through the pointer **front**. To add an element to the queue, the pointers have to be followed until the node containing a pointer of **0** is reached, signifying the end of the queue, and this pointer is then changed to point to the new node. (In some implementations two pointers are kept; one to the front and one to the rear. This saves having to traverse the whole queue when a new element is to be added.)

Using the same table representation of a linked list as in the last Unit, we can similarly keep a second linked list of free space. When a new element joins the queue, we take a node from the free space list, and when an element is deleted from the queue, that node is returned to the free space list by appropriately altering the pointers.

Once again we will illustrate the process of adding and deleting nodes by considering an example of a queue used to hold names.

When the table (which has room for 6 items in the queue) is first initialised prior to entering any names, it will consist of just one linked list of free space, and pointers as shown below:

Address	Name	Pointer
1		2
2		3
3		4
4		5
5		6
6		0

front = 0

nextfree = 1

Figure 25.2 - An empty queue

Adding an element to the queue

Adding an element to the queue is much simpler than adding to a linked list as in the last Unit, because an element can only be added to the end of the list.

After the three names Harriet, Ben and Matthew have been added, the table will be as shown below:

Address	Name	Pointer
1	Harriet	2
2	Ben	3
3	Matthew	0
4		5
5		6
6		0

front = 1

nextfree = 4

Figure 25.3

To add a new name, say Gina, we need to:

```
follow the pointers to the end of the queue
put Gina (the new name) in the node pointed to by nextfree
put 0 in Gina's pointer field to indicate the end of the queue
change Matthew's pointer to point to Gina
change nextfree to point to the next free node
```

We will use the notation **q[p].name** to mean the name in the queue pointed to by **p** in the following pseudocode, which also caters for the case of a full queue and for the special case of adding to an empty queue.

```
begin procedure
    if nextfree = 0 then write 'Queue is full' and exit procedure.
    p = front
    while q[p].pointer <> 0                 (peek ahead to next node]
        p = q[p].pointer                    (advance to the next node)
    endwhile
    q[nextfree].name = new name
    temp = q[nextfree].pointer
    q[nextfree].pointer = 0                 (This is the new end of the queue)
    if front = 0 then front = nextfree      (special case of empty queue)
    else q[p].pointer = nextfree
    endif
    nextfree = temp
end procedure
```

Removing an element from the queue ('Dequeuing')

Elements can only be removed from the front of the queue. To remove Harriet from the queue:

```
copy the name from the front of the queue to a variable (dequeued_item)
change front to the value of Harriet's pointer (to point to Ben)
change Harriet's pointer to point to the current nextfree node
change nextfree to point to Harriet
```

The algorithm for dequeuing an element is shown below.

```
begin procedure
    if front = 0 then write 'Queue is empty' and exit procedure.
    dequeued_item = q[front].name
    temp = front
    front = q[front].pointer
    q[temp].pointer = nextfree
    nextfree = temp
end procedure
```

Use of queues

Queues have a variety of applications. These include queuing items from a processor for output to a peripheral device, and queuing programs which are ready to be run by the computer. If you are working on a multi-user system and you tell the computer to run a particular program, the operating system will add your request to the 'job queue'. When your request gets to the front of the queue, the program you requested will be executed.

Queues are also useful in **simulation** problems.

A simulation program is one which attempts to model a real-life situation so as to learn something about it. An example is a program which simulates customers arriving at random times at the check-outs in a supermarket store, and taking random times to pass through the checkout. With the aid of a simulation program, the optimum number of check-out counters can be established.

Exercises:

1. (a) In the context of data structures, explain what is meant by a queue. (1 mark)

   (b) Briefly describe two distinct applications for which a queue is a suitable data structure. (4 marks)

   (c) Why are queues in computer systems usually implemented as circular queues? (2 marks)

   (d) Describe how a circular queue may be implemented using a one dimensional array. Give algorithms for inserting and removing items from this queue. (5 marks)

   (e) If these algorithms were written as procedures, what parameters would need to be passed between each of the procedures and the calling program? (3 marks)

   London Paper 1 June 1

2.* Explain, with the aid of diagrams, how a one-dimensional array may be used to implement a queue. (4 marks)

   Give algorithms for your implementation which will

   (i) add an item to the queue

   (ii) remove an item from the queue (6 marks)

   JMB Paper 1 1991

3. A buffer provides temporary storage for up to 16 characters at a time. Characters are added or removed from the buffer one at a time. The characters are removed in the same order in which they were inserted. Processing of data in the buffer is controlled by four pointers:

   strtptr - points to the first location in the buffer

   endptr - points to the last location of the buffer

   freptr - points to the next free location in the buffer

   outptr - points to the next character to be removed from the buffer

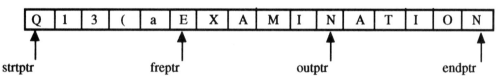

   (a) Write down the characters which are waiting to be removed from the buffer in the order in which they will be removed. (2 marks)

   (b) Describe in detail algorithms to:

   (i) add a character to the buffer;

   (ii) remove a character from the buffer.

   In each case you should test that the buffer is not full/empty as appropriate. (6 marks)

   (c) The buffer is used to hold characters being transferred to a local printer. Explain why the buffer may frequently be full.

   Describe how this problem may be avoided. (7 marks)

   London June 1992

4. Write a program to implement a queue as a linked list held in a table. The program should display a menu of options to allow the user to initialise the queue, add a name, delete a name and print all the names in the queue in the order in which they joined the queue. Include also a 'debugging' option to print the whole table and the pointers. Your algorithms should include the management of the free space in the table, using pointers to the front of the queue and the front of the free space list.

Unit 26 — Stacks

Definition

A stack is a particular kind of sequence which may only be accessed at one end, known as the top of the stack (like plates on a pile in a cafeteria).

Only two operations can be carried out on a stack. **Adding** a new item involves placing it on top of the stack (**pushing** or stacking the item). **Removing** an item involves the removal of the item that was most recently added (**popping** the stack). The stack is a **LIFO** structure — **Last In, First Out**.

Note that items do not move up and down as the stack is pushed and popped. Instead, the position of the top of the stack changes. A pointer called a stack pointer indicates the position of the top of the stack:

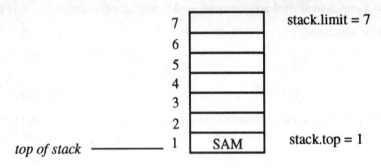

Q1: Is a stack a static or dynamic data structure?

Q2: Show the state of the stack and stack pointer after each of the following operations:

(i)   Initialize the stack

(ii) Add ELAINE

(iii) Add HOWARD

(iv) Remove one item

(v)   Add MICHAEL

(vi) Add TAMARA

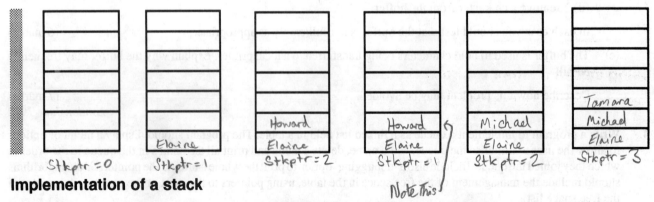

Implementation of a stack

A stack can be represented in memory by an array and two additional integer variables, one holding the size of the array (i.e. the maximum size of the stack) and one holding the pointer to the top of the stack (**top**). **Top** will initially be set to 0, representing an empty stack.

Applications of stacks

Stacks are very important data structures in computing. They are used in calculations, translating from one computer language to another, and transferring control from one part of a program to another.

Example: Suppose a certain computer language allows 3 different kinds of 'scopes'; parentheses ( ), brackets [ ], and braces { }. A scope ender must be of the same type as its scope opener. Thus

> (A+B]   [(A+B])   {A-(B]}

are all illegal.

A stack may be used to keep track of the types of scope encountered. (This is one of the tasks of a compiler). Whenever a scope opener is encountered, it is pushed on to the stack. When a scope ender is encountered, the stack is examined. If the stack is empty, the scope ender does not have a matching opener, so the string is invalid. If the stack is not empty, the stack is popped and the popped item checked to see if it corresponds to the scope ender. If it does, we continue, otherwise the string is invalid. When the end of the string is reached, the stack should be empty, or the string is invalid.

The figure below shows the state of the stack after reading in parts of the string

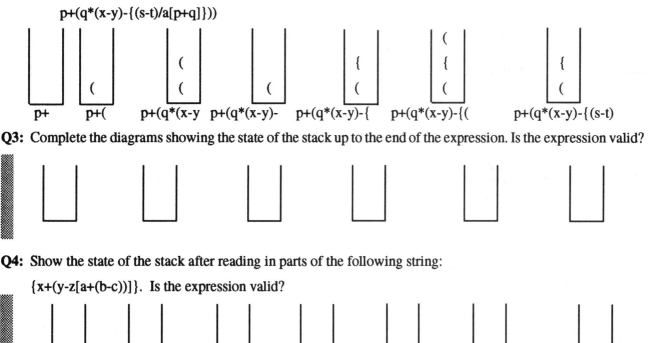

> p+(q*(x-y)-{(s-t)/a[p+q]}))

Q3: Complete the diagrams showing the state of the stack up to the end of the expression. Is the expression valid?

Q4: Show the state of the stack after reading in parts of the following string:

> {x+(y-z[a+(b-c))]}. Is the expression valid?

Using stacks to store return addresses

Stacks are also used to store the return address when a subroutine is called. The principle is shown below:

Instruction Address	Instruction
1	**subroutine** suba
2	....
3	....
4	**return**
5	**begin** { *** MAIN PROGRAM *** EXECUTION STARTS HERE}
6	**call** suba
7	....
8	**end**

The return address (7) will be placed on a stack when SUBA is called and popped when the RETURN statement is encountered.

Q5: Show the contents of the stack as addresses are pushed and popped during the execution of the following simplified program outline.

Instruction Address	Instruction
1	**subroutine** suba
2	. . . .
3	. . . .
4	**return**
5	**subroutine** subb
6	. . . .
7	. . . .
8	**return**
9	**subroutine** sub1
10	. . . .
11	. . . .
12	**call** suba
13	**call** subb
14	**return**
15	**subroutine** sub2
16	. . . .
17	**call** suba
18	. . . .
19	. . . .
20	. . . .
21	**return**
22	**begin**{*** MAIN PROGRAM *** EXECUTION STARTS HERE}
23	**call** sub1
24	**call** sub2
25	**end**

Pushing and popping stack elements

An empty stack will consist of an array of elements (the size of the array is defined as **limit**), and a pointer **top** set to 0. It doesn't matter if the array contains garbage since if the pointer is set to 0, the stack is 'logically' empty.

To push an element onto the stack, we need to test first of all that the stack is not already full, then add 1 to **top**, and place the element in stack(top). The pseudocode is shown below:

```
begin procedure
    if top = limit  then write 'Stack is full'
    else
        top = top + 1
        stack[top] = NewItem
    endif
end procedure
```

To pop an item from the stack:

```
begin procedure
    if top = 0 then write 'Stack is empty'
    else
        PoppedItem = stack[top]
        top = top - 1
    endif
end procedure
```

Exercises:

1. A computer has a stack with data items entering the stack via the input stream and leaving the stack via the output stream. The only operations available are:-

   PUSH -   push the next item in the input stream onto the stack

   POP -   pop the top item off the stack and put it in the output stream

   Given the input stream ABCDE which of the following are possible output streams?

   (i)   ACEDB   (ii)   BCEAD

   (iii) CBAED   (iv)   EACBD

   For the possible output streams show, using the instructions PUSH and POP, how they can be obtained.   (8 marks)
   London Paper 1 June 1989

2. (a) By drawing annotated diagrams show what is meant by

       (i)   a stack

       (ii) a queue   (4 marks)

   (b) How can a stack be implemented using an array? Describe carefully the stack operations of adding and removing items using this representation.   (4 marks)

   (c) The three words 'red', 'amber', 'green' can be written in six different orders. Given the input sequence 'red', 'amber', 'green', show how five of these sequences can be generated using only the stack described above.
                                                                              (4 marks)
   WJEC Paper 2 June 1988

3.* (a) A computer program is to read in a list of integers as follows: the first integer represents a lower limit, the second represents an upper limit, the last is a dummy or rogue value of -1, and the others are actual data values.

       (i)   Design an algorithm, utilising a **while..do** structure, which inputs the lower and upper limits and then counts and finds the arithmetic average of those data values which lie within the specified limits.

       (ii) Show clearly the alterations which must be made to your algorithm if a **repeat..until** structure is used instead.
                                                                              (8 marks)

   (b) With the aid of suitable examples, distinguish between iteration and recursion.   (6 marks)

   (c) Describe the operation of the data structure known as a stack, and hence explain how a stack can be used to store return addresses during the execution of subroutines or procedures.   (8 marks)

   (d) A stack is being implemented in an array of 10 elements. Using pseudocode algorithms show how a data element is

       (i)   added to the stack;

       (ii) removed from the stack.   (8 marks)
   NISEAC Paper 2 1991

4. Explain how the elements in a non-empty queue may be reversed with the aid of a stack.   (3 marks)
   AEB Paper 2 1990

Unit 27 — Binary Trees

Definition

A tree is a dynamic data structure which has zero or more nodes organised in a hierarchical way such that:

- except when the tree is empty, there is one node called the **root** at the beginning of the tree structure

- lines connecting the nodes are called **branches** and every node except the root is joined to just one node at the next higher level (its parent)

- nodes that have no children are called **leaf nodes** or **terminal nodes**.

Note that every tree has only one root, but each node in the tree can be regarded as the root of a **subtree** of the tree. Thus a tree consists of a root and one or more subtrees, each of which is a tree. (This is an example of a **recursive** definition).

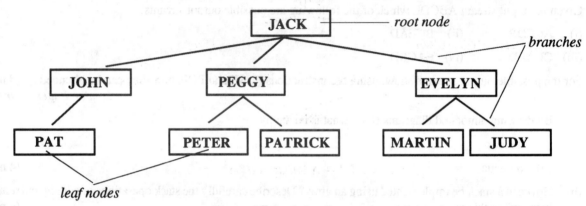

Figure 27.1 - A family tree

Binary trees

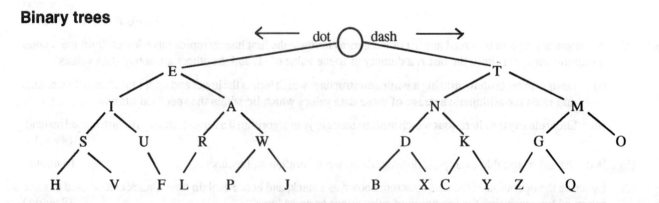

Figure 27.2 — A binary tree for Morse Code

A **binary tree** is a special type of tree in which no parent can have more than two children. A tree can be drawn to illustrate Morse code. Starting from the root, move left if the next signal is a dot and right if the next signal is a dash. (diagram overleaf) The morse code for D, for example, is dash dot dot.

Q1: What is the morse code for L and G?

A **search tree** is a particular application of a binary tree, such that a list of items held in the tree can be searched easily and quickly, new items easily added, and the whole tree printed out in sequence (alphabetic or numeric).

Constructing a binary tree

We could, for example, store a list of names (and, say, telephone numbers or other data as required) in a binary tree. Take the following list of names:

Legg, Charlesworth, Illman, Hawthorne, Todd, Youngman, Jones, Ravage.

In order to create a binary tree that can be quickly searched for a given name, we follow the rules:

1. Place the first item in the root.

2. Insert the items in the order in which they are given, following the **left** pointer if the item comes **before** the current node in alphabetic (or numeric) sequence, and following the **right** pointer if the item comes **after** the current node.

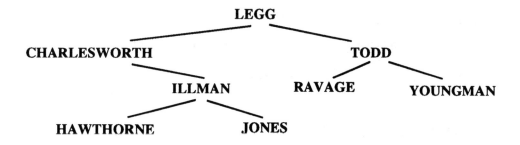

Figure 27.3 — A binary search tree

Q2: Insert the following items into a binary tree for subsequent retrieval in alphabetical sequence: goldfinch, dove, robin, chaffinch, blackbird, wren, jay, sparrow, partridge.

Traversing a binary tree

A binary tree can be **traversed** in a number of different ways; that is, the nodes may be visited in different orders, in order to extract data from the tree. The methods are known as

- preorder traversal
- inorder traversal
- postorder traversal

In each case, the algorithms for traversal are **recursive**, that is, they call themselves. The names **preorder**, **inorder** and **postorder** refer to the stage at which the node is visited.

Preorder traversal

1. Start at the root node
2. Traverse the lefthand subtree
3. Traverse the righthand subtree.

The nodes of the tree below would be visited in the following order: D B A C F E G.

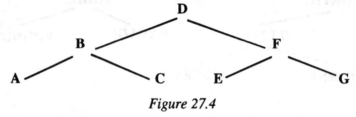

Figure 27.4

Inorder traversal

1. Traverse the lefthand subtree
2. Visit the root node
3. Traverse the righthand subtree.   The nodes are visited in the order: A B C D E F G

Postorder traversal

1. Traverse the lefthand subtree
2. Traverse the righthand subtree
3. Return to the root node.   The nodes are visited in the order: A C B E G F D

Q3: Referring to the tree in Figure 27.3 (LEGG, CHARLESWORTH etc), write down the order in which the data will be listed using:

a)   preorder traversal

b)   inorder traversal

c)   postorder traversal.

In which order should the tree be traversed in order to obtain a list in alphabetical sequence?

Implementation of trees using arrays

Binary trees can be implemented using left and right pointers at each node. A node will consist of:

- a left pointer

- data item

- a right pointer.

	left	info	right
tree [1]	2	Legg	5
[2]	0	Charlesworth	3
[3]	4	Illman	7
[4]	0	Hawthorne	0
[5]	8	Todd	6
[6]	0	Youngman	0
[7]	0	Jones	0
[8]	0	Ravage	0
[9]			
[10]			

A pointer value of 0 indicates a 'nil' pointer

Figure 27.5

Q4: Show how the binary tree structure created in Q2 may be stored in an array similar to the one above.

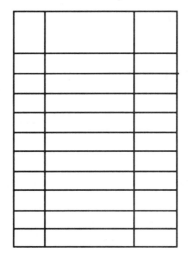

A recursive algorithm for an inorder tree traversal

```
Procedure traverse_from(start:integer);
with tree[start] do
    begin
        if left <> 0 then traverse_from(left); (*endif *)
        writeln (info);
        if right <> 0 then traverse_from(right);  (* endif *)
    end;
end; {procedure}
```

The procedure, when called with the statement **traverse_from(1)** will print out the contents of each node in sequence.

Q5: What is a 'recursive algorithm'?

Recursion

The routine above illustrates just how useful recursion can be to the programmer. The code mirrors the high-level solution arrived at in thinking about the problem, and is far shorter and less complex than a non-recursive solution, which would involve having to store the addresses of nodes that had been visited in order to work back up each subtree.

Summary

A binary tree is an appropriate data structure when a large number of items need to be held in such a way that any item may be quickly accessed, or sequenced lists need to be produced. Additions are easily handled since they require only the adjustment of a single pointer. Different ways of traversing a tree mean that items can be stored in one sequence and retrieved in a different sequence.

A tree structure can be used to hold a **file directory** on backing store, so that any file can be quickly located. Another use of trees is in mapping the access allowed to various files. Access through the tree structure is allowed by passwords typed at a terminal, with a different password for each branch from the root.

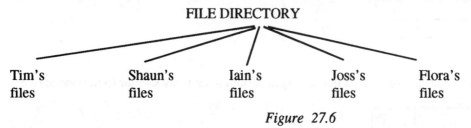

FILE DIRECTORY

| Tim's files | Shaun's files | Iain's files | Joss's files | Flora's files |

Figure 27.6

Exercises:

1. Define briefly with the aid of an example the following terms when applied to a tree structure:

    root, node, subtree, parent, child, leaf   (6 marks)

2. In a perfectly balanced tree of 127 items, what is the maximum number of nodes that would have to be examined to find a given value?   (1 mark)

    What is the average number of nodes that would have to be examined?

3. If items in a list were in ascending sequence prior to being put in a binary tree structure, what would the tree look like? What would be the effect on the time taken to search the tree for a given item?   (2 marks)

4. (a) Explain how a binary tree may be represented in a high level language which supports arrays. Illustrate your answer by showing how the following data may be stored as a binary tree for subsequent processing in alphabetical order. Assume the first data item is the root of the tree and the tree is created by entering the data at run time in the order given: Leeds, Bradford, Halifax, Huddersfield, Batley, Dewsbury, Wakefield, York, Wetherby, Hull, Malton, Scarborough.

                                                                 (8 marks)

    (b) Describe TWO situations in which it would be advantageous for data to be stored in the form discussed in part (a) rather than as a structure in which the data is in a list where the data items are stored in the order of their run time input. Explain clearly the advantages of the tree structure.   (4 marks)

    (c) Use pseudocode, or flowcharts, to describe in detail how the structure described in part (a) can be traversed to output the data in ascending alphabetic order.   (8 marks)

                                                                 AEB Paper 2 1988

5.* Show the resultant binary search tree after the following items have been inserted: 3, 6, 8, 7, 9, 1, 5 and hence show how a data structure to hold such a tree mght be declared in the programming language of your choice.   (5 marks)

                                                                 NISEAC Paper 1 1991

Unit 28 — Hash Tables

Introduction

The idea of taking a primary key value and turning it into a location in a file at which a record is stored was introduced in Unit 9. The same idea can be used to store data in memory in such a way that it can be quickly retrieved. Some compilers use this technique in order to obtain a memory address at which to store variable names and associated information. The **hash table** consists of the variable name and an address (or array subscript).

Hash functions

One of the simplest ways of finding a location from a given key is to use **modular arithmetic** — that is, to divide the key by the number of locations available for storage, and take the remainder as the address. Thus, for a table with 100 locations, a four digit key such as 1537 will be stored at location 37.

Q1: A hash table has 11 locations numbered 0 -10 in which to store a series of 3-digit keys. Use a calculator to generate eight 3-digit numbers (or make them up!) and store them in the table. Store any 'synonyms' in the next free space and mark them with an asterisk.

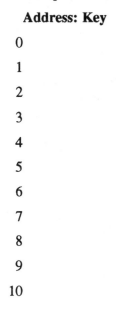

Address: Key

    0
    1
    2
    3
    4
    5
    6
    7
    8
    9
   10

If the key is not numeric, there are various ways in which it can be converted to a number before applying modular arithmetic. An alphanumeric key can be converted to a base 36 number, or alternatively, the ASCII code for each character or digit may be used. For example,

    T I M   converts to   84   73   77

Another technique for hashing is called **folding**. The key is divided into two or more parts and the parts added together. The number 847377, for example, could be split into two parts:

    847
    377

    1224

Modular arithmetic can now be applied. To get an address in the range 0 - 99, for example, take the last two digits.

Q2: A compiler uses a hashing function to store the addresses of variable names. Each letter is first converted to its corresponding ASCII code, according to the table below. The resulting digits are then added together, the sum divided by 197 and the remainder obtained. Thus TIM would be converted to 84 + 73 + 77 = 234. 234 /197 = 1 remainder 37. The required address is therefore 37.

A	B	C	D	E	F	G	H	I	J	K	L	M	N	O
65	66	67	68	69	70	71	72	73	74	75	76	77	78	79

P	Q	R	S	T	U	V	W	X	Y	Z
80	81	82	83	84	85	86	87	88	89	90

What addresses will CHAD and GLENN be stored at?

Buckets

Statistical techniques have shown that in a random file held, say, on disk, the best spread of records is achieved when a prime number is used as the divisor in the modular arithmetic algorithm for calculating the address. However, no matter how clever the algorithm, synonyms are bound to occur, when the calculated address is already occupied by another record.

One way of reducing this problem is to allow several records to be stored in a **bucket** at the same address. A **bucket** is simply an area of disk storage large enough to hold one or more records. Of course, if we allow more than one record in each bucket, we have the added task of searching through the bucket sequentially once we have calculated its address. Moreover, as the disk space fills up, overflow will eventually occur, however large the bucket size.

Q3: A series of keys is to be hashed using two different algorithms to determine which is the most efficient in terms of not causing collisions:

Method 1: 21 locations (0-20) are to be used. Divide key by 20 and take remainder as the address.

Method 2: 7 buckets (0-6) are to be used, with room for 3 keys in each bucket. Divide by 7 and take remainder.

The keys are: 941 004 002 497 999 188 996 061 503 014 309 753 876 501 001

Place the keys in their correct addresses, marking overflowed keys with an asterisk.

Method 1

Address	Number	Address	Number
0		11	
1		12	
2		13	
3		14	
4		15	
5		16	
6		17	
7		18	
8		19	
9		20	
10			

Number in overflow:

Method 2

Address	Number	Address	Number
0		4	
0		4	
0		4	
1		5	
1		5	
1		5	
2		6	
2		6	
2		6	
3			
3			
3			

Number in overflow:

Overflow records are to be' put in the next available bucket. Will location 20 ever be used?

Overflow

The simplest method for dealing with overflow records is to put them in the next available free space, as above. In order to retrieve a record with a given key, the home block is searched first.

If the block is empty, the record or key is not in the file. If the space is **not** empty, the search has to continue sequentially until **either** the key is found **or** an empty space is encountered, when we know that the key is not there.

A slightly more sophisticated method of handling overflow is to add an increasing integer until a free space is found. For example if the record should go in address 50, but this is full, try address 51. If this is full, try address 53, then 56, 60 and so on until a free space is found.

When the last address in the hash table is reached, the search 'loops back' and continues from the beginning of the table. (*Don't forget to mention this point in an exam; it's worth a mark!*)

Deleting records

This poses a problem for deleting records. If for example (using the table for Method 1 in the previous example) we delete key number 503, we will never be able to retrieve 501 or 001!

Q4: What keys will be irretrievable if we delete key 941?

One way round this problem is to *leave the deleted record in place*, and to set a flag labelling it as deleted. In other words, although *logically* deleted, the key is still *physically* present. A '**flag**' is simply an extra variable, say an integer, stored with each record as an extra field. When the file is initialised and contains no records, the flag in each address can be set to 0, meaning that the record position is empty. When a record is written to an address, the flag is set to 1. When the record is deleted, the only change made to the record is to set the flag back to 0. When looking for a particular record, if the record key is found but it has a flag of 0, it is considered to be logically 'not there'. It's as though it's been crossed out, so it is to be ignored, but we can still see that there was a record there at one time. This means the space can be reused if a new record with a key hashing to this address is to be added to the file, but because the space is not actually empty, the search for a record that may have overflowed to the next address will still continue until either the record is found or an empty space is encountered.

Hash files (random files)

The concept of a hash file (or random file) is identical to that of a hash table, the only difference being that a table is normally thought of as being held in memory, whereas a file is typically stored on disk.

Reorganisation

As the hash file fills up, the number of buckets that have to be accessed before a space is found increases until the time taken to insert a new record or find an existing one becomes unacceptably high. Experiments have shown that this stage is reached when the file is about two-thirds full, hence it is wise to allow about double the amount of space initially than the file is expected to occupy.

Thus a file of 50 records would initially be stored in a space of 100 locations. If the number of records then increases to 65 or 70 records, the file needs to be **reorganised** and stored in a space of 150 locations.

Q5: What will be involved in the reorganisation of 70 records from the old file of 100 spaces into the new file of 150 spaces?

Exercises:

1. (a) What is meant by the terms   (i)   hashing algorithm

                                       (ii)   hash address

                                       (iii) hash table?   (3 marks)

    (b) Why do collisions occur when a hash table is used and how can they be handled?   (3 marks)

    (c) Give an example of the use of a hash table in a computer system and explain why its use is more appropriate than other methods.   (3 marks)

                                                             UCLES Paper 2 May 1990

2. A file is to be created that can store up to 100 large fixed length records on a magnetic disk. Each record is to be stored in a separate block on the disk.

    The records have a three digit key field. The location of a record is obtained by a hashing algorithm which involves taking the two right hand digits of the key as the block address. Therefore, for a key of 756 the two right-hand digits give the block address of 56. However, a key of 556 would also give the block address of 56. Collisions can be handled as follows. If the hashing algorithm yields a location that is already occupied, the next location is tested, and so on until the next free block is found into which the record is written.

    (a) The first few records to be written into the file have the following key fields.

        299   496   397   597   300   898

    Draw up a table showing the blocks occupied by these records. Explain how each location is arrived at.

                                                                    (6 marks)

    (b) If the record with key 299 then has to be deleted, explain how this can be achieved without having to reorganise the whole file.   (2 marks)

    (c) If many records are added and deleted it may become necessary to reorganise the file. Suggest how this could be done.   (4 marks)

                                                               UCLES Paper 2 1984

3.* A random access file is being created by hashing the key values of records to produce a block address where the record can be stored. Collisions are said to occur if the hashing algorithm generates the address of a block that is already full.

    (a) Outline briefly a method that can be used to store and retrieve the records that generate collisions.   (2 marks)

    (b) If it is suspected that certain records are far more likely to be referenced than others, what procedures might the system designer adopt to minimise the number of collisions and so maximise the efficiency of future file processing?   (2 marks)

                                                               London Paper 2 1991

Unit 29 — Sorting Files

Introduction

Sorting is a very common operation in data processing applications. It is usually performed by a **utility program** — that is, a commercially written piece of software designed to carry out a frequently performed task. COBOL, a language written specifically for data processing applications, includes a SORT verb, which relieves the programmer from having to write his own file sorting routines. However, it is useful to have some knowledge of how sorting can be done.

Q1: Why is it necessary to sort a transaction file into the same order as a sequential master file before updating the master file?

Q2: Suggest other reasons why it might be necessary to sort a master file.

ASCII characters

Files are sorted on one or more **key fields**, which may be alphabetic or numeric, or include other characters such as spaces, punctuation marks and so on. A question therefore arises as to the order in which character fields will be sorted. Fortunately this is decided by the computer manufacturer so that no ambiguity arises.

A common method of representing characters is the ASCII code (American Standard Code for Information Interchange, developed in 1963). The sequence into which ASCII characters will be sorted is given below:

```
•  !  "  #  $  %  &  '  (  )  *  +  ,  -  .  /  0
1  2  3  4  5  6  7  8  9  :  ;  <  =  >  ?  @  A
B  C  D  E  F  G  H  I  J  K  L  M  N  O  P  Q  R
S  T  U  V  W  X  Y  Z  [  ]  ^  _  '  a  b  c  d
e  f  g  h  i  j  k  l  m  n  o  p  q  r  s  t  u
v  w  x  y  z  {  \  }
```

(• stands for 'blank space')

Thus J.A.Smith will precede JA Smith but follow J A Smith; this can be expressed as

J.A.Smith < JA Smith   and J.A.Smith > J A Smith

Q3: Sort the following keys into ascending sequence, using their ASCII representation: Section 3, SECTION 5, SECTION 17, section 28, SECTION 29.

Internal sorting

When a file is small enough to be held in memory, an **internal** sort is used. There are numerous methods of performing an internal sort, including the **quicksort, treesort, insertion sort** and **bubble sort**. The bubble sort is slow with a large number of items but is a relatively simple algorithm to follow. It is explained below.

Bubble sort

The name **bubble sort** arises from the fact that when the values to be sorted are listed vertically the small values 'bubble up' to the top, or the large values sink to the bottom, depending on the version of the algorithm used. To save space we shall write the values from left to right.

For example, to sort the following values into ascending order: 15 3 11 2 8 19 6

The first two values are compared and if necessary exchanged. The next two values are then compared, and so on.

After the first pass the values will be in the following order: 3 11 2 8 15 6 19

The number 19 has 'bubbled right', (if such a thing is possible !) and is now in its correct position, so the second pass compares only the first 6 numbers. After this pass the values will be in the sequence   3 2 8 11 6 15 19

After the 3rd pass: 2 3 8 6 11 15 19

After the 4th pass: 2 3 6 8 11 15 19

On the 5th pass, no swaps are necessary and the sort is complete. In a list of **n** numbers, a maximum of **n-1** passes is required, but is not always needed so the process can be cut short by setting a flag when a swap is made during a pass, and testing the flag before the next pass. If it has not been set then the sort is complete.

The pseudocode for the algorithm to sort **n** values held in an array **key[1..n]** is shown below:

```
begin procedure
     Set n = number of values to be sorted
     repeat
          flag = false
          for counter = 1 to n-1
               if   key[counter] > key[counter+1]
               then swap the records
                    flag = true
               endif
          endfor
          n = n-1
     until flag = false or n = 1
end procedure
```

Insertion sort

The easiest way to understand this sorting algorithm is to take say 5 cards or pieces of paper each with a number written on them and place them in a random sequence in a line on the table.

```
   [ ] [5] [3] [8] [6] [2]
POSITION  0   1   2   3   4   5
```

Starting with the second card, place it temporarily to the left of position 1, (in position 0) and starting just to the left of the gap, compare each card up to the gap with the card in position 0, moving it along one place if it is greater. Then replace the card from position 0 in the gap.

```
   [3] [5] [ ] [8] [6] [2]        becomes        [3] [ ] [5] [8] [6] [2]
POSITION  0   1   2   3   4   5

                                  and then       [ ] [3] [5] [8] [6] [2]
```

On the next pass, nothing changes. On the third pass

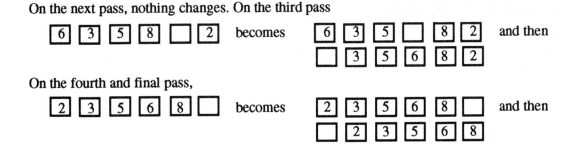

On the fourth and final pass,

In the pseudocode algorithm for this sort shown below, the **n** values to be sorted are held in an array **card[0..n]**, with **card[0]** being used to hold the current card being looked at.

```
begin procedure
     for counter = 2 to n
          CurrentCard:= card[counter]      (start with the second card)
          card[0] = CurrentCard            (place it temporarily in position 0)
          ptr = counter - 1                (point to card just left of the gap)
          while card[ptr] > CurrentCard    (if it's greater than current card,
               card[ptr+1] = card[ptr]      move it along one space)
               ptr = ptr - 1;              (ready to look at next card on right)
          endwhile
          card[ptr+1] = CurrentCard;       (put the card back in the gap)
     endfor
end procedure
```

The insertion sort is considerably faster than the bubble sort, but not nearly as fast as the quicksort, which typically would take about 3 seconds to sort an array of 2000 items that would take a minute using an insertion sort and 5 or 6 minutes using a bubble sort.

Quicksort

The quicksort is a very fast sort invented by C.Hoare, based on the general principle that exchanges should be made between items which are a large distance apart in the array holding them. It works by splitting the array into two sublists, and then quicksorting each sublist by splitting them into two sublists and .... remember **recursion**? The quicksort uses a complex recursive algorithm which starts by comparing the first and last elements in the array. For large arrays, it can be hundreds of times faster than the simple bubble sort.

Extraction sort

If the records to be sorted are of variable length or very long (or of course both) then it is usually a good idea to sort only the keys and store with each key a pointer to the original record address. This means that only two fields (the key and the pointer) need to be exchanged instead of the whole record.

Avoiding sorts

Sorts are time consuming and it may be a good policy to avoid them altogether where possible, either by maintaining the data in the correct order all the time (as in a linear or linked list), or by keeping the items in a data structure such as a **binary tree**. Of course sometimes the data may be required in a different sequence from the one in which it is held and a sort may be unavoidable.

External sorts

When the volume of data is so great that it is impossible to hold it all in memory, an **external sorting method**, which makes use of backing storage, must be used. The basis of all external sorting methods is the process of **merging**; two sorted sequences are merged together to form a single sorted sequence.

Q4: Merge the two sequences (A) and (B) to form a single sorted sequence (C).

    (A)   1   2   8   15   21   23

    (B)   3   9   10   18

Merge sort

This sort uses four files A B C D, and at any time two of these are **transmitting** and two are **receiving**. The roles of the pairs of files change with each pass.

As an example, we shall sort the key values 23 16 57 43 90 13 29 75 36 25 41 82 19

Let A and B be the transmitting files and C and D the receiving files. First of all, write the key values alternately to A and B. We then have

    A: 23   57   90   29   36   41   19

    B: 16   43   13   75   25   82

The keys in file A are merged successively with the keys in file B and placed alternately in the receiving files C and D.

    C: (16,23)   (13,90)   (25,36)   (19)

    D: (43,57)   (29,75)   (41,82)

C and D now contain a set of ordered sequences of keys, each sequence being of maximum length 2.

The process is now reversed, C and D becoming the transmitting files. The sequences in File C are merged successively with the sequences in File D and placed alternately in Files A and B.

Files A and B now contain a series of ordered keys of maximum length 4:

    A: (16,23,43,57)   (25,36,41,82)

    B: (13,29,75,90)   (19)

On the next pass,

    C: (13,16,23,29,43,57,75,90)

    D: (19,25,36,41,82)

and one last pass leaves all the keys in sequence on File A.

Choosing a sort method

Since there are so many different ways of sorting records, which method should you choose for a given set of records? The method chosen will depend on factors such as the number of records to be sorted, whether the computer has sufficient memory to hold all the records at once so that an internal sort can be performed, whether the records are already partially sorted, and the length of the individual records to be sorted (if they are long, an extraction sort may be chosen).

Exercises:

1.   Describe how a file which is too large to be held in memory may be sorted using a merge technique. Assume the availability of four work areas, each of which is large enough to hold the whole file.   *(10 marks)*

                                                               AEB Paper 2 1985

2.   (a)   There are many methods of sorting a set of records into ascending order of key. What factors would you consider in deciding which of these methods is the most suitable for a particular application?   *(4 marks)*

(b) A list of N numbers is to be stored in locations 1 to N of an array in ascending order, by means of an insertion sort as follows. As the numbers are entered, the first is stored in location 1. Then, before each succeeding number is inserted, as many as necessary of those already stored are moved to the next location to leave space in the correct position for the next number.

The numbers 13,11,24,12,20 are entered using this method so that they occupy the locations 1 to 5 in ascending order. Show the contents of the locations immediately **after** each number is inserted (that is, on 5 occasions in all).
(2 marks)

(c) Using pseudocode, or another suitable method, write a detailed algorithm for the process described in (b) above, adding comments to show your method clearly.
(8 marks)

(UCLES November 1992 Paper 1)

3. The algorithm for an insertion sort consistes of two procedures, named insert and sort.

(a) The array CITIES is already sorted alphabetically. It is required to insert the element I into the correct position in the array to create a new sorted array. The algorithm for the procedure insert is:

```
procedure insert(reference CITIES, value j, value I)
    if j = 0 then
        CITIES [1] = I
    else
        if I > CITIES[j] then
            CITIES[j+1] = I
        else
            CITIES[j+1] = CITIES[j]
            insert(CITIES, j-1, I)
        endif
    endif
endprocedure
```

(i) Explain the difference between passing parameters *by reference* and passing them *by value*. (2 marks)

(ii) Show how the procedure **insert(CITIES, 4, I)** operates, given that:

> CITIES[1] = 'BRISTOL'
> CITIES[2] = 'LONDON'
> CITIES[3] = 'NEWCASTLE'
> CITIES[4] = 'NORWICH'
> and   I = 'MANCHESTER'.

You should write down the changes to the contents of the array CITIES and the parameters each time the procedure is called.
(6 marks)

(b) The algorithm for the procedure sort is

```
procedure SORT(reference CITIES, value n)
    if n > 1 then
        sort(CITIES, n - 1)
        insert(CITIES, n - 1, CITIES[n])
    endif
endprocedure
```

The array CITIES2, containing the four elements:

> WARSAW   PARIS   ATHENS   MOSCOW

in that order, is to be sorted.

(i) State the call to the sort procedure.

(ii) Explain how the procedure sort operates on these elements. (5 marks)

(c) State *one* circumstance in which the use of an insertion sort would be useful and *one* circumstance in which it would not be sensible.
(2 marks)

London Paper 2 1992

Section 4 — Databases

Unit 30 — Introduction to Databases

Introduction

In the modern world, many companies rely for their profits not on cheap coal, high quality steel and other such resources, but on **information**. The data and information accumulated by a company represents one of its most valuable assets. In order to gain the maximum benefit from it, the data must be carefully organised so that it can be used in the most effective way possible. This often means maintaining a **database**.

Q1: Identify some of the ways in which access to **information** can be vital to an organisation's success.

The traditional approach

When computers first began to be widely used in business and other organisations, they were viewed primarily as aids to **processing data** rather than as a means of providing information. The payroll was often the first application to be computerised, with the obvious benefit of vastly increasing the speed of producing payslips compared with manual methods. A typical scenario might be something like the following:

> Imagine you work as a programmer in the Finance department of a college, which has recently computerised the payroll operation. A series of complex programs has been written, and data files created. Data is held about each member of staff; their name, salary, national insurance number, bank account details and so on.

> After the system has been working successfully for some time, a change in the conditions of service for lecturers means that overtime pay is to be calculated in a different way, and in order to perform the calculation, extra information has to be added to each lecturer's record in the Employee Master file. Unfortunately, this means that virtually every single program in the payroll system has to be changed, since they all use this file.

> Meanwhile, the head of the Administration department decides to computerise their operation. Their staff need to keep track of which lecturer is teaching what, where and for how long. They also need to know how much overtime is being done by each lecturer. However, they can hardly expect Finance to rewrite their system again, so they buy their own computer (an Archimedes) and write their own programs, even though much of the information needed is common to both systems. What's more, when Miss Babbage marries Mr Boole, Administration are not informed, so her record is held in the two systems under two different names.

> At the end of the year the Principal needs some statistics on who taught overtime on which courses, and how much they were paid. Neither system holds all the information — so you and your opposite number in Administration work through the night trying to find a way of providing the necessary information. There are some red faces when the two versions turn out to be inconsistent. The Principal is not impressed!

Q2: What problems can you identify in the description given above?

The database approach

The scenario described above highlights some of the difficulties which arise when information is held on separate files which are spread throughout an organisation. Often the potential value of the information is lost because it cannot be accessed efficiently or because people in other departments simply do not know of its existence. In an attempt to organise their data more efficiently, many companies have implemented databases.

A **database** consists of a pool of data or information, and software to control access to the data, known as the **Database Management System (DBMS)**. It is intended to overcome many of the problems of the conventional approach.

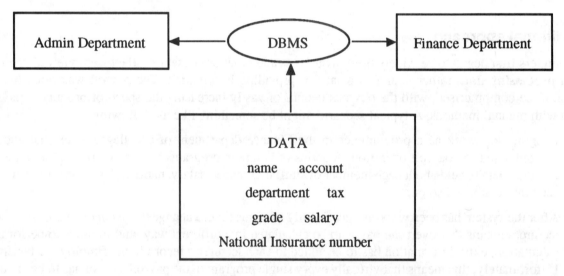

Figure 30.1

This diagam shows the database as a pool of independent items of information. Unlike a conventional file, the database can also specify the **relationships** between various items of data. Thus, for example, a user in the Finance department would be able to access information on which courses a particular lecturer has taught on, and, if relevant, the overtime rate for teaching on a particular course.

Access to the information is controlled by the DBMS, which acts as an interface between the user and the data. Any user may be given access to all or part of the information held.

Advantages of the database approach

1. **Data independence.**

    In a database, the data is held in such a way that changes to the structure of the database do not affect any of the programs that access the data. This is in direct contrast to the non-database approach, where a minor change in a file structure may mean a considerable reprogramming effort.

2. **Consistency of data.**

    Since each data item is held only once, there is no danger of an item being updated on one system and not on another. Thus if employee number 162735, Bloggs Joy, has recently got married and changed her name to Richards Joy, this fact need only be recorded once and all references to employee 162735 will pick up the correct name.

3   **Control over redundancy.**

    In a non-database system, the same information may be held on several different files, which not only wastes space but makes updating more time-consuming. In a database system redundancy is not always completely eliminated, but it is minimised.

4. **Integrity (correctness) of data.**

    The DBMS provides users with the ability to specify constraints on data, such as for example that if a new lecturer is added to the database, his or her national insurance number must be added too. It will then be impossible to store a lecturer's details and omit this item of data.

5. **Greater security of data.**

    The DBMS will ensure that only authorised users are allowed access to the data.

6. **Centralised control of data.**

    In an organisation where the database is used by several departments, one person called the Database Administrator is in charge of the database, and will structure the database with the needs of the whole organisation in mind.

7. **More information available to users.**

    With a database system, users have access to information that was previously held in separate files in other departments, and sometimes on incompatible systems.

8. **Increased productivity.**

    The DBMS provides an easy-to-use query language that enables users to get instant answers to their queries, rather than having to have a special program written by a programmer, which could take days if not weeks.

Disadvantages of the database approach

1. **Larger size.**

    A DBMS is a large program which may require more disk space and a larger, more powerful computer than the system it replaces.

2. **Greater complexity.**

    In order for the DBMS to bring advantages to an organisation, the database must be very carefully designed. This will require considerable expertise and if not done well, the new system may fail to satisfy anyone.

3. **Greater impact of system failure.**

    If the database system fails, everyone using it is affected, not just a single department.

4. **More complex recovery procedures.**

    Recovering from a system failure will require complex procedures to ensure that no data is lost.

Note that these points refer to a large database held on a mini or mainframe computer, rather than a microcomputer database system such as dBase III+, which would not be classified as a 'database management system', but rather a 'file management system'.

Exercises:

1. A kidney transplant service uses database software to match organs to patients requiring transplants. A central minicomputer is used to run the service which provides access to the database 24 hours a day. The system can support simultaneous enquiries from 50 terminals. There are several thousand possible kidney tissue types which the software must match as closely as possible against 3000 patients whose records are stored in the database. Kidneys are best transplanted within 12 hours of becoming available. The software takes a few minutes to produce the 10 best matches in the area local to the donor kidney, and the 30 best matches throughout the country. The matches are ordered according to the best tissue match and the clinical urgency for performing a transplant operation. The software ensures that the surgeons can only access the personal details of their own patients. Surgeons are permitted limited access to the details of other patients so that analysis according to tissue type can be performed but individual patients cannot be identified. Several other applications access the same data, including tissue type statistical analysis, and the analysis of the success of previous transplants.

    (a) Suggest TWO records which may be input to this system. In each case suggest who would be responsible for collecting the data.   (2 marks)

    (b) It is proposed to incorporate an additional minicomputer into the system and a back-up battery power supply. Why would these be desirable?   (2 marks)

    (c) Suggest a reason why the system distinguishes local and national patients. What are the implications of this distinction for the records stored in the database?   (2 marks)

    (d) Suggest a reason why the system restricts the surgeon's access to the personal details of patients. How can this be achieved using a database system?   (3 marks)

    (e) Each patient's record includes name, address, telephone number and next of kin.

         Suggest FIVE other fields of a patient's record which would be required by the system. For each of these explain briefly why it is needed.   (5 marks)

    (f) Describe and justify THREE advantages of the database approach compared with a system where the separate applications access separate files.   (6 marks)

         AEB Paper 2 1988

2. In the database context, what is meant by the term 'data redundancy', and what are the two chief problems associated with redundancy?   (4 marks)

    NISEAC Paper 1 May 1990

3. State what is meant by data independence.   (4 marks)

    NISEAC Paper 1 1991

4.* With reference to a database explain what is meant by data consistency. Explain why the use of a database management system is useful for this purpose.   (3 marks)

    AEB Paper 2 1992

Unit 31— Database Design and Normalisation

Introduction

There are many ways of holding information. For example, consider the following:

"Peter has blue eyes, like the sax player. John's eyes are brown. The trumpeter is the only one with fair hair. Julie is dark, and she is not the drummer, who is the only one with brown eyes."

Q1: List all the instruments played. Who plays drums?

Q2: List the names of all the people with fair hair.

For a computer, this information is more conveniently stored in the form of a table:

Band-member

name	eyes	hair	instrument
Peter	blue	fair	trumpet
John	brown	dark	drums
Julie	blue	dark	sax

A relational database

A relational database is essentially a collection of tables similar to the one above.

These tables are known as 'relations', which is where the relational database gets its name. A **relation** is a two-dimensional table with each column having a distinct name, and each row holding information about a particular item or **entity** in the table. Each row of a relation is technically known as a **tuple**, and each column is called an **attribute**.

Just to add to the confusion, we could also use the terms **file, record** and **field.**

The correspondence between the three sets of terminologies is shown below:

(i)	(ii)	(iii)
relation	table	file
tuple	row	record
attribute	column	field

Q3: What is the name of the **relation** in the database above which contains tuples for Peter, John and Julie?

Q4: How many **fields** are there in each **record?**

Q5: What **entity** is described in the relation, and what are its **attributes**?

From now on, we will refer to tables, rows and columns, which is perhaps the most natural terminology.

Schemas

When a lot of information is held about a number of different subjects, there are several possible ways of organising the data into tables or relations. The organisation of the data in a database into its various tables is known as the **schema.** The schema not only defines what columns go in which tables, it shows the logical relationship between the entities being held.

Designing a database

As an example, consider a certain college which holds information about all its students, lecturers and courses, as follows:

student

student-name	student-no	date-of-birth	sex	course-no	course-title	lec-name	lec-no
Heathcote,R	12345	20-08-77	M	EC6654	A-Level Computing	Glover,T	T345267
Head,J	22433	13-02-77	F	EC6654	A-Level Computing	Glover,T	T345267
Hargrave,R	66688	13-09-54	M	BM3390	HNC Business	Newman,P	T666758
Daley,C	87656	24-12-76	M	HM7756	A-Level Music	Reader,B	T773351

All the data items to be held have been put in the database into one table, holding all the relevant pieces of information. The lecturer name (lec-name) and number (lec-no) refer to the lecturer in charge of the particular course that any student is enrolled for.

Q6: What is the disadvantage of holding the data in one large table?

Primary and secondary keys

The primary key of a table is the column or collection of columns that uniquely identifies a given row. Thus in the **student** table, the primary key is **student-no.** Other columns may be defined as **secondary keys,** and the programmer can instruct the DBMS to build an index for any of these secondary keys. For example, **sex** could be defined as a secondary key, and the DBMS could then quickly find all male students.

Shorthand representation of a database

In order to represent the structure of a database, a commonly accepted notation is to write the name of each table and then within brackets a list of all the columns in the table. The primary key is indicated by underlining the column name or names in the key.

The database above would be represented as follows:

    student(student-name, <u>student-no</u>, date-of-birth, sex, course-no, course-title, lec-name)

Normalisation

When designing tables for a database it is important to make the most efficient use of space, and allow for all possible relationships between data items. It turns out that the best design is one in which each entity is represented by one table in the database. This sounds simple but in practise it requires some thought to separate out the different entities. The process of separating them is called **normalisation.**

There are several aspects of the table **student** which are at present unsatisfactory. For example, what will happen if a student is registered for more than one course? This situation will leave us with several problems:

- how much room should be allowed for multiple courses?

- what happens if one student is registered for more courses than we have left room for?

- how would we be able to determine, for example, all the students who were on a particular course?

The stages of normalisation

There are three stages in the normalisation process to transform a database into what is known as **third normal form**. These three stages transform the data by the application of a set of rules into **first normal form, second normal form** and finally **third normal form.**

First normal form - Repeating group test

If the database is to allow for the fact that a student may take more than one course, it will contain what is known as a **repeating group** of items. That is, the data items **course-no, course-title, lec-name** and **lec-no** will need to be repeated as many times as necessary to hold all the course information about a single student.

The shorthand representation of this table indicates the repeating groups with a line over them:

student(student-name, student-no, date-of-birth, sex, course-no, course-title, lec-name, lec-no)

The first step in normalisation is to remove all repeating groups. This can be done quite easily by holding a separate record for each student/course combination. Thus if a student is on 3 courses, she will have three records in the database.

(Note that for simplicity we are assuming that there is just one lecturer in charge of each course.)

student

student-name	student-no	date-of-birth	sex	course-no	course-title	lec-name	lec-no
Heathcote,R	12345	20-08-77	M	EC6654	A-Level Computing	Glover,T	T345267
Head,J	22433	13-02-77	F	EC6654	A-Level Computing	Glover,T	T345267
Head,J	22433	13-02-77	F	HM7756	A-Level Music	Reader,B	T773351
Head,J	22433	13-02-77	F	AD1121	Pottery	Watts,R	T876541
Hargrave,R	66688	13-09-54	M	BM3390	HNC Business	Newman,P	T666758
Daley,C	87656	24-12-76	M	HM7756	A-Level Music	Reader,B	T773351

Q7: The column **student-no** no longer uniquely identifies a given row. Identify the new primary key of the table and hence write down the shorthand representation of the table.

At this stage it becomes clear that there are two entities involved: student and course. The data can be separated into two tables with the shorthand notation

student (student-no, student-name, date-of-birth, sex, course-no)

course (course-no, course-title, lec-name, lec-no)

The tables are now said to be in **first normal form**.

Definition: A table is said to be in first normal form (1NF) if it contains no repeating attributes or groups of attributes.

Second normal form - Partial key dependence test

The **student** table has another deficiency; it contains a lot of redundant data. Not only is this wasteful of space, but it causes other problems too:

- updating becomes much more time-consuming

- inconsistencies may arise if for example a student name needs amending and we do not update all records for that student correctly.

The problems arise because some fields, for example **student-name**, are dependent on only part of the primary key, **student-no**, and not on the complete primary key. If we can reorganise things so that this does not happen, the table will be in **second normal form**.

Definition: A table is in second normal form (2NF) if it is in first normal form and no column that is not part of a primary key is dependent on only a portion of the primary key.

This is sometimes expressed by saying that **a table in second normal form contains no partial dependencies.**

In order to put the table into 2NF, we first make a list of all the subsets of the primary key (and the list will include the whole primary key).

> student-no
> course-no
> student-no, course-no

Next, we place each of the other columns with the appropriate primary key; that is, place each one with the minimal possible number of columns on which it depends. This gives:

> (student-no, student-name, date-of-birth, sex)
> (course-no, course-title, lec-name, lec-no)
> (student-no, course-no)

Now give each of the new tables appropriate headings, and the shorthand notation for the database becomes

> student(student-no, student-name, date-of-birth, sex)
> course(course-no, course-title, lec-name, lec-no)
> students-registered(student-no, course-no)

Q8: Rearrange the original data into the new normalised tables.

Third normal form - Non-key dependence test

You may have had some discussion about exactly where **lecturer name** belongs. This is an example of an attribute that is not dependent on the key field; it is in fact dependent only on **lec-no**. One problem with this situation (apart from the problem of redundant and possibly inconsistent data) is that it is impossible to record facts about a new lecturer until a relevant course record is entered on the database. To put the table into third normal form, every attribute must be dependent on the key, the whole key and nothing but the key.

In third normal form, there are no 'non-key dependencies'.

In this instance, a new **lecturer** table needs to be defined:

> lecturer(<u>lec-no</u>, lec-name)

Q9: What change has to be made to the **course** table to put it into 3NF?

Entity Relationship diagrams

When designing a database it is often useful to represent in a graphical way the relationship between the various entities in a database. There are three types of relationship - one-to-one, one-to-many and many-to-many.

One-to-one relationships are the least common. An example is 'husband' and 'wife'. Each husband has one wife, and each wife has one husband.

One-to-many relationships are the most common. 'Mother' and 'child' is an example of this type of relationship; each mother has zero, one or more children, but each child has exactly one mother.

Many-to-many relationships are fairly common, and are akin to a 'brother' and 'sister' relationship. Each brother may have many sisters, and each sister may have many brothers.

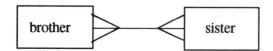

Notice the way that these relationships are diagramatically represented in the so-called **entity relationship diagram**. Another way of drawing these diagrams is to use a single arrow for the 'one' end and a double arrow for the 'many' end of the relationship, as shown below.

Q10: Draw entity relationship diagrams to show the relationships between

    (a)   lecturer and course

    (b)   student and lecturer

    (c)   student and course

Exercises:

1.   Information is to be held by a car-hire firm about cars and all the long-term hirers that a particular vehicle has had. The information to be held about each vehicle is:

        Registration number, make, model, year

    and for each person who hires the vehicle:

        Customer-Number, Surname, Initial, Address, date hired, date returned.

    Design the structure of a database in third normal form to hold this data.   **(5 marks)**

2.   A company selling electrical goods keeps its orders on a database. An order may consist of several lines, as shown below.

Order-number	date	product-code	description	qty-ordered	unit-price
152117	23-5-91	EG8766	CD player	1	299.95
		EG1121	speakers	2	120.00
		CD1127	compact disc	3	9.99

Show how this data would be held in a database in   (i)   first normal form

                                         (ii)   second normal form.   **(5 marks)**

3.   (a)   What is meant by a database system and what are the benefits of using such a system in preference to a number of unrelated files?   **(5 marks)**

    (b)   A librarian in an educational establishment is considering using a database system to hold information about the books and periodicals in the library. She also hopes to hold details of those who are entitled to borrow books (e.g. staff who can borrow books for a month and students who can borrow books for a week before renewal) together with details of the books they are currently borrowing. Books or periodicals may also be reserved if they are currently on loan. Fines are imposed at varying rates depending on the nature of the borrower and the nature of the book.

        Describe the overall design of the database and indicate how the data could be captured and validated.

        Describe typical enquiries that the librarian and a potential borrower might make of the system. Would you expect any restrictions to be placed on access by the borrower, and if so, what?

        What benefits are likely to be gained by the librarian and the borrowers if such a system were implemented?

                                                                      (10 marks)

WJEC AS Level May 1990

4.   A manufacturer of electrical goods maintains a file about the products he manufactures. The records hold details about each product as follows:

        product number (PN)

        product description (PD)

        product cost price (PC)

        product selling price (PS)

and for each component type used in the product

        component number (CN)

        component quantity (CQ)

        component description (CD)

        component cost (CC)

The data is held in fixed length records made up of a fixed number of fixed length fields.

(a)   Explain what advantage there would be in holding this data using variable-length records rather than fixed-length records.   (4 marks)

(b)   State which fields in the above records would be most likely to be stored as variable-length fields, and if this was to be done, what other data would have to be held, and why?   (8 marks)

(c)   Indicate how variable-length records could deal with the fact that different product records might contain differing numbers of component types.   (6 marks)

(d)   Explain briefly why such variable-length records would not be permissible in a relational database.

                                                                     (6 marks)

(e)   In database systems the above records would often be described in the following manner:

        (<u>PN</u>, PD, PC, PS, (CN, CQ, CD, CC))

Using this notation describe the separate records which you would expect to find in a database system holding the same data in third normal form (3NF)   (8 marks)

NISEAC Paper 1 June 1989

5.*   You have been requested to advise on the computerisation of a medium sized bookshop.

    (a)   (i)   Describe briefly two significant costs which the shop will incur after the initial installation of the computer hardware and software.   (4 marks)

        (ii)   Describe briefly **two** benefits which computerisation should bring.   (4 marks)

    (b)   A relational database is to be used. Two entity sets are the books and the publishers.

        (i)   State **eight** attributes associated with the books. Draw a diagram showing the relationship between the books and the publishers.   (6 marks)

        (ii)   State **two** other entity sets which could be related to either or both of the original entity sets. Describe their relationships. Suggest an identifier for each of these two entities.   (6 marks)

AEB Paper 2 1992

6.*   (i)   What is the purpose of normalisation of data?

    (ii)   With the aid of an example, describe the stages in normalisation.   (6 marks)

NISEAC Paper 1 1992

Unit 32 — Database Management

Introduction

We have seen that the pooling of information, software, and computer power is very useful but that it does involve potential problems. There is the danger that one user will damage or change data used by other people without their knowledge; there is the question of how to protect confidential information; there may be problems if more than one person tries to change the same item of data. If a hardware failure occurs, everyone using the database is affected, and recovery procedures must ensure that no data is lost.

In order to minimise the potential hazards, a group known as **database administration** (or a person in charge of the group, known as the **database administrator**) is responsible for supervising both the database and the use of the DBMS.

Database Administration (DBA)

The DBA's tasks will include the following:

1. The design of the database. After the initial design, the DBA must monitor the performance of the database, and if problems surface (such as a particular report taking an unacceptably long time to produce), appropriate changes must be made to the database structure.

2. Keeping users informed of changes in the database structure that will affect them; for example, if the size or format of a particular field is altered or additional fields added.

3. Maintenance of the **data dictionary** (see below) for the database, and responsibility for establishing conventions for naming tables, columns, indexes and so on.

4. Implementing access privileges for all users of the database; that is, specifying which items can be accessed and/or changed by each user.

5. Allocating passwords to each user.

6. Providing training to users in how to access and use the database.

Q1: Do you think that it is necessary to have one person in charge of the database? What would be the alternative?

The data dictionary

The data dictionary is a 'database about the database'. It will contain information such as:

*   what tables and columns are included in the present structure.
*   the names of the current tables and columns.
*   the characteristics of each item of data, such as its length and data type.
*   any restrictions on the value of certain columns.
*   the meaning of any data fields that are not self-evident; for example, a field such as 'course type'.
*   the relationships between items of data.
*   which programs access which items of data, and whether they merely read the data or change it.

The Database Management System (DBMS)

The DBMS is an application program that provides an interface between the operating system and the user in order to make access to the data as simple as possible. It has several other functions as well, and these are described below.

1. **Data storage, retrieval and update.** The DBMS must allow users to store, retrieve and update information as easily as possible, without having to be aware of the internal structure of the database.

2. **Creation and maintenance of the data dictionary.**

3. **Managing the facilities for sharing the database.** The DBMS has to ensure that problems do not arise when two people simultaneously access a record and try to update it.

4. **Backup and recovery.** The DBMS must provide the ability to recover the database in the event of system failure.

5 **Security.** The DBMS must handle password allocation and checking, and the 'view' of the database that a given user is allowed.

(3, 4 and 5 above are covered in more depth in the next unit).

Q2: Distinguish between a **database management system** and a **file management system** such as dBase III+, Smartware II Database, Cardbox or other microcomputer database packages, pointing out the similarities and differences between them.

Querying the database

In order to provide users with a way of accessing the database, a special easy-to-use language is often employed, an example of which is SQL (Structured Query Language). The basic retrieval facility in SQL is the **select** statement, which consists of three clauses in the general form

```
select....
from  ....
where ....
```

The **select** clause specifies columns to be extracted from the table or relation in the **from** clause. The **where** clause specifies the condition that must be met for items to be selected.

For example, to find all the female students in the **student** table given below we could enter

```
select student-name
from  student
where sex='F'
```

student

student-name	student-no	date-of-birth	sex
Heathcote,R	12345	20-08-73	M
Head,J	22433	13-02-73	F
Hargrave,R	66688	13-09-54	M
Daley,C	87656	24-12-72	M

Q3: Use a **select** clause to find all the lecturers on salary grade 13 in the **lecturer** table below.

lecturer

lec-name	payroll-number	department	salary-grade
Glover,T	T345267	Computing	13
Reader,B	T773351	Humanities	23
Newman,P	T666758	Business	12

Query by example

This is the term used to describe another method that is sometimes used to retrieve data from a database. A blank 'form' is displayed on the screen showing one or more tables from the database, and the user fills in the query he wishes to make.

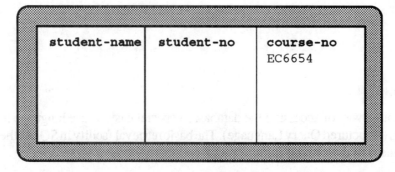

student-name	student-no	course-no
		EC6654

Figure 32.1 — Query by example

In this simplified example, the user is asking for all student names and numbers on course number EC6654.

Q4: Have you used any software which uses 'Query by example'? Describe how you would make a query in a database package with which you are familiar.

Exercises:

1. Most database management packages allow the user to associate conditions with the fields of a record. These conditions are then activated during data entry stage. Data entry is via the keyboard and the fields are displayed on a monitor.

   Three conditions that can be placed on data entry to fields are

   — the data entered must be *unique,*

   — the data must be *verified,*

   — data entry is *prohibited.*

   (a) An application using such a package has records with fields

   <ORDER_NUMBER, PART_NUMBER, UNIT_COST,

   QUANTITY_ORDERED, VALUE_OF_ORDER>

   In this context

   (i) give an example showing why the application would require data entry to a particular field to be unique.

   (ii) what is meant by verification? How might verification be achieved in this case?

   (iii) indicate why entry to a particular field might be prohibited?

   (iv) give an example of a command line a user might enter to obtain information via a query language.
   (6 marks)

   (b) One of the objectives of a database management system is to offer *program-data independence.* What is meant by this term?
   (2 marks)
   London Paper 2 June 1990

2. (a) Explain what is meant by a *database.* What are the benefits and drawbacks, if any, of using a database system?
   (4 marks)

   (b) In a certain city there are eight independent travel agencies named

   ALPHA, BETA, CHARLIE, DELTA, EVERLASTING, FLYME,

   GREATEST, HANGOVER.

   The travel agencies deal with five package holiday operators,

   PRESIDENTIAL, QUALITY, RELAXATION, SUNSHINE, TOURIST,

   who share a common database system. Each holiday operator offers a range of holidays at hotels in various Mediterranean resorts and stores information regarding its holidays and the bookings made on the database. The holiday operators also store the relevant details, such as name and address, of each of the travel agencies with on-line access to the database, including the eight mentioned above.

   Explain how the database would be used when a travel agent selects and books a holiday for a family of three. Give **one** example to show a typical dialogue between the travel agent and the database system, and use annotated sketches to indicate the file transactions which occur.
   (7 marks)

   (c) Subsequent to booking the holiday, the parents find that their teenage daughter wishes to join them on holiday. They then wish to convert their one room booking for three beds into a booking for two twin bedded rooms. Show how the travel agent could interrogate the database to determine whether the original booking could be altered and if so to reserve the new booking.
   (4 marks)
   WJEC AS Level May 1989

3.* A library may use a paper-based record-keeping system, a conventional computer file system or a database management system.

   (a) Describe what is meant by a database and explain the role of a database management system.
   (5 marks)

   (b) Outline the advantages of using a DBMS in an application such as a library.
   (3 marks)
   UCLES Paper 1 May 1992

Unit 33 — Database Security

Sub-schemas

In the traditional file-based approach to data processing, each department had its own files and usually had no access to files belonging to other departments. A database, on the other hand, is used by a number of different applications and will contain a great deal of data that is irrelevant to any one user. In order to restrict access to parts of the database, the DBMS may create different 'views' of the database for each user or user group.

We have seen that the **schema** is a description of the entire database. **Sub-schemas** (also called **internal schemas**) are created to describe the views of the database relevant to particular users.

For example, the employee table in a particular company database may hold details on name, address, date of joining company, post held, salary and other payroll information. However a user in Personnel looking at this table may only be shown name, address, date of joining company and post held. This is their 'view' of the database.

The DBMS performs the mapping required between this view and the database. When an application is added or modified so that a new view is required, an existing sub-schema is modified or a new one added. This will be done by the Database Administrator using a Data Definition language (DDL).

Q1: How will the DBMS identify a user in order to know what sub-schema is to be used?

Access matrices

In many cases it may be useful for some users to be able to see data from parts of the database even though they are not permitted to alter it. The DBMS may use an **access matrix** to define the access rights of different users, as shown below:

	Item1	Item2	Item3	Item4	
User1	W	R	R	-	R = Read access
User2	R	W	-	-	W = Write access
User3	W	W	W	R	
User4	-	-	-	R	

Q2: What access does User3 have to Item2?

As an additional security measure, users may have to type in a password before the computer will execute a certain command.

Locking

When an item is updated, it is read from the database into the user's own memory area where it is updated and then written back to the database. If two users attempt to update the same record simultaneously one of the updates will be lost. Therefore, when a row of a table is to be updated it is **locked** so that no-one else can access it until the update is complete. In some cases the whole table is locked before a user updates an item, but it is more efficient if only the affected record is locked.

There may also be two levels of locking; it may be possible to view but not change the record, or alternatively the user may be denied access altogether while a record is locked.

Deadlock

If two users are attempting to update the same rows, a situation can arise in which neither can proceed.

User1	User2
locks record1	locks record2
tries to access record2	tries to access record1
waits ..	waits ..

DEADLOCK!

The DBMS must recognise when this situation has occurred and take action. One of the two user's tasks must be aborted to allow the other to proceed.

Recovery

Facilities are obviously required to recover data in the event of, say, a system crash which destroys part of the database. At regular time intervals, perhaps weekly, a utility database backup program is run, causing the entire database to be copied, often onto magnetic tape. This utility program comes with the database system and is considered a component of it.

In addition, during regular database processing, every updating transaction is recorded in a transaction file, which is usually also on tape. If part of the database is destroyed, a recovery utility program can be used to generate a new up-to-date copy. The recovery program reads data from the backup and from the transaction log file and using the database system generates a new copy.

Checkpoints

Occasionally a program is run that changes a huge amount of data on the database. Such a program may take several hours to run, and if for some reason it fails near the end, it can be extremely inconvenient to run the whole thing again. Therefore **checkpoints** are taken every half hour or so, recording the entire state of the program and all tables. If the program fails for some reason, the checkpoint/restart program can restart the program from that point.

Exercises:

1. An airline maintains a database of its flight bookings. A travel agent who operates a remote on-line terminal to the database is able to book seats for customers. The agent first checks that an appropriate seat is available and then, if the customer is satisfied, confirms the booking. Finally, the agent makes out the ticket and receives payment from the customer on behalf of the airline. Describe information which the agent must supply to the computer system and the information returned to the agent from the database. Suggest a method of ensuring that a seat cannot be booked by another agent while the first customer is deciding whether to confirm the booking. (18 marks)

    UCLES AS Level Specimen Paper 1989

2. In order to overcome equipment shortages in schools the computer centre of a local education authority have decided to introduce an equipment loan service to link with an existing repair and maintenance facility. The system makes the following services available:

    schools may borrow equipment in an emergency caused by the breakdown of their own standard equipment;

    schools have access to specialised hardware (eg colour printers, robots, interactive video, etc.) which the authority cannot afford to provide to all schools;

    school equipment is maintained on a routine schedule and repaired as required;

    the local authority computer centre maintains accurate records of the overall situation.

    The early analysis of the proposed system's requirements indicates that the use of a database system presents the best approach.

Describe with the aid of a relevant example in each case:

(a)   the advantages of the database approach compared with a system involving the use of separate files. **(4 marks)**

(b)   how the data can be kept accurate and consistent; **(3 marks)**

(c)   what factual information about breakdowns can be obtained; **(6 marks)**

(d)   how unauthorised access to the data may be prevented in a database environment. **(3 marks)**

AEB Sample AS Paper 1989

3.*   Explain, with the aid of an example, the difference between an external schema and an internal schema in the context of a DBMS. **(6 marks)**

NISEAC Paper 2 1992

4.*   A user department complains that response time to database queries is very slow. What can be done to improve response time? Suggest **three** possible improvements. **(3 marks)**

AEB Paper 1 1991

Unit 34 — Database Models

Introduction

To the user, the database appears to be a pool of information from which any item can be selected at will. In practise, different database systems hold the data in different ways. The most important difference is the way the **relationships** between data items are stored.

Data relationships

In database jargon, information is held about **entities**. An entity is a group of objects, people or things. For example, **Lecturer** might be an entity in a college database. **Ship**, **Container**, **Mariner** and **Pension Scheme** might be entities in a dock computer system. Each entity has a corresponding table in the database. Some entities are unrelated, such as **Container** and **Pension Scheme**. Others are related — For example, a ship carries several containers. There are three types of relationship — one-to-one, one-to-many and many-to-many, as discussed in Unit 31.

There are three main strategies for holding these relationships. These are the **hierarchical** database, the **network** database and the **relational** database.

The relational database

This is the most natural way of holding the data and relationships. The entries in each table (relation) are held in random order; they are not sorted in any way. In a one-to-many relationship each 'child' row has a column showing the name or number of its 'parent'. Many-to-many relationships are shown by holding a separate table listing each 'brother' against each 'sister'. The College database used in Unit 31 is an example of a relational database.

Hierarchical databases

This system is based around one-to-many relationships, the most common form of relationship. The 'parents' are sorted into a suitable order. Each parent has a field showing the position of its first 'child', and another field showing the position of the next parent. These fields are called pointers. The children in turn have pointers to the first 'grandchild' and the next child. The last child points back to its parent.

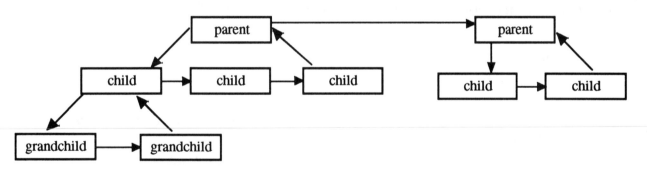

Figure 34.1

Q1: How would the computer list all the children of a particular parent in this system?

The advantage of this system is its speed — it is not necessary to scan the entire database for the information required. The disadvantage of the system is that it is incapable of handling many-to-many relationships properly — in other words, each 'child' can only have one 'parent'. If a child has more than one parent, it has to be placed in a separate database, linked up with the first.

Network databases

This is an advance on the hierarchical model. Pointers are used to indicate relationships, as in the hierarchical model, but it is possible to set up pointers to and from more than one entity, so many-to-many relationships can be implemented. The advantage of this system is that it combines the speed of the 'pointer' system with the ability to hold complex relationships. The disadvantage is that the relationships have to be set up explicitly. This makes the system harder to modify when for example a new entity is added. A large database can also become rather unwieldy, with most of the data being held consisting of pointers to the other items of data! An example of this type of database is the CODASYL DBTG system.

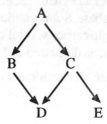   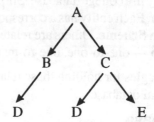

Figure 34.2 — A network   *Figure 34.3 — A hierarchy*

In Figure 34.2, entity D is related to both B and C. In the hierarchy of Figure 34.3, this is not possible, so entity D appears twice; once related to B and once related to C.

Exercises:

1. How does a *hierarchical database* differ from a *relational database*?

2. (i) Explain what is meant by the term 'relational database'.   (5 marks)

    (ii) Describe the following features of database systems:

        sharing of data;   (5 marks)

        differing views of data;   (5 marks)

        security of data   (5 marks)

London Specimen AS Level Paper 1989

3. (a) A local health centre holds records on 10,000 patients who are cared for by 5 doctors and a team
         of health visitors.

    (i) Outline the information which the centre would typically hold about each patient.

    (ii) Estimate the amount of file space which would be required to store all the patients' records, and hence specify
         the hardware and software requirements of a suitable computerised record system for the health centre.

    (iii) Discuss the advantages of such a computerised system over a manual system of record-keeping to the cen-
          tre and to the patient.   (20 marks)

    (b) The centre is considering using a relational database in which to store its data.

         A relation, PHONE, has been suggested in which to hold name, home phone number and work phone extension
         numbers for each doctor. It is assumed that doctors have unique names, will have only one home phone number
         each, and may have several work extension numbers. They may share these work extension numbers.

         A typical instance of this relation is as follows:

Name	H-Phone	W-Ext
BloggsF	234567	3212
BloggsF	234567	3877
GreenG	135791	3001
BrownH	246802	3212
BrownH	246802	3877
YellowF	765432	3002
YellowF	765432	3003

(i)   Discuss which data in this relation are redundant, and hence state how PHONE should be changed to eliminate redundant data.

(ii)   Using the same data, draw instances of the relations which you would use to eliminate redundancy.

(10 marks)

NISEAC Paper 2 June 1990

4.*   Distinguish between the *network* database model and the *relational* database model, giving ONE advantage of each model.

(4 marks)

Section 5 — Systems Development

Unit 35 — The Systems Life Cycle

The role of the systems analyst

The systems analyst has a key role to play in developing computer systems. It is the analyst's job to

- analyse the data processing requirements of the organisation

- decide whether computerisation should be introduced, or the current computer system modified or changed

- specify how the new computer system should work, and what the hardware and software requirements will be

- be responsible for implementing the new system and ensuring that it works efficiently

The systems analyst therefore has to have a good understanding of the nature of the business or organisation by whom he/she is employed, and a thorough understanding of how computers can be used. He or she needs to be an excellent communicator, capable of extracting the required information about the current system from people in the user departments without alienating them.

Q1: Why might people be resistant to the introduction of a new computer system?

Project selection

There may be several reasons why a business decides to introduce computers. Often, one particular area of the business is selected initially for computerisation, for one or more of the following reasons:

- large volumes of data require repetitive processing

- there is a need for better access to up-to-date information on, say, stock levels or sales

- high clerical costs could be reduced by computerisation

- better service to customers could result

- more control over certain areas such as customer accounts could result in an improved cash flow

An additional consideration in selecting what area to computerise first might be the complexity of the project — it is usually better to cut your teeth on a relatively simple task and then apply the experience gained to something more complex.

Overview of the systems life cycle

Commercial systems (payroll, accounts, stock control and so on) all share a common **life cycle** pattern. One method of doing things may work well for a period of time (maybe several years), and then, owing to expansion or changes in the nature of the business, the economic environment, the need to keep up with new technology or other factors, the system may start to deteriorate or seem inadequate. At this point investigations are made, requirements are analysed, a new system is proposed, developed and implemented and the cycle starts all over again.

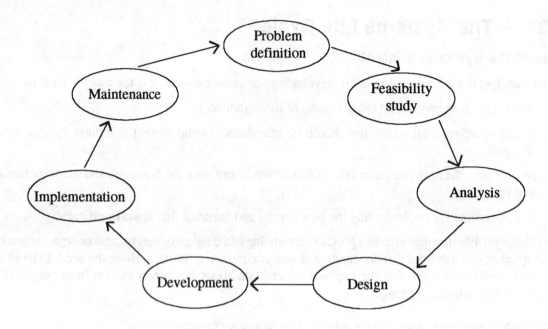

Figure 35.1 - The systems life cycle

The stages in systems development

1. **Analysis**

   The problem must first be identified and defined, and written down in a document called the **terms of reference**. A preliminary investigation will then determine whether the request justifies further detailed investigation and analysis.

   Detailed systems analysis will then follow, involving a thorough study of the current system and a proposed solution to any problems found. Sometimes the systems analyst is asked to prepare a **feasibility study** and a **cost/benefit analysis**. The results of the analyst's work will be presented in a written report to both user and information systems management who consider the alternatives and the resources, such as time, people and money, of the organisation. If a decision is made to proceed, the project enters the design phase.

2. **Design**

   The design stage involves a number of tasks such as designing the output, input, files, database if applicable, system controls and test plan. Input forms must be designed, clerical procedures laid down and all aspects of the design must be documented.

3. **Development**

   There are two aspects to development: program development and equipment acquisition. The systems analyst or sometimes a senior programmer will write program specifications to describe what each program in the system will do and how it will do it. Programmers will then code, test and document the programs.

4. **Implementation**

   This is the phase of the systems development when the new system becomes operational. It is a critical phase of the project, requiring careful timing and the coordination and training of all the user departments involved.

5. **Maintenance**

   All systems need to be **maintained**; that is, performance monitored, modifications made if required, errors corrected, documentation kept up-to-date.

Q2: What circumstances might lead to modifications to a system becoming necessary?

Q3: Stage 3 above describes the development of programs. What alternative approaches could be considered here?

Exercises:

1. The proposed introduction of a computer based system into an organisation can sometimes be a source of concern to employees.

    (a)   State *one* possible area of concern.   (1 mark)

    (b)   For the area of concern you have stated

        (i)   Explain why such a concern might arise   (2 marks)

        (ii)   What steps can be taken in the organisation to alleviate this concern?   (3 marks)
        London Paper 1 June 1989

2. Explain by means of a diagram, or otherwise, what is meant by the **system life cycle**.   (5 marks)
    AEB Paper 2 June 1986

3. Computer systems are often introduced into a business in an attempt to improve efficiency, both in terms of staff productivity and customer services. However, unforeseen circumstances, both organisational and social, can limit the effectiveness of any new system. Discuss briefly why a good technical specification *alone* may not be sufficient to ensure the successful implementation of a computer based system.   (4 marks)
    London Specimen Paper 2 1989

4. People responsible for acquiring computer systems for particular applications are often faced with a choice between a number of different systems. Outline in general terms the criteria which might be applied when making the selection of the most appropriate system.   (5 marks)
    UCLES Paper 1 November 1989

5. Imagine you are a systems analyst working for a large company with its own computing facilities. Your company has just taken over a smaller company. You are asked to examine the suitability of a computerised system developed by the smaller company with a view to making general use of the system throughout the larger company. Describe briefly FIVE factors you would take into account in your evaluation of the system.   (5 marks)
    AEB Paper 2 1988

Unit 36 — Systems Analysis

The stages in the development of a new computerised system were briefly outlined in the previous Unit. Each of these stages will now be covered in more detail, in this and subsequent Units.

The user request (problem definition)

This will be the first formal step in the systems development cycle, but may well be preceded by informal discussions between users and the data processing department. It is, however, essential that before any analysis work begins, the requirements of the new system are written down as the **terms of reference** for any future work. This document is often produced with the assistance of the systems analyst.

The terms of reference may contain

1. Objectives: what the new system must achieve; for example, cost reductions, better service to customers, better management information, ability to handle increased volumes of business.

2. Constraints: any restrictions on cost, equipment to be used, areas of business which are to be left unchanged and so on.

3. Timescale: when a solution is required.

4. Reports or output that is required.

5. Problems that have been identified with the current system.

6. Suggested solutions considered by management.

Q1: Why is it essential for the systems analyst to have written terms of reference before beginning any analysis?

Feasibility study

The feasibility study is concerned with three aspects: technical, social and economic.

Technical feasibility deals with the question of whether the proposed system will achieve its objectives; in other words, will it work? Advances in technology may mean that a system that was not feasible a couple of years ago is now a possibility.

Social feasibility is concerned with the effect on employees and customers of the introduction of a new system. Will it result in redundancies, or a need for retraining or relocation of some of the workforce? Will some jobs be 'deskilled', and will current employees be able to perform effectively any new tasks introduced by the new system? It is essential that user cooperation is secured before changes are introduced. Equally, the effect on customer service has to be considered.

Economic feasibility considers whether the new system will be cost effective. There are two types of cost involved:

- development costs
- running costs

The **benefits** may also be of two types:

- direct economic benefits such as reduced costs
- benefits that are hard to quantify such as improved management information or better customer service

Q2: Name some development costs and running costs incurred in switching over to a new computerised system.

Investigation

Once the decision has been made to go ahead with a system, a much more detailed investigation can take place. The aim is to gain a complete understanding of the existing system, and how it will change in the future. It will cover

- the data — its uses, volumes and characteristics

- the procedures — what is done, where, when and how, and how errors and exceptions are handled

- the future — development plans and expected growth rates

- management reports — requirements for new reports and their contents and frequency

- problems with the existing system

Methods of fact finding

There are a number of ways of finding out about existing procedures and problems. These include

1. observation: spending some time in the department concerned, seeing at first hand the procedures used, workloads and bottlenecks

2. reading the documentation associated with the system

3. asking clerical staff to keep special counts during a trial period to establish where problems might lie

4. questionnaires: these can be useful when a lot of people will be affected by a new system

5. interviews: the most common and most useful way of fact finding. Interviews must be well planned and consideration given to such factors as:

    - whom to interview

    - when to interview

    - what to ask

    - where to hold the interview

Q3: What preparation should a systems analyst make before an interview?

Exercises:

1. An office makes considerable use of a standard microcomputer file management package written by a reputable software house. Why might the office manager be reluctant to change to a new package produced by a rival software house although it offers far more powerful features? (3 marks)
London Paper 2 June 1989

2. Identify the strengths and weaknesses of *interviewing* as a technique for determining user requirements. (3 marks)
London Paper 2 June 1990

3. An enterprising nurseryman runs a successful business selling a wide range of bedding plants, trees, flowering shrubs, and seeds for both flowers and vegetables. He also offers a consultancy service to provide advice and plans for the landscaping and layout of gardens. The nursery occupies a site of approximately two thousand square metres and has about ten large greenhouses and an office. The site holds substantial stock and a security system is in operation. Customers visiting the site are able to park their vehicles nearby. The nurseryman approaches the computer science teacher at the local school to advise him how a microcomputer system might support and enhance his business activities. Assuming that you were the teacher, describe how you would tackle this task. Indicate any assumptions that you would make and explain how you would gather any additional information that was needed. Supposing that a microcomputer system was recommended, suggest a viable configuration and list the possible benefits to the nurseryman and his customers. (20 marks)
WJEC Paper 2 June 1988

4. The Oldways Bus Company operates 200 buses around a town. There are about 30 different routes, and the bus timetables vary according to school terms, national holidays and special events.

Oldways' staff use the bus station as their base. The offices, fuel pumps and the departments of maintenance, cleaning and repair are located within the station.

Payment for the bus service comes in a number of different ways. Most passengers pay in cash on the bus. Some buy monthly travel cards in the bus station. Children's travel to and from school is paid for annually by the Education Department.

Oldways is a successful company, but at present it does not use computers. The management believe that it could significantly increase efficiency if it made sensible use of new technology. Some of the areas where such technology might help are

the cashing-in procedure at the end of each driver shift;

allocation of drivers to shifts;

calculation of wages;

administration of the fuel log, which currently uses a book at the fuel pumps;

bus maintenance and repair schedules, including stock control for parts;

general office tasks.

The Oldways management has asked for a systems analyst to submit proposals for computerisation.

(a) One of the systems analyst's first tasks is to conduct a fact-finding exercise, in which she collects documents, items of data and opinions. Discuss

    (i) the information which should be collected;

    (ii) the methods which could be adopted;

    (iii) the problems which might be encountered. (15 marks)

(b) The systems analyst must suggest those aspects of the company's operations which should be automated, and indicate how far the automation should be taken in each case.

What criteria should she use? (5 marks)
UCLES Paper 2 Nov 1989

Unit 37 — Systems Flowcharts

Systems flowchart symbols

When a systems analyst is developing a new computer system, his ideas need to be written down. Frequently a pictorial representation of how the system will work is easier to understand and take in than a lengthy text. A systems flowchart is a diagram showing an overview of a complete system. It will show

- the tasks to be carried out in the new system, whether manual or by the computer
- the devices (disk drives, tape drives, terminals etc) that are to be used in the system
- the media used for input, storage and output
- the files used by the system

You should be familiar with the standard symbols used in systems flowcharts.

Symbols for operations

start or end

input or output

keyboard input

process

manual operation

sort

off-page connector

Symbols for stored data

on-line storage   disk storage

magnetic tape

visual display

written or printed document

Drawing a systems flowchart

There are many factors to be taken into account when designing a new system. The analyst must establish the following facts:

- Is this a batch, on-line or real-time system?

- How is the data to be captured and input to the system? What manual procedures will be involved, and how will errors be prevented, or detected and corrected if they slip through?

- What is the hit rate on the master files, and what file organisation is therefore appropriate?

- What storage media will be used; disk, tape, or some other medium?

- What will be the output from the system?

- What are the processing steps to be carried out?

Q1: Match the following descriptions with the corresponding systems flowcharts below, adding text to the symbols to make the flowcharts easier to understand.

1. A sequential payroll master file held on tape is updated from a sequential transaction file using the 'grandfather-father-son' method of update, and payslips are produced.

2. A transaction file held on tape is sorted on to a disk file, and a report produced in the new sequence.

3. A collection of input documents is batched, and the batches keyed in and stored on disk.

4. A transaction file held on tape is validated, with valid transactions being copied to a disk file and an error report produced which gives details of invalid transactions.

5. A customer order is keyed in and the stock master file checked to ascertain whether sufficient stock is available. The customer order is stored on an indexed customer order file.

6. Electricity bill payments are read by an OCR device and stored on disk. These transactions are then used to update the indexed customer master file.

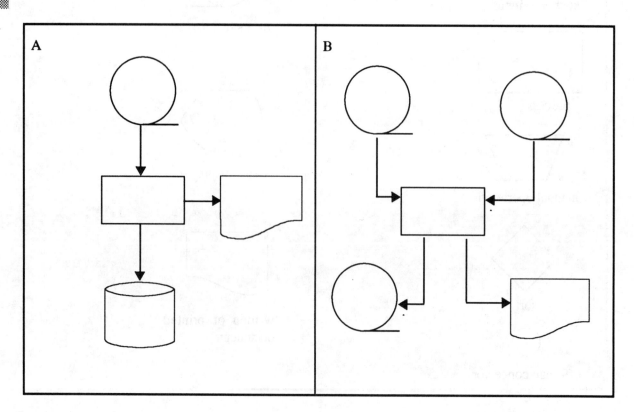

C

D

E

F

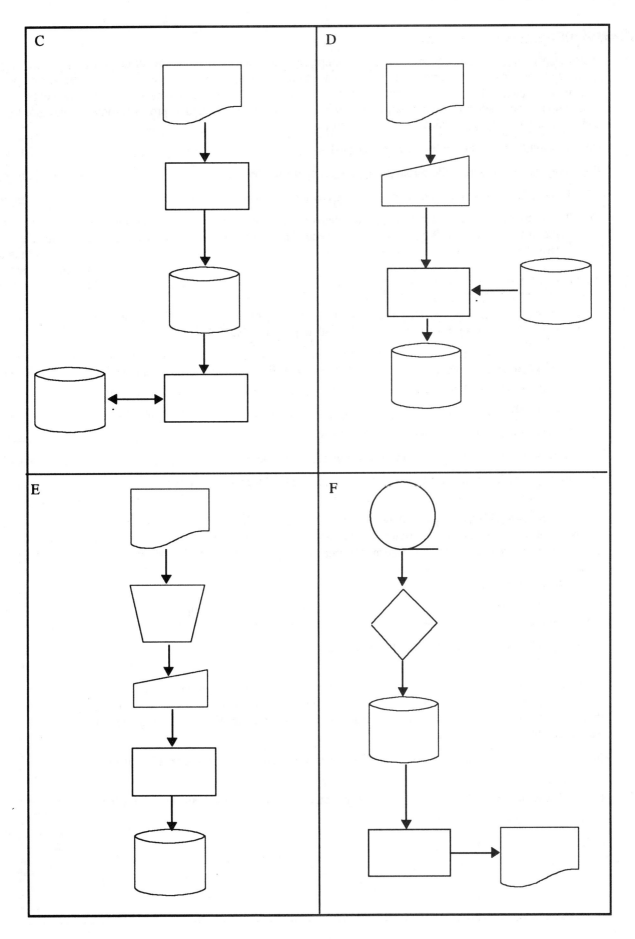

Exercises:

1. A stock master file stored in sequence order of a numeric key is updated by a transaction file using sequential file access. Transaction records, which represent additions and deletions to the stock levels, are collected in batches over a period of time and validated before being sorted into key order. Invalid data is corrected and entered into the next batch of transactions. The ordered transactions are used to update the master file. The update process produces a new master file and a file of all changes to records, for audit purposes.

    (a)   Explain the meanings of the terms underlined.   (3 marks)

    (b)   Why is the transaction file sorted prior to updating the master file?   (2 marks)

    (c)   Draw a data flow diagram, or a systems flow chart, of the system described.   (7 marks)

    (d)   The audit file contains the before and after quantities in stock corresponding to each transaction and monetary value of the transaction. What information is needed in the transaction and master files to derive the audit file information?   (3 marks)

    AEB Sample Paper 1990

2. A sports complex consists of the following:

    5 soccer pitches, 4 squash courts, 4 tennis courts, a multi-gym for up to eight persons, a large sports hall which may be used as four badminton courts or as a five-a-side football pitch or a basketball court.

    Members of the complex may book any facility for an hour up to seven days in advance while non-members may book up to three days in advance. The manager of the complex is considering using an on-line microcomputer system to control the bookings for the activities.

    (a)   Describe the files which would be required and describe how each would be organised.   (4 marks)

    (b)   Draw a systems flowchart for the on-line system.   (4 marks)

    (c)   Describe suitable data entry procedures for this application.   (4 marks)

    (d)   Briefly describe three reports that might be generated by the computer system.   (3 marks)

    London Paper 1 June 1990

3. A firm of specialist cleaners employs staff who are on 24 hour call. Once a job has been completed the staff have to fill in a job sheet which includes information on the duration of the job and details of the amounts of cleaning material used. These sheets are eventually returned to the main office and are used as the basis of transactions to update a direct access stock file. The data on the sheets is also added to the weekly serial transaction file. All data is entered via the keyboard under program control using a predefined screen format.

    Each week this transaction file undergoes further validation and is then used to prepare invoices for the work done. The preparation of invoices requires access to a customer file held as a direct access file by customer reference number.

    Draw a system flowchart to reflect the data processing described above.   (8 marks)

    London Paper 2 June 1989

4.*   A firm assigns a unique 'works number' to each of its employees. The master payroll file is held on magnetic tape in works number order. Each week the master file is brought up to date by adding the details of new employees, deleting the records of employees who have left the firm and amending the records of any employee whose details have changed. This updating is done in batch mode.

    (a)   Draw a systems flowchart for this updating process, from data entry to the creation of a new master file.   (6 marks)

    (b)   What error checks should be included at each stage and what actions should be taken when errors are detected?   (6 marks)

    JMB Paper 1 1992

Unit 38 — Data Flow Diagrams

Nature of a data flow diagram

As an alternative to systems flowcharts, another more recent way of representing a system is by means of a **data flow diagram**. This type of diagram shows how the data moves through the system, and what data stores are used. It does not define what type of data storage is used, or how the data is stored. This type of detail can be determined at a later stage.

Symbols used

Only four basic symbols are used, as shown below.

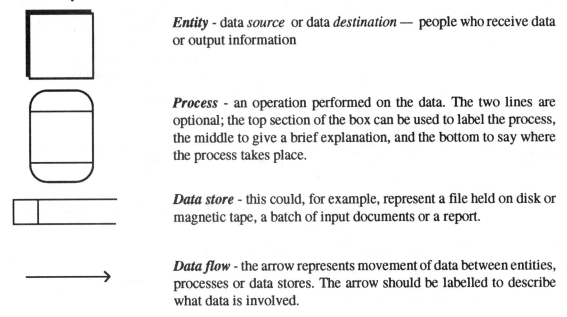

Entity - data *source* or data *destination* — people who receive data or output information

Process - an operation performed on the data. The two lines are optional; the top section of the box can be used to label the process, the middle to give a brief explanation, and the bottom to say where the process takes place.

Data store - this could, for example, represent a file held on disk or magnetic tape, a batch of input documents or a report.

Data flow - the arrow represents movement of data between entities, processes or data stores. The arrow should be labelled to describe what data is involved.

When drawing data flow diagrams, you should stick to the following conventions:

* do not draw data flow lines directly between **data stores** and **external entities**; there should be a process box between them to show the operation performed

* label the data flow lines so that it is clear what data is being transferred.

Example: The payroll system in a certain company may be described as follows:

At the end of each week time sheets are collected and sent to the computer centre. There, the payroll data is entered via a key-to-disk system, verified and validated, producing a new file of valid transactions on disk and an error report. This file is used to update the employee master file, and cheques and payslips are printed. A payroll summary is also printed for the Accounts Department.

Draw a data flow diagram to represent this system.

Solution: Note that different **levels** of data flow diagram are often used. A 'top level' diagram could be drawn as follows:

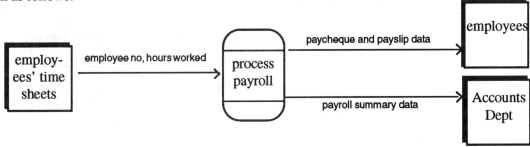

The above diagram can be broken down into greater detail:

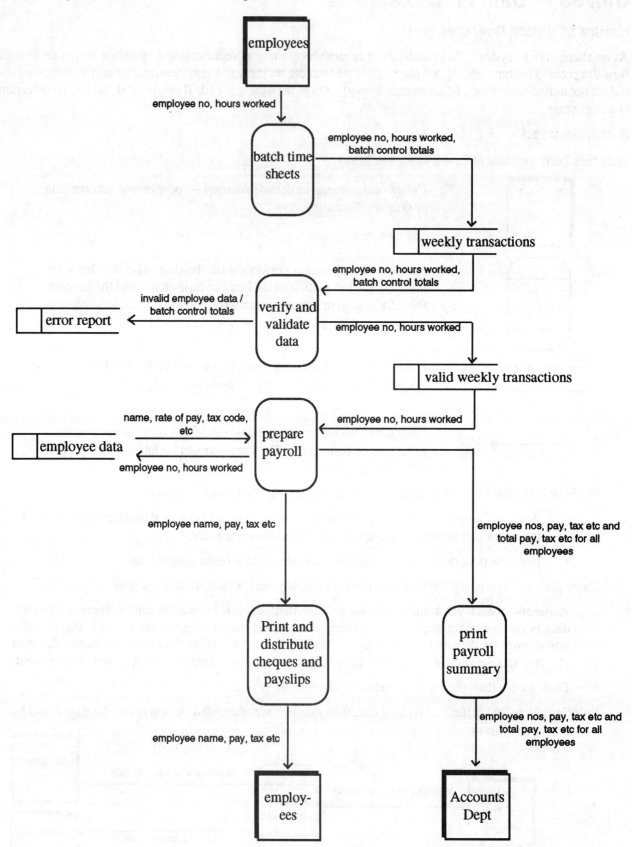

Exercises:

1. A company manufactures and markets screws. The company is considering computerising some of its activities. The departments listed below, with their functions, could benefit from computerisation.

Department	Functions
Ordering	Maintain stock of raw materials.
Production	Arrange production of screws according to known requirements and forecasts; ensure labour and machinery are available.
Sales	Receive orders; make forecasts and market screws.
Dispatch	Make up and send out orders received.
Accounts	Process company's financial transactions.
Planning	Devise possible future developments.

(a) Describe, with the aid of a diagram, the data flow in to and out of the departments, being careful to indicate the direction of flow. (7 marks)

(b) Describe *four* tasks within the departments of the company in which a computer system could usefully be involved. (8 marks)

London Paper 1 June 1989

2. A school is considering implementing a software package to assist in the clerical aspects of producing its timetable. It is intended that the software will check a proposed timetable to identify clashes and, when all clashes have been removed, will print timetables in appropriate formats. This will include the full timetable for the school and individual timetables for each teacher (showing which classes are taught, when and where) and for each room (showing which class and teacher are using that room in each of the 40 periods of the week). Class timetables and timetables for specialist groups within the fourth, fifth and sixth forms will also be needed.

(a) Describe the data which would be needed and how it could be organised in the package. (8 marks)

(b) Discuss how the package could be designed as a collection of modules and how each module would interrelate with the other modules. (6 marks)

(c) Indicate clearly the flow of data from input to output throughout the system. (5 marks)

UCLES Paper 2 May 1990

3. Data flow diagramming is a standard technique used in systems analysis for specifying a system at the logical level. The data flow diagram (DFD) is a graphical representation of a system, and is composed of four elements. State the name and purpose of each of these four elements. (4 marks)

NISEAC Paper 2 June 1990

4.* A large supermarket operates a number of point-of-sale terminals where product details are read from bar codes on the packets and details of non-standard items have to be entered from a keyboard. The price is read from disk and then the product description, quantity, price and amount are printed on the till receipt. The details of the transaction are stored on disk. Specify, diagrammatically or otherwise, the links between the parts of the system in terms of control and the flow of data. (5 marks)

London Paper 1 1991

5.* An Estate Agent has a computerised system which has two files which are referenced and updated by the staff at the Agents. The PROPERTY file stores details about houses, flats etc which are available for sale or rent. The CUSTOMER file stores details about customers who are looking for a property. Prospective buyers are able to use a computer terminal in the Estate Agent's office, if they wish, to browse through the information on properties, and they also receive details through the post from time to time when a new property becomes available.

Draw a labelled diagram showing how information flows between:

vendor (the person who is selling/renting the property)

estate agent

customer

computer (6 marks)

6.* An investigation into the sales and dispatching part of a firm has shown that documentation within that part of the firm flows along certain paths.

A customer sends an order to the sales department. The sales department acknowledges the receipt of the order and raises an internal order form which it sends to the warehouse.

A set of dispatch instructions are sent from the warehouse to the dispatch department who also send a copy to accounts.

Accounts send an invoice to the customer.

The accounts department has a computer sales ledger which receives copy invoices and sends summary financial statements about customers to accounts and also sales summary statements to customers.

Accounts also send notification of current credit limits to the sales department.

Draw a diagram which shows the flow of documents between customers and the firm and between the various departments of the firm. (10 marks)

ACCA Level 1, Business Maths and IT June 1992

7. A manufacturer uses an **on-line computer system** in the running of its buiness. This system maintains four **master files** - a Salesperson file, a Stock file, a Supplier/Price file and a Customer file - all **indexed sequentially** on an appropriate **key**.

(a) Explain clearly what is meant by each of the **four** terms printed in **bold**. (4 marks)

(b) For each of the master files describe **four** fields you would expect to find in the file, indicating clearly which field will be the key field in each case. (4 marks)

(c) When an order is placed the salesperson involved fills out an order form. This form is forwarded to the Sales Office where the order details are keyed in and verified before being validated and processed using the four master files.

    (i) Design a form which could be used by the salesperson to record a firm order. (4 marks)

    (ii) Explain the purpose of data validation and describe **two** different validation checks which might be performed in this case. (4 marks)

    (iii) Represent, by means of a data flow diagram, the way in which a sales order is processed. (4 marks)

    (iv) Design, in outline, an algorithm to show the validation and processing of a single order against the four master files. (10 marks)

NISEAC Paper 1 1992

Unit 39 — System Design and Development

Systems specification

The systems specification must describe how the new system will work. Screen layouts and report formats must be designed, file contents and organisation specified, and each program in the system must be described by means of program specifications, structure charts, pseudocode or flowcharts.

The programmers must then code, test and debug all the programs in the system. In smaller organisations the roles of programmer and analyst may overlap, and in some cases the 'analyst/programmer' may design, code and test the programs.

The 'tools' of the analyst

A tool could be described as something which helps someone to do his job better, faster or more easily. In the case of systems analysis, the tools will help the analyst to

- communicate his ideas more effectively to users and colleagues so as to make sure no misunderstandings arise
- clarify his own ideas and aid in the design of the new system.

Systems flowcharts and data flow diagrams could therefore be described as 'tools' in this sense. **Prototyping**, described below, is a useful tool for both the analyst and programmer.

Prototyping

As in any other context, prototyping means building a working model of a new system in order to evaluate it, test it or have it approved before building the final product. When applied to computer systems, this could involve, for example, using special software to quickly design input screens and run a program (supplied as part of the prototyping package) to input and validate data using the screen format just created. This gives the user a chance to experience the 'look and feel' of the input process and to suggest alterations before going any further.

Some organisations will use prototyping in the analysis stage, others in the design phase. Others may use it almost exclusively, going directly from preliminary investigation, via the prototype, to an implemented system. The analysts or programmers will simply keep refining the prototype until the user says it is acceptable.

Q1: What are the advantages and disadvantages of using prototyping as a tool of systems analysis and design?

Applications generator

Applications generators are software tools which can be used to create complete systems. The user describes the input, output, data and files, and what needs to be done. The applications generator then uses this information to generate a program or suite of programs.

Report generator

This is a useful tool, used to generate reports from information supplied by the user. An example of a report generator is found in dBase III+, which has the capability to generate and store report formats from the menu system. The user simply has to specify the headings, the fields to be printed, the order of the fields, how much space to allow for each and whether totals are required and so on. The program code is then automatically generated.

CASE (Computer-Aided Software Engineering) tools

It has come to be recognised that the design and development of a substantial computer system has much in common with the design and implementation of an engineering project, say for example building a bridge, or on an even larger scale, the Channel Tunnel. A detailed study of user requirements, meticulous planning, rigorous testing and tight control over all aspects of design and implementation are essential prerequisites of success in software projects as well as engineering projects.

A CASE tool refers to any software tool used in the design and development of a system. Special CASE software 'toolkits' can be purchased and would normally contain

- a **graphics tool** specifically designed to aid the drawing of data flow diagrams, system flowcharts and entity-relationship models.

- an **interface generator** to allow the speedy prototyping of screen dialogues, menus and reports.

- a **source code generator** which will generate the source code from a system specification into the source code of the chosen computer language. (It will generally be impossible to generate **all** the code automatically; some will have to be manually coded.)

- a **data dictionary** development tool; this is particularly important in the development of database systems.

- a **project management** tool to allow the scheduling of all activities such as analysis, design, programming and testing, and the allocation of resources such as people and equipment to the project.

The role of applications packages

In some circumstances it may not be necessary to write programs for a new system, if a suitable package exists. In this case the analyst's task will be to evaluate likely packages and ensure that the one chosen is capable of performing the required task.

Q2: What steps could a systems analyst take to find a package suited to the requirements of an organisation?

Choice of processing method

The systems designer will have to decide whether batch processing or on-line processing will be most suitable. This wll depend on such factors as

- how frequently the data changes; is it necessary for data to be completely up-to-date?

- the volume of data input; batch is well suited to large data volumes

- the cost of hardware; on-line systems can be more expensive

- what type of data collection/data preparation facilities will be used

Choice of hardware

The choice of hardware may depend on many factors, including:

- the volume of data

- the number of users

- the location of the users — are they all in one office or spread around the country?

- the type of user — is this a system to be used by the general public, or by technical specialists?

- the nature of the system — batch or on-line

- the hardware currently in use

- security considerations

- the software. In particular, where a software package is to be used, this often dictates the choice of hardware, or at any rate narrows the choice.

Summary: choosing a software solution

Many different solutions to a particular problem will have been looked at before a particular solution is chosen. The criteria on which the the final choice is based will include:

- **usability** — will the users find the system easy to use, will it save them time, cut out tedious repetitive tasks, give them quick access to information they need, or help them in some way? Or will it just give them extra work with no obvious benefits, or produce mountains of paperwork from which it is hard to extract useful information?

- **performance** — will the system function in the way that was intended? Or will it suffer from 'bugs', slow access times when retrieving data from a database, screens that take minutes to change or redraw after a command is typed, hardware that is unreliable?

- **suitability** — does the system really provide a solution to the problem, or was it considered because for example it was the 'cheapest' solution? Will it integrate with existing software, can current manual methods be adapted for the new system?

- **maintainability** — will the system be easy to upgrade the system, add new functionality, make modifications when required?

Figure 39.1 - Is system performance satisfactory?

Exercises:

1. State <u>two</u> advantages and <u>two</u> disadvantages to a company of using application packages bought from an external supplier compared with using internally produced software. (4 marks)

   AEB Sample paper 1989

2. A software house has decided to develop a general software package for theatre bookings. It will consist of a number of interrelated modules. Outline the separate stages that have to be performed, before a working package is ready for demonstration. (8 marks)

   UCLES Paper 2 May 1989

3. Frequently systems development is considered to be a process with a series of stages as shown below:

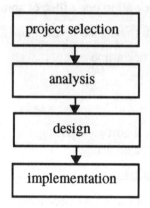

   (a) Describe what happens during the analysis, design and implementation stages. (6 marks)

   (b) Explain why this may be a poor model of the actual process. (2 marks)

   (c) Draw a diagram which better reflects the nature of traditional systems development. (3 marks)

   (d) Outline *two* decisions which must be taken by the project control group. (4 marks)

   London Paper 1 June 1989

4. A builder has formed a partnership with a variety of local tradesmen such as painters, electricians, plumbers and carpenters. In order to expand their business in the area they have decided to offer the residents a contract for regular household maintenance. They are considering using a computer system to help them manage these activities.

   Discuss the various ways in which a computer system could be of use to the partnership, and the types of facilities which would be needed. You should consider

       (i) the input which would be needed and the form of the output which would be useful,

       (ii) the types of hardware needed,

       (iii) the organisation of the data to be held within the system. (15 marks)

   UCLES Paper 1 May 1990

5.* A business is considering computerising the sales accounts of its customers. The system is required to record details of new sales and payments of invoices. In particular the business is considering whether the system should use *batch* or *on-line processing*.

   (i) Distinguish between batch and on-line processing. (2 marks)

   (ii) Describe **four** factors which will be considered when choosing the processing method. (8 marks)

   (iii) Describe **three** checks which should be made to make certain that when payments are received, the account is correctly updated. (6 marks)

   (iv) Describe **two** steps necessary to protect against the consequences of disk failure. Explain and justify how often these should be taken. (4 marks)

   AEB Paper 2 1992

Unit 40 — System Implementation and Maintenance

This is the stage in the systems life cycle when people actually begin to use a new system. There are several tasks to be faced before the changeover is complete.

Installing the hardware

Before a new system can be put into operation, any new hardware will have to be installed. Even if it is only a matter of bringing in a couple of new PCs, this may mean changing office layouts, rewiring, acquiring new office furniture and moving personnel. In the case of a new mainframe, it will probably involve putting in a false floor in a specially designed computer room, laying cables and installing air-conditioning.

Training and education

Everyone involved with a new system will need to be given training in their new role, or in the use of new hardware and software. They will need to have hands-on practice with realistic data before the system goes live.

Creation of master files

Data for all master files will have to be entered before the new system can be used. This usually takes place in two phases: the 'standing data' can be typed in over a few days or weeks, and the rest of the data immediately before the changeover takes place.

Q1: In a new stock control system, what data could be entered in advance on the stock master file?

Q2: What data will need to be entered immediately before the system goes live?

Methods of conversion

There are several choices when converting from an old system to a new one:

Direct changeover. The user stops using the old system one day and starts using the new system the next — usually over a weekend or during a slack period. The advantage of this system is that it is fast and efficient, with minimum duplication of work involved. The disadvantage is that normal operations could be seriously disrupted if the new system has errors in it or does not work quite as expected.

Parallel conversion. The old system continues alongside the new system for a few weeks or months. The advantage is that results from the new system can be checked against known results, and if any difficulties occur, operations can continue under the old system while the errors or omissions are sorted out. The disadvantage of parallel running is the duplication of effort required to keep both systems running, which may put a strain on personnel.

Phased conversion. This is used with larger systems that can be broken down into individual modules that can be implemented separately at different times. It could also be used where for example only a few customer accounts are processed using the new system, while the rest remain for a time on the old system. Phased conversion could be direct or parallel.

Pilot conversion. This means that the new system will be used first by only a portion of the organization, for example at one branch or factory.

Q3: For each of the following examples, state with reasons what type of conversion method would be suitable.

(a) A bakery is introducing a system to input orders from each salesman and use this data to calculate how much of each product to bake each day, and also to calculate the salesmens' commission.

(b) A chain store is introducing EPOS terminals connected to a mainframe computer which holds details of stock levels and prices.

(c) A public library is introducing a computerised system for the lending and return of books.

(d) A large hospital is introducing a computerised system for keeping patient records and appointments.

(e) A College is introducing a computerised timetabling and room allocation system.

(f) A company manufacturing electronic components is introducing an integrated system for production control, stock control and order processing.

(g) A Local Authority is introducing a computerised system for the collection of a new type of tax.

Post implementation review

An important part of the implementation is a review of how the new system is performing, once it has been up and running for a period of time. Minor programming errors may have to be corrected, clerical procedures amended, or modifications made to the design of reports or screen layouts. Often it is only when people start to use a new system that they realise its shortcomings! In some cases they may realise that it would be possible to get even more useful information from the system than they realised, and more programs may be requested. The process of **system maintenance**, in fact, has already begun, and the life cycle is complete.

System maintenance

All software systems require maintenance, and in fact the vast majority of programmers are employed to maintain existing programs rather than to write new ones. There are differing reasons for this, and different types of maintenance.

- **perfective maintenance**. This implies that while the system runs satisfactorily, there is still room for improvement. For example, extra management information may be needed so that new report programs have to be written. Database queries may be very slow, and a change in a program may be able to improve response time.

- **adaptive maintenance**. All systems will need to adapt to changing needs within a company. As a business expands, for example, there may be a requirement to convert a standalone system to a multi-user system. New and better hardware may become available, and changes to the software may be necessary to take advantage of this. New government legislation may mean that different methods of calculating tax, for example, are required. Competition from other firms may mean that systems have to be upgraded in order to maintain a competitive edge.

- **corrective maintenance**. Problems frequently surface after a system has been in use for a short time, however thoroughly it was tested. Some part of the system may not function as expected, or a report might be wrong in some way; totals missing at the bottom, incorrect sequence of data, wrong headings, etc. Frequently errors will be hard to trace, if for example a file appears to have been wrongly updated.

Exercises:

1. Distinguish between the terms 'software maintenance' and 'file maintenance', and for each give one example of an event that would necessitate the maintenance having to be carried out. (6 marks)
NISEAC Paper 1 June 1989

2. In the software life cycle, 'maintenance' falls into three categories, which have been described as

— Perfective maintenance

— Adaptive maintenance

— Corrective maintenance.

Suggest a meaning for *each* of these categories. (6 marks)
JMB Paper 1 1990

3. A retailing company dealing mainly with specialised DIY products has a small number of shops, and a warehouse, situated within a large town. A recent dramatic growth in trade has led the management to review its current practices for maintaining stock and re-ordering goods, with the intention of computerising the system.

A systems analyst is called in to examine the problems and to recommend a solution. The scope of the project is to be limited to stock handling and to the introduction of methods to streamline customer payments.

(a) Describe the ways in which the analyst will set about gathering and recording the necessary information. (3 marks)

(b) After the initial stages some of the problems have been identified as

— products frequently out of stock

— very little inter-store communication about stock items

— store managers have no information about stock on a day-to-day basis

— ordering is done haphazardly.

(c) What *other* information will the analyst need to know before proceeding to the design phase? (4 marks)

(d) Describe, with reasons, what you feel might be a realistic solution in terms of hardware, software, security, implementation and maintenance.

How could the new system be evaluated? (8 marks)
London Specimen Paper 2 1989

Unit 41 — System Documentation

The aims of system documentation

Both systems analysts and programmers are responsible for maintaining standards and documentation on a project. The aims of documentation are:

- To help in the design of the system by working to a set of standards and having available a clear description of the work done so far. The documentation needs to be kept up-to-date throughout the project.

- Good documentation ensures that everyone involved in the system (systems designers, programmers, and users) fully understands how their aspect of the system will work; for example, what data will be input and how, and what information will be available from the system. This allows for any misunderstandings or disagreements to surface before they become deeply entrenched in the system.

- To ensure that the system can be maintained after completion of the system. All too often changes of staff within a company mean that no-one who was involved in the original design or programming of a system is still with the company. It is essential that proper documentation is kept to enable a newcomer to make necessary corrections, alterations or enhancements.

Contents of a documented system

- An accurate and up-to-date systems specification.

- Systems flow chart(s) or Data Flow Diagrams showing the inputs to the system, files required, processes to be carried out, and output from the system.

- A description of the purpose of each program within the system.

- A structure diagram, flowchart or pseudocode for each program in the system.

- Organisation, contents and layout of each file used.

- Layout and contents of all output prints and displays.

- Current version of each program listing.

- Test data and expected results.

In addition, the following items of documentation will need to be prepared:

(a) **A Clerical Procedures Manual**

This details the activities that clerical staff will undertake in preparing data for input to the system, for example batching documents and calculating hash totals. It will also describe what action is to be taken when errors occur — for example when a validation program reports errors.

(b) **Operating instructions**

This gives details to the computer operators of how to run the programs. It may include:

- details of the procedure for starting the program

- details of disks or tapes required

- special stationery to be used

- the number of copies of each report, and who is to receive the output

- backup procedures to be followed

- recovery procedures in the event of hardware failure.

(c) **Data preparation instructions**

This will contain instructions on data entry, showing if necessary how each field should be entered. For example a date field may be entered in various different formats and the correct one needs to be specified.

Documentation for a software package

Documentation for a software package is often divided into two or three separate sections, each perhaps comprising an entire manual. There could be, for example, a **user manual**, describing the various functions that the software performs, what various menu options mean, the format of input, reports that can be printed. The **operations manual** or **technical manual** may give details of how to install the software, the minimum hardware configuration required, how to install a printer to print from the software, and may also give a trouble-shooting guide and a help-line telephone number. A **tutorial manual** may also be included to help users to learn how to use the software.

Exercises:

1. (a) Why do software projects require documentation? Suggest two reasons.

    (b) Name three different documents associated with software projects and describe briefly their specific function.
    (5 marks)
    AEB Paper 2 1989

2. A computerised library system allows books to be borrowed for a set period of time, and borrowers can reserve books, which are out on loan, to be held for them when they are returned. Describe briefly what items of information you would expect to find in the documentation for the library staff. (5 marks)
    UCLES Paper 1 May 1989

3. The information centre of a large organisation has a computerised loan and return system for its books, manuals, journals, tapes etc. However the catalogue for each category still exists as a number of separate card index files. It has been decided to computerise these catalogues to provide users with a single centralised catalogue which can be queried simultaneously by a number of users. The current computer system is not powerful enough to cope with this additional task. A firm of analysts is called in to recommend the steps to be taken and to supervise the transition process.

    (a) What are the likely problems involved in transferring these manual files onto disk? Suggest how these problems could be overcome. (5 marks)

    (b) Why is it important for the analysts to provide documentation for the new system even though it is running satisfactorily?

    Why are professional bodies within the computing industry keen to support documentation standards?

    Outline the content of the documentation that should be given to the staff who use the system at the information centre. (7 marks)

    (c) What changeover method do you think is appropriate in this case? Justify your choice. (3 marks)
    London Paper 2 June 1990

4.* Describe **three** of the features of a software package's operation manual. (3 marks)
    AEB Paper 2 1992

5.* (a) Give **three** items of documentation that you would expect to be included in an applications package.
    (3 marks)

    (b) Give one item of documentation that you would **not** normally expect to be supplied as part of an application package. Justify your answer. (2 marks)
    JMB Paper 1 1992

Unit 42 — Data Security and Integrity

Data integrity

This refers to the **correctness** of the data. The data held in a computer system may become incorrect, corrupted or of 'poor quality' in many different ways and at many stages during data processing.

1. Errors on input. Data that is keyed in may be wrongly transcribed. A batch of transaction data could go astray, or be keyed in twice by mistake.

2. Errors in operating procedure. An update program could for example be run twice in error and quantities on a master file would then be updated twice. Another example might be where the wrong generation of master file was used in processing.

3. Program errors could lead to corruption of files. A new system may have errors in it that will not surface for some time; and errors may be introduced during program maintenance. During modification code may deliberately be inserted for criminal purposes.

4. Errors in data transmission. Interference or **noise** in a communications line may cause bits to be wrongly received. This type of error is usually detected by transmitting a **parity bit** with the code for each character, and other error-checking data such as a **checksum** with each block of data.

5. If master files are not regularly updated the data may simply become out of date — for example, a database of patients at a doctor's surgery will rapidly become inaccurate if it is not regularly updated with new patients arriving, other patients leaving, and other data changing.

Q1: Describe what action can be taken to minimize the loss of data integrity in (1) and (2) above.

Parity checks

A parity bit is an extra bit added to the character code, and set to 0 or 1 so that the total number of 1s in the code is either even, for even parity, or odd, for odd parity. Parity checks are usually used to determine whether the parity of a data item is correct when it is being sent to or from an input, output or storage device, or being sent over a communications line. Odd parity will detect the failure of a transmission line, because all the bits will then be zero.

Note that the character code, including the parity bit, is an example of a **self checking code**.

Q2: Add a parity bit to the start of each of the following codes to maintain odd parity:

110101 001101

Checksum

All the bytes or words in a packet of data may be added together (ignoring overflow) and transmitted with the data. This will then be checked by the receiving device.

Data security

Maintaining data security means keeping data safe from the various hazards to which it may be subjected. These include:

- natural hazards such as fire, floods, hurricanes or earthquakes
- deliberate corruption or destruction of data by malicious or terrorist acts
- illegal access to data by 'hackers'
- accidental destruction of data by hardware failure or program or operator error.

Q3: Suggest measures to minimize the danger of loss of data from natural hazards.

Keeping data secure from fraudulent use or malicious damage

Data may be at risk not only from outside 'hackers' but from employees within the company. Organisations are often exposed to the possibility of fraud, deliberate corruption of data by disgruntled employees or theft of software or data which may fall into the hands of competitors. Measures to counteract these risks include the following:

- careful vetting of prospective employees
- immediate removal of employees who have been sacked or who hand in their resignation, and cancellation of all passwords and authorisations
- 'separation of duties'; ie trying to ensure that it would take the collusion of two or more employees to be able to defraud the company. The functions of data preparation, computer operations and other jobs should be separate, with no overlap of responsibility
- prevention of unauthorised access by employees and others to secure areas such as computer operations rooms, by means of machine readable cards or badges or other types of locks.
- the use of passwords to gain access to the computer system from terminals
- educating staff to be aware of possible breaches of security, and to be alert in preventing them or reporting them. This can include politely challenging strangers with a "May I help you?" approach, not leaving output lying around, machines logged on, or doors unlocked.
- appointing a security manager and using special software which can monitor all terminal activity. Such software can enable the security manager to see, either with or without users' knowledge, everything being typed on any screen in a network. It will also record statistics such as number of logins at each terminal, hours of login time, number of times particular programs or databases were accessed and so on. It will even log the security manager's activities!

Password protection

Most password schemes use tables to store the current password for each authorised user. These tables will be stored on disk and will be backed up along with other vital system files, and in addition may be printed out in a dump of system files. For this reason password lists should not be stored in plain form but should be **encrypted**, and held in an irreversibly transformed state.

Q4: If the encrypted passwords cannot be decoded, how will the system be able to compare a password entered by the user with the coded password held in the password table?

Q5: What happens if the user forgets his password?

When a user types a password at a keyboard, the password is usually concealed in some way, for example by not echoing it on the screen. However, it can still be observed by wire-tapping. Passwords can be protected during transmission by encrypting them, but this is costly.

Q6: Describe briefly another way in which a user's password may be detected by an observer.

Data encryption

The basic idea in cryptography is to take a message in ordinary language, called **plaintext**, and transform it in some way to produce **ciphertext**, which is sent along a communications link. The receiving computer uses another transformation to decode the message.

Classical ciphers use transposition or substitution. In a transposition cipher the letters are rearranged. The message might be written in a grid row by row, and read out column by column.

For example, the sentence "MEET ME TONIGHT AT 8" could be written in a 5 x 4 grid

```
M   E   E   T   •
M   E   •   T   O
N   I   G   H   T
•   A   T   •   8
```

and sent out as MMN•EEIAE•GTTTH••OT8

Q7: Decode the following message using the same grid:LCOLIE••CDK•E•I•NTL•

In a substitution cipher another symbol replaces each plaintext symbol in the ciphertext.

Q8: Decode the following message: X2MM F4P2

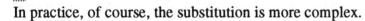

In practice, of course, the substitution is more complex.

Exercises:

1. Describe briefly THREE different kinds of error which may occur due to the INPUT of faulty data.

    (3 marks)
    AEB Paper 2 1989

2. "Information stored in a typical computer system is more secure than information stored in a typical manual filing system".

    Give TWO points in support of this statement and TWO points against. (4 marks)
    AEB Paper 2 1989

3. Read the following scenario and suggest measures that could be taken to improve the security of the computer system.

    A Computer Science student has a temporary job in a large corporation during the summer vacation. One lunchtime while wandering in an unfamiliar part of the building he comes across an unattended terminal in an open-plan office. He is ignored by the only other person in the office, so he sits down and from output lying on the desk obtains the user code for signing on. The system asks for a password and he runs through a list of commonly used passwords (which he obtained from a "Hackers' Bulletin Board"), such as GOD, SEX, SECRET, FRED, GENIUS. After 73 attempts he discovers the correct password, PIGLET. He is then presented with a menu and selects a Database option, and is asked if he would like to Add, Change, Delete or View. He browses through the database for a while and then adds a fictitious record for Mickey Mouse before going off to lunch.

4. When files of data are stored on computer systems there are problems of:

    (i)   users accessing the system and corrupting the data accidentally

    (ii) unauthorised users deliberately corrupting data

    Describe briefly how each of these problems can be minimised. (6 marks)
    London Specimen Paper 1 1989

5. What do you understand by the term data encryption? When might such a technique be used? (2 marks)
    London Specimen Paper 2 1989

6.* Errors in a computer system may arise from

    (i)   hardware faults,

    (ii) operator incompetence or user ignorance,

    (iii) 'bugs' in the software.

    Describe ways of avoiding each of these types of error. (6 marks)
    London 1992 Paper 1

7.* A company has a network of workstations which allows employees to access data held on a central computer. The data is allocated into one of three categories:

    CATEGORY A -   unclassified eg circulation lists

    CATEGORY B -   confidential eg personal data

    CATEGORY C -   company secrets eg business plans

    Describe a security system that would ensure that the data would be protected from unauthorised access

    (i)   at a workstation

    (ii) in the computer room (6 marks)
    London Paper 1 1992

Unit 43 — Backup and Recovery

Introduction

No matter what precautions are taken against fire, flood, power surges, and deliberate or accidental destruction of data, the possibility always exists that data will be destroyed. A simple disk head crash can destroy a disk pack in a fraction of a second. System designers must provide a reasonable backup facility that does not degrade the performance of the system and does not cost too much.

The cost of lack of planning for computer failure can be ruinous. IBM estimates that 70% of organisations that experience a failure (caused by fire, flood, power failure, malice etc) cease operating within 18 months. The main consequence of a computer failure is loss of business, but other problems include loss of credibility, cashflow interruptions, poorer service to customers and loss of production.

Periodic backups

The most common technique used to ensure that data is not lost is to make **periodic backups**, by copying files regularly and keeping them in a safe place. This scheme has several weaknesses:

- all updates to a file since the last backup may be lost
- the system may need to be shut down during backup operations
- backups of large files can be extremely time-consuming
- when a failure occurs, recovery from the backup can be even more time-consuming

A **benefit** of periodic backups is that files which may have become fragmented by additions and deletions can be reorganised to occupy contiguous space, usually resulting in much faster access time.

An important feature of all backup systems is the safe storage of the backup copies: it is usually necessary to store one backup copy in a fire-proof safe in the building, and another copy off-site.

File generations

In the case of sequential file processing, using the 'grandfather-father-son' technique, the previous generation of the master file is always kept as a backup copy, along with the transactions that were used in the update process. Then, if the current master file is destroyed, the situation can be recovered by running last period's master file with the corresponding transactions.

Incremental dumping

Periodic backup of files is not sufficient in systems in which recovery needs to occur quickly and be up to the minute. A more appropriate technique is called **incremental dumping**. During a terminal session, all updated files are marked. When a user logs out, these files are automatically 'dumped' or copied to another disk. In some systems the file directories may be searched even while a user is logged on and modified files dumped more frequently.

Even with incremental dumping, there may be significant activity between the time of the last backup and the time at which a failure occurs. In systems where any loss of transactions would be unacceptable, **transaction logging** may be used. Here, every transaction is backed up as it occurs so that complete recovery can be effected.

Bypass procedures

An on-line system such as a library system for borrowing and returning books, or a banking system, must be able to continue to function even if the main computer fails.

One method is to have intelligent terminals with their own disk storage so that transactions can be stored temporarily and rapidly transmitted to the computer once it is back on-line.

In a real-time banking system, the clerk is allowed to accept withdrawals up to a certain predetermined amount if the computer goes down. In order to give some indication of the customer's current balance, the closing balances are transmitted to each branch during the night, and then printed out at the branches.

Data compaction

It is often useful when backing up from a hard disk to be able to store as much data as possible on the backup medium, such as floppy disk or tape. In MS DOS, all storage devices are defined in terms of **clusters** of fixed length sectors. The sector is always 512 bytes and there may be 1, 2 or 4 sectors per cluster. Hence for every file stored, there will be on average about half a cluster of wasted space.The BACKUP utility program **compacts** the files into a single data file per floppy disk. To use the backup files, a utility program called RESTORE has to be run which restores the data into its individual files.

Data compression

Another technique for saving space when making backup files is called **data compression**. One method of doing this is to use a variable number of bits for each character, with the most frequently used characters having the fewest bits. Another method is to use the '5/10 code' which uses only 5 bits for the 31 most frequently used characters. The 32nd code is used as a switch code to indicate that the following code is for one of the less frequently used characters. This means that frequent characters take 5 bits, infrequent characters 10 bits.

Another application for data compression is in communications, since compressed files are smaller and consequently are transmitted faster.

Exercises:

1. Explain the meaning of the term **incremental dump** in the context of file security. (2 marks)
   AEB Paper 2 1986

2. A bank cashier in a branch uses a terminal linked to a computer based at head office in order to find out the current balance in a customer's account.

   (a) What security checks should be made by the computer system to preserve the confidentiality of the data? (6 marks)

   (b) In order to provide a satisfactory service to customers, it is important that, wherever possible, failures in the various parts of the computer system should not prevent account enquiries from being made in this way.

      (i) Suggest what failures may occur in the system. (3 marks)

      (ii) Describe how the system might be designed so that the effect of such failures on the services provided could be minimised. (8 marks)
      UCLES Specimen AS Level Paper 1989

3. A certain hospital has a large computer system providing many interactive VDUs which are used in the wards, consulting rooms and by the hospital administration.

   (a) Discuss, with reasons, the advantages and disadvantages of such a system compared with a manual system. (8 marks)

   (b) From time to time certain parts of the computer system may fail. If on one such occasion the disk controller fails causing a master file to be corrupted with the loss of a morning's transactions, discuss the steps that could have been taken beforehand to minimise the possibility of vital information being lost. (4 marks)

   (c) Discuss the steps that may be taken to maintain the confidentiality of information in such a system. (4 marks)
   AEB Sample AS Level Paper 1989

4.* An on-line information retrieval system holds confidential personal data.

   (a) What precautions should be taken to

      (i) minimise unauthorised access

      (ii) detect unauthorised access? (4 marks)

   (b) Why might different users be given different access privileges? (2 marks)

   (c) Explain how the data should be recovered after corruption. (4 marks)
   JMB Paper 1 1992

Section 6 — Programming Languages, Compilers and Interpreters

Unit 44 — The Development of High-level Languages

High and low level languages

Computer languages may be classified as being either **low level**, (such as assembly language) or **high level** (such as Pascal, BASIC, PROLOG or 'C').

The characteristics of a **low level language** are

- they are machine oriented; an assembly language program written for one machine will not work on any other type of machine (unless it happens to use the same processor chip)

- each assembly language statement (apart from macros) generally translates into one machine code instruction. Hence, programming is a lengthy and time-consuming business.

Assembly language is generally used when there is a requirement to manipulate individual bits and bytes, write code that executes as fast as possble, or occupies as little memory as possible. An example of an application with all three of these requirements is a **device driver**; that is, a program which allows the computer to interface with an external device such as a printer. When you buy a printer to use with a PC, for example, it will come with an appropriate printer driver supplied on a floppy disk, and the driver has to be installed on the hard disk before the printer can be used.

The characteristics of a **high level language** are

- they are **not** machine oriented; in theory they are **portable** which means that a program written for one machine will run (with minor modifications) on any other machine for which the appropriate compiler or interpreter is available.

- They are **problem oriented**; each high level language has structures and facilities appropriate to a particular use or type of problem. For example FORTRAN was developed for use in solving mathematical problems, whereas COBOL was written especially for data processing applications. Some languages such as PL/1 were developed as **general purpose** languages.

- Statements in a high level language generally resemble English sentences or mathematical expressions and these languages tend to be easier to learn and understand than assembly language. Each statement in a high level language will be translated into several machine code instructions.

Q1: Why are high level languages **not** always 'portable' between different types of machine?

High level languages have many facilities not found in low level languages; for example

- selection structures such as **if .. then .. else, case.**

- iteration structures such as **while .. endwhile, repeat .. until** and **for .. endfor**. Instead of selection and iteration statements, assembly language programmers must use conditional branch statements such as **branch if equal, branch if non-zero**, etc.

- built in routines to simplify input and output (e.g. **readln, writeln** in Pascal)

- built in functions such as **sqr, log, chr**.

- data structures such as **string, record**.

Q2: What are the advantages and disadvantages to a programmer of using a general purpose language such as PL/1 instead of a special purpose language such as COBOL or FORTRAN?

Scientific languages

FORTRAN (FORmula TRANslation) was the first scientific language to be developed, and it has remained popular ever since its invention by John Backus in the 1950s. The features which make it suitable for scientific and engineering applications are listed below.

- It has a large library of inbuilt mathematical functions such as *log, sqrt, sin, arctan* etc.

- Comprehensive libraries of statistical, scientific and engineering routines are readily available, well documented and easy to incorporate into the user's program.

- Double precision arithmetic (using, say, 64 bits instead of 32 bits to represent a real number) means that calculations can be performed with great accuracy.

- Good array handling capabilities mean that it is suitable for solving, for example, large sets of simultaneous equations.

A simple FORTRAN program looks very similar to a BASIC program, and indeed BASIC was originally designed as a simplified version of FORTRAN for teaching students how to program.

```
c    a FORTRAN program to calculate the mean and standard deviation of 2 arrays
c    written by: Gerald Ratzer
     dimension a(100), b(100)
c
     read(5,10)n
 10  format(i2)
     read(5,20)(a(j),j=1,n)
 20  format(10f6.2)
c
     call stats(a,n,amean,sd)
     write(6,30)amean,sd
 30  format(' mean=',f10.3,'standard deviation=',f10.3)
     read(5,20)b
c
     call stats(b,50,bmean,bsdev)
     write(6,30)bmean,bsdev
     stop
     end
c
     subroutine stats(x,m,xmean,sd)
     dimension x(100)
     sx=0.0
     sx2=0.0
     do 7 k=1,m
     sx=sx+x(k)
 7   sx2=sx2+x(k)**2
c
     xm=m
     xmean=sx/xm
     sd=sqrt(xm*sx2-sx**2)/xm
     return
     end
```

Note that variables do not have to be declared in FORTRAN; any variable whose name begins with I-N (the first two letters of INteger) is assumed to be an integer and all other variables are assumed to be real unless specified otherwise.

Q3: How are **comments** identified in FORTRAN?

Commercial languages

The most widely used commercial language is COBOL (COmmon Business Oriented Language), which was developed in the late 1950s. It was designed to be used in data processing and therefore has capabilities which reflect the various stages through which data progresses. The table below illustrates this.

Stages of data Processing	COBOL special features
Input data	Good screen painting utilities such as 'FORMS' in Microfocus COBOL enable the programmer to quickly design input screens
Validate data	COBOL allows statements such as **if** amount **not numeric then perform** error-routine or **if** code **not alphabetic then perform** bad-code-input.
Sort data	COBOL has a **sort** verb which enables a file of data to be sorted using a single statement such as **sort** temp-file **on ascending key** employee-number **using** unsorted-file **giving** sorted-tranaction-file.
Store data on disk or tape	COBOL has excellent file handling capabilities, including in-built facilities to create and access indexed-sequential files. The programmer merely has to declare that the file is an indexed-sequential file and specify how it is to be accessed on that particular run. For example: **select** employee-file **assign to** 'a:empfile.dat' **organization is indexed** **access mode is random** **record is** employee-rec.
write and retrieve records	COBOL has a built-in record structure to enable data to be stored in fields of a record. **Databases** may also be accessed from within COBOL programs
write reports	COBOL has excellent formatting capabilities to enable reports to be laid out in exactly the required format. In addition, **report-writing utility programs** are available to speed this process.

In addition, COBOL aims to be largely self-documenting, with English-style statements, thus easing the task of program maintenance.

COBOL programs are composed of four **divisions**, which always appear in the same order:

The **Identification Division** shows the program name, who wrote it, where and when.

The **Environment Division** specifies the type of computer and peripherals used.

The **Data Division** defines all data files and variables used in the program.

The **Procedure Division** contains the program statements.

PL/1

PL/1 was developed in the 1960s by IBM, and was intended as a general purpose language combining the best features of FORTRAN and COBOL, but although it has its followers, it has generally not been hailed as the complete answer to every programmer's prayer that was originally envisaged. One reason for this is that it is so powerful and incorporates so many features that it is difficult to learn. Most programmers only need capabilities suited to their particular needs and so tend to learn a more specialised language.

Languages used in education

BASIC (Beginner's All-purpose Symbolic Instruction Code) was the first language to be developed specifically for teaching purposes. Its aims were to enable students to learn to write programs in a short time, using only a few simple statements such as **input, write, let, if, for..next** and **goto**.

Unfortunately the inclusion of the **goto** statement led to a lot of novice programmers developing bad programming habits and writing 'spaghetti' programs which are hard to follow and even harder to debug. Later versions of BASIC have encouraged a more structured approach and the language has retained its popularity.

Pascal was also developed as a teaching tool, but from the beginning was intended to encourage structured programming and demonstrate a wide range of techniques for handling data.

Q4: Do you consider Pascal a suitable language for data processing? Justify your answer.

C

C was developed by Dennis Richie at Bell Laboratories in the USA around 1972. It is a block structured language, originally developed for systems programming for the operating system UNIX. It is a relatively low-level language which has many of the advantages of Assembly language (facilitating very efficient programs for operating systems, text processing and compilers) and at the same time has the advantages of a high level language in that it is easy to learn, portable and hides the details of the computer's architecture from the user.

The following ode to C by an unknown author (quoted in the Guardian April 29 1993) fits a well known tune...

> *When I find my code in tons of trouble*
> *Friends and colleagues come to me,*
> *Speaking words of wisdom: "Write in C."*
> *As the deadline fast approaches,*
> *And bugs are all that I can see,*
> *Somewhere, someone whispers: "Write in C."*
> *Write in C, write in C,*
> *Write in C, oh, write in C,*
> *Lisp is dead and buried, write in C.*
> *I used to write a lot of Fortran,*
> *For science it worked flawlessly.*
> *Try using it for graphics! Write in C.*
> *If you've just spent nearly 30 hours*
> *Debugging some Assembly*
> *Soon you will be glad to write in C.*
> *Write in C, write in C,write in C, yeah, write in C.*
> *Only wimps use BASIC, write in C.*

Exercises:

1. In ALGOL 60 a comment starts with the reserved word **comment** and ends with the first following semi-colon (which may be several lines later).

    In ALGOL 68 a comment starts and ends with the reserved word **comment**; these reserved words may be several lines apart. Either or both instances of **comment** may be replaced with a 'cent' sign.

    In ADA a comment starts -- and continues to the end of the line.

    Describe the commenting convention of **one** other high level language with which you are familiar. Discuss the advantages and disadvantages of the commenting conventions of these three languages and the language of your choice.

    (5 marks)

    AEB Paper 2 1990

2. Indicate *three* facilities which you would expect to find in a high level language but not in a low level language.

    (6 marks)

    NISEAC Paper 2 1989

3. Some high level languages have specifications conforming to internationally agreed standards, but it is quite common for individual suppliers to provide extensions to these standards.

    Give an example of an extension to a language standard and state one advantage and one disadvantage of this practice.

    (4 marks)

    NISEAC Paper 1 1989

4.* "The self documenting nature of a high-level language can contribute to program documentation."

    Explain what is meant by the term "self-documenting" in this context, illustrating your answer with examples.

    (5 marks)

    NISEAC Paper 2 1991

Unit 45 — Specialised Languages

Introduction

This Unit looks at just two of the hundreds of programming languages in existence today. Many of these languages were designed with a particular purpose in mind, and contain features suited to a particular application. Some languages subsequently gain wider acceptance (such as 'C'), and others fade into obscurity or continue to be used by only a small minority of specialised applications (such as Forth, which is used for the control of radio telescopes and other process control and machine tool control applications).

Ada

The programming language Ada is named after Augusta Ada Byron, Countess of Lovelace and daughter of the poet Lord Byron. She was a nineteenth century mathematician, an assistant of Charles Babbage (the 'father' of computing), and is considered to have designed the first 'program' for his mechanical computers.

Ada was developed at the initiative of the US Department of Defence (DoD), beginning in 1975, with the primary purpose of producing a common, widely available language appropriate for embedded computer software. An embedded computer is one which is an integral part of some larger system such as a ship, aircraft, missile, robot or washing machine.

The DoD, which is probably the world's largest software user, divides its software into three categories. Scientific, engineering and research applications are generally programmed in FORTRAN, and management information systems and data processing applications were, in 1975, programmed in COBOL, which was considered adequate for its purpose. By far the largest class of software, and the one which accounted for almost all of its serious software problems, was the embedded computer system software, most of which is very large, very complex and very ambitious.

One problem recognised in a 1974 study was that literally hundreds of general purpose programming languages were being used to program the DoD's embedded software. It was not uncommon for a new project to start off with the development of yet another computer language, or the modification of an existing language. Much of the programming had to be done in machine code because of the need for fast execution, efficient utilisation of memory space, and more control of specialised input-output devices such as the monitoring of special sensors or other analogue devices. The software often had to deal with real-time clocks for time-critical processing.

In 1975 the DoD decided that this situation could not continue and that a standardised programming language had to be developed, with the following principal goals:

- the language was to be appropriate for the design, coding and maintenance of reliable embedded computer system software

- it was to be as far as possible machine independent ('portable')

- it was not to contain general capabilities which would not be used in embedded software

- programs written in the language had to be easy to read and maintain, but the language did not necessarily have to be easy to learn or write.

Q1: Contrast the aims of the programming languages BASIC and Ada.

Development of embedded systems

When used for programming weapon systems, development usually takes place on a **host** computer, and programs are tested under simulation conditions. The program is then transferred to the **target** computer, and embedded for example in a missile, where it must be capable of functioning without supervision and be able to recover from run-time conditions that could cause the program (and perhaps the missile!) to crash.

The Gulf war provided spectacular examples of the sophistication of modern weaponry. One journalist described watching a Cruise missile fly *around* his hotel and past his window to hit its target (a Government building) a few hundred yards away. The Patriot anti-missile missile demonstrated the effectiveness of computer-controlled defence systems, as their radar systems counted the number of incoming Scud missiles, allocated a Patriot missile to each, and decided when to blast off and what path to follow in order to intercept them.

Because so much money and effort was put into the development of Ada, it is proving to be a useful language of wide general applicability, both for scientific applications and for business data processing. It is derived from Pascal, but it is a much larger and more powerful language. A sample procedure to perform a bubble sort is shown below.

```
procedure bubble_sort(a: in out integer_vector) is
    previous, current: integer range 1..a'length;
    temp : integer;

begin
    current:=1+a'first;
    for limit in reverse current..a'last loop
        for cursor in current..limit loop
            previous:=cursor-1;
            if a(cursor) < a(previous) then
                temp:=a(previous);
                a(previous):=a(cursor);
                a(cursor):=temp;
            endif;
        endloop;
    endloop;
end bubble_sort;
```

Q2: Describe briefly some of the benefits to the Department of Defence of using a single standardised language for all its embedded system software.

Concurrent programming

From the time when the first computers were designed in the 1940s until quite recently, all computers have been designed in a similar way. The processor is connected to main memory, which holds the programs and data. When a program is executed, instructions are passed to the processor one after the other and executed sequentially.

However, in the real world events do not happen sequentially; they happen **concurrently**, or **in parallel**. Often, when we are using a computer to perform tasks such as processing customers' orders and printing dispatch notes, invoices etc, this is not a problem. Even if several orders arrive simultaneously they can be processed one after the other. In other cases, however, such as the monitoring of a petrochemical plant, every process in the plant must be monitored and controlled at the same time, all the time. Another example is that of controlling a robot, which might have a head, arms and legs which all need to move simultaneously in a synchronised manner.

Q3: Name another application in which parallel processing might be used. Why is there currently such an interest in parallel processing?

Synchronisation

It is possible to write concurrent programs in conventional programming languages and to run them on conventional computers; essentially the programmer writes several programs and the computer runs them 'simultaneously' by running a piece of each one, swapping at very brief intervals, until they are all done. The difficulty of this approach lies in synchronising all the programs so that they all finish at the right time. If one process A needs a result from process B then A has to keep checking to see whether B has the required result ready.

An analogy can be drawn by considering how a sweater is knitted. If it is knitted 'sequentially', the instructions would be along the lines of

```
1.   knit front
2.   knit back
3.   knit sleeve
4.   knit sleeve
5.   sew sweater together
```

It would obviously be quicker, if there were several knitters available, to do the first four steps **in parallel**; the only constraint is that these steps must be completed before step 5 is performed.

The transputer

The INMOS transputer is a high performance single chip computer which is capable of parallel processing; that is, it can execute sequences of instructions in parallel. The programming language **occam** was designed as a concurrent programming language and is therefore particularly well suited to running on a transputer.

Occam

In occam, more than one process may be executing at the same time, and processes can send messages to one another. The **par** construction enables two processes to execute simultaneously. For example:

```
par
  seq
    a := 20
    b :=a * a
  seq
    c := 1
    d := 2 * c
```

200

The **seq** instruction is compulsory whenever two or more processes are to run in sequence. In conventional programming languages, sequence is taken for granted, but because occam allows other modes of execution, sequence has to be explicitly requested.

The **par** instruction states that the component processes are to be executed in parallel. The indentation is used to specify which processes are part of the sequence and which take place in parallel.

Parallel versus sequential processing

As an example of how parallel processing can reduce total execution time, consider how a root of a quadratic equation might be evaluated by a sequential processor. The formula is

```
x := (-b + (b ^ 2 - 4 * a * c) ^ 0.5) / (2 * a);
```

This assignment statement might be calculated by the computer using the following steps:

```
1    b ^ 2
2    4 * a
3    (4 * a) * c
4    (b ^ 2) - (4 * a * c)
5    (b ^ 2 - 4 * a * c) ^ 0.5
6    -b
7    (-b) + ((b ^ 2 - 4 * a * c) ^ 0.5)
8    2 * a
9    (-b + (b ^ 2 - 4 * a * c) ^ 0.5) / (2 * a)
```

On a computer that uses parallel processing, the expression could be evaluated as follows: (the terms **parbegin** and **parend** are used to show where calculations are carried out in parallel)

```
1    parbegin
         temp1 := -b
         temp2 := b ^ 2
         temp3 := 4 * a
         temp4 := 2 * a
     parend
2    temp5 := temp3 * c
3    temp5 := temp2 - temp5
4    temp5 := temp5 ^ 0.5
5    temp5 := temp1 + temp5
6    x := temp5 / temp4
```

The first four operations are performed in parallel, but the remaining five operations must still be performed sequentially.

The disadvantage of using a language that can take advantage of parallel programming is that it is difficult and time-consuming to work out what operations can be done in parallel, and parallel programs are more difficult to debug.

Exercises:

1. An increasing number of computers now have more than one processor so that the execution of a program may be shared between the processors.

    Consider the following segments of code and discuss to what extent a multi-processor system could be employed in their execution.

    (a)   a := 1;

          b := 3;

          c := 2;

          d := 4:

    (b)   x := y * z ;

          w := 2 * x ;

          z := z * 3 ;

(4 marks)

(London Paper 2 June 1990)

2. Rewrite the following expression for a computer that performs parallel processing, using **parbegin** and **parend,** so as to take maximum advantage of parallelism.

```
7 * p * q + 3 / (j + k) ^ (2 - m)
```

(3 marks)

3. A programmer writes the following statements for a parallel processing computer. Why might the program not produce the correct answer?

```
parbegin
    x := y - z
    t := y * z - q
    s := x / 8 + a ^ 3
parend
```

Rewrite the program so that it performs correctly. (3 marks)

4. Comment briefly on the reasons for the continued existence of so many high-level programming languages at the current time. Describe **briefly** a variety of different features offered by high-level languages by selecting relevant statements chosen from **two** distinct programming languages other than BASIC. (8 marks)

WJEC Paper 2 June 1988

5. Name an applications area of computing and name a special purpose language for this area. Give **two** reasons for the suitability of the language for the application. (4 marks)

JMB Specimen Paper 1989

6.* In the 1950s, there were few high level languages. There are now many, with more powerful features.

Discuss **two** factors that have influenced these developments. (4 marks)

SEB Paper 1 1992

7.* When designing the solution to a particular problem a systems analyst may choose between a special-purpose language and a general-purpose language. Give *three* criteria which the analyst might use in coming to a decision. Justify your answer. (6 marks)

London Paper 1 1992

8.* "In the future programming languages will be obsolete because computers will be capable of being programmed in natural language."

State whether you agree with this claim and give **two** reasons to support your answer. (2 marks)

AEB Paper 1 1991

Unit 46 — Fourth Generation Languages

The first three generations

The term 'generation' of computer language is used to categorise the various computer languages that have evolved over the last 50 years. Each generation has involved significant progress in making computers easier to use, so that whereas in the early days of computing it was assumed that only a few elite technical specialists would learn to use computers, their use by a large proportion of the population is now taken for granted.

The generations are defined as follows:

1st generation (late 1940s) — machine code.

2nd generation (early 1950s) — assembly language.

3rd generation (late 1950s through to 1970s) — high level languages.

4th generation (late 1970s onwards) — 4GLs, including a whole range of 'very high level' languages, query languages, and other tools.

What is a 4GL?

One definition of a fourth generation language is that it is **non-procedural** — that is, the programmer or user specifies what is to be done, but not how to do it. Examples of non-procedural commands are

> sort students-file on student-number

> delete current record

> find record for Jo Smith

A fourth generation language is really more than just a programming language; it is an 'integrated development environment', allowing the programmer to build a complete application without writing any traditional 'program code' - though this capability is usually included and used when required.

The following facilities will generally be available in a 4GL, though not every 4GL will contain them all .

- database management system
- data dictionary
- query language
- selection and sorting facilities
- report generator
- screen painting facilities
- text editor
- ability to import and store graphics as a database field
- backup and recovery
- security and password facilities
- links to other database management systems

The database management system is at the heart of a 4GL, and examples include ORACLE, OMNIS 7 and PowerBuilder. All these products enable a programmer to design complete applications including menus, screens and reports in a fraction of the time that it would take using a conventional programming language.

Products such as DBase and Paradox, while not classified as 4GLs, have many features in common with a 4GL (e.g. screen painting and report generating facilities) and serve as examples of a similar development environment.

4GLs and the system life cycle

The traditional approach to systems development was

Initial investigation

|

Feasibility study

|

Analysis

|

Design

|

Development

|

Implementation

|

Maintenance

One problem with this approach is the 'analysis paralysis' syndrome; it is often very hard to envisage in advance how a whole system will be put together, and if no programming can start until the design is complete, some projects will have difficulty in getting off the ground at all. Another problem with the traditional approach is that the user often cannot envisage the problems that will inevitably arise with a new system, and is not satisfied with the result even if it is what he asked for.

When a 4GL is being used, a much greater emphasis can be put on **prototyping**. The user's initial requirements can be incorporated into a prototype and refined until a satisfactory system is evolved.

Prototyping and 4GLs

Prototyping is the process of building a working model of a computer system. The model will demonstrate various parts of the system such as the input dialogues, reports and database operations. Prior to 4GLs, prototyping was not a feasible option because it took too long to produce a prototype in a language such as COBOL.

Prototyping may be used in a number of different ways, and various terms have been coined to describe them, as given below:

- **piloting** — using a prototype to test the feasibility of a design proposal

- **modelling** — a prototype is built to develop an understanding of the user's requirements

- **throw-away prototyping** — both piloting and modelling are 'throw-away prototypes'; once they have achieved their purpose the real system is built, using a 4GL or perhaps a 3GL.

- **evolutionary prototyping** — each prototype built represents a step closer to the final system.

Not all systems lend themselves to prototyping; for example, there would be little point in prototyping a batch processing system with hardly any user interface.

Q1: How might the role of a programmer change with the adoption of a 4GL?

Advantages of 4GLs

1. They allow alternative methods of development such as prototyping.

2. Programmer productivity is increased. One line of 4GL code is equivalent to several lines of 3GL code — some products claim (probably exaggeratedly!) a hundredfold increase in productivity.

3. Systems development is faster.

4. The finished system is more likely to be what the user envisaged, if prototyping is used and the user is involved throughout the development.

5. Program maintenance is easier.

6. End users can often develop their own applications.

7. 4GLs tend to be more portable than 3GLs, which often have a variety of 'dialects'.

8. Documentation is improved because many 4GLs are self-documenting.

Exercises:

1. What is meant by the term **prototyping**? Describe briefly the advantages of prototyping in systems design and development.

2. In what ways do fourth generation languages differ from third generation languages such as Pascal and COBOL?

3. Two programming language environments may be equally capable of supporting the implementation of a program design, but one environment may provide a superior human computer interface for the programmer.

   Describe **three** aspects of the human computer interface which it would be important to assess when making a choice of programming environment. (3 marks)
   SEB Paper 1 1989

4. Good programming languages contain features which encourage the production of programs which are self-documenting, easy to amend, error-free, and inexpensive to produce.

   (a) Discuss the features contained in high-level languages which encourage the production of such programs. Illustrate your answer with practical examples. (12 marks)

   (b) Programmers can use general application packages and software tools such as program generators.

         (i) List the benefits which the use of such tools and packages can bring (5 marks)

         (ii) When can their use be inappropriate? (3 marks)
   UCLES Paper 2 Nov 1989

5* Name **two** distinct examples of Fourth Generation Languages and explain why each can be considered a 4GL.

   (6 marks)
   NISEAC Paper 1 1991

6. A university plans to write software to maintain its students' records. It has chosen a Fourth Generation Language (4GL) which permits the programmer to design screen layouts easily, and to specify the validation to be applied to each field.

   (a) Give **five** fields which would be appropriate for an "Enrolment Details" screen indicating the validation, if any, to be applied to each field. (5 marks)

   (b) The screen has space for 24 lines of text each of 40 characters. Sketch an appropriate data entry screen. Remember to leave sufficient space for an error message adjacent to each validated field. (5 marks)
   JMB Paper 1 1992

Unit 47 — Procedural, Declarative and Functional Languages

Procedural and declarative languages

Human beings possess two different kinds of knowledge:

- **declarative** knowledge — facts about people, objects and events and how they relate to each other

- **procedural** knowledge — how to do things, how to use their declarative knowledge, and how to work things out.

Computers may also be programmed with these two different kinds of knowledge.

High level languages such as Pascal, COBOL or FORTRAN are all examples of **procedural** languages, where the program consists of a sequence of instructions telling the machine what to do. The programmer has to show exactly what steps must be executed in order to solve the problem, and in what order, for any given set of data. As instructions are executed, program variables are modified using assignment statements.

The languages used to write expert systems are quite different. They are called **declarative** languages, and **Prolog** is the best known example.

Prolog

Prolog (which stands for PROgramming in LOGic) is a particular type of declarative language known as a logic programming language. It has the following characteristics:

- instead of defining **how** a problem is solved, the programmer states the facts and rules associated with the problem. A **fact** is something that is always unconditionally true, and a **rule** is true depending on a given condition.

- the **order** in which the rules and facts are stated is not important, unlike the statements in an imperative (ie procedural) language. It is therefore easy to add new rules, delete rules or change existing rules.

Prolog is especially well suited to programming **expert systems**, and it is claimed that it can be up to ten times faster to develop an expert system in Prolog than in, say, C. In an expert system, facts and rules are described in the program to form the 'expert knowledge', and a user can then query the program to obtain answers to problems, given that certain facts or conditions are true. (Expert systems are covered in more detail in Unit 83.)

'Back-tracking' is a built-in feature of Prolog; like Theseus with his ball of string in the Minotaur's maze, who could select a route at a junction and always find his way back if it proved to be a dead end. In a similar manner, Prolog will select a possible candidate for a solution and if that fails, it will backtrack to that point and try another route.

The example of a Prolog program which follows can be used to determine relationships between members of a family — useful perhaps in one of those 500-page family sagas when you can never remember who is related to whom...

The 'knowledge' that has to be programmed is a representation of the family tree below, and rules about relationships.

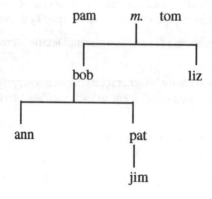

A Prolog program

```
/* Family tree: program by Matthew Todd, 1.12.93 */
/* facts */
    parent(pam,bob).
    parent(tom,bob).
    parent(tom,liz).
    parent(bob,ann).
    parent(bob,pat).
    parent(pat,jim).
    female(pam).
    male(tom).
    male(bob).
    female(liz).
    female(pat).
    female(ann).
    male(jim).

/*rules*/
    grandparent(X,Y):-          (ie X is a grandparent of Y if
        parent(X,Z),                X is a parent of Z and
        parent(Z,Y).                Z is a parent of Y)

    mother(X,Y):-               (X is the mother of Y if
        parent(X,Y),                X is a parent of Y and
        female(X).                  X is female)

    father(X,Y):-
        parent(X,Y),
        male(X).

    sister(X,Y):-
        parent(Z,X),
        parent(Z,Y),
        mle(X).

    brother(X,Y):-
        parent(Z,X),
        parent(Z,Y),
        male(X).
```

Queries can now be made to find out relationships; for example if the user wants to know "Does Liz have a brother?" the query is typed in as

`?- brother(X,liz).`   and the program will respond

`X=bob`

To ask "Who is the mother of Bob?" type

`?- mother (X,bob).`   and the program will respond

`X=pam`

Type   `?- grandparent(bob,who)` and the program will respond

`Who=jim`

`?- brother(Who,ann)`   and the program will respond

`no`   (because ann has no brother)

207

Functional languages

In functional programming languages programs are written as functions to be evaluated. The function expects zero or more arguments and will return a value as the result of its evaluation. The order in which operations are to be executed is not specified.

LISP

LISP stands for LISt Processing. It is an example of a **functional** programming language, and a LISP program consists of a series of function definitions, followed by an expression to be evaluated. It allows relationships to be easily coded; for example, the hierarchy of relations shown below (Figure 47.1) can be represented in LISP with the statement

```
(arthropods(insects(beetles biting flies(mosquitoes midges horseflies)
                                       dragonflies)
          crustaceans(aquatic(shrimps lobsters crabs)
                             land living(woodlouse))))
```

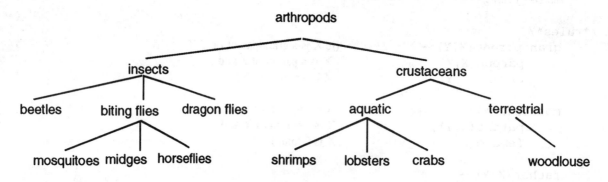

Figure 47.1

A LISP program is itself a LISP list, which means that a LISP program can be treated as data by another program or even by itself. This approach has many benefits: for example

- since data and instructions are in exactly the same format, the declarative knowledge can be easily integrated with information about what actions are to be performed (procedural knowledge)

- a LISP program can actually modify its own program instructions. This is very helpful with an Artificial Intelligence program that is learning to perform a new task

- LISP programs can easily keep track of which instructions have been executed and in what order. This is useful in expert systems, which are expected to explain how they reach a particular conclusion.

Note that functional languages are essentially declarative, though the reverse is not true.

Exercises:

1. Give **three** features of declarative languages such as Prolog, which make them suitable for the creation of expert systems.

    (3 marks)
    AEB Sample Paper 1990

2. Two classes of high level languages are *procedural* and *non-procedural*.

    Give an example of each class of language and explain the main difference between the two classes of language.

    (3 marks)
    SEB Paper 1 1989

3.* Computer languages can be described as imperative, functional or declarative.

    Explain, using examples, what is meant by each of these three terms.

    (6 marks)

Unit 48 — Backus Naur Form and Polish Notation

Meta-languages

In order for a computer language such as Pascal to be translated into machine code, all the rules of the language must be defined unambiguously. Languages such as English, French, or Swahili are not at all precise, which is one reason why it is hard to get computers to understand 'natural language'.

Q1: Punctuate the following:

> TIME FLIES YOU CANNOT THEY FLY TOO FAST

This is fairly baffling for an English-speaking person, let alone a computer whose native tongue is machine code! Not only is English too imprecise to be used as a computer language, it is not even suitable for defining unambiguously the syntax or grammar of a computer language. For this reason, special languages called **meta-languages** have been devised, and Backus Naur form (named after its two originators) is an example of one such meta-language.

Backus-Naur form (BNF)

The structure of BNF is composed of a list of statements of the form

> LHS := RHS

where **:=** is interpreted as **'is defined by'**. **:=** is known as a **meta-symbol**.

Example: <point> := .

<point> is called a **meta-component,** or sometimes a **syntactic variable,** and is distinguished by being enclosed in angle brackets.

The other important meta-symbol is **|** which means **'or'**.

Thus for example a **<digit>** can be defined as

> <digit> := 0 | 1 | 2 | 3 | 4 | 5 | 6 | 7 | 8 | 9

Example: Write down the BNF definition of a numeric variable name, which (in a certain computer language) may consist of a single letter or a letter followed by a digit.

<numeric variable> := <letter> | <letter> <digit>
<letter> := A | B | C | D | E | F | G | H | I | J | K | L | M | N | O | P | Q | R | S | T | U | V | W | X | Y | Z
<digit> := 0 | 1 | 2 | 3 | 4 | 5 | 6 | 7 | 8 | 9

A group of definitions such as the above is known as a **production**.

BNF often makes use of **recursion,** where a statement is defined in terms of itself. For example:

> <variable list> := <variable> | <variable list> , <variable>

Under this definition, is **A,B,C** a variable list? We can show that it is, by the following reasoning:

> A is a <variable> and is therefore a <variable list>.
> A,B is a <variable list> (ie A) followed by a comma and a <variable> and is therefore a <variable list>
> A,B,C is a <variable list> (ie A,B) followed by a comma and a <variable>.
> Therefore, A,B,C is a <variable list>.

Q2: Write down the definition of an integer in BNF.

Q3: The syntax of a real number in Pascal is defined as one or more digits, followed by a decimal point, followed by one or more digits. Write down the definition using BNF.

The process of ascertaining whether a given statement is valid, given the BNF definition, is called **parsing**. The procedure is to work from left to right, replacing meta-variables with more comprehensive meta-variables at each stage.

Q4: An arithmetic expression is defined in BNF as follows:

<expression> := <term> | <expression> + <term> | <expression> - <term>
<term> := <variable> | <term> * <variable> | <term> / <variable>
<variable> := a | b | c | d

Show that a-b is a syntactically correct expression in this language.

Q5: Show that a + b * c is also syntactically correct.

When a compiler checks a statement written in a high level language to see if it is syntactically correct, it will **parse** each statement in a similar manner to that shown above. Compilers will be discussed in detail in the next Unit.

Reverse Polish notation

Reverse Polish (also called **postfix**) notation was developed by a Pole called Jan Lukasiewicz. It is a method of writing arithmetic expressions that is particularly suited to computerised methods of evaluation. We shall see how expressions in reverse Polish notation may be evaluated using a stack.

The way in which we normally write arithmetic expressions is called **infix** notation, and it is not easy for a computer to evaluate such an expression directly. Consider for example the expression

(a + b) * c

210

The sequence of instructions needed to evaluate this is

1. get a
2. get b
3. add them together and store the intermediate result
4. get c
5   multiply by the result of step 3.

In other words, the computer really needs the operands (a, b, and c) and operators (+ and *) in the sequence

>   a b + c *

Q6: What would be the sequence of instructions needed to evaluate the expression b * c ?

We shall see how, in reverse Polish notation, the operator follows the operands — which is the logical sequence, if you are a computer.

Precedence rules

In order to translate from infix to reverse Polish notation, we need to define the order of precedence of operators. This is shown below, in increasing order of precedence.

>   =
>
>   (
>
>   + -)
>
>   * /
>
>   ^   (exponentiation — eg 3^2 means 3^2)
>
>   ~   (unary minus, as in -3 + 2)

Translation from infix to reverse Polish

A computer will use a fairly complex algorithm using a stack to translate from infix to reverse Polish notation. However, it is quite simple to do it manually with the benefit of common sense, a knowledge of the rules of precedence and a few simple rules, given below:

1. Starting from the left hand side of the expression, allocate numbers *1, 2, 3,* etc to operands and operators as follows:

    *   if the next symbol is an **operand**, allocate the next number (*1, 2, 3,* etc) to it

    *   ignore parentheses except in so far as they affect the order of calculation

    *   bearing in mind the rules of precedence, decide which is the next operation which should be performed, and as soon as its operands have been allocated numbers, back up and allocate to it the next number.

eg   *1   5   2   4   3*

      a   +   b   *   c   From the left, allocate *1* to a, *2* to b. Multiplication is done before addition, so keep going and allocate *3* to c. Then back up to allocate *4* to *, and finally *5* to +.

2.   Write down the symbols (operators and operands) in the order of the numbers you have allocated.

Reverse Polish form in the above example is a b c * +

Q7: Translate into reverse Polish notation: (i) $(a + b) - x \wedge y * 3$

(ii) $x = - a + (c - d) / e$

Evaluation of reverse Polish expressions using a stack

Once a compiler has translated an arithmetic expression into reverse Polish notation, each symbol in the expression may be held in an array. The expression may then be evaluated using a stack, scanning the elements of the array from left to right, as follows:

•   if the next symbol is an operand, place it on the stack

•   if the next symbol is an operator, remove the required number of operands from the stack, (two except in the case of a unary minus or exponentiation), perform the operation, and put the result on the stack.

Example: Convert the following expression to reverse Polish notation, and show how the resulting expression may be evaluated using a stack.

$(7 + 10 / 5) + (6 * 2)$

First, convert to reverse Polish:

```
    1    5    2    4    3        9        6    8    7    (allocate numbers to each symbol)
(   7    +   10   /    5   )    +   (    6    *    2   )
```

ie   7 10 5 / + 6 2 * +   in reverse Polish notation.

Using a stack to evaluate the expression, the contents of the stack will be as follows:

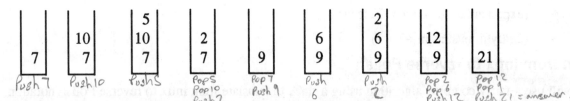

Q8: Convert the following expression to reverse Polish notation and show how it may be evaluated using a stack.

$(5 + 9) / 2 - (2 * 3)$

Exercises:

1. A particular computer language has variable names which must begin with a letter.

   Any following characters can be letters or digits.

   Digits must not be separated by letters.

   e.g. page3 and page32a are valid variable names but page3a2 is not valid.

   Using B.N.F. notation or a syntax diagram define the syntax of a variable name. (6 marks)
   London Paper 1 June 1990

2. The form of arithmetic expressions in a particular programming language is defined by the following rules.

<expression>	::=	<term> | <expression> <addop> <term>
<term>	::=	<primary> | <term> <mulop> <primary>
<primary>	::=	<identifier> | <constant>
<identifier>	::=	<letter> | <identifier> <letter>
<constant>	::=	<digit> | <constant> <digit>
<addop>	::=	+ | -
<mulop>	::=	* | /
<letter>	::=	a | b | c | d | ..... | x | y | z
<digit>	::=	0 | 1 | 2 | 3 | 4 | 5 | 6 | 7 | 8 | 9

   (a) (i) For **each** of the following, indicate whether or not it is a valid expression. For those which are **not valid** explain why.

   half-baked

   farthing = 1/4

   hammond

   m45+a6

   -2

   minutes + hours * 60 (6 marks)

   (ii) The rules do not allow parentheses to be used to enclose subexpressions. Suggest how **one or more** of the rules could be modified to allow for this. (4 marks)

   (b) (i) Write down the reverse Polish form of the following expression.

   jones - sandra * (claire - gareth) - frank / dan * bryn

   (ii) Describe, in general terms, how an interpreter could, during execution of a program, evaluate the expression from the reverse Polish form. (6 marks)
   WJEC Paper 2 May 1989

3. With the following syntax definitions:

   P := aPa \| b

   S := bPPb \| bb

   which of the following strings are correctly formed S expressions?

   bbb, bbbb, babaabab, aabaa (4 marks)
   NISEAC Paper 1 May 1990

Unit 49 — Compilers and Interpreters

Translators

There are two types of translator for converting a high level language such as Pascal into machine code; **compilers** and **interpreters**.

A **compiler** translates a complete program into object code before it is executed, whereas an interpreter analyses the source code statement by statement as execution proceeds, interpreting the meaning of each statement and calling routines to carry out each instruction.

Advantages of a compiler

1. A compiled program will almost always run faster than an interpreted program.

2. The object program (the machine code generated by the compiler) may be saved on disk and run as many times as required without being recompiled.

3. A compiler can give more helpful error messages; if, for example, a keyword (reserved word) is misspelt all through the program, an interpreter will only find the first instance, whereas a compiler will list them all.

4. A compiler will check the syntax of the entire program, whereas an interpreter will only check the syntax of the statements that are executed during that particular run of the program. Certain branches of the program may therefore not be checked until very thorough testing takes place.

5. Commercially produced software can be sold in the form of object code, thus preventing purchasers from listing the source code or making modifications to it.

Advantages of an interpreter

1. Interpreters are very convenient for program development, since making modifications does not mean that the whole program has to be reloaded and recompiled, which can take a considerable time. Many interpreters will allow a program to run up to the point where an error occurs, let the programmer fix the error and then continue to run the program from that point.

2. An interpreter is simpler to write and is usually cheaper to buy than a compiler.

Q1: Some languages have both compilers and interpreters available. If you could use one type of translator for program development and either the same or a different type when the program was fully tested and ready for regular execution, which would you choose for each stage and why?

Cross-compilers and cross-assemblers

Cross-compilers and cross-assemblers are translators which enable a program to be compiled or assembled on one machine, and executed on a different type of processor. This is sometimes useful if, for example, program development is being done on a mainframe for a program which will eventually be run on a microcomputer, or in the development of embedded processor programs.

The stages of compilation

The compilation process has three main phases;

- lexical analysis
- syntax analysis (also includes **semantic analysis**)
- code generation

 In a **single-pass** compiler, each line or fragment of a program goes through each of the phases, producing object code, and then the next line is translated.

In a **multipass** compiler, each phase performs a separate pass over the whole program, with the output of each pass being stored in the computer's memory or on disk. A diagram of a multipass compilation process is shown below:

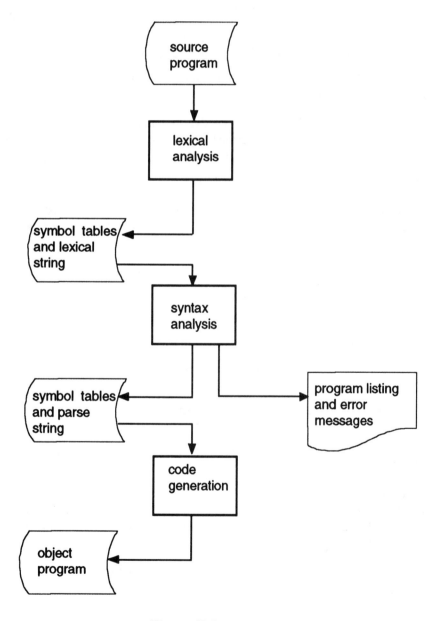

Figure 49.1

Lexical analysis

Lexical analysis performs the following functions.

1. Superfluous characters and spaces are removed. For example, if the user has made a keying error and subsequently backspaced, the line might read

   ```
   wril<-teln  (total_mark,  average); (<- represents a backspace character)
   ```

   This will be converted to

   ```
   writeln(total_mark,average);
   ```

2. All comments, enclosed between such symbols as { }, will be removed from the program.

3. Some **simple** error-checking is performed; for example

   - if the language imposes a limit on the length of identifiers or string constants, the lexical analyser will determine if the identifier is too long

   - an illegal identifier such as 2nd_year (in Pascal) would be flagged as an error

   - the lexical analyser will detect an attempt to assign an illegal value to a constant, such as a value of the wrong type or one that causes overflow or underflow

   (The lexical analyser will not detect misspelt keywords or undeclared variables; this is the job of the **syntax analyser**.)

4. All keywords, constants and identifiers used in the source code are replaced by 'tokens' (unique symbols). For example, numbers will be converted to their run-time representation, and identifiers will be replaced by a pointer to an address in the **symbol table**. Keywords will be replaced by a single item-code.

The symbol table

The symbol table plays a central role in the compilation process. It will contain an entry for every keyword (reserved word) and identifier in the program. The exact format of the entries in the table will vary from compiler to compiler, but typically, entries in the table will show

- the identifier or keyword

- the **kind** of item (variable, array, procedure, keyword etc)

- the **type** of item (integer, real, char, etc)

- the **run-time address** of the item, or its **value** if it is a constant

- a pointer to **accessing information** (eg for an array, the bounds of the array, or for a procedure, information about each of the parameters).

Typical entries in a symbol table might be as given below:

	item name	kind of item	type of item	run-time address or value	pointer
1	read	keyword			
2	pi	constant	real	3.14159	
3	radius	variable	real	(?)	
4	begin	keyword			
5	writeln	keyword			
6	no_sides	array	integer	(?)	(?)
.					
.					

Note that the lexical analyser puts the identifier and its run-time address in the symbol table, so that it can replace them in the source code by 'tokens'. It will not fill in the 'kind of item' and 'type of item'; this is done later by the **syntax analyser.**

Q2: What entries might the lexical analyser insert in the symbol table on analysing the following program? What other functions will it perform? What errors, if any, will be detected in this phase of compilation? (Indicate by ringing them).

```
program lex;
const
      class1=2;
      block_no=1B;
var
      x,y:array[1..10] of integer;
      1st_sum:integer;
begin
      sum:=0;
      ffor i=1 to 100 do
      begin
            readln(x[i],y[i])
            sum:=x[i]++y[i];
      end;
            writeln(class1,block_no,sum)
end.
```

	item name	kind of item	type of item	run-time address or value	pointer
1					
2					
3					
4					
5					
6					
7					
8					
9					
10					
11					
12					
13					
14					
15					
16					

Accessing the symbol table

Since the lexical analyser spends a great proportion of its time looking up the symbol table, this activity has a crucial effect on the overall speed of the compiler. The symbol table must therefore be organised in such a way that entries can be found as quickly as possible.

Q3: Suggest TWO ways of organising the symbol table so that items can be easily added and quickly retrieved.

Hash table organisation

The most common way of organising the symbol table is a hash table, where the keyword or identifier is 'hashed' to produce an array subscript. As with any hash table, synonyms (collisions) are inevitable, and a common way of handling them is to store the synonym in the next available free space in the table. (See also Unit 28, Hash Tables, under 'Overflow' and'Deleting Records'.)

Since keywords are put in the symbol table along with everything else, it makes sense to try to ensure that they, at least, are in their correct position in the table, since they are likely to be looked up most frequently. Therefore, **all** the keywords in the language may be 'pre-hashed' each time the compiler is loaded, and the compiler writer makes sure that the algorithm he or she has used does not result in any collisions of keywords.

Syntax analysis and semantic analysis

Syntax analysis is the process of determining whether the sequence of input characters, symbols, items or tokens form a valid sentence in the language. In order to do this, the language has to be expressed as a set of rules, using for example **syntax diagrams** or **Backus-Naur form**.

Parsing is the task of systematically applying the set of rules to each statement to determine whether it is valid. **Stacks** will be used to check, for example, that brackets are correctly paired. The priorities of arithmetic operators will be determined, and expressions converted into a form (such as **reverse Polish notation**) from which machine code can more easily be generated.

The **semantics** of the program will also be checked in this phase. **Semantics** define the **meaning** rather than the **grammar** of the language; it is possible to write a series of syntactically correct statements which nevertheless do not obey the rules for writing a correct program. An example of a semantic error is the use of an undeclared variable in Pascal, or trying to assign a **real** value to an **integer** variable, or using a **real** number instead of an **integer** as the counter in a **for .. next** loop.

Q4: Give other examples of a semantic error.

218

Code generation and optimisation

This is the final phase of compilation, when the machine code is generated. Most high-level language statements will be translated into a number of machine code statements.

Code optimisation techniques attempt to reduce the execution time of the object program by, for example, spotting redundant instructions and producing object code which achieves the same net effect as that specified by the source program but not by the same means. The disadvantages of code optimisation are:

- it will increase compilation time, sometimes quite considerably

- it may sometimes produce unexpected results. Consider the following program extract, which is supposed to measure the speed of the object program. Assume GetTime is a function which returns the current time set in the operating system:

```
start:=GetTime;
for count:=1 to 100000 do
    x:=0;      {endfor}
finish:=GetTime;
writeln(start,finish);
```

The effect of code optimisation may be to detect that it is quite unnecessary to perform the loop 100000 times to set x equal to 0, and optimise the code so that it is only done once!

Parameter passing mechanisms

You will recall from Unit 17 that a **parameter** is an identifier or value passed between calling program and subroutine. Thus if a procedure **gotoxy(3, 8)** is called, 3 and 8 are the parameters passed to the procedure. (In this example **gotoxy(column, row)** is a procedure which positions the cursor at column 3 row 8 on the screen.)

Different languages employ different mechanisms for passing parameters back and forth between a subprogram and its calling program. Two of these methods are described below.

1. **Call by value.** The actual values of the parameters are placed in memory locations associated with the formal parameters of the subprogram. This is appropriate in the example above, where the values of **row** and **column** will not be changed in the procedure. Call by value is also appropriate for function calls; for example if **sqrt**(x) is a function which returns the square root of the argument, then the function call

    y:=sqrt(b*b-4*a*c)

    will cause the actual value of b*b-4*a*c to be placed in the memory location associated with x. The square root of x will then be calculated and the result placed in y.

2. **Call by reference.** The **addresses** of the parameters, rather than their values, will be passed to the called procedure.

In Pascal, for example, a typical procedure heading is as follows:

```
procedure calc_checkdigit(y:array_n;n:integer; var checkdigit:char);
```

Variable parameters (identified by **var**) are passed by reference — a pointer points to the actual storage location.

Value parameters (which are not changed in the procedure) are passed either by value or by reference depending on the type and size of the parameter. In Turbo Pascal 5, if the value is 1, 2 or 4 bytes, the parameter is passed by value. Arrays or records of more than 4 bytes are passed by reference.

Q5: Why do you suppose arrays are passed in a different way from single variables?

Exercises:

1. (a) An application program is to be developed in a high level language and eventually compiled. The program uses a number of pre-compiled library routines. Describe, with the aid of a diagram, how supporting utility software is used in conjunction with the compiler to produce executable code. (5 marks)

    (b) The compilation process is often viewed as being made up of a number of distinct phases. In this context:

    (i) what is the purpose of *lexical analysis*;

    (ii) what use is made of *symbol tables*;

    (iii) why may a compiler attempt to *optimise code*? (6 marks)

    (c) What is *cross-compilation* and when might it be used? (2 marks)

    (d) Describe one diagnostic utility which can be used to locate errors in a syntactically correct program. (2 marks)

    London Paper 2 June 89

2. The process of compilation involves a number of stages (or phases). Give the name of the stage at which each of the following errors would be detected:

    (a) The compiler cannot recognise the structure of an arithmetic expression due to a missing bracket.

    (b) A keyword in the source program is misspelt.

    (c) An arithmetic operator has operands of incompatible types.

    (d) A compiler created constant is too large to fit into a word of the target machine.

    (e) The name of a variable contains more characters than are permitted in the language definition. (5 marks)

    AEB Paper 2 1989

3. (a) Describe the main differences between an interpreter and a compiler. (3 marks)

    (b) If both a compiler and an interpreter are available for processing a particular programming language, what factors might influence the choice of which one a programmer would use? (3 marks)

    UCLES Paper 2 May 1990

4. Name and state the function of *three* software tools which might be used in the creation of a source program and its conversion to an executable form. (6 marks)

    NISEAC Paper 2 June 1989

5.* A programmer is developing a program in an interpreted version of a language. The program requires a delay in it. This delay is produced using a simple loop which is repeated one thousand times.

    On completion of the interpreted version, the program is implemented in a compiled version of the language.

    Explain why the delay in the program might not function as expected when the compiled version is executed. (2 marks)

    SEB Paper 1 1992

6.* A certain compiler stores user-defined variable names in a symbol table at locations determined by performing a hashing operation on the character codes of the letters in the variable name.

    (a) Explain what is meant by hashing, and state two desirable features of a hashing algorithm in this context. (4 marks)

    (b) Describe a method that the compiler could use to deal with the problem of two variable names hashing to the same address. (3 marks)

    (c) When no further references to a particular variable name are possible, the compiler releases the space in the symbol table. Discuss the problems that need to be overcome in order to achieve this satisfactorily. (4 marks)

Section 7 — Internal Organisation of Computers

Unit 50 — The Processor Unit

The CPU

CPU stands for **Central Processing Unit**. This is the real brain of the computer. All arithmetic is performed here, every program instruction is interpreted and executed here, and every item to be placed in memory or retrieved from memory passes through the CPU. This is the computer. However, the processor would not be much use without memory in which to hold the data and the programs which process the data. The CPU and the main memory of the computer are located in the same physical unit, which is often referred to as the processor unit.

Memory

Computer memory, or storage, can be classified into two main divisions. **Main store**, often just called 'storage', consists of a large number of electronic circuits. If the computer is opened up a number of plastic boxes will be found, most of them housing memory circuits — up to two million in each. It has been predicted that by the end of the century it will be possible to store over a billion circuits on a chip. This is the only type of memory that the CPU can use directly, and therefore all information has to go through main store at some point.

All other types of storage are known as **backing store**, or sometimes **auxiliary storage**, and this includes many devices ranging from paper cards with holes punched in them to laser-scanned compact disks, also known as **CD ROM** (Compact Disk Read Only Memory). By far the most common types of backing store in use today are magnetic disk and magnetic tape.

Q1: What are the advantages and disadvantages of backing store over main store?

Storing characters in a computer's memory

In all modern computers each memory circuit can be either ON, indicated by a 1, or OFF, indicated by a 0. A series of eight circuits in the states ON, ON, OFF, OFF, ON, OFF, ON, OFF can then be depicted as

$$1 \quad 1 \quad 0 \quad 0 \quad 1 \quad 0 \quad 1 \quad 0$$

Data can be stored in memory character by character, with each character being represented by a 'code' consisting of 1s and 0s. Each 1 or 0 is called a 'bit', short for 'BInary digiT'

Q2: How many different 'codes' or combinations are possible with

(i) 2 bits   (ii) 3 bits   (iii) 4 bits   (iv) 8 bits?

Q3: How many bits would be needed to allow a different code for all lower and upper case letters, digits 0 to 9, and all the other characters on a keyboard such as &, <, * etc?

Bytes

Most computers use 8-bit codes to represent each character. Eight bits together are known as one **byte**. This is sufficient to allow a unique code for all the usual characters with one bit, the leftmost bit, to spare. The spare bit may be used either as a **parity bit** (see below) or to give an extra 128 characters. In the latter case, if the spare bit is 0, the code represents a normal character; if it is 1, the code represents a character from the **extended character set**.

When you press a key on the keyboard, the corresponding 8-bit code is generated and sent to the computer. When a code is sent to the printer, the corresponding character is printed. **One byte holds one character.**

Q4: Can you think of any characters that are included in the extended character set?

The ASCII code

Over the years, different computer designers have used different sets of codes for representing characters, which has led to great difficulty in transferring information from one computer to another. Most personal computers (PCs) nowadays use the ASCII code (American Standard Code for Information Interchange), but many mainframe computers use a code called EBCDIC (Extended Binary Coded Decimal Interchange Code — pronounced EB-SUH-DICK or EB-SEE-DICK according to taste). The ASCII codes are shown below.

Character	ASCII	Char	ASCII	Char	ASCII	Char	ASCII
space	0100000	8	0111000	P	1010000	h	1101000
!	0100001	9	0111001	Q	1010001	i	1101001
"	0100010	:	0111010	R	1010010	j	1101010
£	0100011	;	0111011	S	1010011	k	1101011
$	0100100	<	0111100	T	1010100	l	1101100
%	0100101	=	0111101	U	1010101	m	1101101
&	0100110	>	0111110	V	1010110	n	1101110
'	0100111	?	0111111	W	1010111	o	1101111
(	0101000	@	1000000	X	1011000	p	1110000
)	0101001	A	1000001	Y	1011001	q	1110001
*	0101010	B	1000010	Z	1011010	r	1110010
+	0101011	C	1000011	[	1011011	s	1110011
,	0101100	D	1000100	\	1011100	t	1110100
-	0101101	E	1000101	]	1011101	u	1110101
.	0101110	F	1000110	^	1011110	v	1110110
/	0101111	G	1000111	_	1011111	w	1110111
0	0110000	H	1001000	'	1100000	x	1111000
1	0110001	I	1001001	a	1100001	y	1111001
2	0110010	J	1001010	b	1100010	z	1111010
3	0110011	K	1001011	c	1100011	{	1111011
4	0110100	L	1001100	d	1100100			1111100
5	0110101	M	1001101	e	1100101	}	1111101
6	0110110	N	1001110	f	1100110	~	1111110
7	0110111	O	1001111	g	1100111	del	1111111

Parity

For each byte of memory, most computers have at least one extra bit, called a **parity** bit, that is used for error detection. A parity bit can detect if one of the bits in a byte has been inadvertently changed, perhaps because of a chip failure, static electricity or a voltage fluctuation.

Computers use either **even** or **odd** parity. In an even parity machine, the total number of 'on' bits in every byte (including the parity bit) must be an even number. Parity is checked each time a memory location is used. When data is moved from one location to another in memory, the parity bits are checked at both the sending and receiving end, and if they are different or the wrong number of bits are 'on', an error message is displayed.

Q5: In an even parity machine, what will be the value of the parity bit for the characters P and Q?

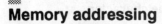

Memory addressing

The memory of a computer can be thought of as a series of boxes, each containing 8 bits (1 byte), and each with its own unique address, counting from zero upwards. The memory capacity of a computer is measured in thousand-byte units called kilobytes — although strictly speaking one kilobyte is equal to 1024, or 2^{10} bytes. For example, a PC with 640K of memory contains approximately 640,000 bytes but, if we wish to be exact, the actual size is 640 x 1024 = 655,360 bytes.

Memory is also measured in **megabytes** (approximately 1 million bytes), or in the case of very large computers, **gigabytes** (1,000,000 K bytes). These measures can be abbreviated to KB, MB and GB.

Q6: What will be the highest address in a computer with 16K of memory?

The data bus and the address bus

The CPU is connected to main storage by two sets of wires, or **buses**. When the CPU wishes to access a particular memory location, it sends this address to memory on the **address bus**. The data in that location is then returned to the CPU on the **data bus**.

Microcomputer buses can typically transfer sixteen or thirty-two bits at a time. A sixteen-bit bus, for example, has sixteen lines and can transmit sixteen bits simultaneously. The larger the number of bits that can be transferred by the bus, the faster the computer can transfer data.

The number of lines in the **address bus** determines how many locations can be accessed. With a 16-bit address bus, the highest location that can be addressed is 65,535 (1111111111111111 in binary!) In the 1970s when IBM brought out their PC, the designers thought it extremely unlikely that a PC would ever have more than 1MB of memory, and that therefore a 20-bit address bus would be quite adequate. Unfortunately time was to prove them wrong, and a major effort had to go into designing new machine architecture to cope with over 1MB of memory.

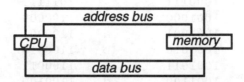

Figure 50.1 — The data bus and the address bus

Word size

The **word size** of a computer is the number of bits that the CPU can process simultaneously, as opposed to the bus size which determines how many bits are transmitted together. Processors can have 8-, 16-, 32- or 64-bit word sizes (or even larger), and the word size will be one of the factors which determines the speed of the computer. The faster, more powerful PCs have 32-bit processors, and most mainframes have 32-bit words. Supercomputers may use a 64-bit or 128-bit word size.

Random Access Memory

Memory may be one of two types, known as RAM and ROM respectively. RAM stands for Random Access Memory, which means that any memory location can be directly accessed by referring to its address. Data and programs are transferred into and out of RAM, and the data in RAM is processed according to the instructions in the program. There are two types of RAM memory chips: **static RAM** is relatively slow, but retains its information as long as the power is switched on. **Dynamic RAM** chips are smaller and simpler in design, and faster in operation, but the information slowly leaks away and has to be refreshed by special regenerator circuits in the CPU. The main memory of most computers uses dynamic RAM chips. Both these types of memory lose all information as soon as the power is switched off.

Memory mapping

Some RAM is given a special function. For example, part of RAM is reserved for the operating system, and some is reserved to hold addresses and parameters used, say, when calling subroutines. This is called a **stack** and is covered later. This allocation of memory to different functions is referred to as **memory mapping**, and a typical memory map for a microcomputer is shown below.

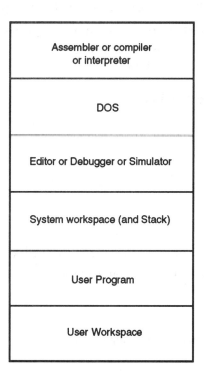

Figure 50.2 — A typical memory map

Read Only Memory

ROM (Read Only Memory) retains information even when the power is switched off, but the information has to be permanently recorded into the circuits when the chip is manufactured, and cannot be changed. ROM is used to store some of the operating system commands, and the instruction set of the computer. In special purpose computers used in video recorders, washing machines and cars, the program instructions are stored in ROM.

It is also possible to buy Erasable Programmable Read Only Memory chips (EPROM), which can be cleared by subjecting them to ultraviolet light, and then reprogrammed.

Cache memory

A **cache** is a small fast memory usually between 1 Kb and 256Kb, too expensive to be used for the whole of RAM, that acts as an intermediate store between the CPU and main memory, and is used to improve the overall speed of the computer. Cache memory can return data to the CPU faster than main memory because:

- it is closer to the CPU
- it may use a dedicated control bus
- it may use higher-speed components

In systems which use cache memory, the most active portions of a program are kept in cache, from where instructions and data can be retrieved faster than from ordinary RAM. Computers using cache memory are exploiting two principles:

- an instruction or item of data that has been accessed once is likely to be accessed again in the near future. (This is known as **temporal locality.**)
- if an item (instruction or data) is addressed at a given memory location, it is likely that other items with addresses near to this one will be accessed in the near future (**spatial locality**).

There are good reasons to expect temporal locality. For example, the existence of loops in a program means that the same instructions will have to be fetched from memory over and over again, and furthermore the data that is operated on may well be the same in many of the instructions.

Q7: Give a reason why you might expect to find **spatial locality**.

Cache memory can also be used as a temporary storage for part of a disk. Disk drives are much slower at storing and retrieving information than memory, so the information that is most likely to be required next from disk is stored in cache from where it can be quickly retrieved.

Exercises:

1. Give an example of the use within a **mainframe** computer system of:

    (i)   RAM;

    (ii) ROM
    (2 marks)
    AEB Paper 1 1990

2. State **one** advantage and **one** disadvantage of using dynamic RAM as opposed to static RAM.   (2 marks)
    AEB Paper 1 1989

3. A dairy farmer who has recently bought his first microcomputer is confused by the terms ROM and RAM in the user manual.

    Write a brief explanation of these terms for the farmer.   (5 marks)
    UCLES Paper 2 Nov 1989

4.* Digital computers use binary codes to represent data. Give **three** reasons why digital computers are based on the binary number system.
    (3 marks)
    SEB Paper 1 1992

Unit 51 — Binary Integers

Introduction

We have seen that each character has a corresponding code, so that if for example the 'A' key on the keyboard is pressed, the code '01000001' will be sent to the CPU. If the key '1' is pressed, the code '00110001' will be sent to the CPU. To print the number '123', the codes for 1, 2 and 3 would be sent to the printer.

Q1: How many bytes would be needed to hold the number three million?

This is fine for input and output, but useless for arithmetic. There is no easy way of adding two numbers held in this way, and furthermore they occupy a great deal of space. Numbers which are to be used in calculations are therefore held in a different format, as **binary numbers**.

Before we look at the binary system, it is helpful to examine how our ordinary decimal or **denary** number system works. Consider for example the number '134'. These three digits represent one hundred, three tens and four ones.

```
100   10   1
-------------------
  1    3   4            100 + 30 + 4 = 134
```

As we move from right to left each digit is worth ten times as much as the previous one. We probably use a **base 10** number system because we have ten fingers, but essentially there is no reason why some other base could not be used. In a later unit we will look at **base 8** and **base 16** number systems, but for now we will study the **binary** system, which instead of using ten digits uses only two, namely 0 and 1.

In the binary system, as we move from right to left each digit is worth twice as much as the previous one. Thus the binary number 10000110 can be set out under column headings as follows:

```
128   64   32   16   8   4   2   1
------------------------------------------
  1    0    0    0   0   1   1   0        This represents 128 + 4 + 2 = 134
```

Q2: Convert the following binary numbers to decimal:

    0011   0110   1010   01000001   01000101

Q3: Convert the following numbers to binary:

    5   7   1   26   68   137

Q4: What is the largest binary number that can be held in 8 bits?

Obviously, using only one byte (8 bits) to hold a number places a severe restriction on the size of number the computer can hold. Therefore two or even four consecutive bytes are commonly used to store numbers.

Q5: Show the number 1 using one byte.

Q6: What is the largest number that can be held in two bytes?

The individual bits of a binary number are numbered as shown below (computers always count from zero instead of one!)

bit number	7	6	5	4	3	2	1	0
binary code	1	0	0	1	1	0	1	1

Bit 0 is sometimes called the **least significant bit** (lsb).

Bit 7 is sometimes called the **most significant bit** (msb).

Binary arithmetic

One advantage of this method of storing numbers is that arithmetic becomes easy. To see how the 'carry' system works, first count from 1 to 16 in binary and complete the table below:

Decimal	Binary	Decimal	Binary
0	00000	9	
1	00001	10	
2	00010	11	
3		12	
4		13	
5		14	
6		15	
7		16	
8			

We can now try some binary addition:

```
    00011001
+   01010110
    ------------
=   01101111
```

Q7: Convert the above sum to decimal to make sure it is correct.

Q8: Add together the binary equivalents of 7 and 9.

Q9: In a certain computer each number occupies one byte. Convert 128 and 129 to binary numbers each occupying one byte and add them together. Comment on the result.

Q10: In a certain computer program the binary numbers representing 20 and 45 are added together giving 65 (01000001). This code is then sent to the screen to be displayed. What will appear on the screen?

Q11: In the question above, what should have been sent to the screen to display the right result?

Negative numbers and sign bits

We now look at ways of representing negative numbers, using only 0s and 1s. One way to do this is to make the most significant bit a **sign** bit; if this bit is 0 then the number is positive, and if it is 1 the number is negative. In essence we are coding a plus sign as 0 and a minus sign as 1. This is known as the **sign and magnitude** representation of binary numbers. For example, using one-byte numbers:

    00000011= 3
    10000011= -3

Q12: Add together these two numbers and convert the result to decimal. Comment on the result.

Two's complement

A much better way of holding numbers is called **two's complement**. Imagine the mileometer of a car, set at 00000 miles. If the car goes forward one mile the reading becomes 00001. If the meter was turned **back** one mile the reading would be 99999 miles. This could be interpreted as '-1' mile.

Two's complement works in the same way:

    11111101 = -3
    11111110 = -2
    11111111 = -1
    00000000 = 0
    00000001 = 1
    00000010 = 2
    00000011 = 3

Notice that if the number starts with a 1, it represents a negative number.

Adding together the binary equivalents for 3 and -3, we obtain

```
        11111101
  +     00000011
      -----------------
  (1)   00000000      The 'carry' of 1 is ignored.
```

The rules for converting a negative decimal number to binary can be stated as follows:

- Find the binary value of the equivalent positive decimal number
- Change all the 0s to 1s and all the 1s to 0s.
- Add 1 to the result.

An even simpler way of changing the sign of a binary number can be stated as:

- Starting from the right, leave all the digits alone up to and including the first '1'.
- Change all the other digits from 0 to 1 or from 1 to 0.

Example: - 00110100 = 11001100

Q13: Convert the following numbers to binary:

(i) - 5   (ii) - 10   (iii) - 20

Q14: What is the largest negative number that can be held in 8 bits, assuming the leftmost bit is a sign bit?

Binary subtraction

The easiest way of performing binary subtraction is to first convert the number to be subtracted to a negative number, and then add it. Thus, to subtract 12 from 15, using 1 byte for each number,

```
   12    =    00001100  in binary
  - 12   =    11110100
   15    =    00001111
        add   11110100
              ------------
              00000011
```

Q15: Subtract 23 from 123 in binary.

Binary multiplication

Binary multiplication is performed by a combination of shifts and addition. First of all, consider how we multiply ordinary decimal numbers. We will multiply 140 by 201.

```
            1 4 0
    x       2 0 1
    ----------
            1 4 0
          0 0 0
        2 8 0
    ----------
        2 8 1 4 0
    ----------
```

Binary multiplication is performed in exactly the same way. We will multiply 6 by 3.

```
            1 1 0
        x 0 1 1
        -----------
            1 1 0
          1 1 0
        0 0 0
        -----------
        1 0 0 1 0
        -----------
```

Notice that to multiply a binary number by 2, it has to be shifted one place to the left. To multiply by 4, shift two places to the left, and so on.

Q16: Multiply in binary: (i) 13 x 4   (ii) 13 x 5   (iii) 13 x 10

Exercises:

1. Convert the following decimal numbers to binary, using an 8-bit byte.

   (i)   77   (ii)   250   (iii)   - 41   (3 marks)

2. Subtract 107 from 115 in binary and convert the result back to decimal.   (2 marks)

3. Find the largest positive number and the largest magnitude negative number that can be stored in 16 bits, assuming bit 0 is a sign bit, assuming the leftmost bit is a sign bit.   (2 marks)

4. Convert to binary and then multiply 9 by 6.   (2 marks)

5. Convert to binary the number 56. Divide the binary representation by 4, leaving the result in binary.   (2 marks)

Unit 52 — Other Data Types and Representations

The hexadecimal number system

In the hexadecimal (base 16) number system, sixteen characters are used to represent numbers:

0   1   2   3   4   5   6   7   8   9   A   B   C   D   E   F

where A to F are used to denote 10 to 15.

Note that F = 15, *not* 16!

The advantage of this system is that it is easy to convert from binary to hexadecimal ('hex'), and it is more convenient to read and write digits in hex notation than a string of binary 1s and 0s.

To convert a binary number to hex, divide it into groups of four, starting at the right hand side of the number. Then write down the hex equivalent of each group of four digits.

Example:	Binary	1001	0010	0111	1100
	Hex	9	2	7	C

Q1: Convert the following binary numbers to hex:

(i) 0111 0101   (ii) 0000 1110   (iii) 1100 1111

Q2: Convert the following hex numbers to binary:

(i) 12   (ii) 2A   (iii) BC   (iv) FF

To convert a hex number into decimal, the same method is used as for converting a binary number to decimal, remembering that the column headings are now powers of 16 rather than powers of 2:

Thus, the hex number 12D is equal to $1 \times 16^2 + 2 \times 16 + 13 \times 1 = 256 + 32 + 13 = 301$.

Q3: Referring to the table of ASCII codes given in Unit 50 (page 223), express the ASCII codes for the following characters in both hex and decimal numbers:

(i) 0 (zero)   (ii) L   (iii) z

The octal number system

In the octal (base 8) number system, only the eight digits from 0 to 7 are used. To convert a binary number to octal, divide the number into groups of three instead of four, starting from the right. Each set of three bits can then be represented by a number between 0 and 7.

Example:	Binary	001	101	111
	Octal	1	5	7

Q4: Convert the following binary numbers to octal:

(i) 001110111000   (ii) 110101010001

Q5: Convert the following decimal numbers to octal:

(i) 256   (ii) 157   (iii) 64

Binary coded decimal (BCD)

In the binary coded decimal system, each decimal digit is represented by its own binary code.

For example,   7   2   1   9   (ie 7219) is represented by
                  0111   0010   0001   1001

Note that the codes 1010,1011, etc do not exist in this system as there are only ten digits (0 - 9) to be represented.

Q6: Write down the BCD representation of (i) 8653   (ii) 2590

Q7: Convert the number 1641 to (i) binary   (ii) hex   (iii) octal   (iv) BCD

The advantage of the BCD representation is the ease of conversion from BCD to decimal and vice versa. For example, when binary numbers have to be electronically decoded for a pocket calculator display, a number held in BCD format simply has to be split into groups of four bits and each group converted directly to the corresponding decimal digit.

A further advantage of the BCD representation is that since each decimal digit is encoded separately, using as many bits as necessary to represent the complete number exactly, no 'rounding' of numbers occurs. Hence BCD arithmetic is used in business applications where every significant digit has to be retained in a result.

The disadvantage of BCD is that calculations with such numbers are more complex than with pure binary numbers. For example, try adding the BCD representations of 1 and 19:

```
We get   0000 0001
         0001 1001
         --------------
         0001 1010      The first digit, 1, is wrong and 1010 is an invalid code!
```

The problem arises because only the first ten out of sixteen combinations of four digits are used to encode the decimal symbols '0' to '9'. Therefore, whenever the sum of two binary digits is greater than 9, 6 has to be added to the result in order to skip over the six unused codes. Adding the binary representation for 6 to 1010:

```
         0001 1010
              0110
         --------------
         0010 0000      ie 20 in BCD which is the correct answer.
```

Q8: Add the BCD representations of 3 and 8.

Boolean values

So far we have seen how a given binary pattern could represent an ASCII character, a binary integer, or a number held in BCD. A Boolean variable (named after the logician George Boole) is one which can only have one of two values, **true** or **false**, represented by 1 and 0. There are many occasions when it is useful to use one binary digit to show whether something is true or false. For example, a particular bit in memory can be set to show whether a disk drive is connected, another can be set if the 'Break' key is pressed, and yet another set if overflow occurs during an arithmetic operation. Single bits used in this way are called **flags**.

Bitmapped graphics

For the sake of completeness one further use of memory is mentioned here. In a bitmapped system for displaying text and graphics on a VDU, the screen is divided up into a grid, and each square on the grid is called a **pixel** (picture element). A low resolution screen may have 320 by 240 pixels, and a high resolution screen may have 1024 by 1024 pixels or more. A monochrome screen will need just one bit in memory to represent each pixel; if the bit is 1, the pixel is on, and if it is 0, the pixel is off. On a colour screen, each pixel may correspond to one byte in memory, giving a possible 256 colours for each pixel. The memory used is additional to the RAM used for programs and data; it is supplied on a graphics 'card' specific to the type of screen.

Q9: Give five different possible interpretations of a given bit pattern in a computer's memory.

Exercises:

1. What is binary-coded decimal (BCD) representation? What are the advantages and disadvantages of BCD? When might BCD be used to good effect? (5 marks)

    London Paper 2 June 1990

2. The list of characters 170788 could represent one of:

    the number of milliseconds since a microcomputer has been switched on;

    the date when a particular file was last accessed;

    a file name.

    Describe the internal machine representation of this list of characters for each application. (6 marks)

    London Specimen AS Level Paper 1989

3. In a 16-bit register represent:

    (i)   9306 in binary coded decimal form

    (ii)   -12 in two's complement form.

    Convert both representations to hexadecimal. Why does the computing industry use hexadecimal (or octal) to represent binary numbers? (4 marks)

    JMB Paper 1 May 1990

4.** A byte consists of eight bits. A particular computer represents both positive and negative numbers, using two bytes for storing integers and four bytes for storing real numbers.

    Suggest a suitable representation which might be used for

    (a)   integers

    (b)   real numbers.

    Illustrate your answers by showing, in hexadecimal notation, how the numbers -256 and 0.625 would be stored. (7 marks)

    UCLES Paper 1 Nov 1989

5. Convert the following into Binary Coded Decimal (BCD).

    194 and 866

    By showing each stage of the working, illustrate how the computer would add together these BCD representations. (4 marks)

    JMB Paper 1 1991

6.* A computer, which uses a 16 bit address bus and an 8 bit memory word, reserves memory locations 0000 to 1FFF for the operating system. What is the maximum addressable memory available to the user? Give your answer in kilobytes.

    (2 marks)

    AEB Paper 2 1993

(** *Leave this exercise until Unit 53 has been covered*)

Unit 53 — Binary Fractions

Fixed point binary numbers

So far we have considered only **integers** — that is, whole numbers. The system can easily be extended to include fractions, as shown by the following example:

```
100   10   1          1/10    1/100
--------------------------------------------------
 1    3    6     .      7        5
```

The number 136.75 represents 1 hundred, 3 tens, 6 units, 7 tenths and 5 hundredths.

In binary, the equivalent column headings are

```
128   64   32   16   8   4   2   1   . 1/2 1/4 1/8 1/16
```

The number 136.75 can be expressed as 136 + 1/2 + 1/4, and using the column headings above converts to

```
128   64   32   16   8   4   2   1   . 1/2 1/4 1/8 1/16
---------------------------------------------------------------------
 1    0    0    0    1   0   0   0   .  1   1   0   0
```

Notice that the first digit after the point (called the 'binary point') is worth one half, whereas in the decimal system the equivalent digit is only worth one tenth. This means that with the same number of digits after the point, the binary system is less accurate. For example, if we write down an amount in pounds to 2 decimal places, the amount is accurate to the nearest penny. If we converted the amount to binary and only allowed two digits after the binary point, we can only hold .00 (0 pence), .01(25 pence), .10(50 pence) or .11(75 pence) as the fractional part, so the amount is only accurate to the nearest 25 pence.

The following table shows some decimal fractions and their binary equivalent:

Binary fraction	Fraction	Decimal fraction	Binary fraction	Fraction	Decimal fraction
0.1	1/2	0.5	0.000001	1/64	0.015625
0.01	1/4	0.25	0.0000001	1/128	0.0078125
0.001	1/8	0.125	0.00000001	1/256	0.00390625
0.0001	1/16	0.0625	0.000000001	1/512	0.001953125
0.00001	1/32	0.03125	0.0000000001	1/1024	0.0009765625

Negative numbers

As in integer representation, negative numbers can be held using two's complement with the leftmost bit being the sign bit. For example, to convert -5.25 to an 8-bit number with the binary point fixed after the fourth digit:

```
calculate +5.25              0101.0100
change 0s to 1s and 1s to 0s 1010.1011
add 1 to rightmost digit             1
result                       1010.1100   (check: this is -8 + 2.75, which gives -5.25)
```

Q1: Using 1 byte to hold each number, with an imaginary binary point fixed after the fourth digit, convert the following decimal numbers to binary:

(i) 4.25   (ii) 7.1875   (iii) 3.5625   (iv) 3.5627   (v) -1.75

Q2: Convert the following numbers to decimal, assuming 4 bits after the point:

(i) 0000000001101000   (ii) 0000000000110010

Q3: What is (i) the largest number   (ii) the smallest positive number that can be held in two bytes, assuming 4 bits after the point?

Floating point binary

Fixed point representation allows the computer to hold fractions, but the range of numbers is still limited. Even using 4 bytes (32 bits) to hold each number, with 8 bits for the fractional part after the point, the largest number that can be held is just over 8 million. Another format is needed for holding very large numbers.

In decimal, we can show very large numbers as a **mantissa** and an **exponent**. For example

$$1{,}200{,}000{,}000{,}000 \quad \text{can be written as} \quad 0.12 \times 10^{13}$$

Here, 0.12 is called the **mantissa** and 13 is called the **exponent**. The mantissa holds the digits and the exponent defines where to place the decimal point. In the example above, the point is moved 13 places to the right.

The same technique can be used for binary numbers. For example, two bytes (16 bits) might be divided into 10 bits for the mantissa (1 sign bit and 9 digits) and 6 for the exponent.

sign	mantissa	exponent
0	110100000	000011

The sign bit (0) tells us that the number is positive. The mantissa represents 0.1101 and the exponent tells us to move the point 3 places right, so the number becomes 110.1, which converted to decimal is 6.5.

Note that the point starts off between the sign bit and the first bit of the mantissa.

Q4: Convert the following binary numbers to decimal:

	sign	mantissa	exponent
(i)	0	101010000	000010

	sign	mantissa	exponent
(ii)	0	110110000	000100

If the *exponent* is negative (indicated by a 1 in its leftmost bit), the binary point is moved *left* instead of right. So, for example,

sign	mantissa	exponent
0	100000000	111110

represents a mantissa of 0.1 and an exponent of 111110 (-2), so the whole number represents 0.001, that is, one eighth or 0.125.

The rules for converting a binary floating point number to decimal can be summarised as follows:

- if the sign bit is 1, convert the mantissa to its equivalent positive number and preface with a minus sign

- place the point between the sign bit and the first digit of the mantissa

- convert the exponent to its equivalent decimal form (positive or negative)

- move the point right if the exponent is positive, or left if the exponent is negative, the appropriate number of places

- convert the resulting binary number to decimal.

Q5: Convert the following binary numbers to decimal:

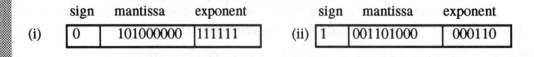

	sign	mantissa	exponent
(i)	0	101000000	111111

	sign	mantissa	exponent
(ii)	1	001101000	000110

Normalisation

The **precision** of the floating point representation described above depends on the number of digits stored in the mantissa. Looking once again at the more familiar decimal system:

the number 34,568,000 can be expressed as $.34568 \times 10^8$, allowing 5 digits for the mantissa,

or as $.3457 \times 10^8$, allowing only 4 places for the mantissa.

Some accuracy has been sacrificed here.

The number could also be written as $.034568 \times 10^9$, but then we need 6 places in the mantissa to achieve the same accuracy. In order to achieve the most accurate representation possible for a given size of mantissa, the number should be written with no leading zeros to the left of the most significant bit.

In binary, the same principle is used. Thus using a mantissa of 9 bits plus a sign bit, the number

0.000001001 would be represented in the mantissa as 0.100100000 , with an exponent of 111011 (-5).

This is known as **normalised form**, and in the case of a positive number, is the form in which the first bit of the mantissa, not counting the sign bit, is 1.

Note that the mantissa of a positive number in normalised form always lies between 1/2 and 1.

Example: Normalise the floating point binary number 0 000110101 000010

Step 1:   Put in the assumed binary point, and convert the exponent to decimal, giving

    0.000110101   Exponent = 2.

Step 2:   Shift the number left 3 places so that the binary point immediately precedes the first 1, and subtract 3 from the exponent.

    0.110101000   Exponent = 2 - 3 = -1.

    Answer: 0.110101000 111111

Q6: Normalise the following numbers, which are held with a 10-bit mantissa and a 6-bit exponent.

    (i) 0 000000110 000111   (ii) 0 000010111 000110

Negative numbers

With negative numbers, the normalised form is the one in which the first bit of the mantissa, not counting the sign bit, is 0. To normalise a negative number, therefore, shift the number left until the first bit (not counting the sign bit) is 0, and adjust the exponent accordingly.

Note that the mantissa of a negative number in normalised form always lies between -1/2 and -1.

Example: Normalise the following number: 1 111100100 000011

Step 1:   Insert the assumed binary point to the right of the sign bit, and convert the exponent to decimal, giving

    1.111100100   Exponent = 3

Step 2:   Shift the number left 4 times so that the first bit of the mantissa is 0, and subtract 4 from the exponent, giving

    1.001000000   Exponent = 3 - 4 = -1

    Answer: 1 001000000 111111

Q7: Normalise the following numbers:

    (i) 1 111110111 000000   (ii) 1 111111010 000011

Converting from decimal to binary normalised form

- convert the number to binary, using a point to indicate the fractional part
- shift the number as many places left or right as necessary to convert to normal form
- *Subtract* one from the exponent for each *left* shift, *add* one for each *right* shift.

Example: To convert -0.375 to binary floating point normalised form:

Step 1: Convert to binary: -0.375 = -(0.25+0.125) = -0.011000000

Step 2: Convert this to a negative number: -0.011000000 = 1.101000000

Step 3: Shift left one place, getting 1.010000000

Step 4: Subtract 1 from the exponent giving -1, that is, in 6-bit binary, 111111

the number is therefore   1 010000000 111111

With negative numbers having a magnitude greater than 1, a better strategy is to convert the equivalent positive number to binary normalised form, and then find the two's complement of the mantissa.

Example: Convert the number -9.5 to binary floating point normalised form.

Step 1: Convert +9.5 to binary: 9.5 = 1001.1

Step 2: Convert to normalised form by shifting binary point 4 places left: 0.100110000×2^4

Step 3: Find two's complement of the mantissa: 1.011010000   Exponent is 4.

Answer is 1 011010000 000100

Q8: Convert the numbers .0625 and -.0625 to binary floating point normalised form, using a 10-bit mantissa and a 6-bit exponent. Then try 27.25 and -27.25.

Exercises:

1. A twelve-bit register in a certain computer is split up such that 8 bits are used in fractional 2's complement representation to represent the mantissa and the remaining 4 bits are used as an integer 2's complement representation for the exponent. Using this register write down the bit pattern which represents the following numbers in normalised form.

   (i) + 1   (ii) - 3   (iii) 0.125   (iv) - 0.25

   You should state any assumptions which you make.
   (4 marks)
London Paper 1 June 1990

2. Illustrate what is meant by normalisation in the context of floating point form.
   (3 marks)
AEB Specimen Paper 2 1990

3.* Numbers can be stored in a computer in either integer form or floating point form.

   Give (i) **two** reasons for using floating point representation,

   (ii) **two** reasons for using integer representation.
   (4 marks)
JMB Paper 1 1992

Unit 54 — Floating Point Arithmetic

Floating point addition and subtraction

Before looking at these operations in binary, we will gain an appreciation of the principles involved in floating point arithmetic by looking at equivalent decimal calculations.

In decimal, when adding two numbers involving decimal points, we first have to line up the points.

For example:

```
            132.156
    +         1.0318
          -------------
            133.1878
```

In their 'normalised form', the two numbers given above would be expressed as

$.132156 \times 10^3$ and

$.103180 \times 10^1$

Clearly we do not simply add the mantissas, and the same principle will hold true in binary. The rules for addition and subtraction can be stated as

- line up the points by making the exponents equal

- add or subtract the mantissas

- normalise the result

Q1: Using the above rules, add together the decimal numbers 1.562×10^4 and 3.128×10^2.

Example: Convert the decimal numbers 0.25 and 10.5 to normalised floating point binary form using a 10-bit mantissa and a 6-bit exponent. Add together the two normalised binary numbers, giving the result in normalised floating point binary form.

Step 1:   The numbers in normalised form are:

sign	mantissa	exponent		sign	mantissa	exponent
0	100000000	111111		0	101010000	000100

Step 2:   Write the mantissas with a binary point, and convert the exponents to decimal, giving

0.100000000   exponent -1   and

0.101010000   exponent 4

Step 3:   Make both exponents 0 and shift the binary points accordingly.

0.010000000 (make the number *smaller* as you *increase* the exponent)

1010.100000 (make the number *larger* as you *decrease* the exponent)

Step 4:   Add: 1010.110000 (check — this is 10.75, which is correct)

Step 5:   Normalise: 0.101011000 exponent 4.

Result is therefore   0101011000   000100

241

Q2: Add together the two binary numbers given below, leaving the result in normalised floating point binary form.

sign	mantissa	exponent
0	110000000	111111

sign	mantissa	exponent
0	110100000	000010

Multiplication of floating point numbers

Again, we will use decimal numbers to illustrate the process. Suppose we want to calculate

$$(5 \times 10^2) \times (7 \times 10^3)$$

This is the same as $\quad (5 \times 7) \times 10^2 \times 10^3$

$$= \quad 35 \times 10^5$$

In other words, we *multiply* the mantissas and *add* the exponents. We can now normalise the result, giving

$$.35 \times 10^7$$

The rules for multiplication can be stated as

- multiply the mantissas

- add the exponents

- normalise the result

Example: Multiply the two binary numbers below:

sign	mantissa	exponent
0	100000000	111111

and

sign	mantissa	exponent
0	101010000	000100

Step 1: Write the mantissas with decimal points, and convert the exponents to decimal, giving

0.100000000   exponent -1

0.101010000   exponent 4

Step 2: Multiply the mantissas. 0.10101 x 0.1 = 0.010101 (in this particular case we are multiplying the second number by the binary equivalent of 0.5, ie dividing it by 2).

Step 3: Add the exponents. -1 + 4 = 3

Step 4: Normalise the mantissa by moving the binary point right, and compensate by subtracting one from the exponent, which becomes 2, or in binary, 000010

This gives the result, ie   0   101010000   000010

Phew!

Q3: Convert the numbers 20 and 2 to normalised floating point form and multiply them together.

Division of floating point numbers

The rules for division can be stated as

- divide the mantissas

- subtract the exponents

- normalise the result

Q4: Using the decimal numbers 126.4 and 0.08, show the main steps required to divide two floating point numbers. (Normalise the two numbers first, and show the answer in normalised form).

Exercises:

1. Using a 10 bit mantissa and a 6-bit exponent, convert to binary normalised form the numbers

    (i)   5.25   (iii) 16.8

    (ii)   -18.75   (iv)   0.25   **(4 marks)**

    Using the representations obtained, perform the following computations:

    (v)   Add together 5.25 and 16.8

    (vi)   Multiply 16.8 by 0.25.   **(4 marks)**

2. Calculate the value of 11.11 (binary) + 11.01 x 2^{-2} and express your answer as a normalised floating point number in the form a x 2^b where the mantissa a is in the range 1/2 <= a < 1.

    All values are positive.   **(6 marks)**
    NISEAC Paper 1 1990

3.* The binary number 1001 0111 0011 can be interpreted in a number of different ways. State its value in denary if it represents

    (i)   an unsigned binary integer

    (ii)   a binary coded decimal integer

    (iii) a two's complement floating point number with an eight bit mantissa followed by a four bit exponent. **(4 marks)**
    AEB Paper 2 1992

Unit 55 — Range and Accuracy of Floating Point Numbers

The range of normalised floating point numbers

We can calculate for a given size of mantissa and exponent the range of numbers that can be held.

The maximum positive number

In a system which stores numbers in a 16-bit word with a 10-bit mantissa and a 6-bit exponent, the largest number that can be held will have the largest positive mantissa and the largest positive exponent.

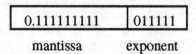

0.111111111	011111

mantissa   exponent

This means that the binary point is moved 31 places to the right, and the number, converted to decimal, is close to 2^{31}.

Q1: Using a 10-bit register with a 6-bit mantissa and a 4-bit exponent, calculate the largest possible positive number that can be held, and convert it to decimal.

The minimum positive number

The minimum positive number that can be held will have the smallest positive mantissa and the largest negative exponent.

Q2: Using a 10-bit register as above, show in binary the smallest positive integer. Convert this number to decimal.

The largest magnitude negative number

This will have the largest magnitude negative mantissa and the largest positive exponent.

Q3: Using a 10-bit register as above, show in binary the largest magnitude negative number and convert it to decimal.

The smallest magnitude negative number

This has the smallest negative mantissa and the largest negative exponent. In a 10-bit register as above, this is

        1.01111   1000   ie 1.1111111101111 after shifting right 8 places

Note that 1.01111 is the smallest negative number in standard form, which requires the first digit after the decimal point to be 0 in the case of a negative number (and 1 in the case of a positive number).

Q4: Find the two's complement of this number and convert it to decimal, correct to 3 decimal places.

The representation of zero

A problem arises in the representation of zero in floating point arithmetic, since zero (000000) is not a normalised number, and therefore does not exist in this system! It has to be represented by the smallest possible positive number.

Q5: How is zero represented in a 16-bit register with 10 bits for the mantissa and six bits for the exponent? What is the decimal equivalent of this number?

In practice, 16 bits does not provide sufficient accuracy for general use, and even the smallest microcomputer will use many more digits for floating point numbers, with 32 being common. The range and accuracy of floating point numbers will typically range from

$+1.5 \times 10^{-45}$ <= positive range <= 3.4×10^{38} with an accuracy of 7 - 8 digits

For increased accuracy, **double precision numbers** are used, taking up double the normal number of bits, which greatly increases both the range and accuracy.

Excess 64 notation

Exponents of floating point numbers are often represented by **excess 64 code**, or **excess 128 code**. With an 8-bit exponent taking values in the range -128 to 127, the exponent is coded as a positive value in binary by adding 128. Thus for example 7 is coded as 128+7 = 135 and -10 is coded as 128 - 10 =118.

Computational errors

In many cases, however many bits are allowed for the mantissa in floating point format, a decimal number cannot be held completely accurately. In 4 bits, for example, we can represent 0.1875 (which is equal to .125+.0625) exactly, but we cannot represent 0.1877 exactly.

Q6: Convert the numbers 0.1875, 0.1877 and 0.2 to binary in a 4 bit register.

The **precision** of a number will be determined by how many bits are used to hold the mantissa. If the mantissa is held in 4 bits, then the smallest mantissa that can be held is .0001 in binary, or 1/16 in decimal. Any number held can only be precise to the nearest sixteenth.

There are a number of errors that can occur during computation. When numbers are held in floating point form, errors can occur owing to **rounding** or **truncation** of values that cannot be represented exactly. These errors can soon accumulate in some calculations to the extent that the final result appears quite inaccurate. An example from business data processing is in the calculation of monthly mortgage repayments, where each payment is calculated from the previous one. If insufficient precision is used, the inaccuracy can be quite significant after a few years! Frequently in commercial data processing calculations are carried out in fixed point integer representation where possible in order to avoid rounding errors. If decimal points need to be used, then fixed point representation may be used, and although rounding will still occur, better precision may be obtained. Another alternative is to use BCD arithmetic.

Overflow

Overflow occurs when a computation produces an answer that is too big to be represented. It happens so frequently with multiplication that double length registers are used to hold the result.

Underflow

If a result is smaller than the smallest number that can be held, an underflow error occurs. Sometimes an error message is given, but sometimes the system simply puts the result equal to zero.

Exercises:

1. If numbers to be represented in floating point format are restricted to a fixed word length, explain how the range of the representation could be increased.

    What other effect would this have on the representation? (3 marks)
    London Paper 2 June 1990

2. Give **two** reasons why fixed point number systems are used in preference to floating point number systems in commercial data processing work.

    Give **one** reason why floating point numbers are used in scientific work. (3 marks)
    AEB Paper 1 1990

3. Two systems store numbers in 16 bit words. The first system uses a fixed point representation with the point assumed to be after the tenth bit (from the left). The second system uses a normalised floating binary point representation with a ten bit mantissa and six bit exponent. Both systems store negative numbers and use two's complement notation.

    Example: The floating point representation of 4 is

    0100000000   000011

    (i)   Compare the range of positive numbers in each system and examine the accuracy of the floating point representation of the largest number in the fixed point system. (6 marks)

    (ii) If in the fixed point system, two successive 16 bit memory locations contain the hexadecimal numbers 00DC and FD40, write down the denary equivalent of both numbers. (4 marks)

    (iii) In the floating point system write down the binary equivalent of the denary numbers 7/32 and -24. (4 marks)

    (iv) Outline the main steps needed to multiply two numbers in the floating point system. Include in your answer the steps required to normalise the result. (6 marks)
    AEB Paper 1 1989

4.* A floating-point number is being held in 5 consecutive bytes.

    (i)   Using a diagram show clearly a possible representation of the number.

    (ii) Explain how your representation will determine both the accuracy and the range of the numbers which can be stored. (5 marks)
    NISEAC Paper 2 1991

Unit 56 — The Fetch-Execute Cycle

Inside the CPU

We have seen that a computer consists of the processor, memory, input and output units. The processor itself consists of two main components:

- the **arithmetic-logic unit (ALU)** in which all arithmetic and logic operations are carried out

- the **control unit,** which coordinates the activities taking place in the CPU, memory and peripherals, by sending control signals to the various devices.

In addition, the CPU contains circuitry controlling the interpretation and execution of instructions. Special storage locations called **registers** are included in this circuitry to hold information temporarily while it is being decoded or manipulated. Some of these special purpose registers are shown in the block diagram and explained below.

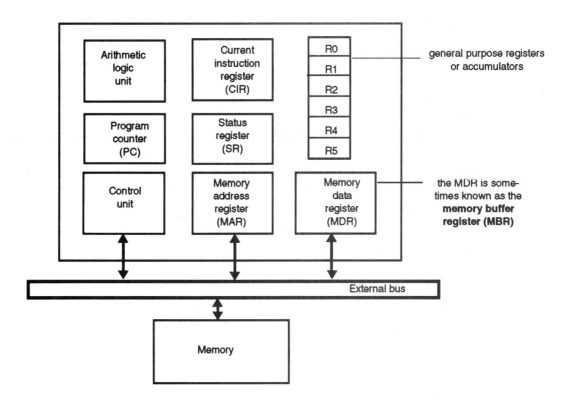

Figure 56.1 — Registers inside the CPU

The registers shown in the block diagram above, which represents a 'typical' computer, each have a specific purpose, which is described below:

- the **program counter (PC)** holds the address of the next instruction to be executed. It is also variously known as the **instruction register**, the **sequence control register (SCR)**, or the **sequence register**.

  When a sequence of instructions is being executed, the program counter is automatically incremented to point to the next instruction — that is, it holds the address of the next instruction to be executed. Depending on the length of the current instruction, this may mean that 1, 2 or 3 has to be added to its current contents. If the current instruction is a branch or jump instruction, then the address to branch to is copied from the current instruction to the program counter.

- The **general purpose registers** are used for performing arithmetic functions. In some computers, there is only one general purpose register, usually called an **accumulator**, which acts as a working area. Other computers have up to 16 general purpose registers.

  For example, an instruction to add the contents of memory locations 1000 and 1001 and store the result in location 1002 might be broken down into the instructions:

  ```
  Load contents of 1000 into the accumulator
  Add contents of 1001 to the accumulator
  Store contents of accumulator in 1002
  ```

- The **current instruction register (CIR)** contains both the **operator** and the **operand** of the current instruction. For example, a machine language instruction to load the contents of location 1000 into the accumulator might be written

  ```
  LDA  1000
  ```

  where LDA is the **operator**, and 1000 is the **operand**.

- The **memory address register (MAR)** holds the address of the memory location from which information will be read or to which data will be written. Remember that both instructions and data are held in memory, so that sometimes the MAR will hold the address of an instruction to be fetched, and sometimes it will hold the address of data to be used in an instruction. Thus when an instruction is to be 'fetched', the contents of the program counter are copied to this register. so that the CPU will know where in memory to get the next instruction from.

- The **memory data register (MDR)** is used to temporarily store information read from or written to memory. The instruction (for example, LDA 1000) is placed here en route to the CIR where it will be decoded. When the instruction has been decoded, the operand, 1000, will be placed in the MAR and the contents of location 1000 will then be copied to the MDR.

  All transfers from memory to the CPU go via the memory data register. Both the memory data register and the memory address register serve as 'buffer' registers to compensate for the difference in speed between the CPU and memory.

- The **status register (SR)** contains bits that are set or cleared based on the result of an instruction. For example, one particular bit will be set if overflow occurs, and another bit set if the result of the last instruction was negative. Based on this information the CPU could make a decision on whether to branch out of a given sequence.

  Status registers (also known as program status words or PSWs) also contain information about interrupts, which are discussed in detail in Section 8, Unit 65.

The steps in the fetch-execute cycle

The sequence of operations involved in executing an instruction can be subdivided into two phases — the **fetch** cycle and the **execution** cycle. In addition to executing instructions, the CPU has to supervise other operations such as data transfers between input/output devices and main memory. When an I/O device needs to transfer data, it generates an **interrupt** and the CPU suspends execution of the program and transfers to an appropriate interrupt handling program. A test for the presence of interrupts is carried out at the end of each instruction cycle.

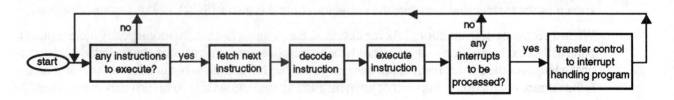

Figure 56.2 — the fetch-execute cycle

How the CPU registers are used

This cycle can be broken down into a more detailed account of how the various registers are used. The diagram below shows a typical sequence of events.

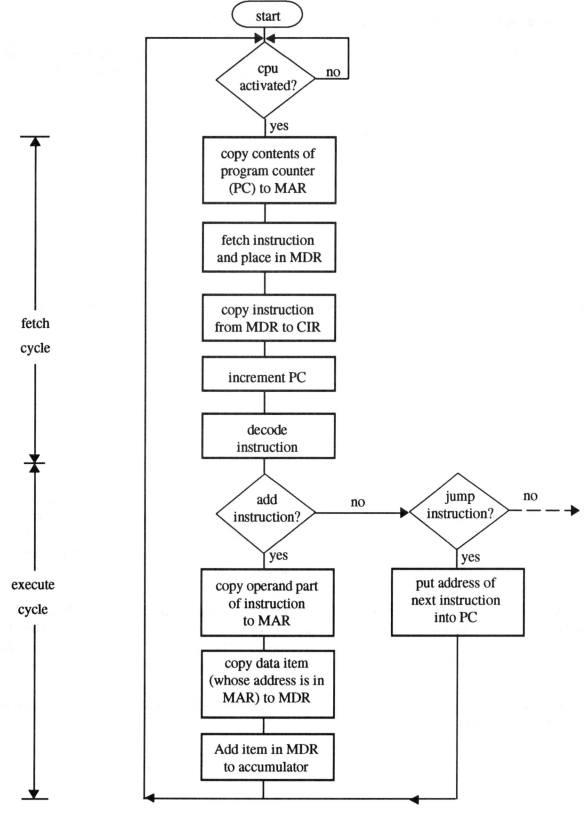

Figure 56.3 — Detail of the fetch-execute cycle

Q1: Describe the sequence of events carried out during the fetch-execute cycle when obeying the first of the instructions below, showing the contents of each of the following registers during the cycle:

> program counter (PC), memory address register (MAR), memory data register (MDR), current instruction register (CIR), accumulator (ACC)

Address	Contents	Type	Comment
500	LDA 1000	instruction	load contents of location 1000 into ACC
503	ADD 1001	instruction	add contents of location 1001 into ACC
506	STO 1002	instruction	store contents of ACC in location 1002
1000	3	data	
1001	5	data	
1002	0	data	

The stack pointer

In addition to the registers mentioned above, most computers use a special register called a **stack pointer** which points to the top of a set of memory locations known as a **stack**. (A stack is a data structure which can only be accessed at the 'top', like a pile of plates). When execution of a program is interrupted for any reason (for example, in a multiprogramming computer another program takes over the CPU), the status of the interrupted program and the current contents of all the registers are saved on the stack, and the stack pointer updated to show where the information is held.

Stacks may also be used instead of general purpose registers to store the intermediate results of arithmetic operations, and to hold return addresses and parameter information when subroutines are called. Whenever a subroutine is called in the program, the contents of the program counter, which contains the address of the next instruction after the CALL, is saved on the stack. A RETURN instruction fetches this value off the stack and loads it into the program counter.

There are also instructions that allow the programmer to push the contents of the accumulator or registers onto the stack and 'pop' them off again.

(Stacks are covered in detail in Section 3, Unit 26).

Recap: the accumulator and general purpose registers

It is important to understand that **all** operations take place in the accumulator or a general purpose register. Thus for example the machine code equivalent of

```
P := Q - R
```

will be something like

```
Load Q into the accumulator
Subtract R from the accumulator
Store the contents of the accumulator in P
```

Q2: Write the machine code equivalent of (i) P := 100;   (ii) NUM1 := NUM2;

Exercises:

1.   List the steps executed during:

   (i)   the fetch phase, and

   (ii)   the execution phase for an unconditional jump instruction.   (6 marks)
                                                                                NISEAC Paper 2 1989

2.   (a)   Describe briefly the function of each of the following registers within the Central Processing Unit (CPU) of a computer:

   Program Counter;

   Instruction Register;

   Memory Address Register;

   Accumulator.   (4 marks)

   (b)   Describe the flow of data within the CPU, and between the CPU and memory, as instructions are fetched and executed.   (3 marks)
                                                                                SEB Paper 1 1990

3.   An 8-bit microcomputer has a 16-bit stack pointer that points to the store location above the top of the stack. The operation PUSH (machine code 07) pushes the content of the accumulator onto the stack and increments the stack pointer. At a certain instant the state of the machine is

value of stack pointer	1234
value of program counter	1233
content of location 1233	07
content of accumulator	07

   Explain what happens as a result of the next **four** instruction executions. What is the final effect on the contents of the immediate access store?   (6 marks)
                                                                                JMB Specimen Paper 1989

4.*   The last instruction in an assembly language program, the HALT instruction, is omitted by mistake. If this error is not detected by the assembler, explain the likely outcome in terms of the fetch/execute cycle if the corresponding machine code program is executed.   (6 marks)
                                                                                NISEAC Paper 2 1992

Unit 57 — Buses and Computer Architectures

Internal and external buses

A bus is a set of wires designed to transfer data, addresses and control information from a specified source to a specified destination. There are two types of buses:

- **internal buses** which connect the various registers and internal components of the CPU

- **external buses** which connect the CPU to main memory and to the input/output units.

A bus may be **unidirectional,** capable of transmitting in one direction only, or it may be **bidirectional**. A **dedicated bus** is a unidirectional bus connecting one source and one destination.

In a **single bus system**, dedicated buses connect each separate unit. This means, for example, that twelve separate buses are needed to connect four units to each other, as shown in the diagram below. The advantage of a single bus system is that it permits simultaneous transfer of data, but it is costly in terms of wires and cables if the distances are long. Also, the number of pins and logic gates on the integrated circuits increase rapidly with the number of external buses connected.

For these reasons, a **shared bus system** is often used, even though simultaneous transfer of data is no longer possible. A further advantage of a shared bus system is that more devices can easily be added.

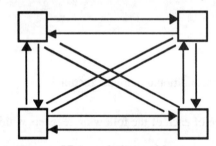

Figure 57.1 — dedicated buses

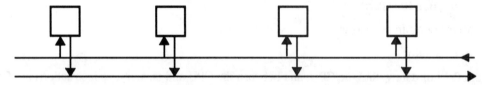

Figure 57.2 — A shared bus system

Control buses

Control buses are used to send control signals between the control unit and the ALU, between the processor and memory, and between processor units and peripherals. Examples of such signals are:

- signals to directly control the operation of the ALU

- signals to indicate a status condition such as 'busy' or 'operation complete'

- signals to indicate that an error condition such as overflow has occurred

- start and stop signals and timing information.

Processor characteristics

The main features which distinguish one processor from another and which determine the performance of each are:

- clock speed
- word size
- architecture

Clock speed

In order to synchronise the various steps carrried out during the fetch-execute cycle, all processors have an internal clock which generates regularly timed pulses. All processor activities such as fetching an instruction, reading data into the memory data register etc must begin on a clock pulse, though some activities may take more than one clock pulse to complete. Typically, the clock pulse rate is between between 4 and 50 Megahertz (million cycles per second). The clock speed, therefore, is one of the factors which will influence the speed at which instructions are executed; a 30MHz processor will in general operate faster than a 20MHz processor.

Word and bus size

Word size was mentioned in Unit 50. Bits may be grouped into 8-, 16- or 32-bit 'words', and processed as a unit during input and output, arithmetic and logic instructions, so that a processor with a 32-bit word will operate faster than a processor with a 16-bit word. However, not all processors with a 32-bit word have a 32-bit **data bus**, and so the data may have to be fetched in, for example, two groups of 16 bits.

Q1: Distinguish between the **data bus** and the **address bus**. What is the maximum address, expressed in hexadecimal that can be directly addressed in a processor with a 16-bit address bus? What is the lowest address? Express the maximum number of directly addressable locations in kilobytes.

Input/Output

In order to communicate with the CPU, input/output units have to be connected to it via an external bus. However, since there is such a wide range of speed (**baud rate**), timing, synchronisation, code conversion requirements and so on, I/O units cannot be connected directly to the bus; instead, each device is connected to its own **interface unit**, which in turn is connected to the bus.

Data may be transmitted in either **parallel** or **serial** mode. A parallel bus with 8 lines can transfer one byte at a time, whereas a serial bus transfers one bit at a time. A commonly used serial interface is the **RS-232C** interface, used for example to connect a modem to the CPU. It normally uses a 25-pin connector.

You may wonder why 25 pins are needed when all the data is being sent down only one line in a serial bus. The other lines are used for control signals, timing signals, secondary data channels, grounding and other miscellaneous functions. Some in fact are not used at all.

Parallel connections can only be used over a short distance; printers, for example, normally use parallel interfaces when the printer is located close to the CPU, otherwise they have to use a serial interface.

Handshaking protocol

Both parallel and serial buses will have a number of extra lines, in addition to the data lines, used for controlling the data transfer. Two or three lines may be used for the **handshaking procedure**. This is the means by which the devices check whether the other end is ready to receive data, or inform the other end that they are ready to receive. The 'conversation' between two devices is along the lines of the following:

Device 1: "Are you ready to receive some data?"
Device 2: "Yes, go ahead."
Device 1: *(sends data)*
Device 2: "Message received, thanks!"

Parallel processing computers

Over the past few decades computers have been getting progressively smaller and faster. However, we are now approaching the theoretical limits of miniaturisation, with components only a few atoms wide on silicon chips, and a single particle of radiation sufficient to alter the contents of memory. Manufacturers are already approaching the limits of the capabilities of single processors, constrained as they are by the finite speed of the electron. Any further increase in speed must come from parallel processing, whereby operations — perhaps hundreds, thousands or even millions of them — are performed concurrently, using separate processors. Parallelism can be achieved either by having more than one **instruction stream** or by having more than one **data element** operated on simultaneously, or a combination of both of these, as described below.

Flynn's classification of computer architectures

Michael J. Flynn (1966) classified computer architectures into four different types:

1. **SISD:** single instruction stream, single data stream

2. **SIMD:** single instruction stream, multiple data stream

3. **MISD:** multiple instruction stream, single data stream (no computer falls into this theoretical category)

4. **MIMD:** multiple instruction stream, multiple data stream

The three existing types of architecture (1, 2 and 4) will now be discussed.

SISD (single instruction stream, single data stream)

An SISD computer is the conventional serial computer in which instructions are executed one by one and a single instruction deals with at most one data operation. However, a degree of parallelism can be achieved using a technique called **pipelining** to speed up the processing. This works as explained below.

Suppose that each instruction consists of four stages; fetch, decode, execute, and write the result to its destination. As soon as the first instruction has been fetched, a second one is fetched while the first is being decoded, and so on as shown in Figure 57.3. Once the pipeline has started there will always be four instructions being processed in parallel.

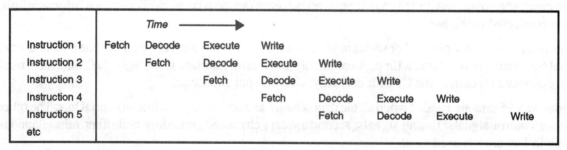

Figure 57.3 - Pipelining

SIMD (single instruction stream, multiple data stream)

In this type of computer, a single instruction may initiate a large number of operations. These **vector instructions**, as they are called, are executed one at a time but are able to work on several data streams at once. The processor is called an **array processor**, and it has several **processing elements** operating in parallel. The processing elements, each consisting of an ALU and registers, are all under the control of a *single* control unit. Each program instruction is transmitted simultaneously to the processing elements.

For example, in the following piece of code:

```
for i:=1 to m do
     x[i] := p[i] + q[i];
```

m processors can work simultaneously, each calculating one element of the array.

MIMD (multiple instruction stream, multiple data stream)

Each instruction stream operates on separate data streams. This class of computer includes multiprocessor systems from linked mainframe computers to large arrays of microprocessors. The processors have to be coordinated as they are all co-operating on a single task; this is distinct from a computer capable of multiprocessing, where all the processors are performing different but unconnected tasks.

Parallel processing is being used for applications such as image processing (for example, images of Mars sent back from a space probe), computer simulations, graphics applications and numerical weather forecasting.

RISC architecture

RISC stands for Reduced Instruction Set Computer, and as the name suggests, a computer with this type of architecture can execute only a small number of different instructions. Research has shown that the average processor spends nearly all its time executing the same few instructions (eg Add, Subtract, Load, Store, Branch) and RISC processors can operate at much faster speeds than conventional procesors. They do this partly by making extensive use of pipelining, and also because the small number of fixed format instructions is faster to decode and execute. Addressing modes are also minimal to reduce complexity and thus increase the speed.

Exercises:

1. (a) The processing unit of a computer contains an 8 bit data bus, a 16 bit address bus, a control bus and a number of registers including a program counter and a stack pointer.

    (i) What is a bus? (3 marks)

    (ii) Explain the functions of a control bus. (2 marks)

    (iii) How many bits will be contained in each memory location? (1 mark)

    (iv) If memory locations 0000 to 0FFF are reserved for the operating system, what is the maximum directly addressable memory available to the user? Give your answer in kilobytes. (2 marks)

    (v) Describe the main functions of the program counter and the stack pointer. (2 marks)

    (b) The computer is called upon to execute the following machine code instructions by automatic sequence control:

    PC = 1000 and SP = 7000

    Memory

Address	Contents		
1000	3E	)	Load into the accumulator the number 8
1001	08	)	
1002	CD	)	
1003	00	)	Subroutine call to address 4000
1004	40	)	

    (i) Describe the action of the fetch-execute cycle in processing the first instruction. Your answer should clearly state the registers utilised. (6 marks)

    (ii) State the contents of the memory locations and registers which will be altered by executing the CALL instruction. (4 marks)
    AEB Paper 1 1990

2. What are the limitations of a conventional processor? Why is there such interest in overcoming these limitations? Outline a technique that may be used to overcome these limitations. (5 marks)
    London Specimen Paper 1989

3.* Temperature measurements taken from a large number of weather stations are sent once a day to a weather prediction program which computes the daily average for **each station** by performing exactly the **same** calculation on each set of readings. Describe briefly a suitable *processor architecture* that would enable the daily average for stations to be calculated **simultaneously**. (2 marks)
    AEB Paper 1 1992

Unit 58 — Assembly and Machine Language

The instruction set

Instructions in machine language are in the form of binary codes, with each different processor using different codes for the instruction set supported by its hardware. The instruction set of a typical computer includes the following types of instructions:

- **data transfer** such as MOVE, LOAD, STORE
- **arithmetic operations** such as ADD, SUBTRACT, MULTIPLY, DIVIDE, SHIFT
- **logical operations** such as AND, OR, NOT, exclusive-OR
- **comparison instructions**
- **branch instructions**; unconditional, conditional, subroutine calls and returns.

Data transfer instructions

Examples of data transfer instructions include:

- moving data from memory to a register
- moving data from a register to memory or to an output unit
- moving data from an output unit to a register.

Typically, two-, three- or four-character **mnemonics** are used for all machine code instructions, such as

```
MOV  R1, R2    Move contents of register R2 to R1
LD   R1, #32   Load the number 32 into R1
STO  X, R1     Store contents of R1 in memory location X
```

Arithmetic instructions

Some microprocessors offer only addition and subtraction as the basic arithmetic operations. Others offer a more comprehensive set such as:

```
ADD        addition
SUB        subtraction
MPY        multiplication
DIV        division
INC        increment
DEC        decrement
NEG        sign change
ABS        absolute value
```

After an arithmetic operation has been carried out, it is often useful to be able to test the result to see whether it was, say, zero or negative, or whether 'carry' or overflow occurred. The status register in some processors includes 4 bits referred to as N, Z, V and C which are set to 1 or 0 depending on the result of the previous operation, as follows:

If result is negative, N = 1

If result is zero, Z = 1

If overflow occurred, V = 1

If carry occurred, C = 1

These bits are called **status bits** or **condition codes**. Conditional branch instructions such as BZ (Branch if zero) check the status of the relevant status bit (often called a 'flag') and branch accordingly.

Carry and overflow

In a microprocessor using 8-bit registers, the range of integers that can be held in one register is from -128 to 127, and if the result of an arithmetic operation falls outside that range, the overflow bit will be set to 1, otherwise it will be set to 0.

Example:
```
        0100 0000    (64)
    +   0100 0001    (65)
        -------------
        1000 0001    (-127)
```

The sign bit has changed to 1, and the result is negative. This situation can be detected by examining the overflow bit, which will have been set by this operation.

The carry bit will **not** have been set, because there is no external carry — that is, all the binary digits still fit into the 8-bit register.

Adding two large negative numbers will cause both the overflow bit and the carry bit to be set, as shown below:

Example:
```
        1100 0000    (-64)
    +   1011 1111    (-65)
        -------------
    (1) 0111 1111    (+127)
```

In some situations the carry bit will be set and the overflow bit will not be set.

Example:
```
        1111 1111    (-1)
    +   1111 1111    (-1)
        -------------
    (1) 1111 1110    (-2)
```

Here, -2 is the correct answer and the carry bit can be ignored.

The overflow bit, then, warns that the sign of the result has been accidentally changed and action must be taken. The carry bit indicates that a ninth bit has been set and action may or may not be needed, as we shall see when performing double precision arithmetic.

Q1: Complete the following additions, showing the status of the carry and overflow bits, and stating whether or not the answers are correct.

```
(i)      0000 0111    (7)       (ii)      1111 1100    (-4)      (iii)          0010 1100
     +   1111 1100    (-4)          +     1111 1000    (-8)             +       0100 1110
         -------------                    -------------                         -------------

         -------------                    -------------                         -------------
     V =      C =    Correct?         V =    C =      Correct?          V =   C =    Correct?


(iv)     0111 1000    (120)      (v)      1110 0001    (-31)
     +   0110 0001    (97)           +    1000 0001    (-127)
         -------------                    -------------

         -------------                    -------------
     V =      C =    Correct?         V =    C =    Correct?
```

Assembly language instructions to add two numbers

The instructions below, which are written in 6502 assembly language, add together two numbers stored in LOC1 and LOC2, leaving the result in LOC3.

```
CLC              clear the carry bit
CLD              clear the decimal bit
LDA  LOC1        load first operand into register A
ADC  LOC2        add the second operand
STA  LOC3        store result in LOC3
```

Note that this particular assembly language only has an 'Add with carry' instruction, automatically adding into the register the contents of the carry bit — we do not want that to happen here, so we first make sure the carry bit is 0. Also, there are two possible modes of addition; decimal mode for BCD arithmetic and binary mode for binary arithmetic, indicated by a 'decimal bit'. We want binary arithmetic here and the decimal bit needs to be set to zero before the operation.

Adding larger numbers

Using only 8 bits restricts us to numbers in the range -128 to 127, which is clearly not enough for many applications. Frequently two or more registers will be used to hold each number, and it is up to the programmer to keep track of where the 'high half' and 'low half' of a two-byte number are stored.

Example: A 16-bit number stored in LOC1 and LOC1 + 1 is to be added to a 16-bit number stored in LOC2 and LOC2 + 1, and the result stored in RES and RES + 1. It is assumed that the high half of each number is in the lower address (though this need not necessarily always be the case). We will also assume that the result is small enough to be stored in 16 bits without causing overflow.

```
CLC                clear the carry bit
CLD                clear the decimal bit
LDA  LOC1 + 1      load low half of first operand into register A
ADC  LOC2 + 1      add low half of second operand
STA  RES + 1       store low half of result
LDA  LOC1          load high half of first operand
ADC  LOC2          add high half of second operand
STA  RES           store high half of result
```

Q2: Dry run the above instructions with the numbers below, showing how the value of the carry bit changes.

LOC1	LOC1 + 1	LOC2	LOC2 + 1	RES	RES + 1
0000 1100	1000 1111	0000 0000	1000 0001		

Exercises:

1.   A simple binary adder forms the sum of two positive binary integers each stored in a single byte. On testing, the sum of 120 and 130 is found to be 250, while the sum of 220 and 230 is found to be 194.

     Explain the most likely reason for this inconsistent behaviour.

     Suggest how this situation is normally detected and how it might be remedied.   (6 marks)

     NISEAC Paper 1 1989

Unit 59 — Shifts, Logical Instructions and Branches

Shift instructions

There are generally 2 or 3 different shift operations available; **logical, arithmetic** and **rotate.**

A **logical** shift right causes the least significant bit (lsb) to be shifted into the carry bit, and a zero moves in to occupy the vacated space.

eg	before	after	carry
	01101011	00110101	1

It is useful for examining the least significant bit of a number. After the operation, the carry bit can be tested and a conditional branch instruction executed.

Q1: Shift the binary pattern 0100 0111 right once and then left once, showing the contents of the carry bit after each shift.

An **arithmetic shift** is similar but it takes into account the value of the sign bit, which always remains the same. Shifting right has the effect of dividing by 2, and shifting left multiplies by 2. In a right shift, if the sign bit is 1, 1 is moved in from the left instead of 0.

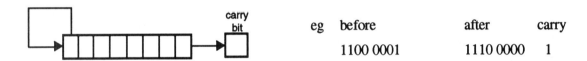

eg	before	after	carry
	1100 0001	1110 0000	1

Q2: Convert the number 12 to binary, and then multiply it by 4 using arithmetic shifts. Convert the result back to decimal.

Q3: Convert the number -16 to binary, and divide by 8 using arithmetic shifts.

It is possible to multiply any two numbers together using a combination of shifts and addition. For example to multiply 12 by 5:

Multiply 12 x 1:	0000 1100
Multiply 12 by 4 with two left shifts:	0011 0000

Add together:	0011 1100

A **rotate** or **circular** shift is useful for performing shifts in multiple bytes. In a circular right shift, the value in the carry bit is moved into the vacated position.

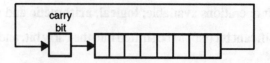

Q4: Show the result of a circular shift on the bit pattern 0100 1100, assuming the carry bit was set to 1 before the operation.

Q5: Assume R1 and R2 are two 8-bit registers being used as a double register to hold a binary integer, with R1 being used to hold the high half of the number. Write down shift instructions which will divide the number by 2, using instructions of the form

```
SRA   Rn    ;arithmetic right shift contents of register n
SRC   Rn    ;rotate right contents of register n
```

Test your instructions with the number 266.

Logical instructions

The instructions OR, NOT, AND and XOR (exclusive OR) have the following effects:

		OR	NOT	AND	XOR
Inputs	— A	1010	1010	1010	1010
	— B	1100		1100	1100
		------	------	------	------
Result		1110	0101	1000	0110

The NOT function can be used to find the two's complement of a number:

```
        A   0110 0111
   NOT A    1001 1000
   add 1             1
        --------------
2's complement  1001 1001
```

The assembly language instructions to carry out this operation would be similar to those shown below:

```
LDA  #01100111B     ;load binary number into accumulator
COMA                ;complement the number in the accumulator
ADDA #1             ;add 1 to the accumulator
```

The OR function can be used to set certain bits to 1 without affecting the other bits in the binary code. For example, a system has eight lights that can be turned on (output 1) or off (output 0), controlled by an 8-bit binary code. At present, lights 1 to 4 are on. We now wish to turn on lights 5 and 7 as well.

Light number	1 2 3 4 5 6 7 8
Present output	1 1 1 1 0 0 0 0
OR with	0 0 0 0 1 0 1 0

Result	1 1 1 1 1 0 1 0

The assembly language code for this operation could be

```
LDA   LIGHT     ;load contents of LIGHT into accumulator
ORA   #1010B    ;OR operation with binary 1010
STA   LIGHT     ;store result back in LIGHT
```

The AND function can be used for masking out certain bits of a number. For example, if we input the ASCII character 3 at the keyboard, the ASCII pattern 00110011 is input. In order to change this to a pure binary number, we need to mask out the first 4 bits.

Q6: Use an AND operation to convert an ASCII digit to a pure binary number.

Q7: Devise an OR operation that will convert a pure binary digit to its equivalent ASCII code.

An XOR function can be used to 'toggle' bits on and off. All 1s become 0s, and all 0s become 1s.

Q8: Use an XOR function to find the 2's complement of a number held in NUM. Store it in NEGNUM.

Conditional branches

These instructions may test the flags in the status register; typical instructions are to 'Branch if the last result was zero', 'Branch if there was a carry' and so on, with mnemonic codes such as BZ, BC etc.

Unconditional branches

An instruction such as JUMP 1000 causes an unconditional branch to an instruction held in location 1000. The contents of the program counter (PC) will be changed to hold the address 1000. In the case of a subroutine call, the return address has to be stored so that control can be returned to the next instruction after the CALL. This is usually done by pushing the address of the next instruction on to the **stack**, and updating the stack pointer. When the RETURN from the subroutine is encountered, the address is popped from the stack and loaded into the PC.

Exercises:

1. (a) The contents of an eight bit register is to be interpreted as a two's complement integer. The register contains 11110101.

    Write down:

    (i)   the effect of carrying out an arithmetic right shift of one place on 11110101,

    (ii) the effect of carrying out a logical right shift of one place on 11110101,

    (iii) the decimal value of the original contents and of the two new bit patterns created by the above shift operations.

    (4 marks)

    (b) Explain how you could transform the byte 10001111 into 11111000 using shift operations.   (1 mark)

    London Paper 2 June 1989

2. The contents of the 16 bit accumulator represent the status of 16 switches. A process can only begin if bits 0, 3, 5, 10, 12 and 15 are set to 1. The status of the other switches has no effect on the process. Write the three key assembly language instructions to check whether the process can take place.   (3 marks)

    AEB Paper 1 1989

3. Most low level languages support the logical operators AND and XOR (exclusive or). These operations can be carried out on a 16-bit register A, using mnemonics of the form:

    AND A, mask   ;mask is a 16-bit pattern

    XOR A, B   ;where A and B are 16-bit registers

    and the result of each operation is left in A. There is also a conditional jump instruction of the form:

    JZ   A, label   ;jump to label if contents of register A are zero.

    Explain how these instructions can be used to:

    (a) test the most significant bit of A;

    (b) check whether the contents of A and B are equal.   (3 marks)

    London Specimen Paper 2 1989

4. The contents of a particular register can be written in hexadecimal format as E6.

    (a) If this bit pattern were to represent in turn

    (i)   an unsigned integer

    (ii) an integer in two's complement form, what would be the decimal value of each representation?

    (b) Write down the contents of this register, in hexadecimal format, after it has been subjected to an arithmetic shift of one place to the right.   (3 marks)

    London Specimen Paper 2 1989

5. Within a register it is sometimes necessary to:

    (i)   test individual bits

    (ii) set individual bits to '1'

    (iii) set individual bits to '0'

    (iv) invert a set of bits.

    Describe efficient methods of carrying out **each** of these four types of manipulation.   (4 marks)

    JMB Paper 1 May 1989

6.* Write assembly language instruction(s) which test whether the contents of the accumulator is zero. What hardware in the processor is used in the actual test?   (4 marks)

    AEB Paper 2 1991

Unit 60 — Instruction Formats and Addressing Modes

Instruction format for an 8-bit microprocessor

Machine code instructions, just like numbers, letters and other symbols, are stored as an arrangement of bits in a binary code. In an 8-bit microprocessor, some instructions may occupy just one byte, while others will occupy two or three bytes. The first byte will always contain the 'op code' — the code for that particular operation or instruction.

Q1: How many different instruction formats are possible if 8 bits are used for the op code?

Zero address instructions

Instructions which occupy one byte do not involve an address — they are instructions such as

```
HALT        ; stop execution
CCF         ; clear the carry flag
CCC         ; clear all status flags
SL          ; shift the contents of the accumulator left one bit
```

PC [| | | | | | |]   op code

One address instructions

One address instructions occupy two bytes; examples of such instructions are

```
ADD   X     ; add the contents of X to the accumulator
LDI   #23   ; load the number 23 into the accumulator
BN    L1    ; branch to label L1 if contents of accumulator are negative
```

PC   [| | | | | | |]   op code

PC + 1   [| | | | | | |]   operand

Two address instructions

Two address instructions occupy three bytes, either because the instruction involves two operands, or because the address of the operand is too large to fit into one byte. Examples of such instructions are

```
LDA MEM2       ; load contents of MEM2 (eg location 0DFF hex) into acc.
ADD C, MEM1    ; add contents of location MEM1 to register C
EXOR A, MASK   ; exclusive OR contents of A with MASK
```

PC   [| | | | | | |]   op code

PC + 1   [| | | | | | |]   low address or operand 1

PC + 2   [| | | | | | |]   high address or operand 2

In the first example above, FF will be stored in PC+1, and 0D in PC+2. The processor will determine from the op code how to interpret all the bytes making up the instruction.

A 16-bit instruction format

Machines which use 16-bit words also make use of 0-address, 1-address and 2-address formats, taking up one, two or three words. However, with 16 bits obviously more information can be stored in each word, and a typical instruction format is shown below.

1-word instruction

0 1 2 3	4 5	6 7 8 9 10 11 12 13 14 15
function code	mode	operand address

The first 4 bits are used for the op code, and bits 4 and 5 are used to indicate the **addressing mode** being used (see below).

Microprocessors may have more than one instruction format for the one-word instructions, depending on the type of instruction being used. Instruction formats indicate not only what operation is to be performed but also how many locations are being used to hold the actual instruction, so that the PC (program counter) can be correctly incremented. The number of memory locations used for the address will depend partly on the mode of addressing being used.

Q2: Does the number of words occupied by an instruction have any bearing on how fast the instruction will execute? Explain your answer.

Immediate addressing

In some instructions, the data to be operated on is held as part of the instruction format. In a 2-byte instruction format, the operand is therefore not an address at all, but a value. Typical instructions using immediate addressing are:

```
LDAI #35H      ; load the hexadecimal value 35 into the accumulator
MVI  C, #8     ; move the value 8 into register C
```

This type of addressing could be used, for example, to initialise a counter to a particular value.

Direct addressing

In this mode, the operand gives the address of the data to be used in the operation. For example:

```
LDA  MEM       ; load contents of location MEM into the accumulator
```

The number of locations which can be addressed using direct addressing is limited, and often more than one word is used for holding the address.

This type of instruction is slow, for locating the data involves three or maybe four memory operations; three to load the 3-byte instruction, and then another to go and get the data to be operated on.

Q3: If 16 bits are allowed for an address, what is the maximum memory address that can be referenced using direct addressing?

Indirect addressing

With this type of addressing, the address of the data in memory is held in one of the registers, and the operand of the instruction holds the number of the register to refer to.

```
LDA   (7)          ; load the contents of the memory location
                     whose address is in register 7.
```

Generally, the 8-bit or 16-bit op code contains all the information needed; what operation is to be performed, and which register holds the data address.

Q4: The store locations 100 and 120 contain the values 120 and 200 respectively. What value would be loaded into the accumulator by **each** of the following instructions?

    (i)   LDAI 100   ;LOAD immediate 100

    (ii)   LDA 100   ;LOAD direct 100

    (iii) LDA (100)   ;LOAD indirect 100

Indexed addressing

This is a variation on indirect addressing, where the operand address is calculated by adding to a base address the value held in an index register. Using this mode of addressing, the address of the operand can be modified by operating on the contents of the index register.

For example, suppose we wish to set to zero the contents of TABLE to TABLE + 99. Using an index register X, the following instructions can be used:

```
     LDA #0          ;load 0 into the accumulator
     LDX #0          ;load 0 into the index register
LOOP STA TABLE(X)    ;store contents of accumulator in TABLE + X
     INX             ;increment the index register
     CPX #99         ;compare X with 99
     BNE LOOP        ;branch if not equal to LOOP
```

Relative addressing

This type of addressing is often used in branch instructions to specify where the next instruction is located relative to the current instruction whose address is held in the PC. An example is:

```
    JMP +10          ;branch to the instruction 10 bytes on.
```

A 'jump relative' with a one-byte operand can only jump forwards or backwards 127 bytes. Relative jumps allow the code to be **relocatable** anywhere in memory (see page 253).

Exercises:

1.   A typical 8 bit microprocessor with a 16 bit address bus uses machine instructions which may be 1, 2 or 3 bytes long. If all operation codes are 1 byte long, use examples to explain why instructions may have:

    (i)   no operand

    (ii)   a 1 byte operand;

    (iii) a 2 byte operand.

                  (3 marks)
SEB Paper 2 1989

2. In a particular assembly language program the following sequence of instructions is encountered:

        ADD +42   ;immediate addressing

        ADD 42   ;direct addressing

        ADD (42)   ;indirect addressing

where ADD means 'add to the accumulator', and the address part of the instruction is to be used as an immediate operand, a direct address and an indirect address respectively.

What will the contents of the accumulator be after executing *each* of these instructions if location 42 holds the value 21 and location 21 holds the value 33? You may assume that the accumulator initially contains zero.   (6 marks)

NISEAC Paper 1 1989

3. (a) Why is it normal to have more than one addressing mode in low level programming languages?   (2 marks)

   (b) Ten characters, held in locations **start** to **start + 9**, are acted upon by the following section of program.

```
            LD    X,#0
            LD    Y,#9
   loop     LD    A,start(X)
            ST    newstart(Y),A
            INC   X
            DEC   Y
            CMP   X,#10
            JN    loop
```

start, newstart are locations in different parts of the memory.

Key

(**reg** represents a register (X, Y or A); **p** represents a memory location; **p(reg)** represents an indexed address).

```
LD    reg,#value      Load value into reg.
LD    reg,p           Load the contents of p into reg.
ST    p,reg           Store the contents of reg into p.
INC   reg             Add 1 to the contents of reg.
DEC   reg             Subtract 1 from the contents of reg.
CMP   reg,#value      Compare value with the contents of reg.
JN    label           Jump to label if the values compared were not equal.
```

   (i) Describe the overall effect of running this section of program.   (4 marks)

   (ii) Suggest an application in which a section of program like this might be used.   (2 marks)

   (iii) With reference to this section of program, discuss the benefits of using indexed addressing.   (5 marks)

UCLES Paper 2 Nov 1989

4.* A microprocessor has an 8 bit data bus and a 16 bit address bus. The operation code of a machine instruction occupies 1 byte. Two machine instructions available to the processor are described below.

Load the accumulator - direct addressing mode   e.g. Load. A 1EF0

Load the accumulator - immediate addressing mode e.g.   Load. A #0F

   (a) (i) What is meant by *addressing mode* with respect to a machine instruction?

      (ii) Explain the difference between *immediate* and *direct* addressing. (You may refer to the examples given above.)   (2 marks)

   (b) If the program counter is currently set at location 1000$_{hex}$ what will it be set at, after the instruction Load. A 1EF0 has been fetched from memory and executed? Explain how you obtained your answer.   (2 marks)

   (c) How much memory, in kilobytes, can be addressed by the processor?   (1 mark)

   (d) What is the maximum number of instructions possible in the processor's instruction set?   (1 mark)

SEB Paper 2 1992

Unit 61 — The Assembly Process

Symbolic addressing

Assembly languages were developed in order to make it easier to write, debug and maintain programs. Using mnemonic codes for each instruction rather than a binary machine code is one obvious way of making instructions more comprehensible.

Another way to make programs easier to write and understand is to use **symbols** instead of actual machine code addresses to refer to locations storing data or instructions. These symbols are also referred to as **symbolic addresses**. Thus, instead of having to remember that location 134 is being used to hold, say, the radius of a circle, the programmer uses an assembly language **directive** to reserve a byte for 'radius' and the name 'radius' is then used in all the assembly language instructions in the program.

```
        LDA  RADIUS    ; load the contents of RADIUS into the accumulator
        .
        .
        HALT
RADIUS:  .RB 1          ; directive to reserve 1 byte of store for RADIUS
```

Labels

Using labels in an assembler program also makes the program easier to understand. Instead of writing

```
        JMP  1000      ; jump to the instruction held at location 1000
```

we would write, for example

```
        JMP  LOOP1     ;jump to the instruction labelled LOOP1
        .
        .
LOOP1   (another instruction)
```

Assembler directives

Directives are instructions to the assembler program itself, which do not have a machine language counterpart. These directives are recognised by the assembler program and action is taken at translation time, not at run time. Different assemblers have different ways of distinguishing directives from mnemonic operation codes — preceding them by a full-stop or an asterisk are two common ways.

Q1: Invent a directive to an assembler to tell it that the program is to be loaded starting at location 150. Then reserve a byte of storage each for variables called A, B and COUNT.

Relocatable code

On some smaller systems, the user has to specify exactly where in memory the program is to be loaded. On larger multiprogramming systems, however, this would be very inconvenient because the operating system would always have to ensure that the program was loaded into the same place in memory. Therefore, most programs are written to be **relocatable** — that is, the operating system decides at run time where the program will be put in memory, and all addresses are worked out relative to the start of the program. As a particular program may be swapped in and out of memory several times before it is completed, it could be relocated several times during one run.

267

Q2: How can the programmer ensure that his program is written in relocatable code?

Macro instructions

A **macro** is a single instruction representing a group of instructions, written either by the manufacturer to perform some common task such as input and output, or by the user. The instructions comprising the macro may be written at the start of the program, and whenever the macro-instruction is subsequently used in the program, the corresponding instructions are inserted into its place by the assembler.

A macro is an example of an **open subroutine**, as opposed to a **closed subroutine** which is entered by using a CALL statement or equivalent instruction, causing a branch to the routine.

Example: A macro to add the contents of two locations and store the result in a third location is defined as follows:

```
.MACRO      ADDUP      NUM1,NUM2,RES
LDA         NUM1
ADD         NUM2
STA         RES
.ENDMACRO
```

In the program, if say the programmer wishes to add the contents of P and Q and store the result in R, she will write

```
ADDUP       P,Q,R
```

At assembly, this instruction is replaced by the three instructions

```
LDA         P
ADD         Q
STA         R
```

Two-pass assemblers

In a two pass assembler, the **source code** (the statements written by the programmer), containing directives, assembler mnemonics and comments, is scanned twice. On the first pass, the following tasks will be performed:

- comments will be removed

- all symbols will be put in a symbol table, giving the name of the symbol and its memory address (either absolute or relative to the start of the program)

- directives will be translated and executed

- macros are replaced by the actual instructions which the macro represents

- any errors found will be put into an error table to be printed out.

On the second pass, the machine code is built up. Thus

- each mnemonic code is replaced with its machine code equivalent, by referring to a table of op codes in memory

- each symbolic address is replaced with its equivalent machine code address by referring to the symbol table created in the first pass

- decimal or character items are converted into machine code and inserted into the instructions using them

- any errors detected during this stage are reported.

Linking loaders

A linking loader (linker) is a program which links together programs which may have been assembled separately. For example, an assembly language program may call a subroutine which performs a sort. The linking loader therefore has to load the sort program into memory at a particular address, and insert this address into the CALL instruction in object code produced by the assembler.

A **relocating loader** can load the object code anywhere in memory, provided the programmer has used no absolute addresses and the object code is in relocatable code.

Exercises:

1. In the context of assembly language programming, contrast the usage of a macro with that of a closed subroutine.

(2 marks)

What implications are there for parameter handling in each case?

(2 marks)
AEB Paper 1 1988

2. Most modern computers store their programs and data in 'relocatable form'.

(a) Explain what is meant by relocatable form and give a benefit of using it.

(2 marks)

(b) Describe a mechanism to support relocatable form.

(2 marks)
JMB Paper 1 May 1989

3. The following is a small section of an assembly language program.

```
;A,B and C are 8-bit registers
;
;EXOR is the exclusive OR operation
;
;inkbd is a subroutine that handles the input of single characters
;from the keyboard. The routine detects a key press and the contents
;of the keyboard buffer are transferred to the register A. The routine
;also provides a simple prompt to the user and takes care of all the
;problems of input-output programming.

            ORG  1000       ;defines the start address for the program
            ctrlc = 03H     ;H means number is in Hexadecimal format
            LOADI C,0       ;C<-- 0
loop:       CALL inkbd      ;calls subroutine inkbd
            MOVE A,B        ;B<--(A)
            EXOR A,ctrlc    ;A<--EXOR of (A) and ctrlc
            JZ A, finish    ;if (A) = 0 then jump to finish
            ADD C,B         ;C<--(C) + (B)
            JUMP loop
finish:     ...
            ...
            ...
inkbd:                      ;the subroutine starts here
```

(i) What does the section of code up to the label **finish** do? (3 marks)

(ii) Explain how this section of code would be processed by a two-pass assembler. (4 marks)

When might an assembly language be used in preference to a high level language? (1 mark)
London Paper 2 June 1990 (part of question)

4.* Explain why an assembler is usually constructed to make two passes through the program. (3 marks)
AEB Paper 2 1993

Section 8 — Operating Systems and Networks

Unit 62 — Using MS DOS

Introduction

This Unit is intended for users of a PC-compatible machine. A knowledge of the most frequently used MS DOS (Microsoft Disk Operating System) commands is useful in order to be able to make the best use of a PC.

Loading the operating system

If the PC has a hard disk, the operating system will almost certainly be resident on it. When you switch on the computer, the small program in ROM will first check the A drive (see diagram) to see if a disk is present. If it does not find one, it will automatically load the operating system from the hard disk.

Q1: What happens if you have a floppy disk inserted when you switch on the computer?

To reload the operating system without switching off the computer, press Ctrl-Alt-Del simultaneously. This will erase all programs and data from memory, but will not affect anything stored on disk.

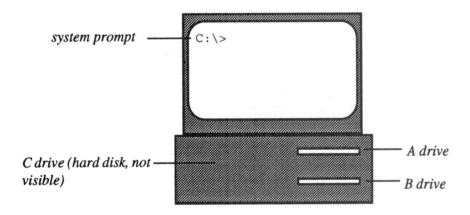

system prompt —— C:\>

C drive (hard disk, not visible)

A drive

B drive

Figure 62.1

The system prompt

Whenever the OS is ready to perform a task it asks you what you want to do next by displaying a **prompt** on the screen. It will look something like this:

```
C:\>
```

The floppy disk drives and hard disk on a PC are given a single letter name starting from A. There may not be a B drive, and the hard disk is usually the C drive. The C:\> prompt means that the OS interprets drive C as the default logical disk drive. In plain English this means that MS DOS will assume it is to use drive C unless you tell it otherwise.

The default logical disk drive

When repeatedly referring to a single disk drive, it is a nuisance to have to specify it all the time. If the disk drive name is omitted it is assumed to be the default logical drive.

To change the name of the default logical drive, at the system prompt type in the name of the drive you require, followed by a colon, and then press Enter.

```
A: <Enter>
```

Files

A **file** is a collection of related items of information and is a unit of storage by which the OS organises and references your data.

Using a computer often involves manipulating files by creating, renaming, making duplicate copies and deleting them. It will not be too long before you delete a vital file that has taken valuable time and effort to create. Only then will you begin to appreciate the value of taking copies of files!

This process is known as **backup**.

Files have to be given names by which they can be referred to, and MS DOS has the following rules for file names.

- They can be a maximum of 8 characters, with an optional 3-character extension, separated from the rest of the filename by a full-stop, eg PAYROLL1.DAT

- Any alphanumeric characters (a - z, 0 - 9) can be used. MS DOS does not distinguish between uppercase and lowercase letters.

- Only the following punctuation marks may be used:

      ! @ % # & ^ ( ) - _ ' { } ~

  (Notice that a space in a filename is **not** allowed).

- All names given to files in the same directory must be unique.

Most software will automatically append the 3 character extension when you save a file. This helps to identify what a particular file is; for example ROBERT.DBF might be a dBase III file, EDWARD.WK1 might be a LOTUS 1-2-3 spreadsheet.

The name that you have given to a file is one of the attributes that the OS looks after for you. Others include the date and time of creation, the date of the last update, and the file size.

Listing your files

Every disk holds a **directory** of files that are currently held on that disk. The OS automatically changes the details in the directory as changes are made to the files. To display the directory of the current default drive, type (using either uppercase or lowercase letters)

      DIR <Enter>

The display includes the name and extension of the files (and sub-directories — see later), the size of the file, and the date and time when last updated. It also shows the number of files present and the amount of space left on the disk.

If you wish to obtain a listing of files that are not on the default logical drive, either change to the drive you require or append the drive name to the command:

      DIR A: <Enter>

Sometimes there will be more files in a directory than can be displayed on a single screen. In such cases, include the PAGE option:

      DIR/P <Enter>

Alternatively, use the WIDE option which will show only the name and extension of each file, but will display five names on each line of the screen:

      DIR/W <Enter>

To direct the output to the printer, type:

      DIR A: >PRN

Wild cards

MS DOS gives you further flexibility with the use of **wild cards**, namely the asterisk (*) and the question mark (?) which enable groups of files to be specified.

The question mark in a name or extension name represents *any single character* in that position, and you can use as many question marks as you need. Thus:

```
DIR PROG?.PAS <Enter>
```

will find the files PROG1, PROG2 and so on.

Using the asterisk instead of the question mark would achieve the same thing in this case, because it represents the character in that position *and all the characters that follow* in the name or extension name.Thus:

```
DIR A:*.DOC <Enter>
```

will find all files with the extension DOC on drive A.

Directory structures

If you want to store several independent groups of files on one disk, MS DOS allows you to create a separate directory for each group of files. This structure is analagous to having different filing cabinets in an office, each concerned with a separate application.

The directory system is most useful on a hard disk, where it is essential to keep applications separate rather than all thrown in together. The disk will have a **root directory**, which will contain an entry for each file in that directory and an entry for each sub-directory that you have created. Each sub-directory will contain details of files and other sub-directories and so on for as many levels as you need.

The diagram below illustrates a possible directory structure.

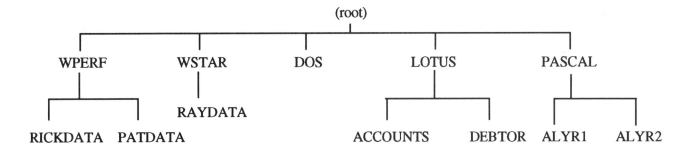

Figure 62.2

Pathnames

When you are in a particular directory you can only directly access files in that directory. To access any other file you must include a **pathname** in the file specification. The **backslash** (\) is used in pathname specifications.

For example, if the default logical drive is A and you wish to access a file called FIRST.DOC in the RICKDATA sub-directory on drive C, the full pathname to access the file would be:

```
C:\WPERF\RICKDATA\FIRST.DOC
```

Changing directories

You can choose any directory to be your current directory using the command CD. To change directory to the RICKDATA directory in the above example, type:

```
CD C:\WPERF\RICKDATA <Enter>
```

You can of course omit the drive name C if you are already in the default logical drive.

To move back up one level of the directory tree, type:

```
CD.. <Enter>
```

To get straight back to the root directory, type:

```
CD\ <Enter>
```

To list all sub-directories of the current directory, use the command:

```
DIR *. <Enter>
```

(Here you are asking for a directory display of all files with any name, but no extension name. All sub-directories come into this category. It is simple to find your way around even a complicated directory structure using the above commands).

Making and removing directories

To make a new sub-directory of your current directory, use the command MD. For example, to make a sub-directory called ROBDATA in the WPERF directory, move to the WPERF directory using the CD command, and then type:

```
MD ROBDATA <Enter>
```

To actually place yourself in that sub-directory, you will need to use the command

```
CD ROBDATA <Enter>
```

To remove a directory, use the command RD. Directories can only be removed if they are empty, so if there are any files in the sub-directory, make a backup copy of any that you need and then delete them all with the instruction

```
DEL *.*                     (see later under Deleting Files).
```

To remove the directory RICKDATA, move to the WPERF directory and type:

```
RD RICKDATA <Enter>
```

The FORMAT command

A new disk cannot have files written to it until it has been **formatted**. The FORMAT command sets up empty tracks and sectors on the disk, and also creates an empty root directory. It erases everything on the designated disk so should only be used on a brand new disk unless you have some good reason for re-formatting a used disk. To format a disk in drive A, type:

```
FORMAT A: <Enter>
```

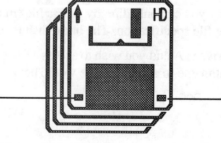

Both high and low density disks have a write-protect tab. If the tab is positioned so that it covers the hole, the disk is NOT write protected.

High density disks have a hole punched out in the bottom right hand corner. They also usually have HD written on them.

Figure 62.3 - High density 3 ½ " disks

On newer computers with high density drives which allow 1.4MB of storage space on a 3 ½" floppy, you need a more expensive high density disk to be able to store 1.4 megabytes of data. To format an ordinary double-sided double-density 5¼" disk, which may only hold 360K, you may need to type:

```
FORMAT  A:/4
```

To format a 3½" disk, if it is not a high density disk, you may need to type:

```
FORMAT A:/T:80/N:9
```

This tells MS DOS to format the disk with 80 tracks and 9 sectors.

The COPY command

The COPY command is used to copy a single file or a group of files from one disk to another. Wild cards and pathnames may be used.

The full syntax of the COPY command to copy a file called FRED.BAS from drive C to drive A is :

```
COPY C:FRED.BAS A:FRED.BAS <Enter>
```

However, if the default logical drive is drive C, and, as in this case, you do not want to change the name of the file at the time of copying, this syntax can be reduced to:

```
COPY FRED.BAS A: <Enter>
```

Q2: What do the following commands do?

```
(i)        COPY *.BAS A:

(ii)       COPY A:*.* C:\DOS

(iii)      COPY C:\WPERF\RICKDATA\*.* A:

(iv)       COPY B:\DOS\*.WK1 C:\LOTUS\ACCOUNTS
```

In practice, the easiest way of copying files between directories is to first place yourself on the destination drive and in the destination directory, and then use the COPY command. That way, at least you know the file will arrive in the right place!

Q3: The system prompt shows B:\>, showing that you are in the root directory on the B drive. Write commands to move to the destination directory and perform the COPY function in (iv) above.

The DISKCOPY command

The command DISKCOPY will make an exact copy of the entire contents of one disk (the source disk) onto another disk (the destination disk). Both disks have to be of the same size and type, so you cannot use DISKCOPY to copy from the hard disk to a floppy disk.

However, you can use DISKCOPY to copy the entire contents of a floppy to another one of the same size even if you have only one floppy drive. To use this command type the following:

```
DISKCOPY <source drive> <destination drive> <Enter>
```

eg   `DISKCOPY A: B:`

or   `DISKCOPY A: A:`

If the source and destination are the same, MS DOS will guide you through the necessary steps.

If you want to copy all files from a 5¼" disk to a 3½" disk (assuming your machine has both drives), rather than using the COPY A:*.* B: command it is often quicker to do the following:

- make a directory on the hard disk and move to that directory
- copy all the files from the source floppy disk to that directory
- copy the files from the directory on the hard disk to the second floppy
- delete the files from the hard disk
- remove the directory you set up for the copy process.

Q4: Assume that drive A is a 3½" drive and drive B is a 5¼" drive. The hard disk is drive C. Write commands to copy all sixty-odd files from the 3½" disk to the 5¼" disk.

Deleting files

There are two commands to delete files, both of which work in the same way. The two commands are DEL and ERASE. For example:

```
DEL FRED.BAS <Enter>
```

```
DEL *.* <Enter>
```

The latter command will delete all files in the current directory so use it with care!

Renaming files

The command RENAME or REN for short allows you to rename files. It is far more efficient to rename a file rather than to copy it and delete the original. To rename a file in the current directory from OLDNAME.DOC to NEWNAME.DOC, type

```
REN OLDNAME.DOC NEWNAME.DOC
```

Displaying or printing the contents of files

It is sometimes difficult to remember the contents of all the files you have created, no matter how carefully you have named them. To display the contents of a file on the screen, use the TYPE command. (You cannot use wild cards with this command). To type the contents of the file AUTOEXEC.BAT in the current directory, type:

```
TYPE AUTOEXEC.BAT
```

If this produces an unintelligible display then you are not displaying a text file.

If the text is scrolling off the screen too fast for you to read it, you can stop it by pressing Ctrl-S. This acts as a 'toggle'; pressing Ctrl-S again will start the text scrolling again. You can keep your finger down on the Ctrl key continuously and press S as required.

To print the contents of a file PROG1.PAS on the printer rather than displaying it on the screen, type:

```
TYPE PROG1.PAS>PRN
```

Many pieces of software come with a file on the disk called 'README' or 'README.DOC' containing instructions about how to use the software. The TYPE command can be used to display such a file on the screen or route the display to the printer.

Another way of sending output to the printer is to press Ctrl-P <Enter>. This sends to the printer everything that appears on the screen until you press Ctrl-P again.

One final tip: pressing Ctrl-Break interrupts the current process and returns control to you. (The Break key is usually located at the top right-hand side of the keyboard.)

Exercises:

1.   Write commands to do the following:

   (i)   Make drive A the current logical default drive.

   (ii)   Obtain a directory listing of the disk in drive A.

   (iii)   Obtain a 'filename only' directory listing of the disk in drive A.

   (iv)   Obtain a directory of all files with the extension .PAS.

   (v)   Copy the file EX1.PAS from drive A to drive B.

   (vi)   Copy the file EX1.PAS from drive A to a second floppy disk to be inserted in the same drive.

   (vii)   Rename the file EX1.PAS, calling it EX2.PAS.

2.   Assume you are in a directory called STUDENT on the hard disk (drive C). Write commands to do the following:

   (i)   Format a new floppy disk in drive A:

   (ii)   Move to a subdirectory on drive C called PASCAL.

   (iii)   Create a new subdirectory called TEMP.

   (iv)   Copy all files from the floppy disk in drive A to TEMP.

   (v)   Copy all files from TEMP to drive A.

   (vi)   Delete all files in the subdirectory TEMP.

   (vii)   Remove the subdirectory TEMP.

   (viii) Obtain a printout of a file called EX3 on drive A.

Unit 63 — Introduction to Operating Systems

What is an operating system?

An operating system is a program or a set of programs that manages the operation of the computer. The most frequently used instructions in the operating system must be stored in main memory and remain there whilst other programs such as application programs are being executed. This portion of the operating system is called by many different names such as **control program**, **nucleus**, **monitor**, **supervisor**, or **executive**.

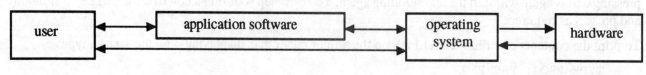

Figure 63.1

Loading an operating system

On all large computers and most micros, the operating system is held on disk and has to be loaded into main memory once the computer has been switched on, before any other programs can be run. The process of loading the operating system is called **booting** the system.

On a microcomputer system, the operating system is usually held on the hard disk if the system has one. Otherwise, it will be held on a floppy disk, which will be known as a **system disk**. On all computers a small program held in ROM (the 'loader') will tell the computer where to look for the operating system, and give instructions for loading at least part of it into memory. Once part of the operating system has been loaded, more instructions can be executed to load the rest of the nucleus. This method of 'pulling itself up by its own bootstraps' is where the expression 'booting' comes from.

In some smaller micros the control program is permanently held in ROM.

Q1: What are the advantages and disadvantages of holding the operating system in ROM?

Modes of operation

Operating systems vary considerably in their capabilities, from relatively simple single user microcomputer systems, to sophisticated mainframe computers. The modes of operation include:

1. **Single program operation.** The OS supervises the loading and running of one program at a time, and the input and output of data from and to peripheral devices.

2. **Multiprocessing.** In larger systems, one computer system may have more than one processor, but may still share all or some of the same memory.

3. **Multiprogramming.** This means that two or more programs are being run concurrently. The operating system has to allocate resources to each program, allowing each one a small amount of processor time before moving on to the next one.

278

There are many different types of multiprogramming system:

- a **multi-user system** allows several people to be running programs simultaneously from different workstations. This is also called a **time-sharing** system, with each user in turn being allocated a **time-slice**.

- a **batch** system where there are few facilities for multi-user, interactive computing, but nevertheless several batch jobs may be processed simultaneously in order to optimise the computer's resources.

- a **multitasking** system which could be, for example, a single user standalone microcomputer running an operating system such as Unix, OS/2 or Windows 3.1, which allows several programs to be running simultaneously. When the term is applied to mini or mainframe computers, it implies the concurrent execution of two or more **related** tasks between which communication is possible. Put in another way, multitasking is taking place when a single job is broken down into stages called tasks which can be simultaneously executed.

4. **Batch processing**. There is no interaction between the user and the computer during batch processing. One or more programs are submitted to the computer as a **job** and put in a **batch queue** until it is their turn to be run.

Various combinations of the above modes of operation are possible. A machine may perform both multiprogramming and batch processing; it may be both multiprogramming and multiprocessing. Batch processing can be done in an on-line mode of operation; a user sitting at a terminal may key in the instructions to run a batch job which executes several programs. The job could for example consist of instructions to run a program to sort transactions, followed by an update program and then a report program.

Program compilations are sometimes run in batch mode; several users may request compilations at the same time, and these requests will be put in a queue to be processed, maybe hours later. Once a program has been compiled it may then be run in an interactive mode.

5. **Real-time processing**. Real-time systems can be of different types; process control, information storage and retrieval, and transaction processing. In any of these systems, the data input to the computer must be processed immediately.

Q2: Give an example of each of the three types of real-time system mentioned above.

In any real-time system a fast response is required, but whereas a few seconds delay may be acceptable in an information retrieval system, response must be instantaneous in a process control system which might for example be monitoring a chemical reaction or controlling a missile.

One feature of such a real-time system is the amount of **redundancy** built into the system. The processor may not be used at its full capacity for a large part of the time, in order that it can respond instantly when required. In addition, since computer failure could have serious consequences, the computer system must be designed to be **fault-tolerant**. This means that when a component fails, its duties must be taken over by other fault-free components of the system. These other components may be used for the sole purpose of improving the reliability of the system.

As well as having duplicate or 'redundant' hardware, a fault-tolerant computer may have alternative software and extra error checking routines, and perform critical tasks a number of times to reduce the probability of error.

The functions of an operating system

Obviously, not all operating systems carry out precisely the same tasks; a single-programming micro will not need to perform all the tasks of a multiprogramming, multi-user mainframe computer. The functions listed below apply to a greater or lesser extent to many computers, and will be explained in more depth in subsequent Units.

1. **Resource allocation and scheduling**. All operating systems must have the ability to load programs into memory and start them running; more complex operating systems have to allocate CPU time, memory and I/O (input/output) resources to different processes running concurrently.

2. **Memory management**. Some or all of the computer's memory will be 'partitioned', with different programs running in different partitions. The operating system decides on how these partitions are organised. Even in a micro which can only run one program at a time, some memory management is required. The operating system, for example, will occupy a different partition from the user's program.

operating system
partition A
program A
partition B
program B
partition C
program C

Figure 63.2 — memory partitioning

3. **Backing-store management**. This includes supervising the creation, updating and deletion of files. A **directory** of files has to be maintained so that they can be quickly located when required.

4. **Input/output control**. Reading from and writing to the various peripherals is controlled by the operating system.

5. **Interrupt handling**. An interrupt may be caused deliberately, as for example in a time-sharing system where a real-time clock generates interrupts at regular time intervals to give the next user processor time. Interrupts may also be caused by program errors, hardware malfunctions, or external events such as pressing the 'Break' key.

6. **Operator interface**. The OS accepts commands from the operator and responds to them.

7. **Security**. Most multi-user systems provide the ability to assign login codes and passwords to different users.

8. **Accounting facilities**. Large systems will keep a record of facilities used by each person, such as processor time, number of pages printed and disk space used.

9. **Utilities**. Most operating systems contain **utility programs** for file management, editing files, reorganising disk space, making backups and so on.

Q3: Name some utility programs provided by an operating system you have used.

Exercises:

1. (a) Name the type of operating system which would be used in computers on a space shuttle. (1 mark)

   (b) State **four** major differences between this type of system and an operating system used for payroll processing.
   (4 marks)
   AEB Paper 1 1990

2. (a) (i) Explain the main characteristics of the following processing methods:

   batch processing

   pseudo real time (or interactive) processing (6 marks)

   (ii) State one advantage of each of these methods in comparison with the other. (2 marks)

   (iii) Batch processing is sometimes performed in an on-line mode of operation. Describe briefly
   this mode of operation. (2 marks)

   (b) A certain computer centre requires programmers to compile their programs using an on-line batch mode of
   operation. However, compiled programs may be run in pseudo real time mode. The justification for this policy
   is that it promotes an efficient overall operation. Discuss the advantages and disadvantages of the policy stating
   whether the claim for efficiency is justified. (4 marks)
   AEB Paper 2 1987

3.* Discuss whether or not there are advantages in using a multi-tasking operating system on a single-user system. You
   should give **two** examples to illustrate your answer. (4 marks)
   SEB Paper 2 1992

Unit 64 — The Operator Interface

Command-driven interfaces

Most large systems use command-driven interfaces; that is, the operator must type in commands rather than choosing from a menu or selecting an icon.

Operator activities include:

- loading jobs or other software
- calling in routines for tracing faults
- terminating jobs, for example if they are 'looping'
- making backups of files and restoring master files in cases of system failure
- using system utilities to reorganise disk space, print file directories, delete unwanted files etc.
- loading tapes and disks as requested by users and by the OS
- loading stationery into the printer.

Job control language (JCL)

A job control language is a programming language used for communicating with the operating system. It has control structures just like any other programming language for sequence, selection and iteration. JCL is particularly important in batch processing, where the user must specify a whole series of programs to be run, and state what is to be done if for example one of the programs results in an error condition. Usually the programmer does not have to be too concerned with the details of the JCL; he or she will write a series of **macro** commands which call in appropriate routines.

A sample JCL program to compile and execute a COBOL program might look something like the following:

```
$JOB USER123   G.MARRIOT
$PRIORITY 2
$COBOL
$INPUT PROG1 (DISK 1)
$LIST LP
$IF ERROR THEN END
$RUN
$MEMORY 50K
$TIME 5
$FILES 'PAYFILE'
$IF ERROR THEN DUMP
$END
```

Q1: Describe briefly the purpose of each statement in the above JCL program. What will happen if more than one user has saved a program with the name PROG1?

MS DOS batch files

MS DOS allows users to specify a series of instructions which are incorporated into a **batch file**, usually identified by a filename extension .BAT. A special batch file called AUTOEXEC.BAT is automatically executed when the computer is booted up. Batch files are often created which perform a simple sequence of instructions such as

```
change to the DB3 directory
run the program called DBASE
On exit from DBASE, return to the root directory.
```

The batch file is then given a name such as DB3.BAT and saved . When the user types the instruction DB3, the operating system looks for a batch file of that name and executes the instructions contained in the file.

Microcomputer operating systems

One of the problems faced by users in the early days of microcomputers, back in the 1970s was the incompatibility of various operating systems. Each different type of computer had a different set of operating system commands; floppy disks could not be transferred from one type of machine to another, and it was difficult or impossible to transfer information from one computer to another.

Q2: Why is it often not possible to transfer a floppy disk from one type of computer to another?

Microsoft's MS DOS

The situation improved somewhat with the release of MS DOS (Microsoft Disk Operating System) by Microsoft Corporation in 1981. It was originally developed for IBM for their first personal computer system (they called it PC DOS) but quickly became an industry standard as other manufacturers adopted it for their PCs. The main problem with MS DOS is that it is unable to reference addresses greater than 1MB, and user memory is limited to 640K. When it was written, a memory capacity of 64K was considered large for a micro, and the systems programmers felt that an addressable storage of ten times that amount would be far more than would ever be needed!

Apple's 'graphical user interface' (GUI)

Early in 1984 Apple launched the Macintosh, which offered a radically different way of using computers by way of a 'graphical user interface' and a mouse. Instead of typing, for example, 'del myfile.doc' to delete a file, the Mac user simply picked up a picture of a piece of paper with the mouse and dropped it into a waste bin on the screen.

Windows and OS/2

MS DOS users wanted something similar, and Microsoft developed a program called Windows. Early versions did not match up to the Macintosh, and in the meantime IBM and Microsoft were developing a new operating system called OS/2 which was launched in April 1987. It was supposed to solve the 640K 'memory barrier', but required a minimum of 5MB of hard disk space and 2MB of memory just to run the operating system. A further disadvantage was that it did not come free with each computer like MS DOS, and consequently it flopped.

Instead, Microsoft's Windows 3.0, much improved over earlier versions, captured the market intended for OS/2. With Windows 3.0 and later releases, a PC can run several programs at once, and each program continues to run inside its own window even if it's 'iconified'. Data can be moved quickly and easily from one application to another, and the use of a menu, mouse and icons to select commands means that is more user-friendly than other operating systems.

UNIX

UNIX is a general-purpose, multi-user, multi-tasking operating system written in C, which has been around since the early 1970s but has only recently gained wide popularity. Unlike virtually all other operating systems, UNIX is available on a wide variety of platforms; that is to say, it can be used on computers from many different manufacturers. This means that UNIX customers can select equipment from various vendors and use the same software on different types of hardware, which is not the case with other operating systems traditionally supplied with the hardware.

The bad news is that although UNIX is available on many platforms, there are some 57 versions available, and this has been a barrier to mass acceptance of UNIX in commercial applications, as there is always the question of which version to go with. UNIX vendors have recognised that the only way that it will become universally accepted is through standardisation and various moves are being taken to achieve this.

Since UNIX predates Graphical User Interfaces (GUIs), it basically uses a command line interface. However a GUI interface called OSF/Motif is available which defines a set of 'building blocks' for GUI applications such as pushbuttons, scrollbars, entry boxes and so on.

Q3: Name any other operating systems which you have heard of or used. What is the advantage to a company of using an **open system** such as UNIX instead of a proprietary operating system supplied with the computer hardware?

Exercises

1. Most computer systems have both an immediate access store and a backing store. When asked to explain why, a student replied that immediate access store has a limited capacity but that backing store does not.

    (a) What limits the capacity of immediate access store? (1 mark)

    (b) Outline **three** other answers the student could have given. (3 marks)
    JMB AS Level May 1989

2. State what is meant by Job Control Language (JCL) and two purposes for which it is used.
    (4 marks)
    AEB Paper 1 1989

3. *Multitasking (multiprogramming)* operating systems are now readily available for *standalone* microcomputers. What is a multitasking operating system and how might a user of a standalone microcomputer make good use of the facilities provided by multitasking? (2 marks)
    London Paper 2 June 1990

4. Explain what is meant by a *window-based interface*. What are the advantages to the user of such an interface? What are the disadvantages, if any? (4 marks)

5.* A computer company has written an operating system which provides a library of pre-written routines for software developers to use. It has also drawn up detailed guidelines for software developers so that all applications packages designed to run on the operating system have a consistent human computer interface.

    (a) Describe **two** advantages that the adherence to detailed guidelines and use of library routines will bring to:

        (i) software developers;

        (ii) users. (4 marks)

    (b) One team of software developers writing application packages to run on this operating system announces that in future they will not be adhering so closely to the computer company's guidelines. Instead they will be writing application packages so that the human computer interface is consistent across a range of operating systems.

        Describe **one** advantage and **one** disadvantage to users which will result from this decision. (4 marks)
        SEB Paper 2 1992

Unit 65 — Peripheral Control, Polling and Interrupts

Introduction

In this Unit we look at the various techniques used by operating systems to optimise the use of input/output devices and memory. A lot of technical terms are introduced and careful study is advised!

Input/Output channels

In early computer systems, particularly in data processing environments where input and output was the major part of the work being done by the computer, systems tended to become 'I/O bound'. While I/O was in progress, processors were tied up and could not perform any other tasks, so that no matter how fast the CPU could operate, it could only transfer data as fast as the peripheral could give it or accept it. In order to overcome this situation **I/O channels** were developed to handle I/O independently of the main processor of the computer system. A channel is a special-purpose computer system which can access main store directly to store or retrieve information.

In modern **interrupt-driven** systems, the CPU executes an instruction to initiate I/O transfer over a channel, and the channel then takes control of the I/O operation, leaving the CPU to carry on with other tasks. When data transfer is complete, the channel issues an 'I/O completion interrupt' to inform the CPU that it is ready for more.

Some I/O channels known as **multiplexor channels** have many sub-channels and can interleave many data streams at once. A **byte-multiplexor channel** interleaves the transmissions of slow devices such as terminals and printers; a **block-multiplexor channel** interleaves the transmission of several high-speed devices such as laser printers and disk drives.

Buffering

A buffer is an area of memory used for holding data during input/output transfers to and from disk or tape, from the keyboard, to the printer and so on. For example, when characters are typed at a keyboard, they are placed in a buffer by an I/O channel, and when the transfer is complete (ie the user presses the <Enter> key) they may be accessed by the CPU. If the CPU happens to be busy doing something else they will remain in the buffer until the CPU is free.

Q1: How could you find out the size of the MS DOS keyboard buffer? How large is it?

Similarly, information that is to be printed is placed in a print buffer which may be up to a megabyte long, located either in the printer or the computer, or both. The CPU then issues the 'start I/O' instruction and the I/O channel transfers the data from the buffer to the printer. This process of being able to perform input and output independently of the CPU is known as **autonomous operation of peripherals**.

Double-buffering

With **single-buffered** input, the input channel deposits data in the buffer, the processor processes it, more data is deposited, and so on. While the channel is depositing data, no processing can occur, and while the data is being processed, no data can be deposited.

A **double-buffering** system allows overlap of I/O operations and processing; while data is being deposited in one buffer, the processor can process data in the second buffer. When it has finished processing this data, it processes the data in the first buffer while the second buffer is filled up.

The diagram on the next page illustrates this process.

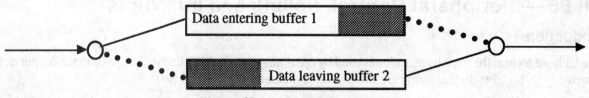

Figure 65.1 — Double buffering

Spooling

Spooling is a technique used to speed up communication between devices which operate at differing speeds. Output to a printer, for example, may be **spooled** (written) to a disk, which is a high speed device. When the printer becomes free, the output will be printed. This technique enables several users who are using a system simultaneously to share the same printer without getting their output muddled up. Each user's output is spooled to a different position on disk, and printed using a queuing system.

Sometimes a single program prints two different reports, sending a line or several lines of one report to Printer 1, then a line of a second report to Printer 2. (It could for example print a payroll slip followed by a line in a summary report). Spooling makes it unnecessary to have two physical printers; both reports will be kept separate on disk and printed one after the other, allowing the operator to change stationery as required.

Polling

Polling is a technique for allowing one unit to check the status of another; the first unit checks whether the second is in a certain status, and if it is not, it carries on with what it was doing. In a multi-user system where several terminals are attached to a computer, the terminals may be polled at frequent intervals to ensure a reasonable response time. Polling takes large amounts of processor time — anyone who has ever tried to make a phone call on a line that is constantly busy will appreciate this fact! An interrupt system is preferable to polling because the request is handled as soon as it occurs, and not when the OS gets round to checking the device. In some cases data can be lost if the request for I/O is not handled immediately.

Timers and clocks

An interval timer is used in multi-user systems to prevent any user from monopolising processor time. After a given time interval, (a 'time-slice') the timer generates an interrupt and the processor is assigned to another user.

A time-of-day clock may keep track of time in increments as small as a millionth of a second.

Q2: What might a time-of-day clock be used for?

Running and blocked processes

Some of the terms that are used in this Unit and subsequent Units need to be carefully defined:

- a **process** is a program actually running on the CPU, even though it might be waiting for I/O at a particular moment.

- a process is **running** or **current** if it is actually using the CPU.

- a process is **runnable** when it *could* make use of the CPU if it was available.

- a process is **blocked** when it is waiting for I/O and could not use the CPU even if it were free.

Interrupt handling

An **interrupt** is a signal generated by an event that alters the sequence in which a processor executes instructions. It is generated by the hardware of the computer system. When an interrupt occurs, the operating system saves the state of the interrupted process and passes control to the appropriate routine.

An interrupt may be initiated by the currently running process (perhaps it has some data to output, for example), or it may be caused by some event which may or may not be related to the currently running process.

Types of interrupt

The following different types of interrupt may occur:

- **interrupts generated by the running process**. The process might need to perform I/O, obtain more storage or communicate with the operator.

- **I/O interrupts**. These are initiated by the I/O hardware and signal to the CPU that the status of a channel or device has changed. An I/O interrupt will occur when an I/O operation is complete, when an error occurs, or when a device is made ready.

- **external interrupts**. These could be caused by the interval timer on expiry of a time-slice, or the operator pressing an interrupt key, or the receipt of a signal from another processor on a multiprocessing system.

- **restart interrupts**. These occur when the operator presses the restart button.

- **program check interrupts**. These are caused by various types of error such as division by zero.

- **machine check interrupts**. These are caused by malfunctioning hardware.

How the interrupt mechanism works

There is a special register in the CPU called the interrupt register. At the beginning of each fetch-execute cycle, the interrupt register is checked. Each bit of the register represents a different type of interrupt, and if a bit is set, the state of the current process is saved and the OS routes control to the appropriate interrupt handler.

Since more than one device may request an interrupt simultaneously, each device is assigned a priority. Slow-speed devices such as terminals and printers are given a high priority, since they are more liable to get behind with what they are doing, and so should be allowed to start as soon as possible so that they do not eventually hold up processing.

In some cases if an interrupt occurs during data transfer, some data could be lost, and so the OS will **disable** other interrupts until it completes its task.

In a large multi-user system there is a constant stream of interrupts directed at the processor, and it must respond as quickly as possible to these in order to provide an acceptable response time. Once an interrupt is received, the OS disables interrupts while it deals with the current interrupt. Since this could mean that interrupts are disabled for a large proportion of the time, the nucleus (ie the part of the OS that is always in main store) on large systems simply determines the cause of the interrupt and then passes the problem over to the specific interrupt handler, leaving itself free to deal with the next interrupt.

A special register called the PSW (program status word) indicates the types of interrupts currently **enabled** and those currently **disabled**. The CPU allows enabled interrupts to occur; disabled interrupts remain pending, or in some cases are ignored.

In smaller systems, the OS handles all interrupts itself, which means that the interrupts are disabled for a larger proportion of time.

Example:

Program A is the currently running process. It needs to retrieve some data from disk, so an interrupt is generated. The interrupt handler changes the status of A to 'blocked', makes a request to the disk drive for data, and invokes a program called the **dispatcher** which selects Job B to run next. After a while, the disk drive has filled the buffer area and generates an interrupt to say it is ready. The interrupt handler is invoked, and changes the status of program A from 'blocked' to 'runnable', but B is left running. One millisecond later B's time up is called by the interrupting clock and the dispatcher hands the CPU back to A, leaving B's status as 'runnable'.

Masking of interrupts

Sometimes it is convenient to have the facility to enable and disable peripherals through program instructions. If for example the programmer did not want I/O from some high-priority device for any reason, a completely automatic interrupt priority system would require physical removal of the peripheral from the system. To allow the user some control, interrupts can normally be **masked** (disabled) using program instructions.

If **all** interrupts could be masked, the user would never be able to regain control if for example his program started looping because of a program error. Therefore, at least one interrupt is normally **non-maskable**.

Exercises:

1. Describe what is meant by 'the autonomous operation of peripherals' explaining why it is necessary and how it is achieved. (3 marks)
    JMB Paper 1 May 1990

2. State *three* advantages of using a system of interrupts rather than a polling system. (3 marks)
    AEB Paper 1 June 1989

3. Outline a method of employing double buffering for processing a serial file as input. (5 marks)
    AEB Paper 1 1988

4. Give *four* distinct examples of errors or malfunctions to which an operating system should respond in a multi-programming environment. (4 marks)

    In the event of one of these errors or malfunctions occurring, describe

    (a) how it would be detected

    (b) what happens when it is detected. (7 marks)
    AEB Paper 1 1985

5. (a) Explain why printers usually contain a buffer store. (2 marks)

    (b) Explain why it is necessary to have two-way communication between a printer and the central processor. (2 marks)
    London Sample AS Paper 1989

6.* (a) When transferring data to a printer, the computer system uses interrupts.

    (i)   What is an interrupt? (2 marks)

    (ii) What is the role of the interrupt in the transferring of data? (3 marks)

    (b) (i)   Give two other examples of the use of interrupts in a computer system. (2 marks)

    (ii) Why is there a system of priorities for interrupts? (3 marks)

    (iii) Explain briefly how an interrupt is detected and identified by the processor. (3 marks)
    AEB Paper 2 1991
    (part of question)

Unit 66 — Multiprogramming Systems

Introduction

Multiprogramming is the term used to describe the technique of having more than one program in the computer's memory at the same time. A CPU running a single program spends most of its time idle, waiting for input or output. Multiprogramming helps to ensure that the CPU runs in the most efficient way possible.

The operating system has various tasks to perform in order to make multiprogramming possible.

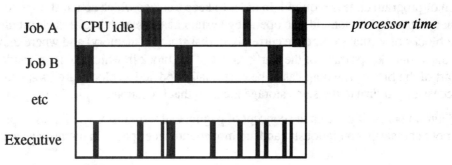

Figure 66.1 — A multiprogramming system

Memory management

In a multiprogramming environment, the operating system has to allocate memory space to the currently running processes. In the earliest multiprogramming systems, main storage was divided up into a number of fixed size partitions, with each partition holding a single job. A job stayed in its partition until it was completed, and the CPU switched between the jobs held in the various partitions. The obvious problem with this system is that it wasted a lot of memory space as it would be unlikely that jobs would exactly fill the fixed partitions.

Q1: Supposing a computer with a usable memory of 360K is capable of running up to 6 jobs at once, but no program is allowed to exceed 200K. Many programs occupy only about 30K or less. How would you partition memory, and what problems can you foresee?

Virtual memory

Modern large computers (and also some micro systems such as Windows 3) operate a system known as **virtual memory management,** which is a much more flexible and efficient way of managing memory. Processes to be run are held on disk, and when a process's turn for CPU time comes round, the operating system transfers a currently running process out of memory to make room for the next one. This enables many more programs to be run simultaneously than would otherwise be possible. In fact, not **all** of the process needs to be in memory even when it is running, so only the section of the program containing the instructions currently being executed needs to be copied into memory. This technique enables a program which is too large to be held in main store all at once to be run, as only part of the program needs to be in memory at any particular time.

It would be impractical to transfer bytes or words one by one as needed, and therefore data is transferred in blocks. There are two possible strategies for doing this; the blocks to be swapped can all be the same size, or they can be of variable sizes. When blocks are the same size they are called **pages** and the associated virtual storage organisation is called **paging.** When the blocks are of different sizes, they are called **segments**, and the associated virtual storage organisation is called **segmentation.**

Paging

Paging means that a fixed number of bytes, generally from 512 to 4K bytes, is transferred to disk each time a new section of program code is required. In order to keep track of which actual storage location any given item of data is in at any particular moment, the operating system has to maintain, for each running process, a 'map' showing which blocks of virtual storage are currently in real storage (memory) and where they are. To refer to a particular item, the system keeps track of the start address of the block in which the item resides, and its displacement from the start of the block. The map has to be continually updated as blocks are swapped in and out, and a block does not necessarily return to the same storage location that it occupied on its last trip to main store!

The diagram below illustrates the concept of paging and virtual storage. Pages of programs A, B and C reside on disk, not necessarily contiguously, and are moved into free spaces in memory as and when required.

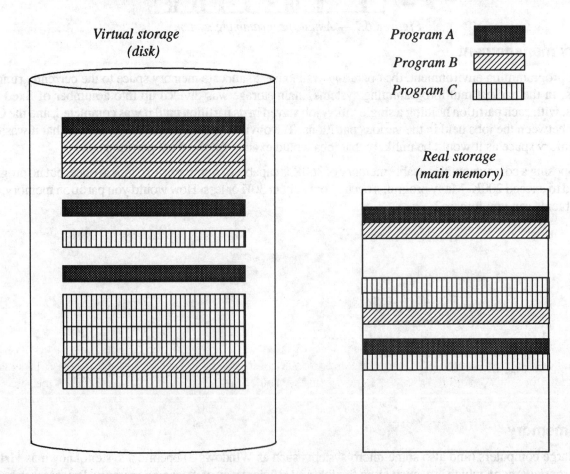

Figure 66.2 — Virtual storage

Segmentation

In segmentation, the programmer or the operating system (or a special utility program) divides the program up into a number of variable size segments which may be loaded into non-contiguous locations in memory. Different segments may have different access rights attached to them so that for example the program instructions could be in a 'read-only' segment so that they cannot be overwritten, and the data could be in a 'read-write' segment.

A program created with many small code segments will require less memory than a program with fewer large code segments, but generally will require more swapping in and out of code and therefore may take longer to execute.

Storage protection

Storage protection limits the range of addresses a program may reference, and is essential in multi-user systems.

If a program occupies a contiguous block of storage locations, storage protection can be implemented by **bounds registers** that hold the lower and upper addresses of the block of storage. As a program executes, all addresses that are referred to in the program are checked to ensure that they are within these bounds. Another method of implementing storage protection is to use **storage protection keys** attached to areas in main store; a program may only reference locations with keys which match the program's key.

Deadlock

A process in a multiprogramming system is said to be in **deadlock** if it is waiting for an event that will not occur. It is akin to the situation of two large lorries each at the head of a stream of traffic meeting on a narrow bridge.

Deadlock can occur because two processes are each holding one resource and requesting the use of a second resource which is held by the other.

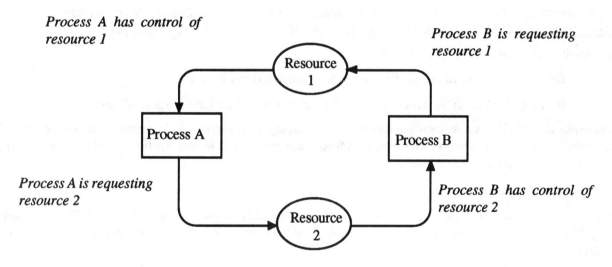

Figure 66.3 - Deadlock

One possible strategy for avoiding this situation is to specify that when a process is denied a resource which it has requested, it must release any other resource it is currently holding. This may result in 'indefinite postponement', as it repeatedly requests and releases the same resources. The operator may have to cancel one of the jobs if this situation is detected.

Deadlock in spooling systems

Deadlock can occur in spooling systems if the operating system does not allow actual printing to begin for any particular job until all the output has been written to the spool file. The situation can then arise where several jobs are still sending output to the spool file, which fills up before any one job is complete. Sometimes this happens because of a programmer error, where the program is in a loop trying to print thousands of pages of repeating data! Recovering from this type of deadlock generally involves restarting the system, which means that everyone has to start their jobs again.

Preempting resources

Most resources in a multiprogramming system are preemptible; that is what makes it possible for several users to receive a reasonable response time. The CPU is preempted by the next user when the current process's time-slice is up or when it becomes blocked waiting for I/O; memory is preempted by the next process waiting to run.

Certain resources may be **non-preemptible**; for example tape drives are normally assigned to one particular program, even when that program is not actually executing. While a tape drive belongs to one process, it may not be given to another process.

Disk drives are sometimes dedicated to single processes, but often contain files belonging to many processes.

Backing store management

One of the tasks of an operating system is to manage all the files on backing store. This includes:

- **access methods** — implementing the various methods of holding files such as sequential, indexed and random.

- **file management** — providing the mechanisms for files to be stored, referenced, shared and kept secure.

- **storage management** — deciding where to put a file on a particular drive, for example.

- **maintaining file integrity** — making sure that data is not accidentally or deliberately corrupted.

As files are added and deleted, the disk becomes **fragmented** with a lot of small spaces but perhaps none big enough to hold the latest file. In **contiguous allocation**, the whole file has to fit into a single space.

Two possible ways of finding space for a new file are

- **first-fit** — put the file in the first space big enough to hold it

- **best-fit** — look for the block which will involve wasting the least amount of space.

More often, the OS allows **non-contiguous** storage, by keeping a 'free space list' containing entries for all the free sectors on the disk. An index entry for each file indicates where the first block of the file is, and pointers in a linked list structure point to subsequent blocks.

Directory structures

On a disk which is capable of holding several megabytes of data and perhaps storing many users' files, it is essential to organise the data so that files can be quickly located and to ensure that each user can only access files which he is entitled to use.

One common way to organise directories is to use a hierarchical or tree structure such as the one shown below. A person signing on to the system with a particular user code and password may be given access to all subdirectories of his own directory, but not to any other part of the file store. The higher up the tree your directory is, the more access rights you have.

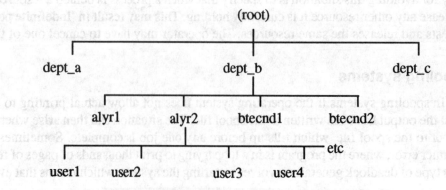

Figure 66.4 — A directory tree

MS-DOS uses a similar tree structure but does not allow for different users to have different access rights since it is a single user system. The directory structure is used mainly as a convenient way of keeping different software packages separate from each other. Any entry in a directory may refer to a file or to a subdirectory.

Directory entries

Each entry in a directory will typically contain the following information:

- the file or subdirectory name
- indication of whether it is a file or directory
- size of the file in bytes
- date and time last used
- address at which the data is stored

Exercises:

1. State **three** advantages of organising the file system of a networked Winchester disk in the form of a multi-level directory.

(3 marks)
AEB Paper 1 1990

2. (a) The term *multiprogramming* is frequently used to describe processing on large computer systems.

    (i) Explain what is meant by the term *multiprogramming*. (5 marks)

    (ii) Describe briefly how it works. (5 marks)

    (iii) Explain why it is useful. (5 marks)

  (b) Two programs which run in a multiprogramming system both direct output to a line printer during their execution. There is only one printer available.

    (i) Explain carefully how *spooling* makes it possible for the two programs to run concurrently.

(5 marks)

    (ii) State the main reasons why such a system uses spooling. (5 marks)
UCLES Specimen AS Level Paper 1989

3. In a disk filing system which uses contiguous allocation of files, two popular algorithms for allocating files to unused disk space are:

    first fit (first block large enough is allocated)

    best fit (block with least wastage is allocated)

Below is a list of files to be stored on disk and a list of unused disk blocks and their sizes. The list of unused disk blocks is sorted by address.

Files to be written to disk	Unused disk blocks and sizes
File 1: 45K	Block A: 75K
File 2: 74K	Block B: 40K
File 3: 35K	Block C: 50K
File 4: 38K	Block D: 35K

Describe what happens when an attempt is made to write the above files using

    (a) first fit

    (b) best fit.

4 marks
SEB Paper 2 1990

4. (a) Memory within a computer system can be shared between various tasks using the technique of paging (virtual memory).

    Explain in detail, what is meant by this and describe how memory references are determined at run time within such a system. (10 marks)

    (b) Sharing data resident on backing storage in a multi-user, multi-tasking environment can lead to difficulties.

    (i) Outline **two** such difficulties that occur within this environment. (4 marks)

    (ii) Outline **three** methods used to overcome such difficulties in the sharing of data within this environment. (6 marks)

    AEB Paper 1 1988

5.* Diagram 1 shows a directory listing. It represents the logical or user view of the files stored on a magnetic disk.

AUTOBOOT

SYSTEM

WORDPRO

DATAFILES

DIARY

Diagram 1

Diagram 2 shows a magnetic disk with files stored on it. It represents the physical or system view of the files stored on a disk.

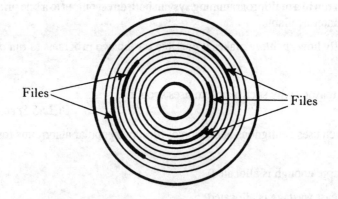

Files   Files

Diagram 2

    (a) (i) Distinguish between the *logical* view of the files and the *physical* view of the files.

    (ii) How does the file management system link the two views? (3 marks)

    (b) Another function of the file management system is to keep track of free disk space. Describe how this might be done. (2 marks)

    (c) While attempting to save a file to disk, a user receives a "disk full" message. On examining the disk's contents, it is found that there is sufficient space on the disk for the file. The filing system in use has no restriction on the number of files stored on a disk.

    (i) What does this suggest about the method used by the operating system to allocate disk space? Give a reason for your answer.

    (ii) Name and describe a method of solving the "disk full" problem. (4 marks)

    SEB Paper 1 1992

Unit 67 — The Scheduler and Dispatcher

CPU management

In a multiprogramming environment, several programs appear to be running simultaneously in the computer. In reality, the CPU can only execute one instruction at a time and the OS must keep switching the CPU between the instructions of the various processes that are running. Deciding which process to run next is the job of the **scheduler**, and will be done in accordance with a **scheduling policy**. This cannot be too complex or the computer will spend more time deciding whose turn it is than getting on with the job! It is not unknown for an operating system to occupy about 90% of the CPU's time, leaving 10% to be shared out among the users. Some compromise has to be reached.

High level and low level scheduling

There are two levels of scheduling:

- **high level scheduling** determines which jobs shall be allowed to enter the queue for resources. Priority may be assigned by the user, who pays a premium to gain fast entry to the queue.

- **low level scheduling** determines which process will be allocated CPU time when it next becomes available, and actually assigns or **dispatches** the CPU to the process. The low level scheduler is also called the **dispatcher**, and is a program which is part of the OS nucleus and therefore is permanently in memory. It makes its decision by choosing the runnable process with the highest priority. The dispatcher will assign its own priorities based on how to make the most efficient use of the computer's resources.

Scheduling objectives

A scheduling policy should try to

- maximise throughput — try to process as many jobs as possible in as little time as possible.

- maximise the number of interactive users receiving acceptable response times (ie at most a few seconds).

- balance resource use — if for example a printer is idle, a high priority could be given to a job that uses the printer.

- avoid pushing the low priority jobs to the back of the queue indefinitely. This can be achieved by giving jobs a higher priority based on how long they have been in the queue.

- enforce priorities — in environments where users can assign priorities to jobs, the scheduler must favour the high priority jobs.

- achieve a balance between response time and utilisation of resources.

Some of these objectives may conflict with each other, making scheduling a complex process!

The dispatcher will use a number of criteria such as:

- how much I/O a process needs

- how much CPU time a process needs

- whether the process is batch or interactive

- the urgency of a fast response

- process priority — high priority processes should be favoured

- accumulated waiting time

- how much more time the process needs to complete, though this is often not known.

Round robin scheduling

In round robin scheduling processes are dispatched on a first in first out (FIFO) basis, with each process in turn being given a limited amount of CPU time called a **time slice** or **quantum**. If it does not complete before its time expires (usually a few milliseconds) the dispatcher gives the CPU to the next process.

In order to do this the OS sets an interrupting clock or interval timer to generate interrupts at specific times. This method of scheduling helps to guarantee a reasonable response time to interactive users. In some systems users who have requested a high priority for their jobs may have more than one consecutive time slice each time their turn comes round.

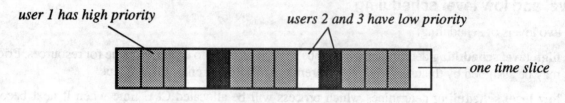

Figure 67.1 - Time slicing

Shortest-job-first scheduling

In this scheduling method, the waiting time or process with the smallest estimated run-time-to-completion is run next. This tends to reduce the number of waiting jobs, and the number of small jobs waiting behind large jobs. Its disadvantage is that it requires knowledge of how long the job will take, so the user has to estimate the job time.

Q1: A user underestimates the job time deliberately in order to get his job a higher priority rating. What action could the OS take if time runs out before completion?

Q2: In a certain operating system jobs are picked off the queue on a first-come-first-served basis. What problems can you foresee? What can be done to improve the situation?

Q3: Job C needs only one hundredth of a second in the CPU to complete. Job D needs 20 seconds. Which should have priority?

Q4: Job E has been in the queue for 4 days — each time it is about to get the CPU another job comes along with a higher priority. What should be done?

296

Multilevel feedback queues

This technique attempts to address the major objectives of a scheduling mechanism, namely:

- to favour short jobs;

- to favour I/O bound jobs in order to get good I/O utilisation;

- to determine the nature of the job as quickly as possible and schedule the job accordingly.

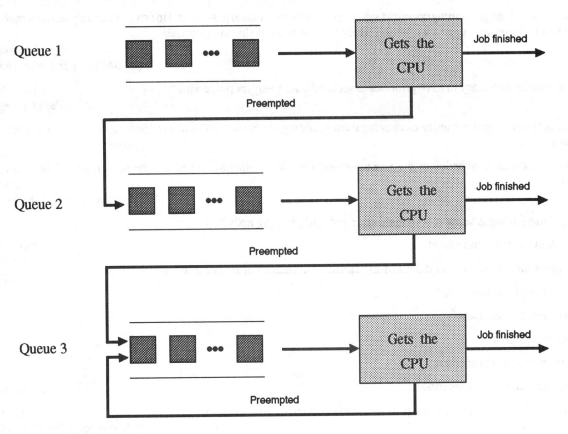

Figure 67.2 — A multilevel feedback queue

The system consists of a number of queues. A new process enters Queue 1 at the back, and moves along the queue until it gets the CPU. If it completes or relinquishes the CPU to wait for I/O, it leaves the queueing network. If the time slice expires before completion, it moves to the back of queue 2.

The time slice in queue 1 is chosen to be large enough so that the great majority of I/O jobs will issue an I/O request before their time slice expires. In Queue 2, jobs receive a longer time slice, but they do not get a turn until the higher-level queue is empty. Thus, a job in this queue may not get the CPU very often but when it does, it will get a longer time slice.

In the bottom queue, the time-slice is longer still, and jobs circulate round-robin until they complete. Once again, though, they are not given CPU time until the higher-level queues are empty. A job which 'voluntarily' leaves the queue for I/O before its time-slice expires will be returned to the same queue that it left, or in some systems to the next queue up.

Three queues are shown in the diagram above but there could be any number of queues.

This system is **a good example of an adaptive mechanism** — one that adapts itself to changing behaviour.

Exercises:

1. Explain carefully how the multi-level feedback queue fulfills the objectives of:

   favouring short jobs

   favouring I/O bound jobs

   determining the nature of a job and scheduling it accordingly.   (6 marks)

2. Explain how a multiprogramming operating system selects the program to pass control to next, indicating the use it makes of priorities in doing so. Suggest a criterion which may be used to allocate priorities.

                                                                                    (3 marks)
                                                                        JMB Paper 1 May 1989

3. Why is it usually necessary to have priorities associated with interrupt processing?   (4 marks)
                                                                        AEB Paper 1 1988

4. In an interactive multiprogramming environment the operating system maintains a list of processes that are ready to use the processor.

   Outline *one* method of scheduling the processor and describe a situation when this method may not be entirely appropriate.   (4 marks)
                                                                        London Paper 2 June 1989

5. Some operating systems support both <u>multi-user</u> and <u>multi-tasking</u> activities.

   (a) Explain the tems underlined.   (4 marks)

   (b) Explain the role of each of the following facilities in such an operating system:

       (i)   peripheral interrupts;

       (ii)   clock interrupts;

       (iii) dispatcher:

       (iv)   memory management;

       (v)   interactive user interface.   (12 marks)

   (c) Discuss the benefit of having a priority system applied to task scheduling.   (4 marks)
                                                                        AEB Specimen Paper 2 1990

6.* At a particular instant during the operation of a multi-access system the situation is as follows.

   A   One program is in main store and is being processed.

   B   One program is being transferred by the disc controller from main store to backing store; this operation was initiated earlier by the processor and the disc controller will interrupt the processor when the transfer is completed.

   C   Several other programs are also in main store waiting to be processed when a time slice is given to them by the scheduler.

   D   Some programs are held in backing store but could continue if loaded into main store and given a time slice.

   E   Some more programs are also held in backing store and are unable to continue until some external activity (e.g. reading a line of data from a keyboard) is completed.

   F   The main store includes between the programs a number of areas which are not currently in use; these vary in size but most are too small to contain any of the programs waiting in backing store.

   Starting from the situation described, suggest the kinds of activity which might subsequently take place and describe in general terms the operation of the multi-access sytem in handling these activities. You should cover the role of the scheduler, the handling of interrupts, and the management of swapping and of the main store.   (10 marks)
                                                                        UCLES Paper 2 May 1992

Unit 68 — Local Area Networks

What is a LAN?

A LAN (Local Area Network) is a collection of computers and peripherals connected together by cables, and generally confined to one building or site. A LAN offers a means of pooling resources and information between a number of users. A central mini or mainframe computer with a number of 'dumb' terminals attached is one form of LAN, but the term is frequently used to describe a number of linked PCs, often with a more powerful computer controlling the network.

A local area network has several advantages over a collection of standalone microcomputers:

- sharing of resources such as disk storage, printers and possibly a large, powerful computer
- sharing of information held on disk drives accessible by all users
- sharing of software
- ability to communicate with other users on the network. This is not important when all the computers are in the same room but can be very useful when they are distributed round a large building.

Q1: What, if any, are the **disadvantages** of networking a collection of standalone micros?

Components of a LAN

All LANs will have at least three basic components:

- **workstations** — PCs or terminals.
- **file server** or **disk server** — a special PC or larger computer where shared software resources are stored, including the network software which monitors network operation.
- **cabling and connection hardware** — this includes the cables that link the computers together, and a special **interface card** or printed circuit board which has to be inserted into each computer on the network to give it a unique identity and allow it to interact with other components of the network.

In addition, LANs may have additional hardware such as printers and extra disk storage. Network printers have to be connected to a computer designated as the **print server** — this may well be the same computer that is designated as the **file server**.

Each workstation on the network may have its own processing power and may have its own disk storage (floppy or hard disk) and its own printer.

Consideration will have to be given to **backup** facilities; some LANs have two file servers, with data being copied at regular intervals (say every few minutes) from one file server to the other, so that if one goes down, the other can take over with the loss of only a few minutes' work.

For making regular backups of files stored on the hard disk, a **tape streamer** consisting of a compact tape cartridge unit with a high storage capacity may be used.

Network topologies

The **topology** of a network is its physical layout — the way in which the computers and other units are connected. There are three basic layouts; **star, bus** and **ring**.

Star network

Each node in a star network is connected to a central microcomputer which controls the network. Network signals travel from the server to the station along each individual station's cable. A **polling** system is commonly used — the file server polls each station in turn to see if it has a signal to send. The server then handles signals as they are received.

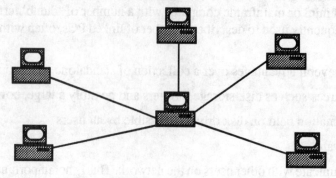

Figure 68.1 — a star network

Advantages of a star network

- if one cable fails, the other stations are not affected

- consistent performance even when the network is being heavily used

- reliable, market-proven system

- no problems with 'collisions' of data since each station has its own cable to the server

- easy to add new stations without disrupting the network

Disadvantages of star network

- may be costly to install because of the length of cable required. The cabling can be a substantial part of the overall cost of installing a network.

A variation of the star topology is the **distributed star** topology. A number of stations are linked to connection boxes which are then linked together to form a 'string of stars'.

Bus network

In a bus network, all the devices share a single cable. Information can be transmitted in either direction from any PC to any other. The problem here is that several stations may want to transmit down the same line simultaneously, and there has to be some strategy for deciding who gets the line. A popular scheme called **Ethernet** uses a collision system known as '**carrier sense multiple access with collision detection**' (CSMA-CD). Before a station begins to transmit, it checks that the channel is not busy; if it is, it has to wait before transmission can begin. Once it begins transmission, it listens for other nodes also beginning transmission. If the transmitted message collides with another, both stations abort and wait a random period of time before trying again.

This system works well if the channels are not too heavily loaded. On the other hand if sixteen students sit down at sixteen computers all at once and all try to load software from the network's hard disk, the whole system more or less grinds to a halt!

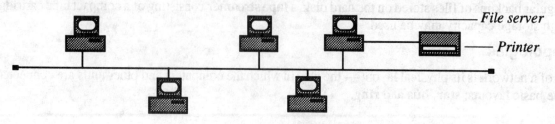

Figure 68.2 — a bus network

The **advantages** of a bus system are that it is

- easy and inexpensive to install as it requires the least amount of cable

- easy to add more stations without disrupting the network

The **disadvantages** are that

- the whole network goes down if the main cable fails at any point

- cable failure is difficult to isolate

- network performance degrades under a heavy load.

Ring network

In a ring network, a series of computers is connected together and there is no central controlling computer. Each computer may communicate with any other computer in the ring, with messages being specifically addressed to the destination computer. Using the 'token ring' system, a 'message token' (actually a unique character sequence) is passed from node to node, and each node has a designated time at which it can remove the token and either add a message together with the addresses of the receiving node and sending node, and some control bits) or take a message from it. A receiving device acknowledges the receipt of a message by inverting a 1-bit field.

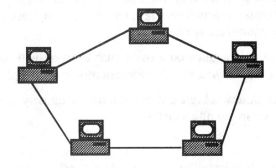

Figure 68.3 — a ring network

The **advantages** of a ring system are:

- there is no dependence on a central computer or file server, and each node controls transmission to and from itself

- transmission of messages around the ring is relatively simple, with messages travelling in one direction only

- very high transmission rates are possible

The **disadvantages** are:

- if one node in the ring breaks down, transmission between any of the devices in the ring is disrupted.

Exercises:

1. What is meant by the term *ring local area network*? Describe briefly how a device connected to the ring sends information
    to another device on the ring. (5 marks)
    AEB Paper 2 1993

2. With the aid of diagrams or otherwise, distinguish between a star and a ring network. (2 marks)
    AEB Paper 2 1992

Unit 69 — Data Transmission

Introduction

In the last Unit we discussed possible configurations for local area networks. Before moving on to wide area networks, we need to look at some of the techniques and hardware used in data transmission in both sorts of networks, and define some technical terms used to describe various characteristics such as speed and methods of transmission.

Communication channels

A communication **channel** is the link between two computers. It could be a cable of some kind, a telephone line, a microwave or a communications satellite link.

Cabling systems

Type of cabling has a major bearing on a network's speed, performance, cost and practicality (a very thick cable being much harder to lay in or along walls). **Twisted pair**, like telephone wire, is the cheapest but has slow transmission rates and suffers from electronic interference. **Coaxial cable** is high quality, well insulated cable which can transmit data much faster and more accurately than twisted pair.

There are two types of coaxial cable:

- **baseband** carries one signal at a time. A bit value of 1 or 0 is sent by the presence or absence of a voltage in the cable. Baseband signals can travel very fast, but can only be sent over short distances. Over about 1000 feet special booster equipment is needed.

- **broadband** can carry multiple signals on a fixed carrier wave, with the signals for 0 and 1 sent as variations on this wave. Data, audio and video transmission can take place simultaneously.

Fibre optic cable represents the latest technological development, being very fine cable that can carry several hundred thousand voice communications simultaneously.

Satellite transmission

Using a satellite dish and a communications satellite, it is possible to send signals over long distances, such as from Britain to America. Communications satellites are placed about 22,000 miles above the earth in geosynchronous orbit (meaning that they rotate with the earth).

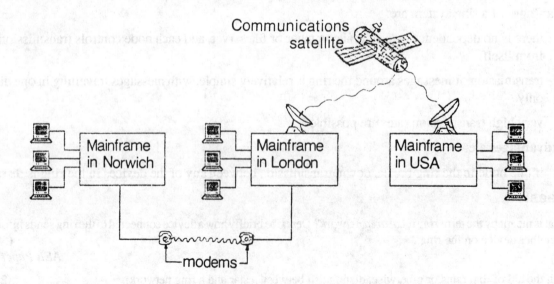

Figure 69.1 — Satellite transmission

302

Microwave transmission

Microwaves are similar to radio waves, and can be used to transmit data between microwave stations. Transmission distance between stations is limited to about 30 miles because of the earth's curvature, since microwaves travel in a straight line. Microwave stations are usually located on hilltops or towers.

Transmission modes: asynchronous and synchronous

In **asynchronous transmission mode**, individual characters are transmitted at irregular intervals — for example, as they are typed by a user. The bits representing the character are enclosed by start and stop bits, and a **parity bit** is usually added to the character code to provide a check against incorrect transmission. A complete character therefore needs ten bits to be transmitted; a start bit, seven bits for the character code, a parity bit and a stop bit. This mode of transmission is used for lower speed transmission, for example on a local area network consisting of a number of linked PCs.

Q1: When one PC communicates with another on a local area network, what information needs to be transmitted in addition to the data to be sent, start and stop bits, and parity bits?

In **synchronous transmission mode**, timing signals synchronise the transmission at the sending and receiving end so there is no need for start and stop bits for each character, only at the beginning and end of the whole block. This mode of transmission is more suitable for longer transmissions such as remote job entry, but requires more expensive and sophisticated equipment.

Simplex, half duplex and full duplex transmission

The direction of transmission may be either:

- **simplex** — transmission can only take place in one direction. This type of transmission could be used for example when the sending device such as a temperature sensor never requires a response from the computer.

- **half duplex** — transmission can take place in both directions but not at the same time, as for example in a citizen's band radio. This type of transmission is often used between a central computer and terminals.

- **full duplex** — data can be sent in both directions at the same time. Most interactive computer applications use full duplex transmission.

Transmission rate

The speed at which data is transmitted is measured in bits per second. Baseband coaxial cable, for example, can transmit up to ten million bits per second over short distances. **Baud rate** is another measure of speed, and is the number of times per second that the signal changes. At speeds up to 2400 bps, usually one bit is transmitted per signal change so baud rate and bits per second are the same thing, but to achieve very high speeds (over 2400 bps) more than one bit is transmitted per signal change, and so the bps rate will exceed the baud rate.

Q2: Using 10 bits for each character (7 bits for the character code, a parity bit and a start and stop bit), at a transmission rate of 2400 bps approximately how long would it take to transmit the text on this page?

Protocol

In order to allow equipment from different suppliers to be networked, a strict set of rules (**protocols**) has been devised covering standards for physical connections, cabling, mode of transmission, speed, data format, error detection and correction. Any equipment which uses the same communication protocol can be connected together.

Manufacturers are gradually incorporating some of these standards in some of their products, but it is unlikely that total standardisation will be achieved for some time, if ever. Where two devices have different protocols they can sometimes communicate via a 'protocol conversion computer'.

The OSI seven layer model

OSI is an abbreviation for Open Systems Interconnection, and a model for OSI (implying that equipment from any manufacturer can be connected to any other manufacturer's equipment) has been under development since 1977. A hierarchy of seven layers has been identified as described below.

a.   Application Layer

This is the highest level, closest to the user. It supports the transfer of information between end-users, applications programs and devices. Several types of protocol exist in this layer, covering specific and general applications such as accounting, entry control and user identification.

b.   Presentation Layer

The aim of protocols in this layer is to ensure that different devices using data in different formats can communicate with each other, for example, handling conversion between ASCII and EBCDIC. It may also carry out encryption to ensure data security during transmission.

c.   Session Layer

The session layer is the user's interface into the network. When a user requests a particular service from the network, the session layer handles the dialogue.

d.   Transport Layer

This layer handles the data transmission between host computers, dealing with addressing and error controls to ensure a high quality data transmission service for the network.

e.   Network Layer

The function of the network layer is to perform the routing of information around the network, connecting adjacent nodes in the network and also carrying out accounting functions to enable the network owner to charge users.

f.   Data Link Layer

The physical data transmission media used in a network are subject to interference which can corrupt data, and this layer handles data transmission errors. The techniques used for receipt and acknowledgement of data by a receiver are handled in this layer.

g.   Physical Layer

This layer is concerned with standards for the mechanical, electrical and procedural aspects of interface devices; for example, the number of pins a network connector should have. It is concerned with how the binary data is transmitted along the communication channel.

Gateways

The term 'wide area network' applies to both national and international networks, and there are hundreds of such networks worldwide, with most major networks being interconnected through a system of **gateways**. A gateway is a computer which acts as a point of connection between different networks.

Exercises:

1. A company is changing its *timesharing minicomputer system* to a *local area network* of microcomputers (stations). The network is supported by two 80Mb hard disk units which are to form part of the common *file server*. The processing power of the server is sufficient to control the operations of the network. The server can also support a number of printers which are centrally available to all users. Each network station is also capable of supporting a local disk drive and a local printer.

    (i)   What is a timesharing minicomputer system?   (1 mark)

    (ii) Discuss the advantages and disadvantages of changing from a timesharing system to a local area network. Would a collection of standalone microcomputers serve the same purpose?   (6 marks)

    (iii) Describe briefly *one* network topology that could be used in this case.   (2 marks)

    (iv) How might the network operating system

          (a)   organise the communication between stations and the server?   (2 marks)

          (b)   handle the problem of allocating the shared central printers amongst the users?   (2 marks)

    (v)   What factors determine the speed at which the network can provide a response to the user?   (2 marks)

    London Paper 2 June 1989

2. The microcomputers (stations) connected to a particular Local Area Network (LAN) share a common cable for transmission of data. Data is sent down this cable either from station to station or from a station to the common filestore.

    (a)   When data is sent from a station it is grouped into a packet. Each packet also contains a header field and a checksum field.

          (i)   What purposes might these two fields serve? How might the checksum field be calculated?   (3 marks)

          (ii) In addition to the original data and the fields mentioned in (i), what other information might you expect to find in the package?   (1 mark)

    (b)   The LAN needs to support many users who may wish to transmit data at roughly the same time. Describe one mechanism that can be used to provide these users with an equitable share of the common cable.   (4 marks)

    (c)   What is meant by the term *distributed data processing*? In what way could such a LAN be said to support such processing?   (2 marks)

    (d)   One of the potential advantages of using a LAN is the ability to link computers from different manufacturers. Discuss briefly the problems that need to be overcome before this goal can be achieved.   (3 marks)

    (e)   Suggest two other advantages of the use of a LAN in a small office or an educational institution.   (2 marks)

    London Specimen Paper 2 1989

3.* (i)   Explain what is meant by the term *handshaking* in the context of data transfer between two devices.

    (ii) Explain why standard interfaces, such as RS232, are often used for the hardware interconnection of devices.

    (iii) Briefly explain the purpose of a protocol in data transmission across a network.   (6 marks)

    London Paper 1 1992

Unit 70 — Wide Area Networks

Introduction

A **wide area network** (WAN) is a collection of computers spread over a wide geographical area, possibly spanning several continents. Communication may be via microwave or satellite link, or by ordinary telephone lines supplied for example by British Telecom or Mercury.

Public and leased lines

A WAN may use either the public telephone lines, dialling up as required, or if communications are very frequent, a **leased line**. This can then be permanently connected and is not charged by the minute, but the subscription charges are obviously heavy.

Q1: Which sort of line (public or leased) would you recommend for each of the following?

(i) a library has several terminals from which it can access databases all over the world to obtain information on publications.

(ii) A travel agent communicates with various airlines via any of several terminals in the office.

(iii) A local newspaper has a communications link with Reuter's, the international news agency.

(iv) A large insurance company with its Head Office in Ipswich communicates with branches in London and other cities via a wide area network.

(v) A major bank has communications links with each of its branches all over the country.

Modems

Telephone lines were originally designed for speech, which is transmitted in **analogue** or wave form. In order for digital data to be sent along a telephone line, it must first be converted into analogue form and then converted back at the other end. This is achieved by means of a **modem** (MOdulator DEModulator). Modems can transmit data at speeds between 300 and about 40,000 bits per second.

With newer digital lines, a modem is not required.

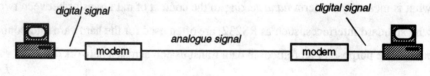

Figure 70.1

Multiplexors

A **multiplexor** combines more than one input signal into a single stream of data that can be transmitted over a communication channel. This increases the efficiency of communication and saves on the cost of individual channels.

At the receiving end, the multiplexor (sometimes called the de-multiplexor) separates the single stream of data into its separate components.

Often a 'front-end processor' or 'communications processor' is connected between the multiplexor and the main computer in order to handle the communications, leaving the main processor free for other tasks.

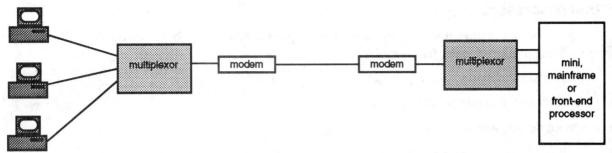

Figure 70.2 — multiplexors and modems

Time division multiplexing

There are two main methods of multiplexing — **time division** and **frequency division**. In **time division** multiplexing, either the bits or characters being transmitted from several terminals are interleaved during transmission. Terminals are polled in sequence, and each terminal is given a time slot whether or not it has anything to transmit. The multiplexor at the other end separates the bits and passes them to the computer.

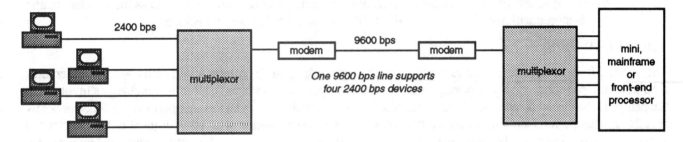

Figure 70.3 — Time division multiplexing

In **statistical** multiplexing, each workstation is still polled, but when a station has data to send, the character, together with the line number, is formed into a data frame by the multiplexor. Stations that are not transmitting are therefore not using up line time.

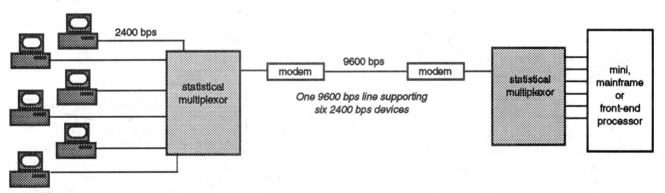

Figure 70.4 — Statistical time division multiplexing

Frequency division multiplexing

In **frequency division** multiplexing, there are several carrier waves each having its own frequency, and each carries one lot of data. The multiplexor at the other end can therefore distinguish between each set of data and separate them out.

Front-end processors

A front-end processor is a computer that is dedicated to handling communications, thus relieving the main computer of many functions. It might handle, for example,

- message assembly/disassembly from/to 'packets' (see below),

- removal and insertion of start/stop bits,

- error detection and correction,

- polling of workstations and

- access security to make sure that a user is authorised to use the network.

Data transfer checks

The following checks may be made during data transmission:

- **parity** checks on each character sent. This involves transmitting an extra bit with each character to make the total number of bits even (or odd, if odd parity is being used).

- a **checksum** may be sent with each block of data transmitted. All the elements in the block (eg words or bytes) are added together (ignoring overflow) to produce a single element known as the checksum, and this is stored with the block and provides a check when the block is transferred.

Circuit switching

The public telephone system is an example of a switched network using **circuit-switched** paths. When a caller dials a number, the path between the two telephones is set up by operating switches in all of the exchanges involved in the path, and the circuit is set up and held for the whole duration of the call, even through periods of silence or heavy breathing. This permits the two people on the phone to hold a conversation with no waiting at either end for the message to arrive. However, because switches are used to connect and disconnect the circuits, electrical interference is produced, and although this is not a serious problem for speech, it may produce corrupt or lost data if the path is being used to transmit computer data. If this is likely to be a serious problem, a leased line may be used instead.

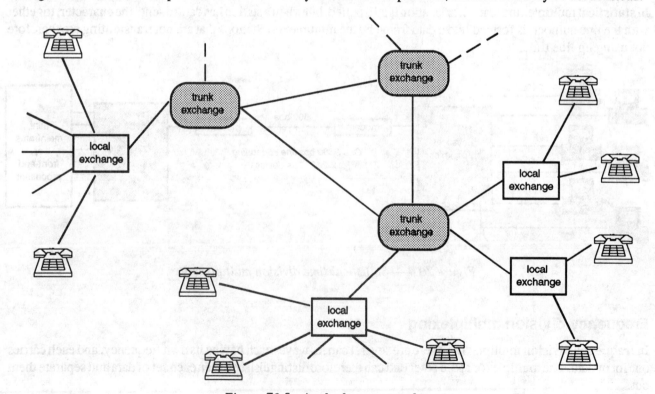

Figure 70.5 - A telephone network

Message switching

Message switching was originally used for the transmission of morse code for sending telegraphed messages as early as 1866, over a century before the days of fax and electronic mail. A batch of messages was relayed to a receiving terminal, where they were manually sorted and stored ready for transmission to the next station in the link to the final destination, in much the same way as letters are sent from the postbox to the main Post Office, sorted and sent on until they finally reach the addressee. In due course the storing and forwarding was automated, and the system is now known as a **message switching system**. Computers are used to store messages on disk while they wait to be sent on to their destinations. The advantage of this system over circuit switching is that unless the lines are completely congested, messages will always be accepted, even though it may not be forwarded for some time.

Packet switching

In a **packet switching system (PSS)** messages are divided into **packets** — fixed length blocks of data of say 128 bytes. As well as the data, each packet also carries

- the source and destination address
- a packet sequence number so that the whole message can be correctly reassembled
- a checksum (longitudinal parity check) for the purposes of error checking.

The PSS (such as the one which in Britain is owned by British Telecom) takes the form of a computer network in which each computer redirects packets it receives to the next computer along an appropriate route to its destination. The packets from different users to different destinations may be interleaved, and all the packets making up one transmission need not necessarily travel by the same route or arrive in the right order. The PSS ensures that they are all reassembled in the correct order at their destination.

The computers in the PSS are able to perform error checking and request retransmission of packets found to be in error. They are also able to perform error correction so that even if a transmission contained some errors, perhaps due to distortion on the line, it may be possible to correct these without having to retransmit.

In order to use the PSS, a user requires a network user identity, which is registered at his/her local packet switch exchange.

Advantages of packet switching compared with message switching

- more efficient use of lines
- cost depends only on the number of packets sent, not on distance so all data can be transmitted at local call rates
- less likely to be affected by network failure because of the multiple routes available to transmit data packets
- better security; data is less likely to be intercepted because the packets may be sent along different routes or be interleaved with other unrelated packets.

Electronic mail

An electronic mail system may be used within an organisation using a local area network, or it may be used for communication all over the country using for example British Telecom's Prestel or Telecom Gold services.

Prestel subscribers pay a subscription rate and charges for time spent using the system, just as telephone subscribers do. Using a telephone line, modem, and either a microcomputer with the appropriate software or a specially adapted TV screen and keyboard, subcribers may call up 'frames' containing for example news, cricket scores or weather forecasts. Prestel is an **interactive viewdata system** so it is also possible to use Prestel to book a holiday or a theatre, or obtain on-line quotes from major insurance companies, for example.

Using the Prestel MAILBOX it is possible to send messages to any other Prestel subscriber.

Typically, the basic services provided by an electronic mail service include

- authentication of sender for security purposes
- notification to sender if message cannot be delivered
- the ability to send the same message to several people
- recording of times of dispatch and receipt of messages
- message filing and retrieval
- automatic accounting and billing of users.

CompuServe

CompuServe is one of the largest international networks. It is advertised as "the world's largest personal information service", and provides access to information on almost any subject. In order to use the CompuServe network, you need a PC, modem and communications software and a membership id, for which a subscription is paid. A monthly member magazine keeps users informed of the latest products and services available on CompuServe.

A typical use of the network might be to gain access to technical support through a software manufacturer's Help line. Many software dealers supply a CompuServe number and a user can dial this number and leave the query in the 'mailbox', and the reply will be sent back in the same way. If you have ever tried to get through to a Help line directly and after finally getting through to some distant city, been put on Hold for up to an hour, you will appreciate the benefits of this service!

Once you are a member of CompuServe, you will have access through 'gateways' to hundreds of other networks so that for example you could get information on University and College places through the UCAS network, or information on, say, travel-related services, or information on UK or foreign companies.

Many networks are used solely for electronic mail, in which case the gateway will be a general purpose computer programmed to receive, store and forward messages.

Exercises:

1. (a) List **two** beneficial effects and **two** adverse effects which *networked* computer systems have had on the 'average' Scottish citizen during the 1980s. (2 marks)

   (b) During the 1990s, most communication systems which rely on *analogue* data transmission will be replaced by *digital* systems.

   Explain clearly what is meant by these two types of data transmission and give **two** reasons for the change from analogue to digital transmission. (3 marks)
   SEB Paper 2 May 1989

2. (a) Data transmission channels can be classified as *simplex, half duplex* or *full duplex*.

   Describe each of these methods and state an application for which each is suitable. (3 marks)

   (b) Why are multiplexors often used when data is being transmitted between computers and distant terminals?

   Describe **two** multiplexing methods. (3 marks)

   (c) Describe the following types of communications links: *circuit switching*; *packet switching*.

   What are the relative advantages and disadvantages associated with each method? (4 marks)

   (d) *Noise* on a telephone line can distort a data signal and result in data bits being incorrectly received. Name and describe two error detection techniques. (2 marks)
   SEB Paper 2 May 19893

3.* A mail order network sets up a wide area network so that members of the public can place orders directly with the company's computer.

One method of communication is to allow the public to connect their microcomputers to the network.

The communication will use a packet switching system.

(i)   State **two** advantages to the company and **one** to the customer of such a system. (3 marks)

(ii) Describe the hardware needed by the public in addition to a basic microcomputer system to allow communication to take place and explain its function. (3 marks)

(iii) Distinguish between serial and parallel transmission. State **one** advantage and **one** disadvantage of serial transmission. (4 marks)

(iv) Explain how packet switching works. Describe the main advantage to the consumer. (4 marks)

(v)   Customers will be able to order goods by entering a code number. There is a likelihood that they will make transposition errors. Explain what a transposition error is and by means of an example give a method that the computer will employ to detect such errors. (4 marks)

(vi) Describe briefly a method of allowing customers without computers to communicate directly with the computer. Give **one** limitation of such a system. (2 marks)

AEB Paper 2 1991

Section 9 — Peripherals

Unit 71 — Input Devices (1)

Historical background

In the early days of computing, and into the 1970s, nearly all computers used 80-column punched cards as input. The data was recorded on cards using a **keypunch** machine, and the cards were collected together and read into the computer's memory by a card reader.

Modern data capture methods

Punched cards have been superseded by a number of different data entry methods, chosen for their suitability to a particular application. There are several alternatives:

- Data may be keyed in from **source documents** by skilled keyboard operators (data prep staff).

- The source documents may be read directly by a document reader.

- Data may be captured directly without the need for any source document, using for example a magnetic strip on a plastic card, a laser scanner or a point-of-sale terminal.

- Graphic input devices may be used to translate drawings or photographs into a digital form that can be processed by a computer.

Key-to-disk systems

In large scale batch processing, where several thousand documents need to be keyed in every day, data is usually entered using an **off-line** key-to-disk system. This has the following components:

- several VDUs or keystations

- a **dedicated** minicomputer

- a fixed disk drive where the data is stored

- a tape drive onto which the completed batches of data are transferred

- a supervisor's console

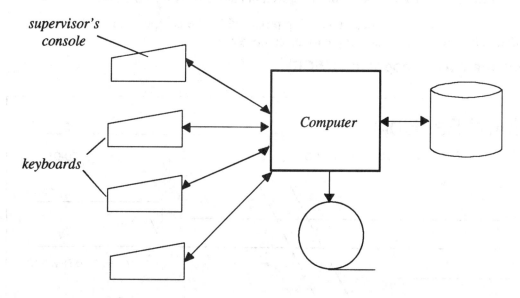

Figure 71.1 — A key-to-disk system

Using a key-to-disk system, each VDU operator loads the data entry program appropriate to her batch of data, and then keys in the data from the source documents. The data is validated by the program as it is being entered, and errors are reported by an audible bleep and an error message on the screen.

313

When the batch of data has been entered and stored on disk, the source documents are passed to another operator who switches her machine to **verify** mode and keys in the batch a second time. Any discrepancies can then be checked and corrected.

Completed batches are transferred from disk to a magnetic tape, which is then physically taken to the main computer for processing. In some systems the transfer to the main computer is done via a data link instead of using a magnetic tape.

The supervisor's console will record the progress of each batch through the system, and also record statistics such as number of keystrokes per hour and number of errors made at each station.

Data entry for interactive processing

With interactive data entry, the person entering the data is communicating directly with the computer which will process the data. This may be any type of computer from a mainframe to a micro, and usually involves keying in data which is then stored on disk. In a sense, then, this is also 'key-to-disk' or 'key-to-diskette' data entry.

Note, however, that the term **key-to-disk system** is generally taken to mean the **off-line** data entry system used in large scale batch systems as described above. A **key-to-diskette system** is a smaller scale operation but is also usually **off-line**, with the diskette being transferred to a larger computer for processing.

Optical character readers

Optical character recognition (OCR) devices are scanners that can read typewritten, computer printed, and in some cases hand printed characters from ordinary documents, by scanning the shape of each character and comparing it with a predefined shape held in its memory. They range from large machines that can read thousands of documents per minute to hand held devices used to scan a printed page.

OCR is most widely used in large scale billing operations such as gas and electricity billing or credit card statements. The statement includes a tear off portion at the bottom of which is printed the customer's account number and the amount owing. A standard typeface known as OCR-A is generally used in the USA, and a similar typeface called OCR-B is common in Europe and Japan. The customer returns this slip with his payment and after the amounts are manually checked the document is read by the computer. Any characters that the machine cannot interpret, or amounts that differ from the printed amount due, are keyed in manually by the operator.

This is an example of a **turnaround** document, being produced by the computer in the first place, sent to the customer and then returned for subsequent input to the computer.

Magnetic ink character recognition (MICR)

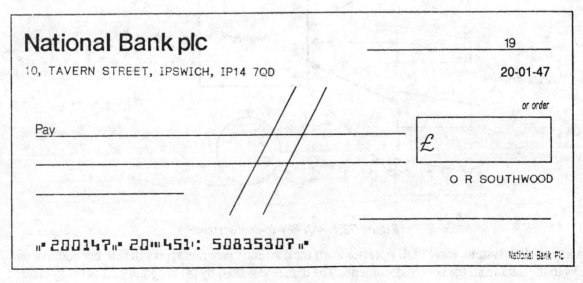

Figure 71.2 — a cheque read by MICR

Virtually all banks use MICR for processing cheques. Special characters encoded along the bottom of a cheque are used to identify the bank number and the customer's account number. When the cheque is processed, the amount is also encoded on it by a bank operator, using a special ink containing ferric oxide which can be magnetized during processing.

MICR devices can process over 1000 cheques per minute. This method of data capture is also used by utility companies (gas, electricity etc), credit card companies and other industries processing large volumes of data.

Q1: Name two advantages, apart from speed, of using MICR as a method of data capture.

Optical mark recognition (OMR)

An optical mark reader is a scanning device which can detect marks made in preset positions on a special form. OMR is frequently used to score multiple choice tests, and also for entering gas and electricity meter readings.

METER READING DOCUMENT						
Account number **5376324**	\multicolumn{6}{c}{Meter reading}

	0	0	0	0	0
	1	1	1	1	1
	2	2	2	2	2
J.L.Sharpe	3	3	3	3	3
76 Boroboro Rd	4	4	4	4	4
	5	5	5	5	5
Ipswich	6	6	6	6	6
Suffolk IP3 6FT	7	7	7	7	7
	8	8	8	8	8
	9	9	9	9	9

Figure 71.3 — An OMR document

Exercises:

1. With the aid of a practical example, illustrate one advantage and one disadvantage of optical character recognition (OCR) in comparison with other forms of computer input. (3 marks)

    AEB Specimen AS Level Paper 1990

2. Select a suitable method of data capture for each of the following applications, with reasons for your choice:

    (a) a theatre booking system

    (b) a telephone company's accounts system for processing customers' payments

    (c) a market research organization employing people to conduct interviews in the street about a range of products

    (d) a salesman going round pubs taking orders for crisps, nuts and other snacks. (8 marks)

3.* An insurance company wishes to enter data from hundreds of proposal forms filled in by customers each day. Describe a suitable method of data input. Justify your choice. Explain a method used to reduce the number of errors made at this stage. (4 marks)

Unit 72 — Input Devices (2)

Magnetic strip card readers

Plastic cards with a magnetic stripe are widely used as cash cards, credit cards and library cards. The magnetic stripe typically holds about 72 characters of information. Most banks now dispense cash via cash machines, known as Automated Teller Machines (ATMs), using a special keypad and a magnetic stripe reader. The customer's card is encoded with

- the customer's account number
- his Personal Identification Number (PIN) held in encoded form
- the bank's sort code
- the customer's withdrawal limit
- the amount withdrawn in the last time period (eg day).

To use the ATM, the customer inserts his card and is then requested to enter his PIN, which is checked against the encrypted PIN held on the card and the PIN held in the customer's record on the bank's computer. The customer then presses a key to indicate the type of transaction he wishes to effect, and if he wishes to withdraw cash, types in the amount. This is checked against the account balance on the bank's computer and the information held on the card. If all is satisfactory the card is returned to the customer and the notes issued.

Figure 72.1 — An Automated Teller Machine

Cash card fraud

Although the banks strenuously deny the existence of 'phantom withdrawals', where a customer's bank statement shows one or more withdrawals that they have not made, about £3 million is lost each year through cash card fraud. One of the most common techniques is 'shouldering'; watching a person key in their PIN and later getting hold of their cash card, probably by theft. There is the possibility of a dishonest postman intercepting a card in the post, and a few days later, intercepting the PIN. Recently a TSB customer had more than £10,000 disappear from her account over a period of time while she was in France, and all her family and close friends came under suspicion. It transpired that a dishonest bank clerk had requested a card for her account number, and had the card and PIN sent to a false address. Installing hidden cameras inside the ATMs could detect 'phantom withdrawals' but the banks say that this is an expensive solution to a problem that doesn't exist!

316

Smart cards

A **smart card** is a plastic card similar to a credit card, but containing a microchip and memory. A new smart card called 'Mondex', soon to be tested out, could soon replace the money in your pocket. It can be used to make purchases, transfer money in and out of bank accounts and even make transactions over the telephone. It works by storing an amount of money on a microchip, which can be topped-up or spent like cash. (See case study at the end of Unit 79.)

As of January 1994, some people will also be using smart cards containing their name and address to pay for electricity; special meters are available which will accept the card instead of cash, and customers will be able to top-up their cards at supermarkets and petrol stations.

Electronic point of sale systems (EPOS)

These systems can be seen at the checkouts of most large modern supermarkets. A laser beam reads the bar code on the item purchased, and the computer to which the scanning device is attached then looks up the price of the item and the description, prints this information on the customer's receipt and adds the amount to the total. Some systems will also adjust stock levels held in the computer's memory. A keyboard is used to enter the numbers for items such as fruit which are not barcoded.

Bar codes on grocery items are 13 digits long; the leftmost digit represents the country of origin (5 for the UK), the next 6 the manufacturer's code and the last 5 are the product number and check digit. The scanner checks the check digit and bleeps if the bar code is not read correctly.

Similar systems are in use in department stores, where the bar codes attached to garments and other goods are usually read by means of a hand held pen or 'wand'.

Figure 72.2 — A typical bar code

Electronic funds transfer at the point of sale (EFT/POS)

Some point of sales systems incorporate an EFT system whereby the customer's bank account is automatically debited when he or she makes a purchase.

The customer passes his bank card through a special reader which reads a number from the card, and the software then connects the terminal via the shop's mainframe computer to the customer's bank's computer. The customer then has to enter a personal identification number (PIN) on a keyboard connected to the terminal, an encrypted (coded) version of which is stored on the magnetic stripe on the customer's card, and this is transmitted to the bank's computer. Assuming the number entered, the encrypted number on the card and the number stored in the bank's computer all match, the transaction can continue.

Details of the transaction are entered by the shop assistant, and if the customer has sufficient funds in his account the terminal prints a receipt and the total is debited from the customer's bank account and credited to the shop's bank account, held in the shop's bank's computer.

Graphic input devices

Graphic input devices are used to transform drawings or photographs into a form that can be processed on a computer. These devices include scanners, digitisers and graphics tablets.

Page and hand scanners

A page scanner is capable of converting a whole page of printed material into a form that can be manipulated by the computer. This is another form of 'optical character recognition' (OCR) available for desktop PCs. A complete OCR package consists of a scanner and software such as Wordscan Plus which runs under Windows 3.1. This particular package allows both text and graphics to be scanned from the same page, whereas some others allow one or the other but not both simultaneously. Most scanning packages give best results with medium to large type size with text either continuous or in simple column structures.

Excellent colour scanners for graphic images are available which will reproduce exactly, say, a colour photograph on the user's screen, where it can be manipulated in any way required. No longer can you trust anything on a printed page!

Hand scanners, which the user passes over a page, are also available for both monochrome and colour applications, and are much cheaper but may give a distorted image if the scanner is not passed over the page at an even speed, and many cannot scan an entire A4 size page at once.

How a scanner works

The scanner shines a bright light onto the image being scanned while the scan head moves from the top of the document to the bottom at a constant rate. As it moves over each 'line' of the image, the scan head collects data by measuring the intensity of the light that is reflected back from the document. Each scanned line therefore results in a stream of data which the scanner converts into digital information, with a certain number of bits representing each tiny area in the scanned picture. For line drawings or text which are only black and white, only 1 bit will be required; for 256 shades of grey, 8 bits will be required. This information is then stored in the computer's memory, and can be saved on disk.

The **resolution** of the scanner is measured in dots per inch (dpi) along the x and y axes, and this can be varied on more sophisticated scanners. The higher the resolution, the sharper the image, but the scanned image will take up more memory.

Three passes of the scan head, one each with a filter for red, green and blue, are required for colour scanning. Each filter eliminates all colours except the one that matches the filter, and the three resulting images are then combined into one complete full colour image.

SPECIFICATION

Optical Scan Resolution	600 x 300 dpi
Maximum Resolution (using software enhancements)	1200 x 1200 dpi
Scanning Modes	24 Bit Colour (16.8 million colours)
	8 Bit Mono (256 greyscales)
	1 Bit Black & White
Typical Scanning Speeds	70 seconds/page colour
(A4 300 dpi image)	14.5 seconds/page greyscale

SYSTEM REQUIREMENTS
Macintosh II, SE30 or Quadra with System 6 + SCSI Interface

Picture courtesy of Computers Unlimited

Figure 72.3 - The Microtek ScanMaker colour flatbed scanner

Graphics tablets

A graphics tablet or digitiser is a flat, square or rectangular slab of material onto which a stylus is placed. The position of the stylus can be detected by the computer and the x- and y-coordinates transmitted to the system.

Tablets can be used for tracing a drawing. The tablet is usually large (say 35cm x 35cm or larger) and very high resolution. The drawing to be copied is placed on the tablet and a stylus used to copy the parts required, which are then shown on the VDU. In some graphics tablets, commands, symbols or a keyboard representation is printed on part of the tablet so that the user can make command selections by touching a specific area of the tablet.

Figure 72.4 — A graphics tablet

Mouse

A 'mouse' is a small device, connected via a cable to a microcomputer, which lies on the desk and fits conveniently under the palm of your hand. On its underside is a large ball bearing which rolls around on the desktop as the the user moves the mouse, and as it moves, the position of the cursor on the screen moves in a corresponding direction and over a corresponding distance. Buttons on the top of the mouse can be pressed to make a selection from a menu, for example, when the cursor is positioned over the correct item. A mouse is also a widely used tool in drawing and painting packages, enabling the user to draw and fill geometric shapes or draw freehand on the screen by controlling the movement of the mouse.

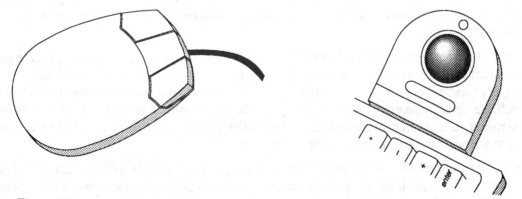

Figure 72.5 — A mouse and trackball mouse attached to the keyboard of a laptop computer

319

Pen/stylus input

September 1993 saw the launch of Apple's Newton Message Pad, a so-called 'Personal Digital Assistant' completely controlled using a pen (stylus) which can recognise handwriting. The Newton's handwriting recognition is writer-dependent and needs to be trained, although it can be configured for a guest user - it comes with a 'handwriting instructor' that teaches users to dot their i's and cross their t's. It has a dictionary of 10,000 words and will convert words that it recognises into type, but since 10,000 words is only a fraction of the average English speaker's vocabulary, unusual words or names can be tapped in manually after summoning the keyboard with a double tap of the pen.

Picture courtesy of Apple Computer (UK) Ltd

Figure 72.6 - The Apple Newton

Light pens

A light pen is a device shaped like a pen, incorporating a light sensor so that when it is held close to the screen over a character or part of a graphic, the object is detected and can be moved to create or modify graphics.

The term 'light pen' is often wrongly used to mean the device which reads a bar code, for example in a library book. This is not in fact a light pen, but a hand-held bar code reader or 'wand'. Do not believe everything you see in print!

Touch screen

A touch screen allows a user to touch an area of the screen in order to enter data, rather than having to type the data on a keyboard. They are widely used in industrial environments such as manufacturing, warehousing and security systems, and also in avionics and medicine. They are very suitable in situations where the operator is moving about and can quickly and easily enter commands by touching the screen. They are less suitable for everyday work in an office, because it is tiring to have to continually reach out to touch a screen.

Touch screens are now available in hand-held portable models and are used, for example, by airlines to receipt bartending, by hospitals to collect information on maternity patients and by local authorities for door-to-door collection of taxes.

There are many different sensor technologies available for different applications. Some respond to pressure, and some use capacitive overlay screens which must be touched by the naked finger. These consist of two primary elements, a glass substrate covered with a tight fitting plastic sheet. Conductive coatings are applied to the inner surface of both elements. Separating the cover sheet from the glass substrate are separator dots, evenly distributed across the active area. Light finger pressure causes internal electrical contact at the point of touch, supplying the controller with the analogue voltage needed for digitisation.

A second type of touch screen uses accoustic wave technology. The screen is a single glass panel with electric transducers in the corners. An interfacing controller sends an elecrical signal to the transducers which convert the signal into surface accoustic waves. These waves are reflected across the active area of the glass by an array of reflector stripes located on the outer edges of the glass. When a finger or pen touches the screen, a portion of the wave is absorbed. The resulting change in the received signal is analysed by the microprocessor in the interfacing controller, and digitised coordinate pairs are transmitted to the computer.

A new and somewhat different technology is used in the Touchmate by Ellinor Touch Technology. An ordinary computer monitor is placed on a force sensing platform, and when the user touches the screen, internal force measurement sensors detect this and measure the location of the touch.

Picture courtesy of Ellinor Touch Technology

Figure 72.7 - The Touchmate Force Sensing Platform and ordinary monitor

Exercises:

1. Cursor keys or a mouse may be used in the following operations:

    (i)   selecting and editing a cell value or formula in a spreadsheet;

    (ii) selecting and editing a shape in a painting or drawing program.

    Give **one** argument in favour of using cursor keys for operation (i) and **one** argument in favour of using a mouse for (ii).

    With reference to the objects involved, explain why the choice between cursor keys and mouse is different in the two cases. (3 marks)
    SEB Paper 1 May 1990

2.* State **two** uses of bar codes in a factory data collection system.

    Give **two** reasons why bar codes are preferred to magnetic stripe in this system. (4 marks)
    AEB Paper 1 1992

3.* Single chip computers embedded into a plastic card of credit card size are used to store personal and financial records. Information can be read from, or stored on, the card using special terminals.

    (a) Outline the advantages and disadvantages of such cards. (3 marks)

    (b) What conditions need to be met for such cards to be widely used? (1 mark)
    London Paper 2 1991

4. Many financial institutions now issue plastic cards which can be used at cash dispensers to withdraw money and, if requested, give details of the holder's account.

    These cash dispensers are available 24 hours a day, 7 days a week. When issued with a card the holder is given a PIN

(Personal Identification Number). On the back of the card there is a thin strip containing magnetically encoded information relating to the holder's account. This strip has three rows on which information can be stored. The financial institutions have adopted two main ways of using the information on these strips.

Method 1 Stores the holder's account number on row 2, and on row 3 a coded version of the PIN together with that account holder's weekly cash withdrawal limit and the money removed so far that week. The system is normally on-line during the day and off-line at night.

Method 2 Stores only the holder's account number on row 2 and leaves row 3 empty. This method requires the system to be on-line at all times. The cash dispensers hold no information of the transactions which have been carried out.

To use the card it has to be inserted into the machine and the PIN entered when requested.

(a) (i) Why must method 2 be an on-line system?

(ii) Why must the PIN on the card in method 1 be held in coded form?   (2 marks)

(b) Give an example of a potential invasion of privacy in this application.   (1 mark)

(c) Give an example of a potential breach of security in this application.   (1 mark)

(d) Describe how the security of **each** of these systems could be broken by the following people and in **each** case indicate what measures could be taken to prevent that breach of security.

(i) members of the general public,

(ii) the bank's computer staff.   (5 marks)

(e) Describe **two** checks which could be held in the rows of the magnetic strip to ensure the data has been read correctly.
                          (4 marks)

(f) Using method 2, when the card holder enters the PIN, what is it checked against?   (1 mark)

(g) Suggest what information could be held in row 1 of the card in both methods.   (2 marks)

JMB Paper 1 May 1989

Unit 73 — Printers

Choosing a printer

Printers come in all shapes and sizes, and the type of printer chosen will depend on several factors such as:

- **volume of output** — for high volumes, a fast, heavy-duty printer is required

- **quality of print required** — business letters and reports to clients, for example, will require a high quality print, probably on special headed stationery

- **location of the printer** — if the printer is going to be situated in a busy office, the noise of the printer is an important consideration

- **requirement for multiple copies** — some printers cannot produce multiple copies

- **requirements for colour** — does the output need to be in colour?

Character printers

Character printers are so called because they print one character at a time, and their rate of printing varies between about 20 and 600 characters per second. This general category of printer is typically used in microcomputer systems or with some minicomputer systems. There are many different types of character printer, some of which are described below.

Dot matrix printer

These are very often used with PCs. A dot matrix printer is an **impact printer**, producing its image by striking the paper through a ribbon. Its print head consists of a number of small pins, varying between 9 and 24 depending on the manufacturer. A 24 pin print head will produce a better quality of print than a 9 pin print head because the dots are closer together.

As the print head moves across the page, one or more pins strike the ribbon and make a dot on the paper. The figure below shows how the letter F is produced.

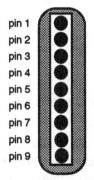

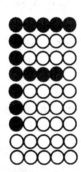

The print head consists of a line of pins. As the 9-point print head moves across the page, it fires the appropriate pins into the ribbon, making a dot on the paper. The two bottom pins are used for lower case letters such as 'p'.

Figure 73.1 — Print head   *Figure 73.2 — Enlarged view of dot matrix character*

In order to produce 'near letter quality' (**NLQ**) print, a line is printed twice, with the print head being shifted along very slightly in the second printing so that the spaces between the dots are filled in. The disadvantage of this technique is that the document then takes approximately twice as long to print. Many dot matrix printers are 'bi-directional', meaning that they can print in either direction, thus eliminating the need to start printing each line from the left hand side of the page.

Dot matrix printers are extremely versatile, with most of them able to print in condensed, standard and enlarged mode, in 'bold' or normal print.

Many dot matrix printers have a graphics mode that enables them to print pictures and graphs by activating individual print head pins separately or in combination to produce any shape or line. With appropriate software any typeface can be produced, and using a special 4-colour ribbon (red, yellow, blue and black), colour output for, say, a graphical presentation can be produced. However the quality of colour is not as good as that produced by other types of colour printer.

One of the main drawbacks of a dot matrix printer is its noise; in an office environment it can be an irritating distraction. Covers can be obtained to cut down the noise, but it is still audible.

```
This is sample output from a 9 pin printer in draft mode.

This is sample output from a 9 pin printer in draft bold.

This is         sample    output  from    a 9      pin
printer in very large mode.

This is sample output from a 9 pin printer in condensed mode.

This is sample output from a 9 pin printer in NLQ mode.
```

Figure 73.3 — Sample output from a dot matrix printer

Ink jet printers

Ink jet printers are a popular type of non-impact printer, with prices ranging between £200 and £1600; a popular colour inkjet printer such as Hewlett Packard's DeskJet 550C costs around £500. They are compact and quiet, and offer resolution almost as good as a laser printer. However, they are slow in operation; a complex combination of text and colour can take up to 8 minutes for a single sheet.

Inkjet printers such as the HP Deskjet fire a droplet of ink at the page by boiling it in a microscopic tube and letting steam eject the droplet. Heating the ink can damage the colour pigments and matching the ink chemistry to the broad range of papers used in the office is a technical challenge. Large areas of colour can get wet, buckle, and the ink may smear. Printing an ink jet colour page can cost as much as 75p if all colour inks are supplied in a single cartridge; more thrifty printers will use separate red, blue, yellow and black cartridges which can be individually replaced. Although ordinary photocopy paper can be used, special smooth-coated paper may produce a more satisfactory result.

Thermal transfer printers

Thermal transfer printers such as Textronix Phaser 200i give high quality colour printing, but are costlier than ink jet printers and slower than black and white only printers at about two pages per minute.

Thermal-wax transfer printers melt and transfer ink contained in coloured ribbons to a carrier drum. The paper passes through the heat source three or four times, depending on how many colours you are using. While plain paper printing gives fair quality, nearly all thermal-wax printers rely on smooth-coated paper. Genicom produces a thermal wax printer costing under £900, which prints on ordinary paper. Each colour page costs about 35p to produce.

Laser printers

Laser printers are becoming increasingly popular, with prices dropping rapidly to around £1000 for a PostScript printer suitable for desktop publishing applications, and under £500 for other models. Laser printers use a process similar to a photocopying machine, with toner (powdered ink) being transferred to the page and then fused onto it by heat and pressure. A laser printer produces output of very high quality at a typical speed in the region of ten pages per minute, and is virtually silent in operation. The main running expenses are the toner, which costs about £75 for a cartridge lasting for around 5,000 copies, and a maintenance contract which is typically up to £300pa.

Q1: Assume you have to choose a printer for use in an office. The software being used includes spreadsheet, database and wordprocessing packages. What questions would you need to have answered before you could recommend a printer?

Chain printers

A chain printer is typical of the type of printer used with a mini or mainframe computer. Characters are embossed on a rotating chain which rotates at very high speed, and each possible print position has a hammer which can fire against the back of the paper, causing the character to print.

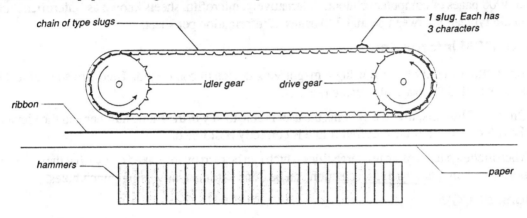

Figure 73.4 — A chain printer

A belt or band printer is similar but instead of a chain, a flexible metal band on which the letters are embossed is used.

These printers are called **line printers** because a complete line is printed in one operation, with one revolution of the chain or belt. They can print at up to around 3000 lines per minute.

High-speed laser printers

For very high-speed, high-volume work, laser printers operating at up to about 400 pages a minute, and costing £100,000 or more, are used. These printers can be set up to print the company letterhead, invoice heading or whatever is required for that particular run, at the top of each page as well as the data to be printed. These printers are usually attached to a dedicated computer and tape drive to maximise the printing speed. They are called **page printers** because they print a page at a time.

Exercises:

1. Suggest **two** types of printer which would be suitable for printing a colour copy of a school magazine. In each case name one major running cost. Compare the advantages and disadvantages of the two types of printer you have selected.

    (7 marks)

2. A printer fails to work as expected when you send a document to be printed. You have checked that it is switched on and on-line, and that it has paper. Give **six** other reasons why it may not be printing correctly (or at all). (6 marks)

3.* (a) State **one** reason other than speed or quality why a non-impact printer might be preferable to an impact printer in an office environment.

    (b) State **one** advantage and **one** disadvantage of a high quality ink jet printer compared with a laser printer.

    (3 marks)

    AEB Paper 2 1991

Unit 74 — Other Output Devices

COM (Computer Output to Microfilm)

Using a COM device, images are recorded onto photographic film which can then be stored and read by a special reader. There are two main methods of capturing the image:

- the output to be filmed is displayed on a VDU, from where it is photographed with a camera onto microfilm

- an electron beam or laser beam writes directly onto special film.

Many different types of film are used, including 16mm and 35mm rolls of cartridge film, with each roll capable of holding over 3000 pages of computer printout. Alternatively, microfilm sheets known as 'microfiche' can be used — these contain typically between 80 and 220 pages of information per sheet.

Retrieval of COM information

Output on microfilm can only be read using a magnifying device of some kind. There are several techniques for enabling the user to find the particular frame required.

- On microfilm rolls, in some systems the user is able to key in the frame number and the viewer advances the roll of film until the required frame is correctly positioned.

- Microfiche systems often use large titles which can be read by the naked eye so that they can be manually positioned. In other systems, selection can be done automatically using punch holes.

Advantages of COM

COM has the following advantages:

- it is very fast, with speeds of over 100,000cps achieved by some microfilmers

- it is cheap and copies can be made easily

- it is very compact, so that information which if stored on paper would amount to a stack several feet high can be contained in a stack of fiches an inch or so in height. Storage and distribution costs are therefore greatly reduced.

Applications of COM

COM is suitable wherever records have to be stored for a length of time, perhaps for legal or backup purposes. It is also used for easy reference to large amounts of data. Uses include

- customers' bank records

- library catalogues

- book catalogues in booksellers

- old invoices and receipts.

Screens

The screen, also called the monitor, CRT (cathode ray tube) or VDU (visual display unit) is an important output device. The most widely used screens are generally equivalent in size to a 12-inch or 15-inch TV screen, and display 80 characters on a line with a maximum of 25 lines. Larger A4 size screens are available and are particularly useful for desktop publishing, allowing the user to see a whole page on the screen. For computer-aided design work even larger screens are used.

Most early screens displayed white characters on a black background, but many newer monochrome screens use green or orange characters which are easier on the eye.

Colour screens are becoming increasingly common, not only for graphics but also for text. It has been found that people tend to be more productive when using colour screens, partly for psychological reasons.

Colour can enhance communication in many ways, such as:

- calling attention to warning messages or specific facts

- making the information more visually appealing

- reducing errors by separating different types of information.

Other screen features include

- the **cursor,** a symbol which indicates where the next character entered will be displayed. This may take the form of a blinking line or square of light.

- the ability to **scroll** the screen, moving the information up or down the screen a line at a time.

- **paging** the screen, bringing up a new page of data.

- **reverse video** — displaying for example black on green instead of green on black.

- **bold** characters appear brighter on the screen.

Displaying characters

A VDU has associated with it a 'display controller' to interpret the information generated by the program to produce the image, and both RAM and ROM. ROM is used as the 'character pattern memory', and holds the representation of each character that can be displayed. (If you want to display Arabic or Russian, for example, a different character pattern memory would be needed). Typically, a 7 x 9 matrix is used to produce each character. Thus the letter A would be displayed as follows:

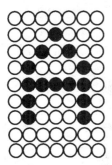

Figure 74.1 — Normal character

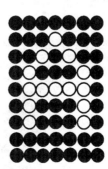

Figure 74.2 — Reverse video

A larger matrix may be used to give a better definition.

Some VDU's are not capable of displaying graphical data on the screen, apart from graphics composed from the extended character set. The RAM associated with the display will contain a map of memory addresses corresponding to character spaces on the screen. Thus on a screen capable of displaying 25 rows of 80 characters, an array of 2000 (25 x 80) elements is required for the memory map. Each element of the array will typically contain 7 bits for the ASCII character code, plus extra bits to indicate reverse video, bold, blinking characters, low intensity display (if the character is to be displayed at less than full brightness) and so on. If a colour screen is being used, then some bits will be used to represent a colour code.

Q1: How many different colours can be displayed if 8 bits are used to represent the colour of a character?

Screen resolution

The **resolution** of a screen is the number of addressable, controllable display or picture elements (pixels). Standard photographic film, for example, has a resolution equivalent to about 2000 x 2000 pixels. Low resolution screens start in the 320 x 240 range, medium resolution 640 x 480, and high resolution screens 1024 x 1024 or more for graphics terminals. VGA (Video Graphics Array) screens, for example, give resolutions of between about 640 x 480 and 800 x 600 pixels, and newer XGA screens, 1024 x 768 pixels in up to 256 colours.

Graphics screens

Screens used for graphics are called bit-mapped displays. There may be two separate display processors, one for text and one for graphics. In character mode, characters and symbols can be read out of memory as a block as described above, and characters are mapped in arrays of memory addresses corresponding to character spaces on the display screen.

In graphics mode up to 16 bits may be allocated to represent each pixel on the screen. IBM's latest 16-bit colour standard allows users to display 65,536 colours simultaneously at 640 x 480 pixels.

Q2: Calculate the amount of memory needed for the memory map for IBM's colour screen described above.

Liquid crystal displays

LCDs are frequently used on laptop computers where weight and size have to be kept to a minimum. They are now available in high resolution and colour, giving a display comparable to a regular CRT display. The viewing angle is, however, more limited.

Picture courtesy of Sharp Ltd

Figure 74.3 — A laptop computer with LCD display

Plotters

A plotter is an output device used to produce high quality line drawings such as building plans or electronic circuits. They are generally classified as pen (vector plotters) or penless (raster plotters). The former use pens to draw images using point-to-point data, moving the pen over the paper. Pen plotters are low in price and hold a large share of the plotter market.

Penless plotters include electrostatic plotters, thermal plotters and laser plotters. They are generally used where drawings of high densities are required, for example drawings of machines, printed circuit boards or maps. Colour electrostatic plotters are increasingly being used in, for example, assembly drawings of machines and building plans, making them easier to read and understand.

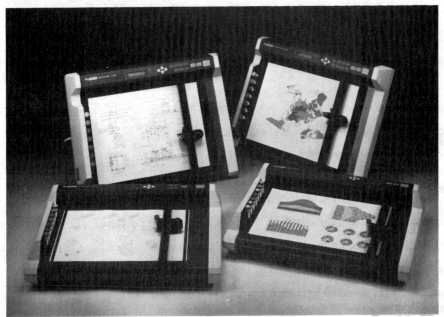

Courtesy of Graphtec (UK) Ltd

Figure 74.4 — Pen plotters from Graphtec

Exercises:

1.   ASCII codes are used both to represent text data internally and to facilitate transfer of data between computers. However the screen representation of the same character may be different on different computers. This is illustrated below for the letter "A".

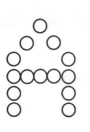

Computer 1

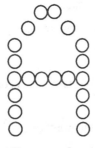

Computer 2

(a)   Explain how the same ASCII code can result in different screen representations on different computers.

(2 marks)

(b)   If text had to be stored by the bit pattern of its characters rather than by ASCII codes, it would take up more storage space. Show this by calculating, for both methods, the storage requirements of an A4 page of text. You may assume the bit pattern for each character is formed by a 5 by 7 grid of pixels as shown for Computer 1 above. State any other assumptions you make.

(4 marks)
SEB Paper 2 May 1990

329

2.   (a)   Describe the functional characteristics of a bit-mapped screen display and its associated memory.   (8 marks)

       (b)   Describe how software may be introduced to emulate a character-based VDU capable of displaying 24 lines by 80 columns of characters.   (4 marks)

       (c)   Describe the functional characteristics of ONE of the following devices, paying particular attention to how they would be used in conjunction with a bit-mapped screen display.

> Mouse
>
> Concept Keyboard
>
> Digitiser
>
> Touch Sensitive screen   (8 marks)

AEB Paper 1 1988

3.   (a)   By far the most common input device is the keyboard.

           For each of the following propositions regarding keyboards,

> — state whether or not you agree;
>
> — give details which justify your answer.

           (i)   Information can be sent directly from the keyboard to an output device such as a printer.

           (ii)   The QWERTY keyboard was designed specifically in order to speed up the process of data entry.

           (iii)   A keyboard buffer may be simulated by the data structure known as a stack.   (12 marks)

       (b)   When a local company installed its computer system the staff was led to believe that this would help reduce the growing amount of paperwork circulating within the organisation. However, in practice this was not achieved, and staff had to deal with more paperwork than ever in the form of reports on every detail of the company's operation.

           (i)   Outline the main features of one permanent form of output, other than printed paper, which would help reduce the bulk of the output.

           (ii)   Discuss briefly an important operational principle which would have limited the volume of output.   (8 marks)

       (c)   Some banks now offer home-banking facilities whereby customers can engage in transactions via a phone at any hour of the day. When using such a facility the customer is not interacting with a person, but with a computer which makes use of voice recognition and speech synthesis.

           (i)   Outline how such systems operate.

           (ii)   Outline the problems which arise with such systems, indicating why they are not more widely used (e.g. in business data-entry systems).   (10 marks)

NISEAC Paper 1 1990

4.*   Human computer interface styles could be classified according to the form of display used:

> character displays
>
> low to medium resolution graphics
>
> high resolution graphics.

       (a)   Describe a typical use for each form of display.   (3 marks)

       (b)   There has been a development from the time when most computers only had character displays, to the present day when high resolution graphics are common. Describe briefly **two** factors that have stimulated this development.   (2 marks)

       (c)   Many groups are carrying out research into new forms of human computer interface. Some are already in use in a limited way.

           Suggest one form of output which may become more widely used in the near future. What benefit would it have over existing forms of output?   (2 marks)

SEB Paper 1 1992

Unit 75 — Disks

Introduction

All types of computer require some form of **backing store** on which to save programs and data. Disks of various types are used on PCs, minis and mainframes, varying in their speeds and capacities but sharing many of the same features. We will look first of all at diskettes used by PCs.

Diskettes (floppy disks)

Floppy disks come in several sizes but the most common are 5¼" and 3½" disks. A floppy disk consists of a thin circular piece of mylar plastic coated with ferric oxide, enclosed in a protective jacket. The disk is read through an opening in the jacket, which in a 3½" disk is protected by a metal sleeve until the disk is inserted into the drive and accessed. Both forms of floppy disk have a **write protect** mechanism, to prevent a disk being accidentally overwritten. A notch can be seen in the side of a 5¼" disk which if taped over prevents the disk from being written to, and a 3½" disk has a small hole in the corner which has to be open for the disk to be write-protected.

Formatting a disk

Before a disk can be used it must be **formatted**, a process which marks out **tracks** and **sectors** on one or both surfaces of the disk. Typically a disk may be formatted to hold between 9 and 18 sectors and 40 or 80 tracks, giving capacities between about 360K and 1.44 MB (though several manufacturers have now developed 4MB drives). Disks of a higher quality (high density disks) are required, for example, to be able to hold 1.44MB rather than 360K or 720K, and not all PC disk drives will read high density disks. The following table shows the various tracks and sectors on disks supported by MS DOS.

size of disk	capacity	no. of tracks	no. of sectors
5¼"	360K	40	9
5¼"	1.2MB	80	15
3½"	720K	80	9
3½"	1.44MB	80	18

Figure 75.1 — Storage capacities of floppy disks

Storing data on a floppy disk

When the disk is inserted into the drive and data is to be written to it the disk starts to rotate at about 300 revolutions per minute. Data is stored on tracks, character by character using the same code (eg ASCII) used to store characters in main memory. The read/write head rests on the surface of the disk and moves backwards and forwards to access different tracks.

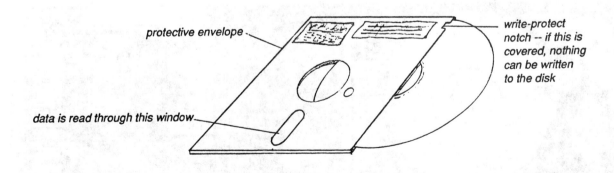

Figure 75.2 — A floppy disk

331

Hard disks

The hard disks used with PCs (also called Winchester disks) consist of one or more disk platters permanently sealed inside a casing. A hard disk for a microcomputer typically stores between 80MB and 400MB of data, though disks with higher capacities are available.

With hard disks, the read/write heads do not actually touch the surface of the disk but 'float' on a cushion of air about a millionth of an inch above the surface. Any tiny particle of dust on the surface of the disk or accidental jolting of the disk which causes the head to come into contact with the disk surface (a 'head crash') can cause damage to the disk and loss of data.

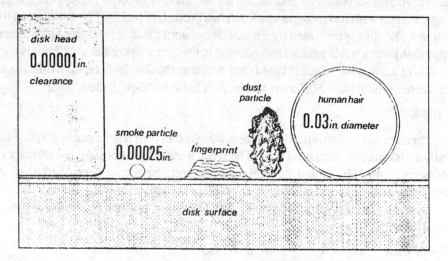

Figure 75.3 — Disk head clearance

Access times

The time required to access and retrieve data depends on three factors:

- **seek time** — the time it takes to position the read/write head over the correct track

- **latency** — the time it takes to rotate the disk until the correct sector is under the read/write head

- **data transfer rate** — the time it takes to transfer data from disk to main memory.

Hard cards

Hard cards consist of a hard disk mounted on a circuit board which can then be installed in an expansion slot in a PC. They provide an easy way to expand the storage capacity of a PC and are convenient if, for example, there is not room to install another disk drive.

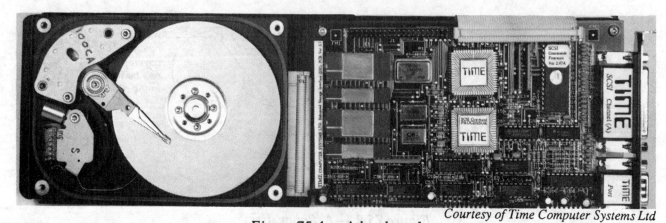

Courtesy of Time Computer Systems Ltd

Figure 75.4 — A hard card

Disks for minis and mainframes

Large computers may have dozens of disk drives, each capable of storing hundreds of megabytes of data. **Removable disks** (also called exchangeble disks) are gradually being replaced by higher capacity and more reliable fixed disks, which are sealed inside the disk unit.

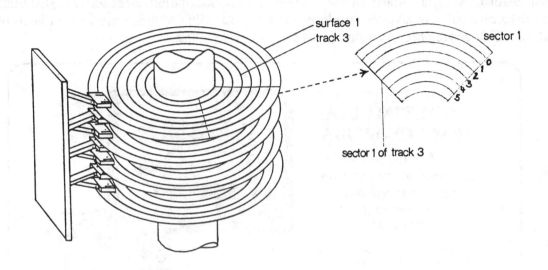

Figure 75.5 — Disk drive

Organisation of data

As with floppy disks, each track is divided into sectors. All the tracks of the same number are considered to be part of the same **cylinder** — for example all the Track 5's on each surface form cylinder number 5. If there are 200 tracks on each surface, there are 200 cylinders. Data is recorded cylinder by cylinder to minimise the movement of the read/ write heads, thus cutting down on seek time. There may be any number of 'platters' in a disk drive, from one to about ten or more.

CD (Compact Disk)

Compact disks can be divided into three basic categories:

- Read Only
- Write Once, Read Many (WORM)
- Erasable

CD-ROM

CD-ROM (Compact Disk Read Only Memory) is a digital optical storage system belonging in the first category above. A 5 ¼" CD (which is made of plastic and looks exactly like an audio CD) can store about 550 - 600 MB of data, including sound, motion picture video, animated sequences, text and graphics.

The production of a CD involves making a master disk with the aid of a laser beam which burns tiny holes in the surface of the disk. The presence or absence of a hole corresponds to a digital 0 or 1, and the information can be read by a laser beam in an optical disk reader. The production of the master disk is expensive but mass production of a CD brings the production cost down to about £1 per disk. The main cost is in the collection of the data to put on the disk.

CD-ROM drives are increasingly being built into PCs, much like a floppy disk drive.

Uses of CD-ROM

In March 1991 British Telecom launched the Phonedisk, which is a CD containing all the information from 99 BT phone books (17 million entries). It runs on a standard CD drive on any IBM compatible PC, costs £2,200 a year and is issued quarterly.

Another example of a CD-ROM application is the Software Toolworks Multimedia Encyclopedia, which contains all 21 volumes of the Academic American Encyclopedia. This includes the full text of nearly 33,000 articles, as well as a comprehensive index of all titles, words, pictures and maps. In addition, there are thousands of pictures, hundreds of sounds and digitised animations, and dozens of video clips.

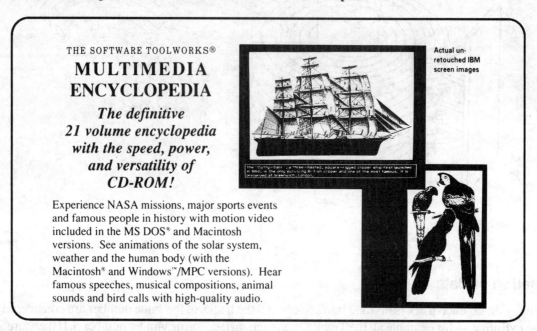

THE SOFTWARE TOOLWORKS®
MULTIMEDIA ENCYCLOPEDIA
*The definitive
21 volume encyclopedia
with the speed, power,
and versatility of
CD-ROM!*

Experience NASA missions, major sports events and famous people in history with motion video included in the MS DOS® and Macintosh versions. See animations of the solar system, weather and the human body (with the Macintosh® and Windows™/MPC versions). Hear famous speeches, musical compositions, animal sounds and bird calls with high-quality audio.

Actual un-retouched IBM screen images

Figure 75.6 - A multimedia encyclopedia held on CD-ROM

Q1: Name some other uses of CD-ROM.

Other Read Only systems

Two other (incompatible) systems are now being sold as multimedia platforms; Philips has developed Compact Disc Interactive (CD-I) and Intel has produced Digital Video Interactive. Both these systems can combine text, full-screen full-motion video and sound. Most of the software currently available for CD-I can be described as 'edutainment' - *Dark Castle*, *Interactive Golf* and *A Visit to Sesame Street* being examples.

WORM devices

WORM stands for Write Once, Read Many, so these disks can be used for archiving large quantities of data. There is no standardisation in this technology, with disks varying in size (5 ¼" and 12") and capacity (approximately 5MB to 10GB) and prices in the range £50 to £700 for one disk.

Erasable disks

This is the latest development in CD technology. The disks can be written to and erased just like floppy disks, but store a massive 650MB on a 5¼" disk and cost around £75. The heat of a laser beam is used to change the magnetic field of the disk, so that billions of spaces are created, all with a plus or minus load, which function like the holes in a CD. These could provide the equivalent of enormous hard disk capacity for personal computer use.

Ramdisks

A 'ramdisk' is not really a disk at all; it is an extra memory chip which the user can access in the same way as an ordinary disk is accessed — for example, it could be referred to as Drive D. The user could, for example, create a wordprocessed document or write a program and save it on drive D (the ramdisk) temporarily, reaping the advantage of faster access. When the computer is switched off, however, the information will be lost, and therefore it must be copied to a floppy disk or hard disk before the end of the session if it needs to be retained.

Exercises:

1. A particular disk drive has the following characteristics:

    — 512 characters per block
    — 64 blocks per track
    — 800 tracks per surface
    — 10 data surfaces per pack.

    For this drive, how much data (in Kbytes) may be stored on:

    (i)   one track

    (ii) one cylinder

    (iii) one pack   (3 marks)

    NISEAC Paper 2 1990

2. A student using a computer network has the choice of loading programs from:

    a ramdisc;

    a floppy disc;

    a 160 megabyte Winchester;

    an optical disc.

    (a) The double-sided floppy disc has a total maximum formatted capacity of 720K. The disc is formatted with 80 tracks each side, with 9 sectors per track.

       (i)   What is a track?

       (ii) Why are tracks divided into sectors?

       (iii) How many bytes are there on each sector?   (3 marks)

    (b) Suggest a suitable alternative device for taking backup copies of the Winchester. Explain the principles of its operation.   (3 marks)

    (c) Explain what is meant by a ramdisc. State with reasons, **one** advantage and **one** disadvantage to the student of using the ramdisc.   (3 marks)

    (d) Explain how individual bits are written to and read from the optical disc. State **one** advantage and **one** disadvantage of using optical discs over magnetic discs.   (5 marks)

    (e) A teacher saves a datafile on the Winchester so that some students may access it and update it. Outline **two** distinct problems which could arise and suggest suitable methods for solving them.
                                                                             (6 marks)
    AEB Paper 1 1990

3.* (a) State *three* differences between floppy-disk drives and hard-disk drives.

    (b) Name *two* other media which are commonly used as secondary storage.   (4 marks)
    London Paper 2 1992

Unit 76 — Magnetic Tape

Uses of magnetic tape

Magnetic tape is now principally used as a backup medium. It is a convenient and cheap medium for backing up hard disks on micro, mini and mainframe computers.

Tape reels

Conventional magnetic tape comes in reels of up to 3,600 feet and is made of mylar plastic coated with an oxide material. Data is written in **frames** across the tape, with one frame representing one byte. The frames form **tracks** along the length of the tape, with nine tracks being commonly used, giving eight data tracks and one parity track. When the tape is read, the parity bit is checked by the tape unit, and if the frame does not contain the correct number of bits, the block is read in again. If the tape unit fails after a certain number of attempts to read the data correctly, the operator is alerted.

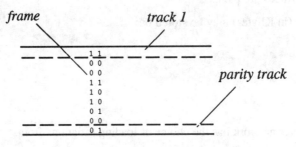

Figure 76.1 — Magnetic tape

The **packing density** varies between 800 and 6250 characters per inch, with some tapes able to store 100MB of data per reel. It is possible to achieve data transfer rates of 1.2MB per second on the latest tape drives. It is not true to say, therefore, that tapes are slower than disks! In many instances the reverse is true.

Q1: Name some advantages and disadvantages of magnetic tape compared with non-exchangeable hard disk.

Reading data from tape

Tape decks are read from and written to at very high speed, 200 inches per second being common. Data can only be transferred when the tape is running at full speed and so when, say, a READ instruction in a program is encountered, the tape has to be accelerated to its working speed before a block of data can be read in, then after the data has been read, decelerated until it comes to rest. For this reason, the blocks of data on the tape are separated by **inter-block gaps** of between half an inch and an inch. These gaps are effectively wasted space, and so it is common practice to write several records in one block. When the first READ statement is encountered, a block of data containing, say, 20 records is read into a buffer area in memory. The next 19 READ statements do not require a physical reading of the tape; the records are merely transferred from the buffer store in the computer's memory. This not only reduces wasted space on the tape but also speeds up data transfer, since the tape does not have to start and stop so often.

Tape is a **serial** medium, meaning that data can only be read from a tape in the same sequence that it was written. Data cannot be read from and written to the same tape in one run, so if a master file held on magnetic tape needs to be updated, each block of records is read into memory, updated if necessary, and written out to a second tape. Records which do not need to be changed are copied over to the new file.

Q2: How are records **deleted** during a tape update ?

Streamer tape

Unlike conventional tape, streamer tape does not allow for stopping and starting between data blocks. Streamer tape is either a quarter inch or half inch wide, and although it has inter-block gaps, it passes over these without stopping. Long data blocks of up to sixteen kilobytes are used to attain a high rate of data transfer.

Streamer tape is available in cartridges, typically about the size of a video cassette or smaller. Tape cartridge units provide a convenient method of backing up all types of hard disk, and are becoming increasingly popular because they can store more data and take up less space than conventional tape.

The photograph below shows a DMT 780C cartridge tape drive from Anritsu Corporation which has a tape length of 1020 feet, a recording capacity of 525MB, uses a recording density of 16,000 bits per inch, and transfers data at 2MB per second. Data is transferred in blocks and 'read-after-write' checks are performed to ensure correct data transfer — as soon as data is written, it is immediately read back and checked against what was written. If the two sets of data do not match, the data is rewritten and error checking repeated, giving an unrecoverable error rate of 10^{-14} bits or less.

Courtesy of Anritsu Corporation

Figure 76.2 — A cartridge tape drive from Anritsu

337

Header labels and trailer labels

In addition to data, each tape file will generally contain a header record (header label) at the beginning of the file and a trailer label at the end of the file. The header label will contain

- a field identifying the record as the header label
- the file name
- the date written
- the purge date, before which the information on the tape cannot be overwritten

The trailer label will contain

- a field identifying the record as the trailer label
- a count of the number of records on the file
- the reel number if the file occupies more than one reel of tape

Exercises:

1. Find some computer magazines and look up the details on some of the latest backing storage units. Compare the prices, speeds, capacities, physical size, capabilities and convenience of various different devices.

2. Consider the following storage systems:

   (i) floppy disk;

   (ii) hard disk;

   (iii) magnetic tape;

   (iv) optical CD-ROM.

   (a) Identify **four** characteristics which could be used to compare and contrast these systems.   (2 marks)

   (b) Evaluate the suitability of each of the above storage systems for the backup of 50 megabytes of data.
   (4 marks)

   (c) Which of the four storage systems would be most suitable for spooling output to a printer? Explain your answer.
   (2 marks)
   SEB Paper 1 1990

3. (i) What is the purpose of the interblock gap on magnetic tape?

   (ii) Why are interblock gaps not needed on magnetic disks?   (5 marks)
   NISEAC Paper 2 1992

4.* A magnetic tape is 90 metres long and can hold 500 characters per cm.

   Data is held in fixed-length records of 250 characters with several records per block. Each inter-block gap occupies 1 cm.

   (a) State *two* items of information, other than the data of the records, which would usually be held on the tape.
   (2 marks)

   (b) Calculate the storage capacity of the tape if:

   (i) 4 records are stored per block

   (ii) 6 records are stored per block.   (2 marks)

   (c) Describe factors which might influence the choice of the number of records per block.   (2 marks)
   London Paper 2 1992

Section 10 — Computer Applications and Social Implications

Unit 77 — Computers and Multimedia in Training and Education

Computer-based training (CBT)

CBT is training via a computer system. This may be a business PC, or a terminal linked to a mini or mainframe computer. It can be used to to train people in hundreds of different skills, from using a wordprocessing package to learning to fly a jumbo jet. Here, the occupants of the flight simulator appear to be in the cockpit of a real aircraft, with instrument panels, sound, views and motion all simulating the genuine article.

Benefits of computer-based training

- For an employer, a major benefit is cost. Employers do not have to pay for accommodation, travelling or salaries while staff attend a course. The investment in a suitable training package may quickly pay for itself, especially if suitable hardware is already available.

- It means that staff can train when they want, often at their own desks on the computer which they will eventually be using. Without CBT, when new members of staff join a company they may have to wait until there are sufficient numbers to justify a course. With CBT they can start on their training immediately.

- Students can study at their own pace, and repeat sections of the material that they find difficult. Some CBT products have checks built in so that they can monitor individual performance.

- Real life situations can be simulated and the student can learn without the danger of performing live experiments; such as in the aircraft simulator mentioned above.

Q1: Describe briefly other situations in which it is convenient to learn on a simulated model rather than 'going live'.

Interactive Video simulations

New laserdisk technology combined with the processing speed obtainable from parallel processing is enabling a whole range of computer simulation software to be used in training.

One such simulation has been developed to help train fire officers. The Iccarus group, which developed the software at Portsmouth Polytechnic's School of Architecture, included a programmer, a graphic artist, a psychologist to give advice on the user interface and an Artificial Intelligence expert, working closely with the West Midlands Fire Brigade. The software was written in LPA Prolog, chosen for its flexibility and good graphics capability.

The complete system consists of an Apple Macintosh equipped with a transputer for parallel processing, a Laserdisc player which provides motion video and stills, a compact disk player for the audio sound track, and two monitors. The first screen provides a layout of the building and gives command and confirmation information in the form of text and graphics, and the second shows still pictures and motion video. Fire footage was obtained by torching an old cinema that was due for demolition.

Parameters can be specified for different simulations, altering for example the layout of the building, opening or closing doors, or including hazards like flammable gas cylinders.

The simulation starts with a series of stills showing the officer on the way to the fire, with radio messages from HQ and the scene of the blaze coming in. When the officer arrives at the scene, he can look around, deploy personnel, ask for more pumps and so on. The simulation also includes 'stressors', such as a journalist suddenly interrupting and asking for a news update, or a distraught person coming forward to say that there is someone trapped in the building.

The computer stores all the officer's commands, resources used and when they were deployed, so that later he can hear a replay of messages received and his responses, and analyse his decisions. He can also try out the effect of different actions.

The production version of the complete system will cost around £10,000 — cheap when you consider that a major fire costs around £10,000 per minute, and that the West Midlands Fire Service alone spends around £1 million annually on training.

Types of computer-aided learning (CAL) package

Computer-aided learning can fall into any of the following categories:

- tutorials
- drill and practice
- simulation
- games
- tests

Q2: What facilities would you expect to find in a software package that allowed a teacher to write computer-based tests (i.e. tests that the student would answer by sitting at a computer, which would ask questions and accept answers)?

Many software packages come with a 'tutorial' disk which helps users to learn how to use the software. A spreadsheet tutorial disk, for example, will put a simple spreadsheet on the screen and instruct the user where to enter given figures or labels, and inform him if he goes wrong. A series of 'lessons' guides the user through the basic features of the spreadsheet.

No amount of explanation here can act as a substitute for experience, so look for the 'tutorial' option on a spreadsheet, wordprocessor or database, for example, and try it out!

Authoring software

'Authoring' packages such as Authorware Professional and Tencore are available which allow courseware designers to write sophisticated **interactive multimedia training systems (IMTS).** The term 'multimedia' implies that the courseware will include some or all of the following: text, graphics, animated graphic sequences, video clips, scanned photographs and sound, either taped or synthesised. Authoring software allows the programmer to quickly design screen layouts and friendly user interfaces including pushbuttons and 'hot spots' that the user can point to using a mouse, incorporate questions and if..then..else structures according to the answer given by the eventual user, import graphics, sound and video clips and design animated sequences. Designing and implementing such courseware is a lengthy and expensive process, requiring a team of people including a subject matter expert, an instructional designer, a graphic designer, a programmer and a project manager.

Hardware and software requirements for IMTS

In order to implement such a system, a 'multimedia PC' is needed. This implies a PC with a large hard disk (graphic images and sound use up huge amounts of disk space), lots of memory (at least 8 MB), a sound card (such as 'Soundblaster') and speakers for playing back sound, a high resolution screen with the ability to display say 32,000 colours and usually a CD-ROM drive. Apple Macintosh and many PC manufacturers now produce such systems. Software such as Video for Windows allows video clips to be replayed. In order to capture the video and digitise it, a video recorder needs to be connected to a computer with a video capture card, but no special hardware is required to replay the stored video clip.

Q3: Mention some **disadvantages** of computer-aided learning as opposed to conventional classroom learning.

Computers in education

Computers are increasingly being used in schools in five main areas:

- as a teaching aid in many different subjects

- in monitoring progress and testing pupils

- for electronic mailing systems, both inside the school and to communicate with other schools or organisations

- to assist in administration

- for careers advice, or helping to find a place in a College or University.

Q4: Name some administrative tasks in a school that could be performed by computer.

Exercises:

1. Describe a computer assisted learning package with which you are familiar. Your answer should indicate the purpose of the package, and the benefits and possible drawbacks that come from using such a package. (9 marks)
    WJEC Paper 1 June 1988

2. Two of the general areas of computing are:

    (i) training using Computer Assisted Learning (CAL),

    (ii) business and commerce.

    (a) For **each** area describe a specific, non-trivial computer application and the hardware requirements.

    (6 marks)

    (b) Describe the human-machine interface you would use for **each** application, clearly explaining how your choice overcomes the problems of communication between the computer and the user(s).

    (c) For **each** application describe the main features of the documentation, appropriate for the user(s) and for system maintenance. (4 marks)

    (d) For each application describe the specific features of the programming language(s) or package(s) that are necessary to implement the application. (4 marks)
    JMB Paper 2 May 1989

3.* A computer-assisted learning package is required to help children with reading difficulties to learn to spell. The package should present the child with a picture of an object (for example, a cat) and a spoken word ('cat'), to which the child needs to supply the correctly spelled word (C A T). If the child experiences difficulty, hints can be given, and after three attempts the correctly spelled word should be displayed.

    (a) Suggest a sensible way of setting about designing such a package. (3 marks)

    (b) Describe possible forms of interface suitable for this application. (3 marks)

    (c) Explain how the data could be organised and accessed. (3 marks)

    (d) What advantages do you think such a system might bring for the children and their teachers? (3 marks)
    UCLES Paper 2 1992

4. **Case study: Multimedia system used in medical training**

An article in the Guardian of December 9 1993 illustrates an excellent use of training with an interactive multimedia system. The system, called Cytovision, costs £11,000 and runs on an Apple Quadra attached to a laser disk player. It is used to train lab technicians to recognise normal and cancerous cells when they examine slides under a microscope.

A demonstration of the software might start with a look at some of the 3,500 digitised photographs of microscope slides. Many can be enlarged by clicking on a lens icon; all are more stable images than under a microscope, and unlike a book, they appear to emit light in a realistic way.

The package moves the viewer backwards and forwards between the macroscopic and the microscopic, from purple views of invasive carcinomas to how to take a cervical smear. Students can study a picture or document and, coming on something unfamiliar, click on it for fresh screens of information. The searching can be repeated ad infinitum and what makes for a fascinating browse among rotating diagrams, brisk text and stunning photos is, more importantly, a magnificent tool for study. The package includes half an hour of video sequences that are almost up to TV quality.

Death rates from cervical cancer have declined by 15% since screening became general in 1986, and most of the women who do die have not presented themselves for tests. Nevertheless, the good news can be made better, and training has been very variable. The National Screening Programme is a new scheme which must depend on lowly paid cytoscreeners to do preliminary checks on the five million slides taken every year from women aged between 20 and 64.

Training is a problem and computers may be able to solve it. Many laboratories have little if any slack in the system and find it difficult to devote time to training. Quality of tuition varies, and so do slide collections. Some laboratories receive little abnormal material and find it difficult to establish a teaching collection. No two students are likely to receive the same training.

Questions:

a. Why is this described as a 'multimedia' system?   (2 marks)

b. What type of software could be used in the development of the system? Describe briefly the facilities that you would expect the software to offer the programmer.   (5 marks)

c. What are the advantages to

    (i)   the hospital

    (ii)   the laboratory staff

    (iii) the general public

           of adopting this sytem for training laboratory staff?   (6 marks)

d. Briefly describe **five** features which you would take into account when evaluating the quality of an interactive multimedia training package.   (5 marks)

e. Name and describe briefly the characteristics (eg physical size, storage capacity, read/write capabilities) of a suitable medium for the storage of large quantities of data such as the abnormal slides in this application so that it can be viewed on a computer screen. Describe how data is stored and retrieved.   (6 marks)

f. In the early stages of the development of a new computer system, a **preliminary analysis** and **feasibility study** will normally be conducted. Describe briefly **five** items you would expect to find in the preliminary analysis and feasibility study which preceded the development of the software package for training the cytoscreeners.

                                                                                                                       (5 marks)

g. Name **three** other areas where computers are commonly used in hospitals, and for each application, describe briefly **one** advantage of using computers.   (6 marks)

                                                                                                                   (Total 35 marks)

Unit 78 — Computers and the Disabled

How can technology help?

About ten percent of people in Britain have some kind of disability. For many of them, new computer technology can dramatically improve their quality of life, their ability to communicate and their opportunities for independence and employment.

Today there are systems based on personal computers that can talk, listen, teach, communicate and translate. People with control over just an eyelid or a toe, for example, can communicate by means of the proper equipment attached to a PC.

Voice synthesizers

Many manufacturers have produced special equipment for people who are either unable to speak, or who have been profoundly deaf from an early age and need special help in learning to speak.

IBM's SpeechViewer software, which runs on a PS/2 and consists of twelve modules accessible from a main menu, is a tool for speech therapists and teachers of the deaf. It provides visual feedback on a screen for elements of speech such as loudness, pitch and timing. This enables people who have a speech disorder or impaired hearing to see a visual representation of their speech. Patterning modules use graphical displays so that the student can match his speech with the 'correct' pattern.

For people unable to speak, a wide variety of speech synthesizers has revolutionized their ability to achieve and communicate their full potential. The world famous Cambridge physicist Professor Stephen Hawking, although unable to speak and with severely restricted movement, is able to prepare and deliver his lectures using a special keyboard and voice synthesizer.

A different type of device called a 'Touch Talker' is available to help disabled people of all ages and abilities. It consists of a portable computer in the form of a 'tablet' about 13" by 9", onto which different picture overlays can be placed. The computer enables the user to store information of his choice and recall it at will to be spoken by the voice synthesizer.

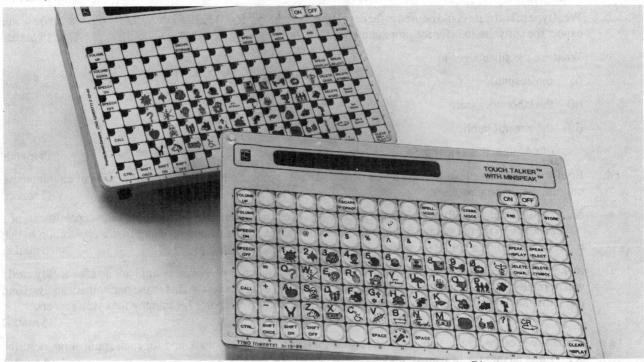

Picture courtesy of Liberator Ltd

Figure 78.1 — Touch Talker

For example, to create a message "What time are we going home?" the computer is programmed as follows:

1. Select STORE

2. Select a series of pictures or icons to represent the sentence: question mark, sun (or whatever symbol you choose to represent time), house.

3. Select END

4. Spell in the sentence W-H-A-T T-I-M-E A-R-E W-E G-O-I-N-G H-O-M-E

5. Select STORE.

To recall the message, the user selects the pictures that represent the message and the device then says "What time are we going home?"

The user can use any amount of imagination to build up messages from the set of pictures on his template. For example, Tuesday could be represented by a pancake (or by association, any food), Wednesday by a knot (tying the knot = WEDding = WEDnesday).

Q1: How could you represent the other days of the week?

Q2: How could you say "Shall we go to Macdonald's for lunch?"

Computers for people with severely limited movement

Devices such as the TouchTalker are also designed for people without touch capabilities who have a simple body movement that can be utilised - for example, head movement, brow-wrinkle, puff-sip, or the raising of a finger or a knee. Letters from the users of these devices testify to the dramatic improvement they can bring to a disabled person's life: "Words cannot express the change that has occurred in our lives since my daughter obtained her TouchTalker. Years of frustration have disappeared in seconds..."

These devices change lives, but they are not cheap. A TouchTalker retails for around £2500.

Special Wordprocessing packages are available for people who cannot easily type at a keyboard. In one such package, a cursor moves down a grid of letters and the user indicates when it is opposite the row with the desired letter. The cursor then moves along this row until the user selects a letter, which is then displayed in a different area of the screen. At this point the computer starts to 'guess' the word or phrase. If "Th" has been typed the computer might guess "Thank you " or "They" etc and the user can confirm or select the next character.

Q3: Describe a keyboard which has been specially adapted for use by a disabled person.

Computers for the blind and visually impaired

In addition to voice synthesizers and a variety of Braille and other special keyboards and printers, there are some interesting systems for enabling blind people to read screens and written text. One such device is the Optacon, a compact, portable reading system which converts the image of a printed letter or symbol into a tactile form that can be felt with one finger. Different type styles, symbols and languages can be read with the Optacon because it reproduces exactly what is printed in enlarged vibrating form, which is felt as a 'buzzing' sensation by a user. An experienced blind user can even tell when his print ribbon is getting worn! A special attachment on a typewriter enables a blind person to read what is being typed, and other lens modules allow a VDU screen or a calculator to be read.

Picture courtesy of Sensory Visionaid

Figure 78.2 — The Optacon

Access to terminals by blind people has opened up an enormous number of job opportunities, as well as enabling them to carry out a myriad of everyday tasks such as reading a bill or bank statement, recipe book or telephone directory.

Telecommunications equipment

Carrying on a telephone conversation is no longer an impossibility for deaf people, thanks to literally dozens of special services and equipment provided by British Telecom and many other organizations. Some of these such as the electronic mail box system **Telecom Gold** are in wide general use but are particularly useful for deaf people. Profoundly deaf people can also communicate using text terminals, typing a message to another person with similar equipment and seeing both incoming and outgoing messages displayed on a screen. **Fax** (facsimile transmission) is another example of visual image transmission.

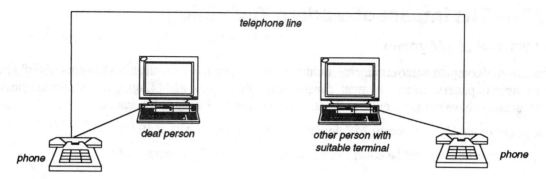

Figure 78.3 — Typing over the phone using text terminals

A system developed at British Telecom involves the use of a video camera and a digitizer connected to a telephone line, so that a person can communicate over the phone with someone who has similar equipment using sign language or lip-reading. The digitised picture of the person's hand or face is sent down the telephone line and displayed on the receiver's screen.

Future developments

This unit has described just a few of the hundreds of computer applications that have been developed for disabled people. Research work now being carried out means that better and more sophisticated devices are constantly being put on the market, dramatically improving the opportunities for people suffering from all types of disability, however severe, to live a full and active life.

Exercises:

1. Consider the possibility of a computer system able to accept directly the input of ordinary human speech. Describe briefly one way in which such a speech recognition system could be of benefit to an individual and one way in which it could be damaging to society.

(2 marks)

AEB Paper 2 1989

2. **Case study:** **Blind engineer wins achievement award**

In 1992 a young woman aged 22 and almost completely blind from infancy, won an award for her inspiring achievements. She graduated from Exeter University with a First Class Honours degree and is now employed by Rolls Royce as a design engineer, working on the design of aero engines. She has some peripheral vision with which she can read magnified words on a screen, and also uses a talking calculator, a braille printer and an embosser for making diagrams she can trace with a fingertip. A closed circuit television operated with her bare foot magnifies lists of figures such as temperatures, speeds and pressures of engines under different flight conditions.

Questions:

a. Describe briefly **three** ways in which computer technology can help blind and partially sighted people at work in addition to the ways described in the case study.

(6 marks)

b. Identify **three** general ways in which computer technology has improved the quality of life for disabled people. Describe in detail the operation of TWO specially adapted pieces of hardware and/or software in use by people suffering from different disabilities.

(7 marks)

c. Computer technology is available to help many disabled people, but is sometimes very expensive. Do you think it should be freely available to those who need it? Give arguments for and against.

(2 marks)

(Total 15 marks)

Unit 79 — The Impact of Modern Technology

Computers and employment

The introduction of computers into commerce, industry and government organisations has undoubtedly caused far-reaching changes in patterns of employment, causing hardship to some and bringing new opportunities to others. Perhaps the changes have not been quite as drastic as some people forecast: for example

"Unemployment in the UK will rise to 25% by 1990" (Jenkins and Sherman 1979)

"Employment as we know it will be down to 10% in 30 years' time" (Stonier 1979)

Q1: Read through the list of statements below, and indicate your opinion on each with a number 1-5, where 1=strongly agree, 2=agree, 3=don't know, 4=disagree, 5=strongly disagree.

Over the past decade, the widespread use of computers has

1. put many people out of work

2. changed the nature of many people's work

3. resulted in a de-skilling of some jobs

4. made some people's jobs more interesting

5. resulted in an increase in the total number of unemployed people

6. enabled some organisations to operate more efficiently

7. resulted in an increase in the number of bankruptcies

8. created many new job opportunities

9. made some people's work environment more pleasant

10. forced people to learn new skills

In the 1950s and 1960s when computerisation was just beginning, computers were largely used to replace clerical or routine manual tasks. There is no doubt that an enormous number of clerical jobs has disappeared since the introduction of computers. In banks, for example, clerical staff manually prepared customers' bank statements, counter staff counted out cash for customers making withdrawals, payroll clerks prepared payslips for thousands of employees.

On the other hand, banks in particular were scrupulous in avoiding redundancies wherever possible. Natural wastage (resignations and retirements) have been used to reduce staff where necessary, and staff have been retrained for other and perhaps more interesting jobs. Lower level posts such as that of cashier have been broadened and may now include dealing with post, filing, typing and answering customers' queries. This benevolent treatment of employees by banks has been made possible by the enormous increase in business done by financial institutions over the last 15 or 20 years.

Q2: Name another category of work, other than routine clerical tasks, where computerisation has resulted in huge job losses.

Jobs in computing

Surveys of employment trends in the UK show that while jobs in manufacturing industries continue to decrease, jobs in service industries such as retailing, hotels and catering, banking, building societies, insurance and leisure will continue to increase. In computing (which is itself largely a service industry) the number of jobs available to programmers, systems analysts, data processing managers, systems programmers and network staff is rising steadily. The number of computer operators and data preparation staff, however, is declining.

The role of many programmers has changed recently with the increased use of software packages. The ability to code programs is often less important than the ability to understand the users' requirements and install and implement a suitable set of packages.

The electronic office

The advent of personal computers has brought about a revolution in office life.

- **word processing** is a much more efficient operation than typing. In addition to all the benefits of easy editing, storage and retrieval of documents, wordprocessing is now **integrated** with other packages such as spreadsheets and databases

- **databases** have largely replaced manual filing systems, providing fast and easy access to information that in the past would have been time-consuming or impossible to obtain

- **desktop publishing** allows the production of high quality newsletters, brochures or manuals within the organisation, where previously the work would have to have been sent out to a printer for layout and typesetting. **Scanners** may be used to capture graphics, photographs or text from other sources.

- **spreadsheets, accounts software, job-scheduling software** and numerous other applications packages have made the jobs of planning, budgeting, monitoring and accurate record keeping far easier.

- **local area networks** mean that people can share software, data and hardware such as modems and laser printers.

- **wide area networks** allow people to communicate across the world via electronic mail, and access on-line databases anywhere in the world.

On-line databases

One example of an on-line information retrieval system is the (American) Dialog Information Retrieval Service, which covers nearly 400 databases with 329 million records. Many public and College libraries subscribe to this service, and this gives the user access to information on any subject under the sun for a dial-up fee of a few pounds. In addition, an electronic mail facility allows a user to send mail instantly to any other DIALMAIL user, or to send output from a query to any other electronic mail system.

A somewhat more local and possibly more useful service in the UK is the General Academic Index, which is held on CD-ROM. This is designed to meet the needs of academic and public library researchers in the UK and Europe. It provides indexing of approximately 350 major scholarly and general interest journals and newspapers published in the US, Canada and Britain from 1989 onwards. A subscription costs about £1,400 pa and monthly updates provide users with the most current information.

To use it, you are presented with a screen asking what to search for. Type in, say, 'Computers and the Police' and after a few seconds three references (in this particular case) are given on the screen:

```
1.   Community Policing (European Community). (Includes related article on Customs
     Intelligence network.) Computing, Feb 4 1993 p18(2)
2.   Joining Forces (UK Police Use of Computers) Computing, Feb 4 1993 p 9(2)
3.   Police computer fuels fear of 'European Connection'. (Civil rights concern
     over invasion of personal privacy.) New Scientist Jan 4 1992 p14(1)

          Press Enter for Abstract
```

You can then select a reference and see a brief resume of the article. If you want to see the full article, the librarian will obtain it for you.

Electronic mail

Electronic mail gives the ability to send and receive messages over a local area network as well as communicating with separate computer systems via a modem. The Quickmail electronic mail package is an example of such a system, allowing users to send messages, documents and computer files around a local area network and across the ocean; just the thing for a firm in Suffolk, say, with a head office in London and a sales office in California.

Within the local area network, say on three floors of a building, messages can be sent to any colleague by selecting their name from an 'address book' held on disk. A flashing icon appears on the receiver's screen, and he can then load the Quickmail software and read the message. If the message is not read within 10 minutes a message "Please wake up!" scrolls across the top of the screen. The sender can also be notified as soon as the message has been read.

When someone wishes to contact the California office, messages can be given graded priorities, so that 'Urgent' messages are sent immediately and 'Normal' messages are saved on the Quickmail server until 6pm when the cheap rate starts.

Other facilities include

- the ability to enclose up to 16 files with the message, so that previously prepared documents, spreadsheets or programs can be transmitted with the message
- the ability to send the same message to a group of people, with a copy to another selected group of people
- create different 'directories' of people in, for example, different working groups
- 'unsend' messages before they are read
- check the mail 'log' to see a record of all messages sent and whether they have been read
- create customised 'forms' on which to send out messages

Q3: With the proliferation of desktop PCs and the increasing use of online databases, it has become feasible for many people to work from home. What are the advantages and disadvantages of this to (a) the employer and (b) the worker?

Health and safety in the office

Health and safety at work is not a subject which most office managers would regard as being of great significance to them. Who ever heard of an employee getting caught in the paper shredder or electrocuting themselves on their VDU?

Nevertheless, there are more subtle dangers which arise from the constant use of a keyboard and VDU. These include

- RSI (Repetitive Strain Injury). This is a disorder of the arms and wrists which can be caused by using a keyboard for long stretches of time without regular breaks. The sufferer at first feels pain in the arms and wrists which may worsen to the point where even picking up, say, a kettle may be impossible. Moreover, the condition is very difficult to cure. In one recent case, a journalist sued his employers for £250,000 for loss of earnings over an extended period due to RSI.

- eyestrain. Problems of glare, flicker and focus all contribute to this problem.

- radiation. Some studies show a possible link between VDU use and miscarriages or chromosomal defects.

Safety and the law

A European Community directive on the health requirements for working with VDU's became law in December 1992. It includes various clauses such as those outlined below.

- Employees work must be planned in such a way that VDU work is periodically interrupted by breaks or changes in activity

- All employers must undertake an analysis of workstations to evaluate the risks to eyesight, physical problems and mental stress, and take appropriate action to remedy any risks found.

- Technical requirements for the design of workstations are laid down — for example, the keyboard must be separate from the screen, the chair must allow freedom of movement, be adjustable in height and tiltable.

Several firms are developing software to help ensure these requirements are adhered to. Computer Systems has developed a package called Tempus which, after a pre-set time, puts a message on the screen advising a break. The system keeps a log to record when screen breaks have been recommended and whether they were taken.

The AEB has produced an Interactive Multimedia Training package on diskette entitled 'Working With Display Screen Equipment' which combines graphics, animation and interactive questions and answers in an entertaining manner.

Computers and the police

Computers are widely used in crime detection. Computerised files of fingerprints enable known criminals to be identified, and databases of stolen cars help in the recovery of vehicles. In a 1991 case, computers helped to catch Rodney Witchelo, the man responsible for contaminating Heinz baby food jars, forcing the company to destroy 100 million jars of food worth £32 million. He attempted to blackmail the company, demanding that they pay large amounts of money into a Halifax Building Society account, which they did, under police supervision. Hundreds of police watched all the cashpoint machines in a targeted area, and the Building Society computers were specially programmed to slow down their response to Witchelo's requests for cash so as to give the police time to identify him. The plan worked, and he was eventually caught.

How reliable are computers?

In some of today's computer applications, our lives may depend on the computer functioning correctly. Can testing be sufficiently rigorous to eliminate the possibility of failure? The answer is probably "No".

One example of reliance on computer technology is the system used by the Airbus 320, known as a 'fly by wire' aircraft, in which three computers control all the flight surfaces and the engines. If there is disagreement among the computers they will make a majority decision as to the appropriate course of action, and if the computers disagree with the action of the pilot then the computer decision will be accepted. In order to minimise the possibility of software error, the three computers were programmed by completely different teams of software engineers, in the hope that any errors which crop up in one would not be repeated in the other two.

In June 1988 when the Airbus A320 crashed spectacularly at an air show while making a low-level pass over spectators, the pilot reported that his instructions to gain altitude had been overruled by the on-board computer. On another occasion, an Indian Airlines plane on a routine flight crashed in perfect weather as it was coming in to land, and an independent investigator found that the A320 did not obey the pilot's commands in the last few seconds before impact.

In hospitals, cases have been reported of people receiving the wrong doses of radiation owing to computer malfunction. In other cases, we could be at risk from criminal or terrorist activity, for example by interfering with the control systems of a nuclear power station.

Impact of technology on society in general

No one in a modern industrialised society is unaffected by computers. In the supermarket, bank, library, hospital and travel agency, we take their presence for granted. Computerised bills and statements, personalised letters inviting us to participate in yet another million pound draw, join a new private health scheme, make a charity donation or add our names to the electoral roll, remind us that our names are on computer databases all over the country. Even at home, we program the washing machine, microwave and video recorder with varying degrees of ease and frustration.

Has all this added up to a better quality of life for everyone? Most people would agree that, were computers to be phased out completely, our high standard of living would no longer be possible. On the other hand, some wistful husbands, back from a hard day at the office, might yearn for the good old days when the little wife was back at home, pulling the home baked bread out of the oven and warming his slippers by a roaring fire. More likely today he will be pulling the Marks and Spencer's ready cooked lasagne out of the freezer and wrestling with the controls on the microwave.

Q4: In what ways have computers improved the quality of life for the ordinary person? Are there any ways in which the use of computers has contributed to a supposed decline in our quality of life?

Exercises:

1. Describe by means of examples the way in which the introduction of a computer into an office can eliminate some jobs, transform others and create some new jobs. (5 marks)
    AEB sample paper 1990

2. Many commentators have suggested that computers have become *essential*, both to maintaining and enhancing the quality of our lives. By describing *one* application and speculating on future trends, discuss critically whether you feel that these assertions are true. Your answer should reflect on whether the perceived benefits, or drawbacks, apply to society as a whole, a sector of society, a particular organisation or to the "individual". (15 marks)
    London Paper 2 June 1989.

3. A firm employs 2000 workers to assemble railway locomotives. Each worker has a particular job on an assembly line.

    The firm plans to make more flexible use of the workforce by introducing a computerised task-allocation system.

    The proposed system stores details of the firm's operations, including records of the orders not yet completed and their completion dates. The system also stores information about the skills of each worker.

    Each day, workers register their arrival and the system then allocates tasks which meet the particular needs of the day.

    (a) Suggest ways in which the worker might

        (i) register for work;

        (ii) receive instructions from the computer system (4 marks)

    (b) Discuss the social, economic and other implications of the introduction of the new system for

        (i) the management,

        (ii) the workforce

        (iii) customers,

        (iv) others who might be affected. (16 marks)
    UCLES Paper 2 Nov 1989

4. Far greater attention is now being given to the potential health hazards of working with computers. Identify two such hazards and explain briefly how their effects can be alleviated. (4 marks)
    London Paper 2 June 1990

5. **Case study: The cashless society**

National Westminster Bank has developed an alternative to cash — a plastic card with a microchip which stores "electronic money" and can be topped up over the phone. A year-long trial of the card, called **Mondex**, will take place in Swindon in 1995, involving about 10,000 people, and will be run in conjunction with Midland Bank and British Telecom.

The system lets people add money to their card by using adapted cash dispensers or telephones to access their accounts. Once charged with money, the card becomes the equivalent of cash.

Payments are made by slipping the card into a retailer's terminal. The sum is transferred from the card to the retailer without need for time-consuming authorisations or signatures. Provided there is enough money on the card, the transaction will take place.

Payments between individuals are carried out by inserting the card into a pocket-sized electronic wallet and making six keystrokes. Customers and retailers can deposit electronic money into their bank accounts over the phone. The system is not intended to replace credit cards, but is designed for both small and large payments. Small traders, for example a newspaper vendor, could have a battery-powered terminal.

At the moment, cash is still used for 90% of all transactions in Britain, and handling the cash costs the banks more than £4.5 billion a year. The Mondex card would be quicker and more convenient to handle than cash, but if the card was lost or stolen, the money on it would be lost as it would be in a missing wallet. However, cards could be 'locked' to prevent unauthorised use by tapping in a four-digit personal code. Once locked, the money could not be spent without re-entering the code.

Initially, cash dispensers would be adapted to give customers the choice between drawing physical or electronic money. The telephone, however, would be the most important access point. BT is planning to adapt its payphones, and special phones for home use are being designed. Customers will insert the card into the phone, triggering an automatic call to the bank's computer system. After a prompt, the customer will tap in his PIN, and transfer money to the card or vice-versa.

Mondex is a multi-currency system, capable of holding five separate currencies on a card simultaneously. Other British and foreign banks will be invited to join Mondex in due course to create a "global payment scheme".

(Adapted from an article in the Guardian, December 10 1993)

Questions:

a.   "Britain will become a completely cashless society". Give **two** reasons why this statement may be true and **two** reasons why it may never come true.   (4 marks)

b.   Give **one** advantage and one disadvantage to members of the general public of using a Mondex card rather than cash.   (2 marks)

c.   Give **one** advantage to the banks, and **two** to retailers, of the use of these cards rather than credit cards.
                                                                                                                                                                (3 marks)

d.   Give **three** distinct items of information which each card will have encoded on it.   (3 marks)

e.   The system will use a wide area network. Give **three** reasons for choosing a *packet switching* network for the wide area network rather than *message switching*.   (3 marks)

f.   Give **two** precautions the bank could take to minimise disruption to the system caused by hardware failure.
                                                                                                                                                                (2 marks)

g.   Describe briefly **two** security risks in this sytem, and **two** ways in which these risks can be minimised.
                                                                                                                                                                (4 marks)

h.   What additional item of hardware will users need to have in the specially adapted home telephones to enable them to transmit their requirements over the network? What is the function of the additional hardware?   (2 marks)

i.   Name and describe briefly **two** checks that can be made to ensure that the data is correctly transmitted.
                                                                                                                                                                (2 marks)
                                                                                                                                                      (Total 25 marks)

Unit 80 — Artificial Intelligence and Expert Systems

Definition of artificial intelligence

Conventional data processing is concerned with inputting and processing data in the form of facts and figures in order to produce operational or management information. **Artificial intelligence**, on the other hand, is based on **knowledge**. A widely accepted definition of artificial intelligence is based on a test devised by Alan Turing in 1950:

Suppose there are two identical terminals in a room, one connected to a computer, and the other operated remotely by a person. If someone using the two terminals is unable to tell which is connected to the computer and which is operated by the person, the computer can be credited with intelligence.

Competitions are regularly held in which judges "talk" via terminals to a mixture of computer systems and people and try to guess which is which. In one such contest held in Boston in August 1991, where questions were limited to a small range of specific topics, two people and six programs were tested aginst six judges.

Four programs convinced at least one judge that they were people. Two judges mistook one of the people, Cynthia Clay, for a program. They didn't believe anyone would know *that* much about Shakespeare.

Q1: Write down three questions you could pose in order to distinguish between the computer and the human.

Following on from this idea we could say that artificial intelligence is the science of making machines perform tasks that would require intelligence if done by people. Artificial intelligence covers such fields as expert systems, problem solving, robot control, intelligent database querying and pattern recognition. Pattern recognition includes speech comprehension and synthesis, image processing and robot vision. Getting a computer to communicate in 'natural language' is yet another field of research.

One aspect of artificially intelligent computers is that they should be capable of learning, and therefore improving their performance at a given task. Computers have been successfully "trained", for example, to recognise (with as much accuracy as a human being) a face as either male or female, and to be able to recognise an Underground train station as being "crowded" or not.

Neural computing

The technology that makes this possible is neural computing, the revolutionary process that mimics the way the human brain works. By imitating the way that thought processes pass through the neurons and synapses of the brain, reinforcing some signals and dissipating others, neural computers enable machines to retain the most important information and discard the rest. This self-teaching ability sets them apart from traditional computers which cannot reprogram themselves.

Neural computing is being used in a wide variety of applications. Bass the brewers for example, has built (with the aid of scientists at Warwick University) a machine that can sniff the beer and decide if it is up to scratch. Its artificial nose makes a complex series of judgements based on electro-chemical stimuli received by its gas sensors. By detecting an over-active yeast or a weak crop of hops at an early stage in the fermentation process, the "nose" could save the brewers from having to throw away a whole batch of 345,600 pints of beer.

Bankers, stockbrokers and insurance agents are all experimenting with the possibilities of neural computing. TSB has been applying the system to forecasting the risk on insurance premiums, and is now seeing how it can be used to detect fraud. The computer can be trained to alert bank staff when an unusual transaction appears in a client's account. Bankers also hope to train computers to tell them how much money to load into their cash dispensers (the amount varies from day to day and location to location).

Not all banks, however, have had happy experiences with neural computing. One large bank reportedly lost millions of pounds before closing down its neural network in 1993. The problem with a technology still in its infancy is its unpredictability; it is difficult to know whether results will justify the expenditure.

Expert systems

Expert systems are computer programs that attempt to replicate the performance of a human expert on some specialised reasoning task. Also called **knowledge based systems,** they are able to store and manipulate knowledge so that they can help a user to solve a problem or make a decision.

The main features of an expert system are:

- it is limited to a specific domain (area of expertise)
- it is typically rule based
- it can reason with uncertain data (the user can respond "don't know" to a question)
- it delivers advice
- it explains its reasoning to the user.

An expert system has the following constituents:

- 'the knowledge base' that contains the facts and rules provided by a human expert
- some means of using the knowledge (an 'inference mechanism' or 'inference engine')
- a means of communicating with the user (the 'man-machine interface' or 'human-computer interface').

The knowledge base

The knowledge base will store knowledge in different forms, namely FACTS and RULES. For example:

THE BASIC FEE FOR A 10 WEEK COURSE IS £25	**FACT**
THE COURSE CODE FOR C PROGRAMMING IS EEC5012	**FACT**
IF STUDENT IS UNEMPLOYED THEN THE BASIC FEE IS WAIVED	**RULE**
IF STUDENT IS UNDER 18 THEN ALL FEES ARE WAIVED	**RULE**
ALL COURSES WITH CODES STARTING WITH 'E' CARRY AN EXTRA CHARGE OF £15	**RULE**
EEC5012 IS A 10 WEEK COURSE	**FACT**

Knowledge like this can be stored in a knowledge base, and the expert system should then be able to make deductions. If we supply the information that Jo Bloggs wishes to enrol for C Programming, the expert system should guide us through a series of relevant questions and deduce the fee to be charged.

Q2: What questions will the system need to ask to establish the fee for Jo Bloggs?

In practice there may be hundreds or thousands of facts and rules. When the program runs it does not simply start at the first rule and run through them all; it makes deductions as it goes along, finding out what else it needs to know before providing an answer. The way in which it does this is called the 'inference mechanism'. Part of the inference mechanism may be represented in rules — for example

IF AGE OVER 18 THEN CHECK EMPLOYMENT STATUS.

Methods of reasoning fall into two categories: **deduction** and **induction**. Using deduction,we start with statements which are true in general, and make specific deductions from them: e.g. given that

> All mammals suckle their young

and > Whales are mammals

we can deduce that

> Whales suckle their young.

Using induction, we use facts like "All the swans I have ever seen are white" to induce that "All swans are white". Of course sometimes, as in this case, these generalizations turn out not to be true.

Some types of knowledge are rather indefinite and difficult to store in an expert system. For example:

"This patient reminded me of one I saw a few months ago"

"Sometimes coffee seems to keep me awake at night"

"He is tall"

Q3: Write down some facts and rules that you would give to an expert system designed to predict student grades in A-Level Computing.

The man-machine interface

This describes the way in which the user interacts with the system by asking questions, supplying answers, requesting explanations, and so on. An inflexible interface will be like the traditional menu-driven programs where the user has to know what to enter and has little opportunity for error or variation. A better interface will be nearer to natural language and will let the user feel in control and well-informed throughout.

Software that allows you to build an expert system for some particular purpose is sometimes called an "Expert System Shell", and the package Crystal is one example. This package allows you both to build the expert system and then use it to seek advice.

Uses of expert systems

Expert systems are best suited to fields of study where a well-defined set of rules exists or can be written down. Medical diagnosis and geological exploration have both proved suitable domains, and the construction industry is making increasing use of expert systems to carry out part of the tasks traditionally done by quantity surveyors. The expert system ELSIE, which runs on almost any PC with a hard disk, will come up with a cost for a new building after asking the user a series of questions about type of ground, facing required, floor space, number of storeys, whether a basement is required, heating requirements and so on.

Facilities of an expert system

In summary, a good expert system should be able to

- allow a user to specify the parameters for a problem
- ask relevant questions and draw inferences from the replies
- be capable of handling incomplete or imprecise information
- allow the user to change parameters to explore 'what if' situations
- make reasonable guesses or deductions
- explain how it reaches its conclusions

Developing an expert system by prototyping

The person who carries out the tasks of defining a problem, constructing a suitable system, acquiring the knowledge to go into the system and developing the system is called a **knowledge engineer**. His job is analagous to that of a systems analyst.

Expert systems are nearly always built using **prototyping**, whereby a trial model is developed so that users can try it out and evaluate it. This differs from the method of first producing a complete and correct specification, in that the **product** and not the **design** is checked and tested by the user.

Exercises:

1. As a systems analyst for a multinational pharmaceutical company you have been commissioned to produce a report outlining the benefits, and drawbacks, of introducing expert systems. Outline the possible contents of such a report and include in your answer sections on

    (a) the essential features and underlying philosophy of an expert system

    (b) the problems to be tackled in designing and building an expert system

    (c) references to the experiences of other users. (15 marks)
    London Paper 2 1991

2. What is meant by *artificial intelligence* (AI)? With reference to **one** example, give **one** advantage and **one** disadvantage of an AI approach. (5 marks)
    AEB Paper 1 1992

3. A hospital consultant, who specialises in liver disease, is interested in developing an expert system to assist in diagnosis. A computer specialist is contacted with a view to creating an appropriate system.

    (a) (i) Report on the types of issues they would need to discuss.

    (ii) Indicate the steps the computer specialist would need to take to design the expert system. (14 marks)

    (b) Suggest how such an expert system could be of benefit

    (i) to patients

    (ii) to hospital doctors (6 marks)
    UCLES Paper 2 May 1989

4.* State **three** of the main features of an expert system. Suggest one class of applications for which expert systems are particularly well suited. (4 marks)
    AEB Paper 1 1991

5. **Case study: Expert system in the Department of Social Security**

Three computer firms have spent two years researching and developing a new expert system for use by the Department of Social Security. Claimants may soon be interviewed by computer instead of filling in forms or having face-to-face interviews. The machines will give an audio-visual presentation and incorporate touch-screen technology that can be used even by those who have no experience of computers.

Currently, several million people have face-to-face interviews in Britain's 600 benefit offices to see if they qualify for social services, unemployment benefit, or local council-related support. With the new system, guiding the public through a question-and-answer dialogue to see if a person is eligible would be undertaken by an on-screen interviewer — an actress "deliberately selected to appeal to all members of the public".

If questions are not fully understood, the claimant can select an option by touching the screen for the presenter to explain the questions more fully. The result is an "expert" who is immune to frustration, unlike its human counterpart.

The system, which is designed to relieve the stress of endless form-filling, can assess customers' entitlements and needs, providing an instant response and recommendation. Customers can even explore "what if" scenarios.

A decision has not yet been taken, but the Department of Social Security is considering the scheme.

(Adapted from an article in The Sunday Times, November 21 1993)

Questions:

a.   What is the term used to describe software which stores the knowledge of a human expert and is then able to answer questions? In what way does this type of software differ from an "artificially intelligent" computer system?
(2 marks)

b.   What are the two types of knowledge stored? Give an example of each type of knowledge applied to the application described.
(4 marks)

c.   Give **two** advantages of having an actress ask the questions to elicit information from potential claimants, rather than having written questions appear on the screen. Give **one** disadvantage.
(3 marks)

d.   Give **two** examples of questions that the actress might ask, and explain how the respondent would give the answer to the computer.
(4 marks)

e.   The system will incorporate touch-screen technology. Explain how **two** different types of touch-screen technologies work. What is the advantage of using touch-screen technology in this application?
(5 marks)

f.   Give **two** examples of "what-if" scenarios that a customer might explore in this application. Name another type of software that also allows "what-if" scenarios to be explored.
(3 marks)

g.   Give **one** reason in each case why there might be resistance to the introduction of such a system from

(i)   members of the public

(ii)   members of staff at benefit offices.
(2 marks)

Give **one** reason in each case why the system might be welcomed.
(2 marks)
(Total 25 marks)

Unit 81 — Computer-aided Design and Manufacture

CAD systems

CAD (Computer-Aided Design) systems generally consist of of a complete hardware and software package, ranging from micro systems available for around £1000 to sophisticated systems used in aircraft and automobile design, costing hundreds of thousands of pounds.

These systems act as tools for the designer, not replacing his skills but aiding him in the fast and accurate production of drawings. The benefits of CAD can be summed up as:

- accuracy
- repeatability
- speed and flexibility of production.

Specialised hardware for CAD systems

A CAD workstation may be a standalone system, possibly linked to other workstations so that peripherals can be shared, or it may be connected to a mini or mainframe computer. Either way it will have, in addition to its own or a shared processor, input and output hardware chosen from a range of devices available, some of which are described below:

- a high resolution CRT display — typically between 1024 by 1024 and 4096 by 4096 pixels. Most graphics systems use colour screens.
- sometimes a separate monitor is used for displaying the commands entered by the operator.
- a keyboard for entering commands.
- programmable function box to allow the operator additional control of functions performed on the screen.
- a joystick.
- a graphics tablet, which contains a grid that corresponds to the resolution of the CRT. Thus, using a hand-held cursor, stylus (similar to a pen) or mouse, any x and y coordinates on the tablet can be mapped directly onto the screen.
- a light pen, an input device which allows the user to interface directly with the CRT display. It allows the user to pick a point or character on the screen and cause some action to be taken.
- a flatbed or drum plotter, which may have up to ten pens of different colours to produce high quality coloured drawings.
- a printer. Ink-jet, laser and thermal printers are among the options for output.

CAD software

CAD systems obviously vary enormously in their capabilities. The more sophisticated systems allow a user to:

- draw straight lines and polygons, shading them if required
- draw mathematically defined curves including circles, arcs, ellipses, parabolas and hyperbolas
- move sections of a drawing to different locations
- scale an object (i.e. increase or decrease its size)
- rotate an object
- zoom in on a section of a drawing.

Having made two-dimensional drawings of an object, the software can then show the object in three dimensions, rotate it, shade it, show a view from any angle and shrink or expand it along a given dimension. Properties such as centre of gravity can be calculated. The drawings can be stored in a library on disk for future use. Large aerospace companies, for example, have libraries on disk containing over a million drawings.

359

Bitmapped versus vector-based graphics

There are two different kinds of graphics; **bitmapped** (also known as pixel-based) and **vector-based** (also known as object oriented). Paint programs and scanners produce bitmapped images in the form of a collection of pixels, the smallest visual unit that the computer can address. These applications create images by altering the colours or attributes of each individual pixel, and the amount of memory taken up by the image is dependent on the resolution of the display adapter where the image was first created. As a result, finished bitmap images are difficult to edit when you transfer them from one application to another. If you increase the size of a finished bitmap image, you see unsightly white spaces and jagged edges. If you greatly decrease the size of a finished bitmap image, parts of the image may 'smudge' because of the compression involved. Distortion can occur if you transfer bitmapped images to another computer that has a different display resolution.

(i)   (ii)   (iii)

Figure 81.1 - Bitmapped graphic image created in a PAINT package: (i) original size, (ii) expanded, (iii) shrunk

Object-oriented graphics, on the other hand, have none of these limitations. The information used to create and represent a drawing is real geometric data, rather than graphic data. For example, a line is defined by its endpoints, length, width, colour, and so on. A CAD program (and object oriented graphics software such as CorelDRAW!) then uses this information to create a representation of the line on the computer screen. Since this method of storing information has nothing to do with the resolution of a given display adapter, line-art is considered to be **device-independent**. No matter what computer you use to create an object-oriented graphic, you can stretch, scale and resize it flexibly without distortion. Object-oriented graphics also tend to create smaller files than bitmapped images because the computer does not have to store the attributes of each individual pixel.

(i)   (ii)   (iii)

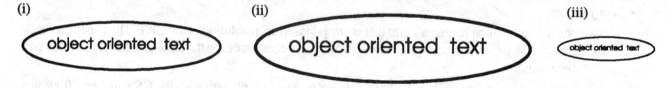

Figure 81.2 - an object oriented graphic created in CorelDRAW!: (i) original size, (ii) expanded, (iii) shrunk.

Another characteristic of CAD programs is the degree of accuracy that can be attained. Since a CAD program works with real geometric data, you can easily draw lines that meet exactly at a point, or move a line to a precise location, or draw an arc of an exact degree. When you zoom in on a portion of a line, no degradation occurs, and you can get an infinite degree of magnification. (The resolution of the laser printer may, as in this case, make the image appear less than perfectly smooth.) Using bitmapped graphics, by contrast, a line degrades when you zoom in and you see the individual pixels.

CAM (Computer-aided manufacturing)

This is the other side of the CAD coin. A complete CAD/CAM system will enable, say, an engineering component to be designed and manufactured using numerically controlled machine tools. The computer performs calculations for defining the tool path and generates the instructions necessary to produce the part. An interactive CAM system will first simulate the machining operation so that the user can make sure the tool does not collide with clamps or fixtures, and make any necessary adjustments before going 'live'.

One of the great benefits of CAD/CAM is 'flexible manufacturing', enabling product changes to be made quickly and inexpensively. Not only is a much wider range of products easily produced, but manufacturers are able to respond quickly to current demands, making modifications to their products without the delays that would previously have resulted from a change in setup.

Exercises:

1. Outline four features provided by a general purpose graphics package. (4 marks)
   NISEAC Paper 1 May 1990

2. You have been asked to evaluate a microcomputer system for its graphics capability. List *three* features which you would examine in performing the evaluation. (3 marks)
   London Paper 1 June 1989

3. Discuss **two** of the following computer applications:

   (a) computer aided design (10 marks)

   (b) computerised stock control and financial accounting (10 marks)

   (c) word processing and electronic mail (10 marks)

   Your answer should include:

   (i) why a computerised system is used in the particular application

   (ii) the hardware which is a specific feature of the application

   (iii) the software used in the application

   (iv) the effects of using computers on the people who work in the application described, and on society in general.
   AEB Paper 2 1986

4.* Outline an application for which a graphics package would be useful. (3 marks)
   London Paper 1 1992

5. **Case study: Rearranging the Office Furniture**

   Carleton Furniture is a company who provide furniture for customers such as British Gas, British Telecom, BP and ICL. Services include floorspace planning, full refurbishment and furnishing offices. Typical contracts deal with the refurbishment of large government offices and the furnishing of student residential halls.

   When an important customer recently asked for a special order, Carleton Furniture responded within hours. The speed of response - just over a year ago it would have taken a week and a half - won the £150,000 order. The detailed specification of a desk, drawn and fully costed, had taken half a day.

   Even more important, the specification put together at such speed actually worked. The people who had to execute the design by cutting the metal and fitting parts, knew their system would not design something that could not be built.

   Carleton designers rely on a computer-aided design product, but design is only part of the story. It has also capitalised on its ability to produce quick CAD drawings to launch a specialised service in space planning. A recent £800,000 order was won because the company was able to produce a space-plan within a very tight deadline, partly because it could read in existing measurements from the client's own AutoCad package.

   The company spokesman offered some emphatic do's and don'ts for companies setting out to implement CAD software. "Don't underestimate the culture change that needs to take place within the business", he said. "It's taken us a year longer than we expected. Do make sure you get on with your suppliers. At the end of the day you're investing a great deal: if you can't get on with them, don't do it, however good the software."

   Questions:

   a. Outline **six** features of a Computer Aided Design system. (6 marks)

   b. Describe briefly **three** advantages to the company of using this system. (3 marks)

   c. What sort of 'culture change' do you think would take place in a company as a result of the introduction of such a system? (3 marks)

   d. Why is it so important to 'get on with your suppliers'? (3 marks)

   e. Describe the difference between bitmapped graphics and vector-based graphics. Why do CAD systems use vector-based graphics? (5 marks)
   Total 20 marks

Unit 82 — Robotics and Process Control

What is robotics?

The word 'robot' comes from the Czechoslovakian word 'robotnik', meaning slave. Robots come in many different forms and shapes, but they all have the same basic components:

- **sensors**, which capture information from the environment

- a **microprocessor** to process the information

- **actuators** to produce movement or alter the environment in some way, for example by turning an electronic switch on or off.

Robots may be used for spray painting, spot welding and assembling cars. They are also used as security devices inside homes and office buildings, as vehicles in space exploration, as intelligent wheelchairs for disabled people, and as underwater maintenance workers for oil rigs. Hundreds of other applications also use robots in one form or another.

A recent application of robot technology is for testing blood samples in pathology labs. The lab is based on a car factory production line, with blood samples being carried round on a track. As they go, robots read bar codes on the test tubes telling them which tests to apply to which samples. At the end of the process, the system automatically writes a report on the blood, and deposits the samples in a fridge for storage. The system, which costs round £1m to install, is being put into use in many hospitals, and is expected to recoup its cost over three to five years. In hospitals which rely on human laboratory technicians, blood samples are sometimes lost, wrongly diagnosed or not tested at all. At a large hospital performing over a million tests a year, even a 1% error rate means 10,000 tests a year have to be repeated, and the new system, while not expected to replace staff completely, will free them to concentrate on the less tedious and repetitive tasks.

Input — Process — Output

The inputs are provided by sensors which detect changes in the system such as temperature, speed, position, etc. These are all things which change continuously in time. **Transducers** convert them into voltages which change continuously, i.e. **analogue** voltages. However, computers work in discrete digital values and it is therefore necessary to convert the analogue changes into a form which the computer can understand. This is usually achieved by passing the information provided by the sensors through a circuit called an analogue-to-digital converter.

The processing is carried out by the computer on the basis of its program in order to achieve a predetermined output.

The computer will then send signals to appropriate output devices, such as motors and heaters which control the process. The system must work in real time as the computer is affecting the situation in the real world, and it therefore forms a **closed loop**. The computer must be able to react quickly to any changes produced by its own output.

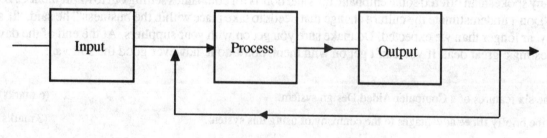

Figure 82.1 — A closed loop

Since the computer is continuously monitoring the real world throughout the process, it cannot be used for anything else, and therefore many process control computers are **dedicated systems** which can be used only for this process.

Analogue input

A simple example of an analogue input device is a joystick or thermometer. The BBC Model B micro, for example, has four 'analogue-to-digital' converters, each of which accept a voltage and give out a whole number depending on how large the voltage is. The voltage might be controlled by the position of the joystick, or the computer could be attached to a speed sensor or a piece of machinery.

Sensors

Using different types of sensor, robots can see, hear, smell, touch and taste their environment. For a robot to see, for example, cameras can be attached to its processor, enabling it to perform such tasks as recognising and sorting components on an assembly line. Microphones, in conjunction with speech recognition software, can enable a robot to respond to spoken instructions. One robotic system, endorsed by the American Spice Trade Association, measures the 'heat' of hot peppers, based on the amount of capsaicin that the peppers contain.

Q1: Would you define the following as robots? Justify your answers.

(a) A self-steering container vessel.

(b) A neural implant to overcome paralysis.

(c) A system of sensors in a building which controls the heating and lighting, dependent on whether there are people in the area.

(d) An underground train that maintains a minimum distance between itself and the next train on the track.

Why use robots?

1. Robots can work in environments hazardous to humans, or perform dangerous tasks such as disarming live bombs, working in a radioactive environment or sending information back from the surface of Mars.

2. They can tirelessly perform repetitive and monotonous tasks, lift heavy loads and reach long distances. They are used, for example, by the US Navy to scrape and repaint ships.

3. Labour costs can be substantially reduced, and robots are now widely employed in car manufacturing as well as many other industries, including printing and publishing. Robots can carry tons of paper coming off presses, bind and trim books and apply book covers. It has been estimated that each industrial robot will replace an average of six workers.

4. Quality of work is consistent. A robot is never distracted or bored, never loses concentration or makes a mistake. In welding work, for example, a robot quickly puts the right size weld in the right place at the right time with predictable accuracy and consistency.

5. Increased productivity. Robots will work for 24 hours a day, work faster than humans and do not go on strike or demand higher wages.

On the negative side, robots are expensive to buy, and even more expensive to install. Existing facilities have to be modified and installation costs can be as much as three times the robot's purchase price. No industry can afford to underuse its robots. (The computer industry, by contrast, estimates that 80% of people who own computers use them for less than twenty minutes a day).

Q2: Can you think of any other disadvantages of using robots?

Q3: Discuss the advantages and disadvantages of using robots for applications such as the following:

Landing an aircraft, waitressing, coal mining, controlling a Challenger tank, brain surgery, guarding a prison.

Teleoperators

Many mobile devices described as robots are in fact controlled by humans rather than by processors, and are really **teleoperators**. They have important practical applications, such as in undersea exploration, rescue and recovery, disarming bombs or handling radioactive material.

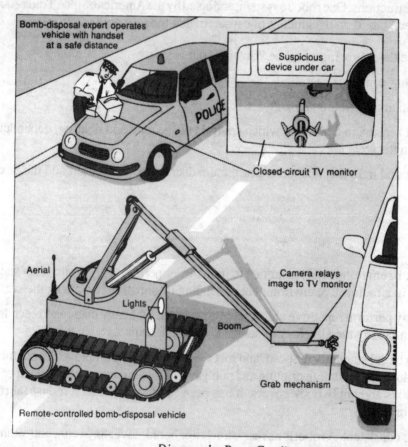

Diagram by Peter Gardiner, New Scientist 'Inside Science' Number 38

Figure 82.2 — Teleoperators can take risks while controllers look on from a safe distance

Feedback

Feedback occurs when the output of a process is used to modify its own input.

Robots may operate in one of two different modes:

- **open loop mode.** Here, there is no feedback and the robot simply goes through preprogrammed motions or actions. If it were programmed to spray paint a car, it would go through the motions, regardless of whether the car was correctly positioned or whether it had run out of paint.

- **closed loop mode.** Here, a system of feedback is used so that sensors send back signals to the computer, which can take appropriate action. For example, a robot may have to line up one component with another before inserting a bolt. A camera may capture the necessary image, and the processor then has to transform this data into information so that the robot knows what action to take.

Artificial Intelligence and Robotics

The abilities of robots are being greatly extended by advances in artificial intelligence (AI). AI is a mode of programming that allows a robot to operate on its own, to learn, adapt, reason and improve its own performance. **Pattern recognition**, for example, is an important field of study in improving robot vision.

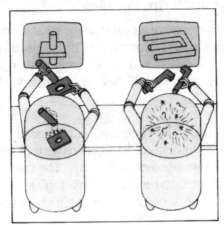

Perceptual understanding requires a robot to store an internal model and use it for the performance of a task, interpreting its sensory feedback in terms of the model.

Diagram by Peter Gardiner,
New Scientist 'Inside Science' Number 38

Figure 82.3 — An intelligent robot

Process control

Computers used in the control of real-time processes (for example, in the chemical or nuclear energy industries) need a **multi-level interrupt system** and a **real-time clock**. The 'real-time clock' implies that the computer's internal clock co-ordinating the activities of the computer is calibrated to be correct to time in the real world. Using the multi-level interrupt system, process interrupts are usually dealt with straight away while an operator interrupt is given the lowest priority. In summary:

- the computer must be capable of responding to events that are triggered by time, for example recording process variables at regular intervals (**time-initiated events**)

- the computer must be able to respond to incoming signals from the process (**process-initiated interrupts**). Depending on their relative importance, the computer may be required to interrupt its current task to carry out the higher priority task. It must, therefore, be capable of interfacing with **sensors** to permit process monitoring

- the computer must be interfaced to **actuators** and have the software capability to direct the hardware devices to carry out tasks

- as the control computer will invariably be connected to other computers, it must be able to handle events related to the computer itself, such as data transfer

- the computer must be able to respond to **operator initiated events**, i.e. accepting input from the operator, and outputting commands to trigger operator action. For example, the computer might guide the operator through the correct system start-up conditions.

Q4: Give an example of   (a) an operator-initiated event
                             (b) a time-initiated event
in a computer-controlled system for developing photographic film.

Computers in partial control

In many modern car production plants, the complete production process is controlled and monitored by computer. In one part of the plant engines of the various types used in the different models are either assembled on site or brought in from another factory. Each engine is placed on a trolley which will carry it around the factory. The trolley carries a magnetic code which can be detected by sensors located around the site so that the computer can continually monitor the position of each engine in the factory. Similarly as the body panels are pressed from sheets of steel, they are placed on another trolley which is coded with a model type and colour.

As the body moves around the plant the computer can automatically sense what model it should be and send appropriate signals to welding robots, paint machines, etc. The computer will also ensure that each car receives the appropriate engine, trim and so on. It is possible to minimise wastage of material such as paint by ensuring that, for instance, several blue cars are produced consecutively, even if they are different models.

Computers in total control

In Helsinki, the underground trains are entirely controlled by computer, with no need for a driver. The trains are controlled in such a way as to make maximum use of a system called regenerative braking. The timing is such that as one train slows down, its energy is used to accelerate another train away. The trains are precisely positioned against the platforms to prevent heat loss along the tunnels, and doors in the platform are aligned with the train doors to allow passengers to get on and off. A built-in safety feature makes it impossible for the station doors to open unless there is a train at the platform.

Exercises:

1. Robots are commonly used in car construction and assembly. Describe briefly **four** factors which have led to the implementation of these new techniques in car production. (4 marks)
    AEB Paper 2 1990

2. A computer is being used to control an industrial process. What is meant by *feedback* in this context and why is it an essential element of such a control system? (4 marks)
    London Specimen Paper 1 1989

3. A water company uses computer-controlled equipment to monitor and control the quality of drinking water. Sensors are placed in various positions on the equipment to take digital measurements every minute. The computer has been programmed to respond to feedback from the sensors and input from the operator.

    (a) What data is likely to be captured by the sensors? (2 marks)

    (b) Describe situations in which the computer will respond to

    (i)   feedback

    (ii) input from the operator (4 marks)
    London Paper 1 1991

4.* Computer systems are widely used for process control in industries such as the chemical industry. Explain why this is so and describe the organisation of such systems, including the types of hardware needed to capture and process the data. (7 marks)
    UCLES Paper 1 May 1992

5.   Case study: Robots on guard

Three-wheeled robots are learning to find their way around the Los Angeles County museum, one of America's largest museums. Each robot has a central computer that has been programmed with a set of highly accurate maps of the building showing the position of all doorways, walls, desks and any other permanent obstructions.

When a robot is told to go to a particular place, it works out the best route from the appropriate maps. It has an ultrasonic navigation system which it uses to check the exact position of a doorway before trying to go through it. It also has a collision-avoidance system to help it get round any obstructions that are not shown on its maps.

The robots can be equipped with a number of sensors, including microwave or infrared to detect movement. They can monitor temperature and humidity as well as check for fires, smoke or a build-up of gases. Some have closed-circuit TV cameras that can send back pictures to the security centre from which they are operated.

The computer controlling the robot's sensors uses "fuzzy logic" software which gives the robot a primitive sense of "suspicion". This works by analysing temperature, humidity, smoke and gas readings, so it can reach a conclusion about the probability of a fire.

At the museum, the robots go on duty seven days a week at about midnight and patrol seven of the museum's fifty galleries, concentrating on those containing the valuable collection of European paintings dating from the 17th century. The robot's main task is environmental monitoring — looking for changes in temperature or humidity which could damage the collection.

Similar robots employed elsewhere have more than covered their £50,000 cost by discovering escaping steam, dangerous fumes and leaking water pipes.

(Adapted from an article in The Sunday Times, December 5 1993)

Questions:

a.   What hardware is needed to convert the information collected by the robot's sensors into a form that the computer can process?   (2 marks)

b.   Describe the difference between 'open loop mode' and 'closed loop mode'. In what mode is the robot acting when it finds its way around obstacles?   (5 marks)

c.   Describe with the aid of an example what is meant by a **process-initiated interrupt** in the context of the case study.   (3 marks)

d.   Describe briefly **two** other hazards which the museum needs to guard against in addition to those mentioned. How effective would the robots be in protecting the museum's collection in each of these cases?   (4 marks)

e.   Describe briefly **three** other situations in which robots similar to those described above could play a useful role.   (3 marks)

f.   Give **three** examples of situations in which different types of robots have replaced human workers. In each case, state why robots are employed. (Choose a different reason in each case.)   (6 marks)

g.   Give **one** argument to support the idea that the introduction of robots in industry has contributed to the overall level of unemployment, and **one** argument which contradicts this theory.   (2 marks)

(Total 25 marks)

Unit 83 — Protection of Information and Computer Crime

Personal privacy

The **right to privacy** is a fundamental human right and one that we take for granted. Most of us, for instance, would not want our medical records freely circulated, and many people are sensitive about revealing their age, religious beliefs, family circumstances or academic qualifications. In the UK even the use of name and address files for mail shots is often felt to be an invasion of privacy.

With the advent of large computerised databases it became quite feasible for sensitive personal information to be stored without the individual's knowledge and accessed by, say, a prospective employer, credit card company or insurance company to assess somebody's suitability for employment, credit or insurance.

Q1: Do you think that personal data about people such as might be held on police, hospital or inland revenue files should be made available to a government department for any reason? Justify your answer.

The Data Protection Act

The first concerns about the need for 'data protection' were voiced quite soon after the introduction of computers into commerce and industry, but more than 20 years passed before any legislation came into force. Public pressure for legislation gradually increased in the 70s and early 80s, and with the prospect of 'joining Europe' not too far away, the Government also had to look at the consequences of not conforming with European legislation on data protection. The Council of Europe Data Protection Convention set up in the late 1970s allowed participating countries to refuse to transfer personal information to non-participating countries, and this could have put Britain at a disadvantage in trade and lost international contracts. Each country has to ratify (confirm their acceptance of) the Convention by signing twice, once when they agree to legislate and once when the legislation is passed.

The Data Protection Act became law on 12th July 1984. It contains eight **principles**, summarised as follows:

1. Personal data must be obtained and processed fairly and lawfully.

2. Personal data must be held for specified purposes.

3. Personal data must not be used for any reason incompatible with its original purpose.

4. Personal data must be relevant and adequate.

5. Personal data must be accurate and up-to-date.

6. Personal data must not be kept longer than necessary.

7. Personal data must be made available to the individual concerned and provision made for corrections.

8. Personal data must be kept secure.

'Personal data' means any data relating to a living person who can be identified from it — for example, by name.

The Act established the office of **Registrar**, whose duties include administering a public register of Data Users, investigating complaints and initiating prosecutions for breaches of the Act. All Data Users have to register, giving:

*   their name and address (or that of their company)

*   a description of the data held and its purpose

*   a description of the sources from which the data is obtained

*   a description of the persons to whom it is intended to disclose data.

Exemptions from the Act

- The Act does not apply to payroll, pensions and accounts data, nor to names and addresses held for distribution purposes.

- Subjects do not have a right to access data if the sole aim of collecting it is for statistical or research purposes, or where it is simply for backup.

- Data can be disclosed to the data subject's agent (e.g. lawyer or accountant), to persons working for the data user, and in response to urgent need to prevent injury or damage to health.

Additionally, there are exemptions for special categories, including data held

- in connection with national security
- for prevention of crime
- for the collection of tax or duty.

Q2: Under the Data Protection Act, the user has the right to see his personal data. Suppose when he sees it, it is in the form of a name and a list of unintelligible numbers. What further action can he take?

Q3: A person who has not declared all his income wishes to know whether the Tax Office suspects him of tax evasion, and asks to see his personal data file. Will the Tax Office have to show it to him?

Computer Fraud

There are two opposing views about fraud in general; one that since few cases are reported it is quite rare and not a serious problem, and the other that it is widespread but that firms tend not to report it. Recent statistics suggest that losses for 1989 alone were in the region of £1 billion, but that only one in ten cases were reported. 44% of cases were uncovered by accident, and 13% had been going on undiscovered for more than three years.

Q4: Why do firms not always report suspected cases of fraud ?

Programmers and other computer personnel, if they are so inclined, are often well placed to commit fraud if the controls within the company are at all lax. Anecdotes abound of successful frauds eventually discovered, some of which are given below:

- *Two clerks in a bank who worked for the section that handled mutilated cheques deliberately mutilated their own cheques so the computer would reject them. When they got them back, they literally threw them away. They were inevitably caught because the bank's accounts wouldn't balance.*

- *An outside consultant who found a blank form used for adding a new employee to the company payroll used it to add himself. Since he was doing a six-month study in the computer department, he could just pick up his cheque as it came off the computer.*

- *An army programmer set up an entire imaginary base, with 200 men on it. He opened 200 bank accounts for their pay cheques and the whole scheme worked beautifully until he realised that he had to keep the fraud going for ever; no one had questioned an extra 200 men, but questions would certainly be asked if they all disappeared! He considered having them desert en masse, dropping an imaginary bomb on the base, having them wiped out by an imaginary case of food poisoning, and eventually gave himself up in despair.*

- *In one incident at Heathrow Airport the cargo system was reprogrammed to divert a £2 million consignment of cannabis so that it bypassed customs examination.*

- *Students at Thames Polytechnic were invited to break the security routines on the DEC System 10 as part of their course on Systems Security. They managed to get into a secure file containing their examination marks, alter the marks and return the file to its original place.*

Hacking

'Hacking', or obtaining illegal access to data, is a well publicised form of computer crime. Senior managers have been slow to take the problem seriously, partly because they did not understand computers and failed to appreciate what could be done with them. One expert described a US bank's system as 'a training ground for hackers'. A case was reported in October 1990 of hackers blackmailing several clearing banks by demanding money to show how they broke their computer security!

Other forms of computer crime

Fraud is only one example of computer misuse. Another is use of computer time for non-company purposes — there are several cases on record of private computer bureaux operated on company computers.

Malicious damage is not uncommon, and ranges from starting fires to deliberately destroying data. In one incident in the US a delivery driver was dismissed, and his fiancee, who happened to be the firm's tape librarian, wreaked her revenge by substituting blank tapes for the master files, all properly labelled. When several generations had been updated and were blank she quit her job.

Viruses

A computer 'virus' is a computer program that is able to copy itself without the user intending it, and without most users noticing it. There are many different types of virus — some which infect only floppy disks, others which infect hard disks as well. If the hard disk is infected with a boot sector virus, then the virus will copy itself into memory every time the machine is booted up, and then infect any floppy disk which is inserted into a drive by copying itself to the diskette as soon as it is accessed either for reading or writing. When the same diskette is used on a different machine, that machine's hard disk will become infected and so on.

Types of virus

There are now several hundred known viruses, with more appearing every month. Two categories of virus are **time-bombs** — triggered by a particular date such as Friday 13th or April 1st — and **logic-bombs** triggered by a set of conditions such as the number of files on a disk or a certain combination of letters being typed. Some of the common viruses are

- **Italian (also called Ping Pong, or Bouncing Ball)**. Once every half hour a bouncing dot is triggered, bouncing off the edge of the screen and passing through any text on the screen, replacing letters with random characters.

- **Stoned** — corrupts the file allocation table, causing file directory entries to be deleted on floppy disks so that users' files are effectively lost.

- **Datacrime** — a particularly vicious virus which operates between October 13th and December 25th, reformatting the hard disk with consequent loss of all data and programs stored.

Viruses have been around since 1986 but were then extremely rare; by 1991 they had become a genuine problem in both corporate and academic environments.

Getting rid of viruses

Software such as 'Dr Solomon's Anti-Virus Toolkit' can be bought which will check any disk for known viruses and get rid of them. Of course, the floppy disk containing the anti-virus software should be write-protected before use or it may itself become infected!

There are a number of precautions that a company can take to slow down the spread of viruses.

- Viruses are frequently spread unwittingly by hardware engineers who move from machine to machine, or software salesmen running demonstration programs. The most obvious precaution to take before a demonstration program is shown is to make sure it is write-protected so that no virus can be written to it, and the same precaution should be taken by an engineer before he inserts his disks into a machine.

- No floppy disks should be brought in from outside (e.g. games, disks brought back from a training course, disks containing sample software, etc.) and inserted into a machine without first being checked by a virus checker program. The virus checker may be installed on all machines, or held on one machine where disks can be taken and checked (a 'sheepdip station').

- Whenever new software is purchased, the diskettes that it came on should be write-protected before putting them into the disk drive. This will mean that the distribution diskette will not become accidentally infected.

- Blank formatted disks can be 'innoculated' against boot sector viruses such as Italian and Stoned by using anti-virus software. This means that even though they are write-enabled, they will not get infected by those viruses.

Crime prevention

Most firms have introduced stringent precautions to ensure the security of their computer systems, and indeed under the provisions of the Data Protection Act they are legally required to do so. ('Data must be kept secure'.) A Corporate IT Security Policy needs be laid down and clearly understood by all employees. It should specify exactly what each end-user is permitted to access and to change, and who is authorised to give that permission.

Legal provision to enable computer criminals to be prosecuted is described in the following paragraphs.

The Computer Misuse Act 1990

This Act made it a criminal offence for anyone to access or modify computer-held data or software without authority, or to attempt to do so. It created three specific offences to deal with the problems of hacking, viruses and other nuisances which have plagued computer users. These are:

- unauthorised access to computer programs or data

- unauthorised access with a further criminal intent ('ulterior intent')

- unauthorised modification of computer material (i.e. programs and data).

To prove the first offence, it is necessary to show that the access was deliberate and unauthorised and that the alleged miscreant knew it was unauthorised. Unauthorised access covers both access from outside and authorised users who deliberately exceed their authority.

In order for the 'ulterior intent' offence to be proved, it has to be shown that the accused deliberately accessed a computer without authority, knowing he was unauthorised, and that he had the intention of using the information gained (either at the time or later) to commit some further offence.

'Unauthorised modification', for example, covers the **deliberate** introduction of a virus into a system, or the creation and distribution of a new virus, even if the perpetrator cannot know in advance which computers it will end up on.

Q5: In which of the following scenarios is the Computer Misuse Act being contravened, rendering the culprit liable to prosecution?

A user on a network dials a wrong number in error and finds he has accessed a local government department computer.

He now decides to explore a little further, and after some while comes across a record pertaining to a parking ticket which he has not paid. He deletes this record.

A Computing student attends a course at a local College, where she unwittingly picks up a computer virus from a PC and copies it to her school's network.

A student discovers a way to log on to fellow students' user areas. He does so, and for a prank, changes all their passwords so that they cannot get into their own user areas next time they try to log on.

An employee in a Personnel Department logs on to her computer, browses through some employee records on the company database and finds that a colleague has a criminal record. She decides to ask for some small favours in return for keeping the information quiet.

Software copyright laws

Computer software is now covered by the Copyright Designs and Patents Act 1988 and has the same status as a literary work, retaining copyright for 50 years after publication. Plato and Shakespeare will undoubtedly still be going strong but will Windows, Lotus 123 and WordPerfect still be valued products halfway through the 21st century??

Provisions of the Act make it illegal (for copyright protected software) to

- copy software
- run pirated software
- transmit software over a telecommunications line, thereby creating a copy.

Exercises:

1. The terms 'hacking' and 'computer virus' have recently been widely used in the press and television programmes.

    (a) Write a simple explanation of these terms in a form which would be understood by a non-specialist person.
    (4 marks)

    (b) Briefly describe why hacking and computer viruses are undesirable. Identify precautions which can be taken to discourage them. *(4 marks)*
    UCLES Paper 1 May 1990

2. Why is it desirable to have legislation to control the use and the storage of personal data on a computer?

    List the main provisions that you would expect to find in such legislation. *(7 marks)*
    London Sample AS Paper 1989

3. What kinds of people are most commonly involved in computer crime? Summarise the main types of computer crime and account for its increased incidence. What steps are being taken to counter its growth?
    (6 marks)
    WJEC AS Level May 1990

4. Write an essay about computer based crime and how it may be combatted. You are advised to restrict your answer to considering at most three specific areas of crime. *(15 marks)*
    London Paper 1 1991

5. Describe **three different** major ways in which computers may assist police in their task of combatting crime.

    Give **two** reasons why the storing of information on a police computer constitutes a potential danger for the individual in society. *(5 marks)*
    AEB Paper 1 1992

6.* The illegal use of computer systems is sometimes known as computer-related crime.

   (a) Give **three** distinct examples of computer related crime   (3 marks)

   (b) Give three steps that can be taken to help prevent computer-related crime.   (3 marks)

JMB Paper 1 1991

7.* (a) Name two examples of computer applications in which personal data are stored.   (2 marks)

   (b) Describe briefly the chief ways in which such data can be protected from access by unauthorised people.

(4 marks)
UCLES Paper 2 November 1992

8. **Case study: Market research survey**

The National Readership Survey is a survey about the newspapers and magazines people read (and the ones they don't), how much television they watch, and how much they listen to the radio. The research is used by publishers and editors to help them identify, for instance, what people of different ages are interested in, so they can produce newspapers and magazines to suit their readers.

The people to be interviewed (35,000 annually) are a cross-section of the population, and in order to make sure that a representative sample is chosen, interviewees are asked questions about their age, occupation, income and other descriptive details. They are also asked for their name and telephone number.

Each interviewer is equipped with a battery-powered laptop computer with a single floppy disk drive, and a modem. The program for each particular survey is posted to them in advance together with a list of addresses to visit and a list of questions to ask. The interviewer types the respondent's answers straight into the computer from where the data is saved on to the floppy disk. Each evening the data is transferred by telephone link to the company's mainframe computer. The data is analysed and distributed within two weeks of collection.

Questions:

a. How can a householder be sure that the interviewer is genuinely employed by a Market Research Organisation?
(1 mark)

b. Name **two** advantages of entering the data straight onto the computer rather than onto handwritten forms.
(2 marks)

c. Describe briefly **two** advantages and **two** disadvantages of using laptop computers that have only a single floppy drive and no hard disk. In each case say whether the advantage or disadvantage is to the Market Research Company or the interviewer.   (4 marks)

d. Describe briefly **two** ways in which the data collected could be corrupted by the time it is stored on the mainframe computer. In each case give **two** precautions that could be taken to lessen the chance of corruption.   (6 marks)

e. The interviewees' names, addresses and telephone numbers are stored on the mainframe computer system, but held separately from the answers given in the interview and not linked to them in any way. Why are interviewees asked to supply this information? Explain why names and addresses are held separately from the rest of the data.
(3 marks)

f. The survey includes questions on which articles people read in newspapers (eg home news, foreign news, sport, computers, finance etc) and also questions on major purchases made by the members of the household over the past year or two. How would this information be useful to the organisations who use the data?
(2 marks)

g. Describe briefly **two** ways in which the data could be lost **before** it is transmitted to the mainframe. Describe briefly **three** precautions that may be taken to ensure that data is not lost **after** it is stored on the mainframe.
(5 marks)

h. Draw a diagram to show the flow of data and the processes that take place between the time when a member of the population is interviewed and the time when he or she might read the results of the survey they took part in.
(7 marks)
Total 30 marks

Bibliography

Recommended texts

The following textbooks are recommended as general texts that cover comprehensively all or part of the Advanced Level and BTEC Computing syllabuses:

Computer Science by C.S.French (DPP)

Understanding Computer Science for Advanced Level by Ray Bradley (Stanley Thorne Ltd)

Computing by Nick Waites and Geoffrey Knott (Business Education Publishers Limited 1992)

Computing Science by Peter Bishop (Nelson)

Revision Text:

A-Level and AS-Level Computer Science by David Bale (Longman Revise Guides)

Further reading

The following books have been used as source material during the writing of this book and/or provide useful additional reading material for both lecturers and students:

Section 1 — Introduction to Computers and Business Data Processing
Data Processing and Information Technology by C.S.French (DPP)
Data Processing by Graham Lester (PP)
Computer Concepts by Shelly, Cashman and Waggoner (Boyd and Fraser Publishing Company)

Section 2 — Programming in Pascal
Pascal Programming by B.J.Holmes (DPP)
Pascal — An Introduction to Methodical Programming by William Findlay and David A.Watt (Pitman)
The Complete Guide to Software Testing by William Hetzel (Collins)

Section 3 — Data Structures
M205 Mathematics: A Second Level Course. Fundamentals of Computing (The Open University)
Data Structures using Pascal by A.Tenenbaum and M.Augenstein (Prentice Hall)
Advanced Turbo Pascal Programming and Techniques by Herbert Schildt (Osborne McGraw-Hill)

Section 4 — Databases
Microcomputer Database Management using dBase III+ by Philip J. Pratt (Boyd and Fraser)
Database Management by G.C.Everest (McGraw Hill)
Data Analysis for Data Base Design by D.R.Howe (Edward Arnold)
An Introduction to Database Systems Volume 1 by C.J.Date (Addison Wesley)
Open University M357 Data Models and Databases course, Blocks 1-4 OU Press

Section 5 — Systems Development
People and Computers — How to evaluate your company's new technology by Chris Clegg et al (Ellis Horwood Limited)
Management of Systems (ICSA Study Text) (BPP)
Structured Systems Analysis: Tools and Techniques by C.Gane and T.Sarson (Prentice Hall)

Systems Analysis for Profitable Business Applications by Ralph Cornes (Prentice Hall)
Systems Development using Structured Techniques by Malcolm Bull (Chapman and Hall)
Computer Security by Michael B. Wood (NCC)
Security of Computer Based Information Systems by V.P.Lane (MacMillan)
Systems Analysis and Design by W.S.Davis (Addison Wesley)

Section 6 — Programming Languages

Developing Expert Systems for Business by G.Benchimol, P.Levine and J.C.Pomeroll (North Oxford Academic)
Expert Systems - an Introduction for Managers by Anna Hart (Kogan Page)
Understanding Artificial Intelligence by Henry Mishkoff (Macmillan)
Artificial Intelligence and PROLOG on microcomputers by J.McAllister (Edward Arnold)
An Introduction to Fourth Generation Languages by Diane Meehan (Stanley Thornes)
Ada - An Introduction to Program Design and Coding by S.Amoroso and G. Ingargiola (Pitman)
A Tutorial Introduction to Occam Programming by D. Pountain and David May (BSP Professional Books)
Prolog Programming and Applications by W.D.Burnham and A.R.Hall (MacMillan)
Understanding and Writing Compilers by Richard Bornat (Macmillan)

Section 7 — Internal Organisation of Computers

Computer Architecture and Organisation by John P. Hayes (McGraw-Hill Inc)
Computer Architecture and Organisation by Theodore H. Meyer (Dilithium Press)
Understanding Microprocessors by Don L. Cannon and Gerald Luecke (Tandy Corporation)
Programming the 6502 by Rodnay Zaks (Sybex)
32-bit microprocessors edited by H.J.Mitchell (Collins)
Elements of Computer Organization by Gideon Langholz et al (Prentice-Hall)

Section 8 — Operating Systems and networks

An Introduction to Operating Systems by Harvey M. Dietel (Addison-Wesley)
Business Data Systems by H. D. Clifton (Prentice-Hall)

Section 9 — Peripherals

Computer Peripherals by Barry Wilkinson and David Horrocks (Hodder and Stroughton)
(Note: the best source of up-to-date information on peripherals is computer magazines and catalogues)

Section 10 — Computer Applications and Social Implications

The CAD/CAM Primer by Daniel J.Bowman (Howard W. Sams & Co. Inc.)
Robotics by Anne Cardoza and Suzee J.Vlk (TAB Books Inc)
Robotics Science edited by Michael Brady (MIT Press)
Fundamentals of Robotic Systems by Harry Poole (Van Nostrand Reinhold)
Computer Insecurity by Adrian R.D.Norman (Chapman and Hall)
Computers by Larry Long and Nancy Long (Prentice-Hall)
GCSE Computer Studies - An Application Approach by Paul McGee and Gareth Williams (Longman)
Computers at Work by Peter Bishop (Edward Arnold)
Manufacturing Systems by D.J.Williams (Chapman and Hall)
A Practical Guide to the Computer Misuse Act 1990 by Tony Elbra (NCC Blackwell)
PC Viruses by Dr. Alan Solomon (Springer-Verlag)

Answers to starred exercises

Unit 1

6.   A hard disk:

 holds much more data, e.g.100-400MB as opposed to a floppy which holds typically around 1MB

 cannot be removed from the computer

 is sealed and therefore less prone to damage

 has much higher data transfer speeds.

7.   A CD ROM can hold around 500MB and more. Data can only be written once to a CD when it is manufactured, unlike a hard disk. A CD ROM is removable.

 Applications: holding an encyclopaedia, library reference material, list of all books currently in print, catalogue of art works etc.

Unit 2

8.   The text will probably be legible, but all the formatting (e.g. centering, tabbing) will be lost and many strange happy faces and other characters will be embedded in the text. This is because these represent the control characters that the wordprocessor uses to tell it when to tab, centre, start a new paragraph, embolden and so on.

9. (a) So that you do not lose too much work if the power suddenly goes off or someone unplugs the computer.

 (b) Save your work frequently yourself using the appropriate command.

 (c) Number of words typed per minute.

Unit 3

6. (a) Spreadsheets are useful because they are a powerful tool for recording and analysing any type of numeric or financial data. Automatic recalculation of fields containing formulae allows mistakes to be quickly rectified and 'what if' situations to be explored.

 (b) An analysis or graph created in a spreadsheet could be incorporated into a wordprocessed report. Alternatively, a graph could be exported to a presentation graphics package for, say, a sales presentation.

 (c) Text and labels need to be entered. Sometimes figures are required to many decimal places, sometimes to the nearest whole number, sometimes preceded by a £ sign. Dates may be required in an American (mm/dd/yy) or British (dd/mm/yy) format.

Unit 4

5. (a) An operating system could provide **icons** representing software packages and **mouse support** so that the user can load software by clicking on the icon. It could provide easy ways of copying files, by using a mouse to move a filename from one directory list to another. **Editing facilities** in all types of software could be provided so that the mouse is used, for example, to highlight text, and a **menu** of options allows the user to select cut and paste facilities.

 These facilities are needed because it is hard to remember the correct syntax for performing infrequently used commands. Computers are no longer the province of the trained expert; people from many different skill areas want to use, for example, wordprocessors, spreadsheets and databases and do not want to learn complex operating system commands.

 (b) The effectiveness of such interfaces could be assessed by the number of copies of a package like Microsoft Windows, which uses these techniques, which are sold worldwide.

Unit 5

5.   A **spreadsheet** could be used. Current seat sales, running costs and admission prices could be entered and a formula used to calculate the current profit (or loss). He could then try out the effect of various price increases and possible loss of seat sales, and the spreadsheet would automatically recalculate the profit/loss using the revised figures. This is termed a 'what if' series of calculations.

Unit 6

5.   The bank's computer could update the customers' accounts using a transaction file created during the day, print out customers' bank statements and print management reports, for example on the number of transactions and the total amount of money involved.

6.   In batch processing, many transactions are collected up, possibly over a period of time, and all processed at the same time. In real time processing, each transaction is processed as it occurs and master files updated instantly.

 A payroll is suitable for batch, with weekly hours for each employee being recorded on paper and the documents batched and processed weekly. Advantages of batch for this application: more thorough validation and error checking is possible, including verification. Data can be processed in off-peak period making efficient use of computer time. Disadvantage: if someone needs to be paid immediately (e.g. they have been fired), this could cause a problem.

Unit 7

5. Verification means that the data is entered a second time and compared with what was entered the first time. For example a second keypunch operator may enter a batch of data and it will be compared to what is already stored on the disk. Validation is performed by means of a computer program; e.g. weekly hours could be checked as being in a particular range, or a customer number could be validated by means of a check digit.

6. (a) The computer could be used for a wordprocessing package to produce a catalogue of items sold. Data would be item code, description, model, colour, size, etc and price. Data would initially be captured from lists maintained in the old manual system, and typed in via the keyboard. Thereafter the catalogue file (document) would be updated from time to time when prices changed or stock changed. The catalogue would be printed using a high quality printer.

    It could also be used for an Accounts system, including Purchase Ledger and Sales Ledger. Purchases and sales would be recorded, and also expense items such as electricity, payroll etc for the General Ledger. The output would be a set of company accounts, printed in report format.

    (b) Advantages: less tedious repetitive work, more accurate calculations and accounts. Disadvantages: new skills have to be learned, could make a mistake and wipe valuable information.

    Privacy: password system essential so that only authorised people can see salaries etc.

    Fraud: a clever dishonest person can probably defraud any sytem, computerised or manual. If the computer system has a record of all transactions and more than one person checks the accounts all should be well.

    (c) For: could have on-line stock control system integrated with purchase ledger and sales ledger . Against: small computer systems are more likely to be succcessfully implemented, larger projects run the risk of failing because the software doesn't work as expected, or new methods are not well understood, and the business can suffer as a consequence.

Unit 9

6. 800 customers is 80% of capacity. Therefore, 1000 customers is 100% of capacity. The 5-digit customer number has to be hashed to produce a 3-digit address, so the last 3 digits could be taken as the addesss (i.e. divide by 1,000 and take remainder to give address between 0 and 999.

    23456 / 1000 = 23 remainder 456. Address = 456.

Unit 10

5. The grandfather file is still uncorrupted. A sensible first step would be to take a copy of this since it may be a bug in the updating program that is corrupting the files. Then, the transactions that were originally used to update the grandfather file are used to update it and recreate the master file. Finally update the Father file with the corresponding transactions to recreate the working copy of the master file.

6. There are 10 records on the master file but only the records 45, 123, 246 and 400 are updated. Therefore the hit rate is 4/10 = 40%.

Unit 13

6. (a) is invalid (should be **value >= 100.0**)

    (b) is valid

    (c) is invalid, because the variables in the square brackets have to be 'ordinal type variables'; basically **integer** or **char**. (There are other ordinal types such as **Boolean**, but **string** is not an ordinal type).

    (d) is invalid (should be **not mark >80**)

Unit 14

6. Program maintenance means fixing bugs which may surface from time to time, making modifications to suit changing user requirements, making changes to accommodate new hardware, adding in extra reports that users may want, changing the way the software processes data because of increased volumes of transactions, etc.

Unit 17

6. Parameter passing means passing variable contents or addresses between the calling routine and the called subroutine. For example, to call a subroutine which adds up two numbers and returns the result you might write

    ADDUP (num1, num2, result)

    num1, num2 and **result** are parameters. The main advantage of parameters is that the subroutine is completely self-contained, uses variable names which are independent of those used in the main program, and can be made to perform the same instructions on different variables by calling it with different parameters.

Unit 20

5. Program test data is used to try and ascertain whether the program works correctly for all circumstances. Test data should include both valid and invalid data, and data which is at the extremes of permissible values (e.g. if a range check in the program tests that MARK is between 0 and 100, test it with values of MARK equal to -1, 0, 20, 20.5, 100, 101 and ABC).

Unit 24

3.(a) (i)   Algorithm using **while..do**:

```
TotalValue = 0
NoOfValues = 0
read LowerLimit
read UpperLimit
read DataValue
while DataValue <> -1 do
  if DataValue within limits
  then    add 1 to NoOfValues
          add DataValue to TotalValue
   endif
   read DataValue    {**}
endwhile
if NoOfValues>0
then Average = TotalValue/NoOfValues
else write 'No values entered'
endif
```

If a **repeat .. until** structure is used, the algorithm won't work if the first data value is -1, because the loop will be performed once and the program will encounter another read statement at the line marked {**}.

After the line 'read UpperLimit' substitute

```
repeat
 read DataValue
 if DataValue within limits and <>-1
 then    add 1 to NoOfValues
         add DataValue to TotalValue
  endif
until DataValue = -1
```

(b) Iteration means looping using for example **while, repeat** as in the examples above.

Recursion implies that a procedure calls itself. A recursive procedure must have a stopping condition so that it doesn't continue calling itself for ever. (see example in Unit 18, calculating a factorial).

(c) A stack is a first-in, last-out data structure. When a procedure is called, the return address is put on the top of the stack. If this procedure then calls another procedure, the new return address is added to the top of the stack, and so on for each procedure called. When a procedure finishes, the top address in the stack gives the address that it should return to.

(d)(i)   Add an element (NewEl) to a stack:

```
if    stack is full
then overflow = true
else overflow = false
     increment TopOfStackPointer
     stack(TopOfStackPointer) = NewEl
endif
```

(d)(ii)   Remove an element from a stack:

```
if    stack is empty
then underflow = true
else
  underflow = false
  PoppedEl=stack(TopOfStackPointer)
  decrement TopOfStackPointer
endif
```

Unit 25

4.   A queue can be implemented as an array of a fixed size and pointers to the front and rear of the queue. Using the array as a circular structure the queue can wrap around to the top of the array. Two other variables Size, giving the current number of elements in the array, and Limit, giving the dimension of the array (ie the maximum size of the queue) are also required.

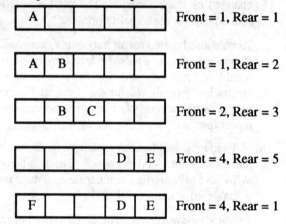

(i)   To add an item to the queue:

```
if Size = Limit then
    QueueFull = True
else
    if Rear = Limit
    then Rear = 1
    else Rear = Rear + 1
    endif
    Queue(Rear) = NewElement
    SizeOfQueue = SizeOfQueue + 1
endif
```

(ii)   To remove an item from the queue:

```
if Size = 0 then
    QueueEmpty = True
else
    Item = Queue(Front)
    SizeOfQueue = SizeOfQueue-1
    if Front = Limit
    then Front = 1
    else Front = Front + 1
    endif
endif
```

378

Unit 27

5.

	Left Ptr	Item	RightPtr
1	6	3	2
2	7	6	3
3	4	8	5
4	0	7	0
5	0	9	0
6	0	1	7
7	0	5	0

The tree can be represented as 3 arrays called LeftPtr, Item and RightPtr. The items are put into the array Item in the order in which they are given. The other two arrays are used to show which elements are pointed to on each side. For example the first item, 3, points to 1 on the left (the 6th item), and points to 6 (the second item) on the right. So LeftPtr = 6, RightPtr = 2.

To hold the tree in a data structure in Pascal, an **array of records** could be used:

```
type
Node = record
   LeftPtr     :  integer;
   Item        :  integer;
   RightPtr    :  integer;
end;
var
Tree: array[1..7] of Node;
```

Unit 28

3. (a) The record that generates the collision can be stored in the next available space on the file. When retrieving the record, the address is generated, and if there is a record at that address, but not the required record, the file is searched sequentially until the record is found or a blank address encountered, wrapping round to the first address when the end of file is reached.

(b) The records that are most likely to be referenced should be stored first. Also the algorithm should be chosen carefully so that a minimum of collisions occurs when these particular records are stored.

Unit 30

4. Data consistency means that data such as a person's address, salary grade, department etc is the same wherever it is held. In a DBMS programs and data are independent, the data is only held once and can be accessed by people from many departments in an organisation. A DBMS will not allow two people to update a record simultaneously; a system of record locking will be used.

Unit 31

5.(a) (i) Two significant costs:
software maintenance, hardware maintenance. (Could also mention staff training, cost of disks, tapes, but NOT creation of master files, transfer of data which takes place **before** installation.)

(ii) Benefits: greater financial control on stock levels, accounts, sales analysis. Better customer information and service.

(b) (i) attributes:
ISBN, publisher, author, title, date published, qty in stock, price, category (fiction, biography etc).
BOOKS <<-------------------->PUBLISHER

(ii) ORDERS < ----------------- >> BOOKS
Identifier: account number
PERSON <------------------->> ORDER
Identifier: Name and address

6.(i) Purpose of normalisation: to establish which are the entities in the database, and which attributes belong to which entities. Also to define the relationships between the entities and thus to define the tables required in the database so as to minimise duplication of data.

(ii) First normal form; remove repeating groups (eg in a database about students and courses, do not have a record showing one student and three courses that he or she attends. Second normal form: each column in the database must be dependent on the whole of the primary key, not just a portion of the key. Third normal form: The table contains no attributes which are not dependent on the key (no non-key dependencies). Use example in text to illustrate.

Unit 32

3. (a) A database is a collection of data, organised in such a way that the relationship between items in the database is clearly defined and such that users can query the database to get different types of information according to their needs. The DBMS acts as an interface between the user's view of the data and the way in which the data is actually held. It restricts an individual user's view of the data to what he/she needs to know, and protects the database from accidental or deliberate corruption or data theft.

(b) In a library, users and librarians can look up details on a particular book, see whether the book is in or on loan, look up books by a particular author etc. Also librarians can get lists of overdue books, send out reminders, see how many books a borrower already has out.

Unit 33

3. An external schema is the users' view of the data. He/she will have access to only parts of the database as determined by the datadase manager. The internal schema is the way that the database is logically structured.

4. To improve response time: use more powerful processor, reorganise the database, possibly index fields on which queries are frequently made, delete unwanted records, run a utility program to de-fragment the disk so that access time is decreased, make tables/fields read-only where possible so that other users are not locked out when a query is being made reschedule activities so that certain time-consuming operations are performed in off-peak periods. (Any three of these will do.)

Unit 34

4. A network database model can support many-to-many relationships by the use of pointers. Relationships have to be set up explicitly, and the user must know what linkages have been established in order to know how to access the data. A relational database consists of a number of tables or 'relations' each holding data about a particular entity. An advantage of a network database is that access to data is fast. An advantage of the relational database is that new entities can more easily be added, or existing tables changed.

Unit 37

4. (a) Flowchart is shown opposite.

(b) Error checks at STAGE 1 (see flowchart) will include validation checks on transactions: eg valid transaction code (**Add, Delete, Change**), check digit on employee number, checks on various fields of a new employee record such as character check on Sex (M/F), range check on salary grade, valid date check for joining date, etc. Batch checks such as checking number of records in batch, control totals and hash totals may also be performed.

An error report will be produced listing errors, which will then be manually checked and the information corrected and re-keyed.

Error checks at STAGE 2 will include checks on errors such as attempting to delete or amend a non-existent employee record, or attempting to add a record for an employee already on file. A report will be produced listing such errors, and the transaction in error will be ignored in the update process. The data prep supervisor will probably read the report and reconcile the errors before having the original document re-keyed.

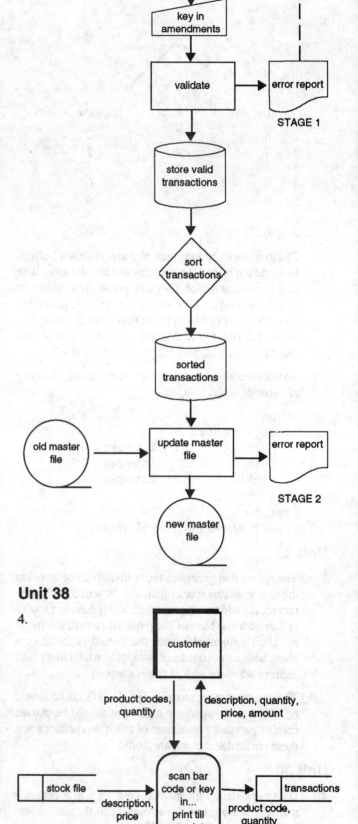

Unit 38

4.

380

5

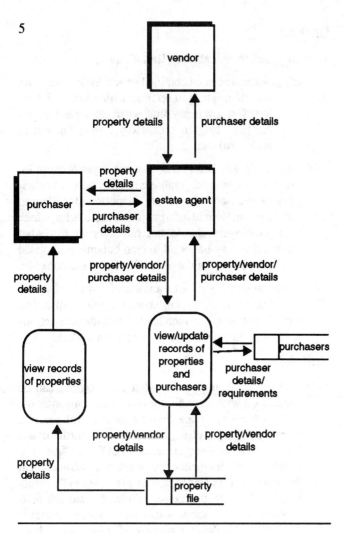

6. Read each paragraph and build up the diagram. After the first paragraph it looks like this:-

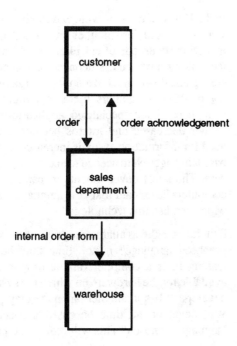

.. and when it is completed, the diagram will look something like the one below, though of course you may have placed the boxes differently.

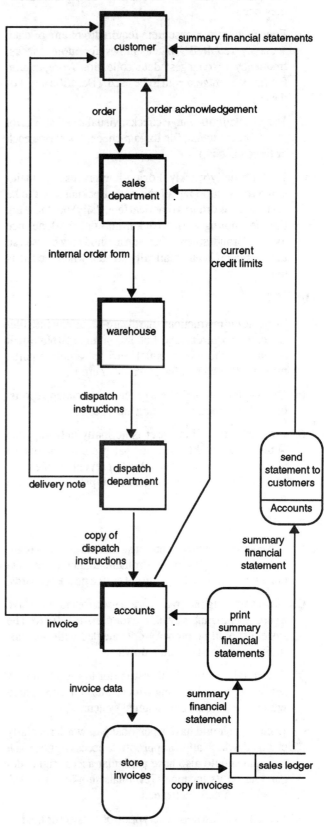

Unit 39

5.(i) Batch: transactions collected over a period of time and processed together. On-line: transactions processed as they occur.

(ii) Four factors: response time required; volume of data; accuracy required - batch allows for more checks; frequency of changes; data collection / preparation facilities; storage media to be used. (Describe any 4 of these.)

(iii) Use check digits; range checks; visual checks; control totals / batch totals; file lookup check. (Describe each of three checks.)

(iv) Backups daily/weekly. For on-line processing, maintain a transaction log all the time. Backups need to be performed as often as practical (e.g. daily) but these are time consuming so a full backup may only be done once a week. Grandfather-father-son method may be used so that a backup is automatically created when the file is updated.

Unit 41

4. Installation instructions, hardware requirements, file/ directory requirements, hot line number. (Note that features of the **user** manual such as sample reports, tutorial etc are not what is wanted here.)

5.(a) Description of facilities eg menus; specimen reports; tutorial; instructions for data entry, etc.

(b) Program listing. Purchaser is normally only supplied with an executable file, so that program cannot be altered in any way. This helps to prevent people from 'pirating' code and creating a new improved version to resell.

Unit 42

6.(i) Have a maintenance contract so that hardware is regularly serviced. Buy from a reliable manufacturer. Do not allow people to have cups of coffee near keyboards.

(ii) Have a training program to train users/operators. Have a supply of manuals available for users to refer to. The system should be properly documented with operator instuctions clearly written down.

(iii) Thorough testing of software prior to installation. A period of parallel running with results being compared with those produced by manual system.

7.(i) Each user should have a personal password, regularly changed, which allows appropriate access rights. Each terminal should also have particular access rights depending on its location. Terminals should not be left switched on and unattended.

(ii) Security lock on door, encryption of passwords held on file, password system on operator's console.

Unit 43

4.(a) (i) See answer above. (Unit 42 qu.7)

(ii) Software can be obtained which records statistics on who has logged on from which terminal, how long for, how many times a user attempted unsuccessfully to gain access (by typing the wrong password) etc.

(b) Users are given different access privileges because for example senior management will need access to company secrets, and the payroll department will need access to confidential information about salaries, which other employees should not have access to. Other information may be for all to read but only authorised people to change; eg the price of an item on a stock file.

(c) A transaction log of all transactions which have occurred since the last backup should be held on disk. The most recent backup is then loaded, and the transactions applied to the master file to bring it up to date.

Unit 44

4. "Self-documenting" means that the program can be understood without additional written documentation. A high level language permits meaningful variable names such as student_name, date_of_birth. It has English-like statements such as (in COBOL) "Add 1 to counter", or statements that resemble mathematical formulae such as (in Pascal) "a:=(b+c)/(x+y)". Structures such as If..then..else, While..do, etc are self-explanatory. Comments can be included wherever necessary to explain the purpose of procedures or lines of code.

Unit 45

6. In the 1950s, computers were extremely expensive and were only used for 'number-crunching' applications involving thousands of calculations. As the hardware technology advanced, silicon chips replaced valves, costs came down, and the number of organisations that could afford computers increased, more languages were needed for specialised applications. As costs further decreased and micros became common, the need for information systems increased and new database languages were needed to access large amounts of data. The latest developments in parallel processing computers has meant that new languages are required which can use this technology.

7. Criteria: are the available programmers expert in the proposed language? If not, time may be wasted in leaning it. Is a compiler for the proposed language available for the hardware on which the system is to be developed? If not, another language may be selected. Will development time be cut if a special-purpose language is chosen? This will reduce the project cost.

8. Agree: natural progression from 1st to 5th generation language. Also a lot of work is being carried out in artificial intelligence, neural networks etc which is moving in that direction.

OR Disagree: natural language is extremely ambiguous; "We're having the Smiths for supper tonight" and therefore not suitable for computers. Natural languages vary between nations and dialects would make the problem even worse. In contrast, Pascal is the same all over the world; a universal language, understood by all Pascal programmers.

Unit 46

5. SQL (Standard Query Language) is a 4GL. It is a non-procedural query language, specifying what has to be done but not how to do it. Other database products such as Omnis 7, Paradox for Windows and Access are sometimes referred to as 4GLs because they include screen painting facilities, report generators, selection and sorting facilitiesand can be linked to other database management systems.

Unit 47

3. Imperative: program consists of a logical sequence of steps to be carried out. eg Pascal, COBOL, BASIC.

Functional: program consists of a series of function definitions followed by an expression to be evaluated. eg LISP.

Declarative: programmer states the facts and rules associated with the problem. The user can then interrogate the program to get it to deduce new facts. e.g. PROLOG.

Unit 49

5. The delay may be very much shorter as the compiled version will run faster. Also, if an optimising compiler is used, the loop may be performed only once or not at all if there is no 'point' in performing it that the compiler can detect.

6.(a) Hashing means using the characters of the variable name to generate an address in the symbol table where the variable name will be stored. Two desirable features: that it should generate a minimum of collisions, and that every address in the table can potentially be generated.

(b) The compiler could put the second variable name in the next available free space in the table. If the end of the table is reached, it should scroll round to the beginning of the table.

(c) The variable name must not be physically deleted as then a 'synonym' that had been stored in the next free space would not be found. Instead, the variable should be flagged as deleted so the space can be re-used.

Unit 50

4. The binary system uses only 2 digits, 0 and 1 and the circuits inside a computer can represent these numbers by either conducting or not conducting a current. The computer uses 'bi-stable' devices, which can be either on or off, to represent 1 and 0. This is therefore a very convenient way of representing data. Secondly, if the denary system were used, components would need to be able to represent 10 different 'states', and slight changes in performance might result in the computer confusing one state (say, 6) with another state (say, 5 or 7). Thirdly, magnetic storage devices are able to use magnetic fields of two possible polarities (north and south) as bi-stable devices to represent 0 and 1.

Unit 52

6. The maximum address that can be held in 16 bits is FFFF, ie 1111 1111 1111 1111. But 0000 to 1FFF are used by the O/S, leaving FFFF-1FFF = E000. This is

$$1110\ 0000\ 0000\ 0000 = 111000 \times 2^{10}$$
$$= 56 \times 2^{10} = 56\text{Kbytes}$$

(Remember that 2^{10} bytes = 1KB)

Unit 53

3.(i) Floating point form allows real numbers (with a decimal point) to be held more accurately. It also allows a greater range of numbers to be held.

(ii) Integer arithmetic is performed faster than floating point arithmetic. No rounding errors occur with integer representation.

Unit 54

3.(i)

2048	1096	512	256	128	64	32	16	8	4	2	1
1	0	0	1	0	1	1	1	0	0	1	1

2048 + 256 + 64 + 32 + 16 + 2 + 1 = 2419

(ii)   1001 0111 0011

      9   7   3   = 973

(iii)   1001 0111   0011

$$= 1.001\ 0111 \times 2^3 = 1001.0111$$

First bit represents the sign bit, so take 2's complement to translate it to a positive number.

$$-\ 0110.1001 = -6.5625$$

Unit 55

4.(i) The number could be held with a 12-bit mantissa and an 8-bit exponent. The first bit of both parts of the number will be the sign bit.

    0   00101000000   00000011

  sign bit   mantissa   exponent

(ii) The more bits that are allowed for the mantissa, the greater the accuracy that will be obtained, because more 'binary places' are used. The more bits that are allowed for the exponent, the greater the range of numbers that can be represented.

Unit 56

4. The computer will not be able to detect where the program instructions end and where the data (or other memory contents) begin. Therefore the PC (program counter) will be incremented to point to the next memory location beyond the end of the program. This will be interpreted as an instruction, fetched and placed in MDR. It will be decoded if possible, and executed. At this point memory will start to be corrupted by the execution of spurious instructions. Sooner or later a memory location will be reached which cannot be interpreted as an instruction and the program will halt with an error message.

Unit 57

3. A parallel processor architecture using array processing. (Single instruction multiple datastream.)

Unit 59

6. For example:

```
CMP  #0        ; compare with value 0
BNE  LABEL     ; branch if not equal
```

The ALU and status register are used in the test.

Unit 60

4. (a) (i) Addressing mode:

Absolute addresses (physical memory addresses) may be accessed in a number of ways and the addressing **mode** is indicated in the operand of an instruction.

(ii) Immediate addressing: The actual number to be loaded is specified, eg hex 0F.

Direct addressing: The address of the operand is specified, eg 1EF0

(b) This is a 3-byte instruction (1 for op code, 2 for address) so PC will be incremented by 3 to be 1003 hex.

(c) 0000 to FFFF = 64KB

(d) 1 byte allows $2^8 = 256$ op codes.

Unit 61

4. A 2-pass assembler can deal with forward references. On the first pass symbolic labels and their addresses are entered into a symbol table. On the second pass the symbolic address operands are replaced by their machine equivalent.

Unit 63

3. Multi-tasking in this context means that one user is able to perform several tasks at the same time; or more accurately, switch between them at will, for example having several programs running simultaneously in a Windows environment. This can have advantages if for example you want to type text using a word-processor, create a picture using a Paint program, and combine the two in a Desktop Publishing package. If you are writing a user guide to a database package for example, you can have the database running in one window and write about it in another window. You can switch to File Manager, or back to the operating system, to list directories or make backups without quitting the software you are running. All these examples illustrate advantages of a multi-tasking environment. On the negative side, the computer will need more memory and will probably run slower than one which does not permit multi-tasking.

Unit 64

5. (a) (i) Advantages to software developers:

Development time will be shortened because use can be made of the pre-written library routines.

They are saved the trouble of drawing up their own guidelines for consistent user interface, and able to make use of good ideas already tested.

(ii) Advantages to users:

Software is much easier to learn if packages have the same 'look and feel', eg F1 always used for Help, identical icons for sizing windows, closing windows etc.

Users familiar with one package will be at ease with any other package, and with all new versions of software. They will be able to 'guess' the effect of many functions.

(b) Users who switch between operating systems will not have to learn different versions of the software. However if they work only on one operating system with software from many manufacturers, they will have to learn a different HCI which could cause confusion and frustration.

Unit 65

6. (a)(i) An interrupt is a hardware-generated signal which causes the execution of the program which currently has control of the CPU to be suspended.

(ii) When a computer needs to transfer data to the printer, the currently running process will generate an interrupt The interrupt handler will then call the appropriate routine to check the status of the printer (e.g. ready or not) and initiate the data transfer. A further interrupt will be generated when data transfer is complete.

(b) (i) program check interrupts, e.g. overflow or underflow

external interrupts generated by the expiry of a time-slice.

(ii) Each peripheral device is given a priority rating so that if interrupts occur simultaneously, the device with the highest priority will be serviced first. In general slow speed devices are given high priority because if they are continually interrupted they may hold up processing — for example if more data needs to be read in before processing can continue.

(iii) A special register in the CPU called the interrupt register is checked at the beginning of each fetch-execute cycle. Each bit in the register represents a different type of interrupt, and if a bit is set, the state of the current process is saved and control is passed to the appropriate interrupt handler routine.

Unit 66

5.(a) (i) Logical view is how the files appear to the user to be stored; i.e. one after the other. For example if a directory listing is requested, they will be listed in this order. The physical view is where the files are acually physically held on the disk.

(ii) The file management system keeps a table which specifies where each file is physically located.

(b) The file management system could keep an entry for every block (or sector or cluster) on the disk,with an entry of 0 for a free block (or sector or cluster).

(c) (i) It suggests that possibly the file can only be stored if there is enough contiguous space free on the disk to store the whole file.(ie the file cannot be split and stored in scattered free blocks). It may be using 'first fit' which will result in a lot of small blocks being left free.

(ii) The system could use 'best fit' which allocates the area on disk which will waste the least amount of space. Alternatively it could allow non-contiguous allocation of free blocks.

Unit 67

6. The program currently being processed could **complete**. An **interrupt** will then be generated and the **scheduler** will bring in one of the other programs waiting in main store, maybe on a **round-robin** or **shortest job first** basis. Before the time slice expires, the transfer of the program referred to in B may be

completed, generating an interrupt. The program which has control of the CPU may execute until its **time slice** expires, or until user input is required, for example, when one of the other programs may get processing time. The first program may be **swapped** out of memory and stored on disk (**virtual storage**), with the system keeping track of where it is located. One or more **pages** of the new program may then be swapped into a free area of memory. If a currently executing program **needs user input** from a keyboard, say, an interrupt will be generated and control will pass to another program.

Unit 69

3.(i) Handshaking is the means by which devices check whether the other end is ready to receive data, or inform the other end that they are ready to receive data, or acknowledge that data has been received and are ready to accept more.

(ii) Standard interfaces are used so that hardware from different manufacturers can be connected together. The RS232 interface conforms to an internationally agreed standard; various bodies such as the Electronic Industries Association have been set up to try to acheve uniformity in communications equipment.

(iii) Standard communications protocols are adopted so that equipment from any manufacturer will be usable on a variety of different networks. 'Open systems networks' are not limited to one manufacturer's equipment, and a standard protocol for Open Systems Interconnection (OSI) has been defined although many of the standards have not yet been implemented.

Unit 70

3.(i) Advantages to the company: reduces paperwork, rapid sale/customer analysis, better stock control. Advantages to customer: rapid response to orders.

(ii) Modem will be needed. This translates the digital signal to analogue for transmission over the phone line. A modem at the other end will translate back to digital.

(iii) Serial: one bit at a time. Parallel: many bits transmitted simultaneously down individual wires. Advantage of serial is that data can be transmitted over much longer distances. Disadvantage: slower transmission rates.

(iv) In packet switching, data is broken up into fixed length packets of say 128 bytes, with the data in each packet accompanied by source and destination address, and packet number. The packets are dispatched by any route connecting computers in the PSS, and are reassembled at the receiving end. The main advantage is that data can be sent at local call rates, and is therefore cheap.

(v) A transposition error means that two digits or characters are written down in the wrong order eg 13579 is written 13759. A check digit could be added to the code number; eg modulus-11 check digit where weights of 2,3,4 etc are given to digits of the code, starting with the leftmost. (Give a worked example.)

(vi) Voice recognition could be used. Most voice systems have to be 'trained' to the user's voice and the system could be unable to recognise some voices eg with a foreign accent.

Unit 71

3. A key-to-disk system could be used. This system consists of a number of keystations connected to a dedicated computer with disk and tape drive. Data is keyed in, stored on disk and later transferred to tape and thence to the main computer for processing. Suitable and cost effective for high volumes of batch processed work by skilled operators. **Verification** could be used to reduce errors (another operator keys the data a second time, and it is compared with what is already stored on the disk.)

An alternative acceptable answer would be OCR.

Unit 72

2. Large bar codes may be printed on cardboard boxes stored in a warehouse, and these can be read by a hand-held laser beam by someone walking or driving round the warehouse to count stock.

A bar-coded tag can be attached to an item in the process of manufacture (eg a sweater) and read at every stage of manufacture, as part of a production control system. Bar codes are cheap and easy to print and can be read from a distance with a laser 'gun'.

3. (a) Advantages: A lot of information can be stored on the card, and can be kept by the card holder. Easy way of having data (eg medical record) available wherever you are. Could be used as an identity card holding scanned photograph. This could be used to combat credit card fraud. Can be used as replacement for cash (eg Mondex card). Disadvantage: the card could be lost or destroyed accidentally and might be hard to replace. Cannot read data without special equipment.

(b) The cards would need to be cheap, robust, easily replaceable, difficult to forge, secure against fraudulent use and convenient to use. Special terminals would have to be widely installed to read the cards.

Unit 73

3. (a) Quieter.

(b) Advantage: much cheaper, can get portable models. Disadvantage: tendency to smudge, leave paper wet

and buckled. Also slower in operation.

Unit 74

4. (a) Character displays: inputting programs, querying a database.

Low to medium resolution graphics: paint packages, graphs from spreadsheet packages.

High resolution graphics: CAD systems eg for designing aircraft.

(b) Two factors: memory has become much smaller and cheaper. (Much more video RAM is required for a graphics display than a text display.) Processor speed has increased enormously so that screens can quickly be redrawn. Magnetic media such as disk hold far more data and so are able to store high res. graphics.

(c) Voice output, useful for visually impaired people, or people receiving computer instructions for a task which requires them to be looking at something else, eg a machine.

Unit 75

3. (a) Floppy disks have a capacity of typically 1MB, whereas hard disks store typically 80-400MB. Floppy disks can be removed from the computer and are easy to post or carry from one computer to another, whereas hard disks are usually sealed inside the computer. Data transfer speeds from hard disks are much faster than from floppy disk.

(b) Magnetic tape, CD ROM.

Unit 76

4. (a) Header label containing file name, date written.

(b) (i)   12,000 records

(ii)   13,500 records

(c) The memory size of the computer; since it has to be capable of holding a complete block of data in its buffer area. The limitations of the software; it may allow blocksizes of 1, 2, 4, or 8 records only, for example.

Unit 77

3. (a) Advice should be sought from a subject expert (e.g. nursery school teacher) on how children learn to spell, what words to select, how to grade them in difficulty, how to match them with reading schemes, etc. A suitable length of lesson needs to be determined taking into account concentration span. The hardware needs to be identified. A visit to a local school to spend time in a classroom would be a sensible first step.

Suitable software such as an authoring package or programming language then needs to be selected, and the sequence in which the information will be presented and response to user input decided.

(b) A keyboard, graphics screen and a computer with a sound card may be used. Since the child presumably cannot read, all instructions will have to be given verbally using the stored spoken text. Feedback in the form of "Well done" or "No, try again" can also be spoken, but backed up with graphics of say happy face or sad face.

(c) The data could be organised on a random access file, and a random number generator used to generate the address of the next word to be selected. This way, the child gets a different selection of words each time the program is run. Different files could be used to store words at each level of difficulty.

(d) The computer is endlessly patient and children can repeat lessons over and over again if they are having difficulty. The lessons can be done at any time while other children may be working on other programs to suit their particular needs. The teacher has more time to give individual attention where needed.

Unit 80

4. The knowledge base containing the facts and rules provided by a human expert.

some means of using the knowledge (an 'inference engine')

a means of communicating with the user, and the ability to explain how it reached a particular conclusion.

Expert systems are well suited to fault diagnosis (eg of cars) or medical diagnosis.

Unit 81

4. A graphics package would be useful in designing a book cover. A picture can be 'painted', different text fonts and colour combinations can be tried out, the picture (or a representation of it if for example a photograph will be used in the final version) can be sized and the best overall design decided upon. This can then be printed out.

Unit 82

4. Computers are used because they can work 24 hours a day with absolute accuracy, can do monotonous, dangerous or unpleasant tasks, and once set up and installed are more economical than human operators.

A computer used for process control must have **sensors** to permit process monitoring, **transducers** to convert the information collected by the sensors into voltages, **analogue-to-digital converters** to change the information to binary form. It also needs **actuators** to direct the

hardware to carry out tasks, and a **real-time clock**s so that it can respond to events in real time.

Unit 83

6.(a) Using a stolen cash card to obtain money from a bank's cash machine.

Hacking into someone's private electronic mailbox and leaving messages.

Fraudulently altering a company's computerised accounts and siphoning off funds into a personal account.

(b) Fraud can sometimes be combatted by rigorous auditing procedures, and ensuring that no one person is in sole control of the system. Hacking can be discouraged through the use of a strictly enforced password system where passwords have to be changed regularly, and a record is kept of all attempts to log on to the system. Combatting cash card fraud is difficult; alerting the public to the problem and urging care that no one is watching the PIN being typed in could help.

7.(a) Credit card companies store data on customers.

Colleges store data on students.

(b) Access matrices can be used on database systems so that only authorised people signing on with a particular user id and password can access the data. Physical access to buildings and computer rooms can be restricted to prevent entry by unauthorised people. Laws can be put into effect forbidding the sale of personal data and making it a criminal offence not to keep data secure.

Index

Symbols

1NF   147
2NF   148
3NF   149
4GL   203
5/10 Code   191

A

Access matrix   156
Accounting facilities   280
Accounting functions   304
Accumulator   248, 251
Actuator   362
Ada   198
Adaptive mechanism   297
Address bus   224
Addressing
   direct   264
   immediate   264
   indexed   265
   indirect   265
   modes   263
   relative   265
   symbolic   267
ALU   247
Analogue signal   306, 363
AND   260
APPEND   87
Apple Mac   283
Apple Newton   320
Application packages   5
Applications generator   177
Argument   77
Arithmetic shift   259
Arithmetic-logic unit   247
Array   71, 98
   two-dimensional   73
Array processor   254
Artificial intelligence   354
ASCII character sequence   135
ASCII code   81, 223
Assembler directives   267
Assembly language   46, 256
ASSIGN statement   87
Assignment statement   51
Asynchronous transmission
   mode   303
ATM   316
Attribute   145
Authoring software   341
Autonomous operation of peripher-
   als   285

B

Back-tracking   206
Backing store   2
Backing store management   292
Backup   190
BACKUP utility program   191
Backus-Naur form   209
Bar code   317
Baseband   302
BASIC   196
Batch cover note   24
Batch header check   26
Batch header slip   24
Batch processing   21, 24, 279
Batch register   24
BCD   233
Best-fit   292
Bi-directional   323
Binary
   arithmetic   228
   fixed point   236
   floating point   237
   integers   227
   multiplication   231
   numbers   227
Binary coded decimal   233
Binary search   104
Binary tree   126
   traversal   128
Bit   222
Bitmapped graphics   234, 360
Black box testing   94
Block packing density   35
Block structure   75
Block-multiplexor channel   285
Blocked process   286
Blocking factor   35
Blocking strategy   35
Blocks   35
BNF   209
Boolean   50, 55
Boolean values   234
Booting   278
Bottom-up design   66
Bps   303
Branch instruction
   conditional   261
   Unconditional   261
Breakpoint   59, 91
Broadband   302
Bubble sort   136
Bucket   132
Buffer   285

Auxiliary storage device   2

Bus
   address   224
   control   252
   data   224
   dedicated   252
   external   252
   internal   252
   shared   252
   size   253
Bus network   300
Bypass procedures   190
Byte   50, 223
Byte-multiplexor channel   285

C

C   196
Cabling systems   302
Cache memory   226
CAD   359
CAL   341
Call by reference   219
Call by value   219
CAM   360
Carrier sense multiple access   300
Carry   257
Cartridge tape   337
CASE statement   67
CASE tools   178
Cash card fraud   316
CBT   340
CD (Compact Disk)   333
CD-ROM   333
Centralised data processing   22
Changeover
   direct   181
Character   50
Character pattern memory   327
Check digits   27
Checksum   186, 308
Chr   81
CIR   248
Circuit switching   308
Circular queue   117
Circular shift   260
Clerical procedures manual   184
Clock speed   253
Closed loop mode   364
Closed subroutine   268
Cluster   191
Coaxial cable   302
COBOL   195
Code generation   215, 219
Code optimisation   219
Collision   37
COM   326

Computer Science

ISBN: **1 873981 19 8** • Date: **1992** • Edition: **4th**
Extent: **656** • Size: **275 x 215 mm**
Lecturers' Supplement ISBN: 1 873981 41 4

> *Courses on which this book is known to be used*
> A Level Computing; BTEC National and HNC/D Computer Studies; City & Guilds; BCS; AS Level
> Computer Science; BSc Applied Science.
> **On reading lists of ICM, IDPM, BCS and ACP**

This book provides a simplified approach to the understanding of Computer Science.

Notes on the Fourth Edition

This edition contains changes in content and layout which are aimed not just at covering the material on the
latest syllabuses but at assisting the reader's study **for the latest examinations**. Parts targeted at
contemporary computer applications and applications packages have been introduced. This reflects a
significant shift in emphasis in examinations over recent years. Graphical User Interfaces (GUIs),
development methodologies, desktop computers, applications packages and databases have been given
more emphasis to reflect the examination requirements of developing and using computer systems.
Obsolete material has been removed.

Contents:

Foundation Topics • Applications I: Document Processing • Storage • Input and Output • Applications II:
GUIs and Multimedia • Computer Systems Organisation I • Programming I • File and File Processing •
Applications III: Spreadsheets • Logic and Formal Notations • Computer Arithmetic • Computer Systems
Organisation II • Software • Applications IV: Applications Areas • Programming II • Databases and 4GLs •
Applications V: Information Storage and Retrieval • Systems Development • Applications VI: Business
Industrial Computing • Computers in Contexts • Revision Test Questions.

Review Comments:

*'I think the presentation is superb and content perfect for my course work.' 'Good basic book –
recommended by all academic staff in the department.' – Lecturers*

ELBS

Also available as ELBS edition
in member countries at local
currency equivalent price
of £3.00

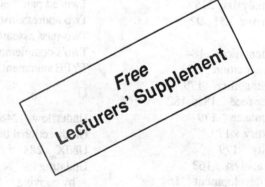

Introductory Pascal

BJ Holmes

ISBN: **1 85805 007 3** • Date: **1993** • Edition: **1st**
Extent: **242 pp** • Size: **245 x 190 mm**

Courses on which this book is known to be used

A Level Computing, BTEC HNC/D Computer Studies, BTEC First IT, GCSE Computing, City & Guilds 7261, IDPM Foundation, Access to HE/Computing, NCC.

The aim of this book is to introduce students to computer programming skills using Pascal. No prior knowledge of computing or computer concepts is assumed. Having covered the ground of this book students will be well placed to progress to *Pascal Programming* by the same author.

The author has used Turbo Pascal Version 5.0 from Borland International in the preparation and compilation of all the programs listed in this book.

Review Comments:

'Price excellent, pace and coverage of topic very good, readability very good.' 'An excellent introduction at a reasonable price.' 'An excellent book for students who have not programmed a computer before.'
– Lecturers

Tackling Computer Projects
A step-by-step guide to better projects

PM Heathcote

ISBN: **1 85805 002 0** · Date: **1992** · Edition: **1st**
Extent: **240 pp** · Size: **275 x 215 mm**

Lecturers' Supplement ISBN: **1 85805 002 2**

> *Courses on which this book is known to be used*
> A Level Computing; BTEC National and Higher National Computing.

The aim of this book is to provide students with a comprehensive and practical guide on how to tackle a computing project for an Advanced Level or BTEC National computing course, using either a programming language or a software package. It will also be useful to students doing a project for a GCSE computing course or a Higher National computing course, since the principles remain the same at any level.

Students very often find it difficult to think of a suitable idea for a computer project, and having come up with an idea, find the analysis and design stages extremely difficult to get started on. This book gives them plenty of ideas for possible projects with advice on what constitutes a suitable project and a complete specimen project of each type (programming and package implementation) together with advice on how each stage (analysis, design, etc) is tackled.

The first project is implemented in Pascal and the accompanying listing is used to illustrate many useful techniques in Turbo Pascal such as pop-up windows and the use of function keys. The second example illustrates how to tackle a project using a software package instead of a suite of programs. Borland's Paradox database (Version 3.5) has been used, but the actual package is not of any significance here as the emphasis is on how to analyse, design, test and document the system.

Contents:
Part 1 – Choosing a Project. Analysis. Design. Using a Package. Pascal Techniques. Testing. The Report
Part 2 – Specimen Project 1 – Gilbert and Sullivan Society Patrons List Analysis. Design. Testing. System Maintenance. User Manual. Appraisal.
Part 3 – Specimen Project 2 – Short Course Database Analysis. Design. Testing. System Maintenance. Appraisal. User Manual. Appendices: Paradox Script. Test Runs. Turbo Pascal Editing Keys and Blank Forms

Review Comments:
'It is ideal for our BTEC students to help them to tackle programming projects in a realistic and down-to-earth way, encouraging good practice - very readable too!' 'It tackles areas other texts ignore eg testing approaches and creation of a user manual, etc'. 'Well thought out and thorough advice for students on their project work for A Level - in fact for any level later too!' 'This is just the book required for students. It fills a gap in the market since other texts devote at most a single chapter to this 'grey area'. 'It is an excellent aid and should sell very well.' – Lecturers

Free Lecturers' Disk